EMERGENCY PRESIDENTIAL POWER

THE NEED FOR THIS BOOK

WAS ANTICIPATED BY A GRANT

FIGURE FOUNDATION

EMERGENCY PRESIDENTIAL POWER

FROM THE DRAFTING OF
THE CONSTITUTION TO
THE WAR ON TERROR

CHRIS EDELSON

The University of Wisconsin Press

The University of Wisconsin Press
1930 Monroe Street, 3rd Floor
Madison, Wisconsin 53711-2059
uwpress.wisc.edu

3 Henrietta Street
London WC2E 8LU, England
eurospanbookstore.com

Printed in the United States of America

Library of Congress Cataloging-in-Publication Data

Edelson, Chris.
Emergency presidential power: from the drafting of the Constitution
to the War on Terror / Chris Edelson.
p.   cm.
Includes bibliographical references and index.
ISBN 978-0-299-29530-1 (cloth: alk. paper)
ISBN 978-0-299-29533-2 (e-book)
1. War and emergency powers—United States.
2. Executive power—United States.
3. War on Terrorism, 2001–2009.
I. Title.
JK558.E34   2013
352.23′5—dc23
2013010416

For

KITS

the only one I'd trust with absolute power

CONTENTS

FOREWORD

Louis Fisher

In this book Chris Edelson confronts the growing independence of presidents over what he calls emergency power: power related to national security, foreign policy, and war that responds to claims of an imminent threat or crisis.[1] This type of presidential power is dangerous, especially when presidents act unilaterally, in secret, and on the basis of false, deceptive, and unreliable information.

Beginning with President Truman's use of military force against North Korea in June 1950, presidents have systematically circumvented Congress, violated statutes and the Constitution, and undermined democratic government. Even before Truman, presidents invoked threats to national security—sometimes real, sometimes exaggerated—to justify emergency power. Sometimes they acknowledged constitutional checks and balances. For example, President Lincoln sought retroactive congressional approval to make legal the actions he took at the beginning of the Civil War. At other times, presidents claimed power that could not be checked by other branches.

Presidents who concentrate power in the executive branch threaten the rule of law, the system of checks and balances, and individual rights. Post-9/11 presidents have been among the worst offenders. Among the wrongs that result from these presidential initiatives: claiming that support from the UN Security Council and NATO countries is a constitutional substitute for authority from Congress, detaining suspects (including U.S. citizens) without charging them and subjecting them to trial, using torture during interrogations, conducting warrantless surveillance, and relying on secret legal memos to carry out targeted killing without judicial process or legislative controls. Unilateral executive actions regularly inflict harm on the nation and the political system. Eventually they come at a high cost to presidents and their parties.

Emergency Presidential Power: From the Drafting of the Constitution to the War on Terror offers important assistance in understanding the legitimate sources and limits of executive power. It sheds light on emerging legal and political issues that flow from inflated claims of presidential power. The need to heighten our understanding applies not merely to public officials and specialists. It must reach the general public. Without that knowledge the aspiration for self-government through elected officials is in jeopardy. Although the United States frequently announces its desire to spread democracy to other countries, there is serious concern about the health and future of democracy at home.

Edelson provides the foundation for understanding the dangers of presidential power by presenting in clear terms the constitutional principles that were established in 1787 and how they apply to political decisions today. It is often argued that the Framers' decision to adopt eighteenth-century principles has no application to contemporary times. Yet the Framers fully appreciated the dangers of unchecked executive power. They saw the pattern in other countries of executives going to war not for the national interest but for reasons purely private and personal. As John Jay explained in Federalist No. 4, executives engaged in wars "not sanctified by justice or the voice and interests" of their people, leading to heavy loss of life and national treasure. We have seen that same pattern from 1950 to the present time.

Questions about human nature that concerned the Framers in 1787 apply equally well to the last six to seven decades. From 1789 to 1950, no president claimed the right to take the country from a state of peace to a state of war. They knew that the Constitution left that decision solely to Congress. Starting with Truman and continuing up to Barack Obama, presidents have assumed they have the power to use offensive military force against other nations that have not attacked or threatened the United States. The Framers believed in 1787 that such decisions must be made through a deliberative process by Congress to avoid costly and ill-advised military adventures. That lesson applies particularly to American wars from Korea to the present time.

The value of Edelson's book is that it puts within easy reach both clear analysis and access to original documents to permit readers to form an independent judgment. By providing these documents, Edelson leaves it to the reader "to decide which arguments are best and how emergency presidential power should be defined." As he explains, presidents may decide to act unilaterally but it is their burden to persuade "Congress, the courts, the press, the people" that their actions are justified. That requirement helps preserve popular government.

One of the many themes in Edelson's book is that many "emergencies" are contrived events, heightened in public furor by misleading presidential statements. President Polk was determined to gain territory from Mexico. On December 2, 1845, he advised Congress about diplomatic efforts to determine the boundary between Mexico and Texas. Nevertheless, on May 11, 1846, he told Congress about military hostilities between U.S. and Mexican soldiers in disputed territory and announced that Mexican forces "have at last invaded our territory and shed the blood of our fellow-citizens on our soil." He produced no evidence that the territory belonged to the United States, but Congress authorized war.

In 1898, after the battleship *Maine* exploded while sitting in the Havana harbor, a naval board of inquiry concluded that the blast resulted from a mine placed outside the ship. Within a short time Congress declared war on Spain. The board failed to acknowledge that other U.S. ships had experienced spontaneous combustion of coal in bunkers placed next to magazines filled with ammunition, gun shells, and gunpowder. Several weeks before the *Maine* exploded, an investigative board warned the Secretary of the Navy about spontaneous coal fires that could detonate magazines.

The escalation of the Vietnam war after 1964 relied on statements by the Johnson administration that the North Vietnamese had committed two attacks on American destroyers. We now know the second "attack" did not occur. It consisted of late signals coming from the first. The Bush administration in 2002 issued six arguments why Iraq possessed weapons of mass destruction and could inflict even greater damage on the United States than the 9/11 attacks. All of the executive claims about aluminum tubes, uranium ore from a country in Africa, the presence of Al Qaeda in Iraq, the existence of chemical and biological weapons, mobile labs carrying biological agents, and drones capable of delivering WMDs were empty of evidence.

Advocates of unchecked presidential power often point to the actions of Abraham Lincoln at the start of the Civil War. He withdrew funds from the Treasury without an appropriation, raised the militia, ordered a blockade, and suspended the writ of habeas corpus. At no time, however, did he claim his actions were fully constitutional. He did not invoke "inherent," "plenary," "exclusive," or "preclusive" authority. As Edelson demonstrates by including Lincoln's speech to Congress on July 4, 1861, Lincoln believed "that nothing has been done beyond the constitutional competency of Congress." In that manner he publicly acknowledged that he had exercised the Article I powers of Congress and for that reason needed Congress to pass legislation to make his actions legal, which Congress proceeded to do.

Edelson rejects an argument frequently used to expand presidential power. In the *Curtiss-Wright* case of 1936, the Supreme Court in dicta claimed that the president possesses "plenary and exclusive power . . . as the sole organ of the federal government in the field of international relations." To support that assertion, the court referred to a speech given by John Marshall in 1800 when he served as a member of the U.S. House of Representatives. Edelson points out that Marshall in his speech never assigned to the president plenary control over foreign affairs. Instead, the court took Marshall's language out of context and misrepresented what he said and what he intended. At no time in Marshall's long public career did he adopt or promote the position attributed to him in *Curtiss-Wright*.

The Nazi saboteur case of 1942, relied on by the George W. Bush administration after the 9/11 terrorist attacks to create military tribunals without seeking statutory authority, is carefully analyzed by Edelson. He reviews the many defects in the 1942 procedures. Neither the military trial of eight German saboteurs nor the court's decision in *Ex parte Quirin* (1942) provided reliable precedents for the initiatives taken by the Bush administration. As Edelson notes, Justices Scalia and Stevens in their dissent in the 2004 *Hamdi* case dismissed *Quirin* as "not this Court's finest hour." Two years later, in *Hamdan v. Rumsfeld*, the court struck down the claim by the Bush administration that "inherent" powers were available to the president to create military tribunals. As a result, Bush had to come to Congress and seek legislative authority.

It is often argued that the freedoms of speech and press apply in times of peace but not in times of war. That was the position of Justice Oliver Wendell Holmes, Jr., in a series of decisions after World War I. Zechariah Chafee, Jr., in a penetrating critique in the *Harvard Law Review* in June 1919, defended the right of citizens to not only criticize government in time of peace but particularly in time of war and emergency conditions. He argued that the First Amendment declared a national policy that favored broad discussion of all public questions. The First Amendment protected not merely an individual's interest in speaking out but also society's interest in hearing criticism about the commitment of military forces. Democratic government requires impassioned debate that directly and forcefully challenges the government. This type of criticism is not seditious. It is a citizen's duty.

Chafee insisted that the First Amendment "is just as much a part of the Constitution as the war clauses, and that it is equally accurate to say that the war clauses cannot be invoked to break down the freedom of speech." For those who believe that the Bill of Rights should be placed on the shelf during time of war and emergency, he insisted that the first ten amendments to the Constitution "were drafted by men who had just been through a war." Once government has decided to use military force, Chafee said "there is bound to be a confused mixture of good and bad arguments in its support, and a wide difference of opinion as to its objects." Truth can be sifted out from falsehood "only if the government is vigorously and constantly cross-examined, so that the fundamental issues of the struggle may be clearly defined, and the war may not be diverted to improper ends, or conducted with an undue sacrifice of life and liberty, or prolonged after its just purposes are accomplished." In short, free speech and press are more important during time of war than in time of peace, because during time of war the government is capable of committing the greatest injustices on the people.

We now find ourselves in a vaguely defined war against Al Qaeda and other terrorist organizations, a state of emergency that has no clear end point. If we defer to those who insist that this crisis requires us to subordinate individual rights to presidential power, we will find that the "temporary" condition becomes the norm. As Edelson suggests, all Americans have a role to play in defining the scope and limits of presidential power. He provides the intellectual tools needed to equip citizens for this task. As presidents continue to claim broad, even unchecked power in the context of this open-ended effort sometimes called the "war on terror," we cannot depend only on members of Congress or judges to counter those claims. Ultimately, it will be up to us.

ACKNOWLEDGMENTS

I began writing this book in the winter of 2009–10 when I could not find a suitable book to use for a new class I was teaching on emergency presidential power and the war on terror. I am grateful to the American University students in Government 296 and Government 226 who offered comments on this book as I wrote it.

I am also grateful to Todd Eisenstadt and Meg Weekes for their support of this project. I deeply appreciate Louis Fisher's comments and advice. My wife, Jen Stark, was involved at every stage of this project. I am also grateful for the extremely helpful comments and suggestions made by Michael Genovese and Mitchel Sollenberger.

I also want to acknowledge the influence of my parents, Peter Gordon and Rae Edelson, who shaped my views about writing and about presidential power. I am certainly grateful, at the very least, to both of them. Finally, I am grateful to Gwen Walker at the University of Wisconsin Press for her essential support of this project.

EMERGENCY PRESIDENTIAL POWER

INTRODUCTION

Americans understandably think of the U.S. Constitution as a document that defines (among other things) the scope of presidential power in war and peace, calm and crisis. If you follow political debate about constitutional interpretation, which focuses on distinctions between "activism" and "strict construction," the process of defining presidential power would seem easy: just turn to Article II of the Constitution, which addresses executive power, and see what it has to say. Reality, it turns out, is more complicated. As one scholar notes, "the text and history of Article II fail to offer decisive guidance regarding presidential power."[1] When presidents want to take action, it is not always clear whether the Constitution provides the authority they desire. Some presidents are reluctant to act without clear constitutional or statutory authorization, but most presidents have not viewed their authority as restricted to the plain text of the Constitution or the explicit approval of Congress. When asked to review presidential actions, the Supreme Court has been unable to develop a "magical formula" to define the scope and limits of presidential authority.[2]

One area of special difficulty is the question of presidential authority to respond to national security threats: what powers do presidents have to respond to emergencies like war, rebellion, or the threat of terrorist attack?[3] Article II makes no express provision for such emergency presidential power—in fact, what emergency power the Constitution does provide seems to be assigned to Congress by Article I.[4] Presidents may and often do cite congressional authority as a basis for responding to threats to national security. When congressional authority is lacking, however, presidents often claim the right to take unilateral action. During crises, "presidents generally have not hesitated to do whatever, in their view, needed to be done."[5] Faced with a document that does not provide clear instructions and faced with crises that demand or seem to demand immediate action, presidents have found ways to justify actions not expressly authorized by the Constitution or statute.

The central problem this book addresses is this: given that the Constitution does not expressly provide for emergency presidential power in the absence of congressional authorization but presidents, in practice, do independently exercise such power, how do we define its scope and limits? In answering this question, I consider actions taken by each branch of the federal government. Presidents often do whatever they believe is necessary, but Congress and the courts do not always agree with them. All three branches of the federal government can and do play a role in defining emergency power. I will frequently use excerpts from Supreme Court opinions as guideposts for assessing the nature of emergency power—not because the Supreme Court necessarily has the last word on the matter but because the court has, since *Marbury v. Madison*, identified its duty as "say[ing] what the law is."[6] Court opinions highlight some of the central issues involved in assessing emergency presidential power, and they tell us what the justices think about these issues—including when the court thinks presidents have acted appropriately and when presidents have exceeded their authority. That does not mean the court always provides the right answers or even asks the right questions, but these opinions offer a useful window into the ongoing debate and discussion.

As noted and as is discussed in detail throughout this book, presidents have historically exercised power beyond what is expressly assigned to the executive branch by the text of the Constitution—often to the satisfaction of Congress, the courts, and the people. That does not mean, however, that all justifications for such actions are equally valid. For instance, presidents, members of Congress, judges, and scholars have recognized implied emergency presidential power that is linked to express powers and limited by contrary provisions of the Constitution.[7] On the other hand, arguments for inherent executive power, unmoored from and unlimited by the Constitution, are far more controversial.[8] This book aims to consider the strengths and weaknesses of different justifications offered for presidential power during war or other national security crises. I refer to this as emergency presidential power because presidents often assert authority to take unilateral action when necessary to protect national security, especially when there is no time for deliberation and/or, in their view, Congress is not equipped to respond.

Most observers agree that the president has at least some unilateral ability to take action necessary to respond to crisis, even though the Constitution is silent on the matter. However, there is disagreement as to the scope of such power.[9] Advocates for broad presidential power argue that the president has "plenary" or absolute power when it comes to defending the nation—that decisions in this context are for the president alone to make. Others conclude that presidents can initially act independently when they believe it is necessary to defend the nation; however, their actions must be retroactively approved by Congress and are subject to review by the courts. Some arguments, of course, are more persuasive than others, and one's conclusion about which argument is best may depend on constitutional text, court precedent, congressional action, and past presidential practice, as well as context—the specific reason why presidential authority is claimed in different cases. This book presents and explains the various arguments offered for specific presidential actions while offering different ways to consider the questions at stake but ultimately leaves it to you to decide which arguments are best and how emergency presidential power should be defined.

One may reasonably ask if, in the end, presidents do whatever they believe is necessary, why it matters how they justify their actions. First, presidents may act unilaterally, but, unless they achieve permanent dictatorial power, ultimately they must persuade others—Congress, the courts, the press, the people—that their actions are justified. As we will see, presidents have sometimes been able to do so, but not always. The justifications presidents offer for their actions are also important because they may be cited as precedent in the future. Lincoln's decision to order a naval blockade of the Confederacy is cited as support for broad presidential authority with regard to deployment of the military in the context of the war on terror. Franklin D. Roosevelt's decision to try captured Nazi saboteurs before a military tribunal is improperly cited as precedent for the decision to do the same with suspected terrorists.

The challenge for the Framers of the Constitution and for Americans today is to balance competing considerations. After the failure of the Articles of Confederation, which did not provide for an executive, the Framers realized it was necessary to create the presidency. The new president would have to have enough power to carry out the responsibilities assigned to the office and to resist encroachment from the other branches of the federal government, but there would also have to be limits on presidential power. The president would not be a king, as Alexander Hamilton explained in the Federalist Papers.[10] Unlike the eighteenth-century British monarch, the American president would share war power and power over foreign affairs with Congress, as part of the system of checks and balances the Framers developed. In the twenty-first century, this balancing continues. As Supreme Court Justice David Souter put it, "the Constitution embodies the desire of the American people, like most people, to have things both ways. We want order and security, and we want liberty."[11] Defining the scope and limits of emergency presidential power requires Americans to balance liberty and security, to make sure the president has enough authority to deal with threats to national security without taking on so much power that the system of checks and balances fails and liberty suffers.

Some of the discussion so far may seem fairly abstract, but the reward of unraveling the mysteries of emergency presidential power is that we can begin to arrive at answers—or at least possible answers—to specific questions we face today. Can the president decide to hold suspected terrorists indefinitely without charges? If suspected terrorists are prosecuted, can presidents order their trial before military tribunals instead of civilian courts? Was the Bush administration justified in authorizing waterboarding? If the president decides that the best way to prevent future terrorist attacks is by secretly listening to millions of telephone conversations and reading millions of e-mails, can he (or, at some point, she) order these actions? Was President Obama justified in authorizing the killing, without trial or hearing, of a U.S. citizen who was a suspected terrorist?

This book addresses each of these questions. Since the question of emergency presidential power begins with the Constitution itself, we start by considering how the Framers understood that power, to the extent that such inquiry produces useful guidance. We then examine how presidents have actually exercised and justified emergency power and what role Congress and the Supreme Court have played in defining such power.

As we will see, emergency presidential power is not a new idea. However, the way in which it is used in the twenty-first century, especially in the context of the war on terror, presents new challenges. If, in the past, one way to limit presidential power was by publicly debating the justifications presidents gave for using emergency power, what happens when power is exercised in secret, with justifications initially provided only in classified memoranda? If one way to limit emergency power is to require that it be temporary, that it be used only for as long as a particular crisis demands, what happens when crisis is open ended, when Americans find themselves in a war against terrorism that has no clear end point?[12] Defining the scope and limits of emergency presidential power becomes especially important, though also more difficult. Although we begin by considering how power has been defined and used historically, the ultimate goal is to develop a framework for emergency presidential power that meets the challenges of our time.

1

THE CONSTITUTION
AND EMERGENCY PRESIDENTIAL
POWER

One scholar has observed that, considering the constitutional framework, "[one] would marvel at how much Presidents have spun out of so little" in terms of defining presidential war power.[1] The observation applies with even more force to emergency presidential power—the Constitution does not expressly grant *any* such power to the president. The only explicit reference in the Constitution to emergency power of any sort appears in Article I, section 9: "The privilege of the writ of habeas corpus shall not be suspended, unless when in cases of rebellion or invasion the public safety may require it." Since this provision, known as the Suspension Clause, appears in Article I, which deals mainly with congressional power and its limitations, the Supreme Court has concluded that the emergency power to suspend the writ of habeas corpus belongs solely to Congress.[2] One could also describe the power "[t]o provide for calling forth the militia to execute the laws of the union, suppress insurrections and repel invasions" or the power to declare war as emergency powers because these powers could be used to respond to threats to national security.[3] However, like the power to suspend habeas corpus, these powers are expressly assigned to Congress—in Article I, section 8, of the Constitution.

And yet, despite the lack of any express authorization in the Constitution, presidents have independently exercised emergency power, and courts and scholars have justified its use in varying degrees.[4] If the Constitution does not directly identify any emergency presidential power, where does this idea come from? Without clear guidance from the Constitution, how can we know the scope as well as the limits of such power? Why should *any* unilateral emergency presidential power be recognized?

Although the Constitution does not specifically assign the president any independent emergency power, scholars cite several reasons for concluding such power exists. At the outset, it may be useful to categorize the various justifications for emergency presidential power that we will encounter throughout this book.

LIMITED UNILATERAL EMERGENCY PRESIDENTIAL POWER SUBJECT TO RETROACTIVE CONGRESSIONAL APPROVAL

Some scholars conclude that only strictly limited emergency presidential power exists—the power only to repel sudden attacks or invasions. This, its proponents argue, is a form of implied emergency power: if the nation has a right to defend itself against sudden attack or invasion, then *someone* in government must be able to exercise this right, and it makes sense, as a matter of both logic and historical record, that the president, as commander in chief of the military, would exercise the national right of self-preservation. Such power is said to flow from the president's enumerated powers and is limited by other provisions of the Constitution, including the Bill of Rights, and by the other branches of the federal government.

Along these lines, the political scientist Louis Fisher describes emergency presidential power as simply the power "to take actions necessary to resist sudden attacks either against the mainland of the United States or against American troops abroad."[5] Fisher points to records from the Constitutional Convention in Philadelphia: in debating the language of the Declare War Clause, delegates noted that the president would have "the power to repel sudden attacks."[6] Fisher concludes that the president possesses limited implied emergency power to act unilaterally in order to defend the nation; however, the president must seek retroactive approval from Congress, which may either vindicate or censure the president's actions.[7]

Advocates of this view of emergency presidential power emphasize that it permits the president to act promptly to defend the nation when necessary while preserving the rule of law by subordinating the president to legal authority and congressional review.[8] They often point to President Lincoln's actions during the Civil War to illustrate the way in which implied emergency power can work.[9]

BROAD UNILATERAL EMERGENCY PRESIDENTIAL POWER DEFINED BY THE PRESIDENT

Critics of a limited definition of emergency presidential power argue that the approach Fisher describes unwisely hamstrings the president and may expose the nation to danger. They argue for a broader vision of emergency presidential power. John Yoo, a law professor and a former attorney in the Office of Legal Counsel,[10] disagrees with Fisher's analysis of the debate at Philadelphia and concludes that the Framers meant to give the president "plenary" or complete constitutional power to take any military actions needed to defend the nation.[11] For Yoo, such actions are not limited to responding to sudden attacks. The president can authorize *any* action he or she believes necessary to defend the nation, including ordering preemptive military action. Congress cannot limit this authority; such decisions regarding the use of military force, in Yoo's view, "under our Constitution are for the president alone to make."[12] Under this approach, the president, rather than Congress or the courts, defines the scope and limits of emergency power.

Advocates of broad emergency presidential power, like Yoo, often base their claims in inherent rather than implied powers. Inherent powers have been defined as "[p]owers over and beyond those explicitly granted in the Constitution or reasonably to be implied from express powers."[13] They may also base their argument on the sole organ doctrine, a theory that the president exercises "plenary and exclusive power . . . in the field of international relations."[14] As discussed in chapter 5, the sole organ doctrine depends on a misreading or distortion of a speech then–U.S. Representative John Marshall gave in defense of President John Adams's authority to carry out a treaty passed by the Senate.[15] Presidents may also invoke the state secrets privilege, discussed in chapter 14, to shield claims of broad emergency power from review by the courts or Congress.

Advocates of broad emergency presidential power argue that such power is necessary in order to defend the nation, especially against twenty-first-century threats that demand immediate action.[16] Their approach suggests that the United States exists in a state of ongoing emergency that requires a president with the authority needed to deal with threats that are always present. Critics charge that this approach threatens to place presidents outside the rule of law, allowing them to wield unchecked power.[17]

EMERGENCY PRESIDENTIAL POWER
AUTHORIZED IN ADVANCE BY CONGRESS

As David Gray Adler observes, claims of unilateral emergency presidential power may be ambiguous and difficult to evaluate, "but what is clear is that Congress may, by statute, vest emergency powers in the president."[18] Indeed, an influential Supreme Court opinion concludes that "[w]hen the President acts pursuant to an express or implied authorization of Congress, his authority is at its maximum, for it includes all that he possesses in his own right plus all that Congress can delegate."[19] Even advocates of broad emergency presidential power acknowledge that advance congressional authorization of presidential action is "welcome."[20] However, even when presidents claim to act pursuant to congressional authorization, there can be questions as to the legitimacy of presidential action: did the president *really* act pursuant to congressional authorization, or does the president's claim rest on a misreading of statutory authority? Even if Congress did grant the president power to act, Congress itself may overstep the bounds of the Constitution by authorizing presidential action that conflicts, for example, with protections in the Bill of Rights.

How can we assess the strength of the various approaches used to define emergency presidential power? This is ultimately a problem of constitutional interpretation: the question is what amount of emergency power does the president have under the Constitution. Of course, one solution would be to say the president simply has no such power[21]—but the consequences would be a president powerless to respond to direct attacks against the United States without prior congressional authorization.[22] If we accept that there must be some emergency presidential power, we can begin to assess its scope and limits by considering various methods of constitutional interpretation, including what the Framers intended and how presidents, legislators, courts, and scholars have defined it. Most of this book is devoted to considering this question—how presidents, legislators, courts, and scholars have defined implied emergency presidential power. To provide a foundation for assessing their conclusions, we begin by considering the intellectual world the Framers inhabited and the influences that shaped their understandings of presidential power.

In 1952, Supreme Court Justice Robert H. Jackson concluded that it was pointless to turn to historical evidence when considering questions of presidential power because "[j]ust what our forefathers did envision, or would have envisioned had they foreseen modern conditions, must be divined from materials almost as enigmatic as the dreams Joseph was called upon to interpret for Pharaoh."[23] For Jackson, turning to scholarly analysis offers no help since it "only supplies more or less apt quotations from respected sources on each side of any question. They largely cancel each other."[24] The historian Jack Rakove argues that Justice Jackson "overstated the point."[25] It may not be possible to use historical evidence to provide indisputable answers to specific questions of constitutional meaning, but, Rakove claims, we can at least draw on historical sources to arrive at a "range of [constitutional] meanings."[26] In other words, as a first step in dealing with difficult constitutional problems—such as assessing the scope and limits of emergency presidential power—we may begin by considering whether a preferred interpretation put forward today is "plausible" given "the prevailing ideas of the time [when the Constitution was drafted]."[27]

This is not to dismiss Justice Jackson's perspective out of hand; as we will see, his conclusion that judges and presidential advisers are guided by practical "real world" considerations in defining the contours of presidential power is a useful hypothesis to examine as we assess both presidential actions and scholarly justifications. We will return to this point throughout the book. For now, however, we will consider Rakove's suggestion that something may be gained by considering the historical context of the Constitution, including the influences that shaped the Framers' understanding of executive power.

The Framers were both familiar with and influenced by European writers like John Locke, Charles de Secondat (the Baron de Montesquieu),[28] and William Blackstone.[29] These thinkers provided general principles—the idea that a separation of government powers would protect liberty, that foreign affairs was uniquely the province of the executive, and that at times the executive would need to take extralegal action in order to respond to an emergency.[30] The Framers sometimes built on and sometimes diverged from or reinterpreted these ideas, and they were also influenced by recent history in the colonies and in Britain. The seventeenth-century Stuart monarchs in Britain had claimed a "divine right" to rule that supported broad royal "prerogatives"—absolute powers, including emergency powers, that could not be challenged.[31] But their approach pitted them in civil war with advocates for parliamentary supremacy who ultimately won out, first taking the extraordinary step of executing one intransigent king and later inviting monarchs with more limited power to rule as Parliament's guest.[32]

Although royal power was reduced after the Glorious Revolution of 1688, British kings retained some prerogatives, including the power to initiate war.[33] Even John Locke, who endorsed parliamentary supremacy, recognized a need for royal prerogative and concluded that what he called the "federative power" over foreign affairs, including matters of war and peace, ought not to be given to the legislature; the executive should have both the executive and federative power.[34] Montesquieu, an eighteenth-century observer and admirer of the British system of constitutional monarchy, endorsed (like Locke) a separation of powers with regard to the legislature, executive, and judiciary.[35] Like Locke, he accepted certain prerogatives as essential to executive power.[36] These ideas were well known to the Framers and shaped their thinking, though they did not accept each premise relied on by Locke and Montesquieu. They expressly rejected the position of Locke and Blackstone that all power over external affairs be vested in the executive.

The Framers were also influenced by their own experiences with drafting state constitutions and the Articles of Confederation. These were practical "experiments" with republican theories of government, and the Framers learned from their successes as well as their mistakes. The early state constitutions of 1776, written by revolutionaries who had taken up arms against an overbearing monarch and royal governors, not surprisingly provided for executives with sharply limited powers.[37] State governors were deprived of prerogatives that had been wielded by royal governors. The Articles of Confederation, written in 1777, did not provide for an executive at all; the Continental Congress exercised executive power.[38]

During the Revolutionary War, the failure to provide for a capable executive proved costly. Government had trouble carrying out its functions. The Continental Congress was unable to carry out basic administrative tasks, and inefficiency threatened the war effort.[39] In an effort to address these problems, the Continental Congress created four executive departments in 1781 to carry out functions such as managing finances and conducting foreign affairs.[40]

When the Framers took up the question of defining executive power, in 1787, experience taught them to balance competing concerns. They did not want an all-powerful monarch who would re-create the excesses of the Stuart monarchs.[41] But the Articles of Confederation had gone too far in reacting against the idea of monarchy: the failure to provide for an executive at the national level left government dangerously inefficient, unable to perform its functions. The Framers also had Locke's and Montesquieu's idea of separation of powers in mind. To them, this did not mean a formalistic division of carefully insulated powers, and it did not mean, as the state constitution writers in 1776 had believed, a focus on protecting the judiciary and legislature from the executive. In 1787, the concern was with concentrating power in *any* one branch, as Montesquieu had warned. In a republic, the Framers believed, it was not likely that the executive would present the greatest threat to liberty—it was the legislature that was most to be feared. In fact, one important factor motivating the Framers as they described the powers of the federal government "was the desire to enable the executive to resist legislative encroachments."[42]

Different Framers had varying ideas as to how to define executive power. Alexander Hamilton and others were drawn to the idea of an "energetic" executive—one person who could act quickly to respond to crises and who was given power sufficient to defend against encroachment by Congress.[43] George Mason favored the idea of a "plural executive" that would avoid vesting executive power in any single person, either by dividing power among multiple executives or by creating a council of advisers to the president that would possess independent power.[44] Mason and others also worried that the president could be dominated by the Senate, a body that they saw as possessing legislative, executive (with regard to appointments and treaties), and judicial (through impeachment trials) power.[45]

Various questions and possibilities swirled around the debate in Philadelphia: how should control over foreign relations and war, Locke's "federative powers," be assigned—should these powers belong to the president or to Congress? How could the Framers ensure that the president would be powerful enough to withstand congressional encroachment? How could they construct a system that would prevent power from being concentrated in the hands of one branch?

These questions were answered, of course, by the Constitution itself, specifically in Articles I and II, which mainly address congressional and presidential power, respectively. In the areas of foreign relations and war, the Constitution divides power between the two branches. For example, Congress is assigned the power to declare war, while the president is made "Commander in Chief of the Army and Navy of the United States, and the Militia of the several states, when called into the actual service of the United States." The president is given power, with the advice and consent of the Senate, to make treaties, subject to approval by two-thirds of the Senate.

In arguing for ratification of the Constitution in the Federalist Papers, Alexander Hamilton, John Jay, and James Madison described, among other things, their views of executive power. As we will see, the Federalist Papers are still cited as a source to guide debate over the scope and limits of presidential power today. Hamilton is generally the favorite of those who favor broad executive power, although his position is more nuanced than it may seem at first glance. It is easy to see why Hamilton appeals to backers of broad emergency power; in Federalist No. 70, Hamilton declares that "[e]nergy in the Executive is a leading character in the definition of good government. It is essential to the protection of the community against foreign attacks. . . . A feeble Executive implies a feeble execution of the government."[46] Hamilton even invokes the example of dictatorship, noting that the ancient Romans sometimes would "take refuge in the absolute power of a single man, under the formidable title of Dictator . . . as against the invasions of external enemies who menaced the conquest and destruction of Rome."[47] Hamilton concluded that "unity" in the executive was essential; while some, like George Mason, favored a plural executive, Hamilton defended the Constitution's decision to place executive power in the hands of a single president.[48]

As we'll see, defenders of broad executive power emphasize Hamilton's praise for an energetic executive, one person who can act quickly and decisively (in contrast with multiple executives or a dilatory Congress) to respond to emergencies, especially when it is necessary to defend the United States against attack. However, they tend to overlook evidence that Hamilton acknowledged limits on executive power. In arguing for a single executive instead of a plural model, Hamilton explained that one benefit is that it is easier to hold a single person accountable: "one of the weightiest objections to a plurality in the Executive . . . is, that it tends to conceal faults and destroy responsibility."[49] It would be easier, Hamilton argued, to hold a single executive accountable for overreaching or abusing power; in this way, his argument acknowledges the importance of setting and enforcing limitations on executive power.

Moreover, in responding to concerns that the president would wield the powers of a monarch, Hamilton explained in Federalist No. 69 that there were important differences between a president and a king. Kings were hereditary monarchs, while presidents would be elected for finite terms of office. Presidents could be removed from office and then prosecuted and punished by the law, while kings were "sacred and inviolable." British kings could exercise an absolute veto over legislation, while the president's veto could be overruled by Congress. While the British model assigned Locke's federative powers to the king, the Constitution did not; the president could make treaties only with the advice and consent of the Senate, subject to agreement by two-thirds of the members of that body, whereas the British king was "the sole and absolute representative of the nation in all foreign transactions" and could independently enter into treaties. In addition, while the British king could declare war, raise armies and navies, and make rules to regulate the military, the president could do none of these things—power under the Commander in Chief Clause "would amount to nothing more than the supreme command and direction of the military and naval forces, as first General and admiral of the Confederacy."[50]

Poor health prevented John Jay from writing more than a few of the Federalist Papers, but in Federalist No. 4 he made an important contribution to the debate over presidential war power. Jay warned that:

> absolute monarchs will often make war when their nations are to get nothing by it, but for the purposes and objects merely personal, such as thirst for military glory, revenge for personal affronts, ambition, or private compacts to aggrandize or support their particular families or partisans. These and a variety of other motives, which affect only the mind of the sovereign, often lead him to engage in wars not sanctified by justice or the voice and interests of his people. But, independent of these inducements to war, which are more prevalent in absolute monarchies, but which well deserve our attention, there are others which affect nations as often as kings; and some of them will on examination be found to grow out of our relative situation and circumstances.[51]

The Framers hoped to navigate a middle path between on the one hand the danger of concentrated power associated with monarchy and on the other hand the danger of a feeble executive. In Federalist No. 4, Jay explained why it was important to be cautious about giving too much war power to a president. While the Articles of Confederation had proved that it was necessary to have an executive, the lesson of monarchs who abused war power served as a cautionary tale to the Framers in creating the presidency.

James Madison similarly spoke to the concern about creating a government of excessive power when he responded to critics who insisted the Constitution failed to respect the principle of separation of powers because the three branches of the federal government were not sealed off from one another in airtight compartments, each left to its own distinct and independent sphere of authority. In Federalist No. 47, Madison explained that the separation of powers doctrine was not intended to create this kind of formalistic government. The point was to create a system of checks and balances that would guard against the concentration of power in any one branch: "[t]he accumulation of all powers, legislative, executive and judiciary, in the same hands . . . may justly be pronounced the very definition of tyranny."[52] Madison expected that, in a republic with a "carefully limited" executive branch, the legislature was the most to be feared.[53] "Parchment barriers" between the different branches were not enough to guard against concentrated power—instead, each branch would be provided with the motivation and power to check the other branches.[54]

Madison's discussion of the separation of powers as a way to prevent power from concentrating in any one branch points to an important dilemma that the Framers sought to resolve: how to create a federal government that was strong enough to carry out the important responsibilities assigned to it, while still ensuring that its powers were limited. Turning to Hamilton once again, let's consider Federalist No. 23. As we'll see, like Federalist No. 70, No. 23 is often cited by supporters of broad executive power—for one thing, it contains the robust assertions that the federal government "ought to be clothed with all the powers requisite to complete execution of its trust" and that the powers necessary to defend the nation ought to be assigned to the federal government "without limitation."[55] At first glance, Federalist No. 23 looks like an excellent candidate to be recruited in support of a strong executive with plenary power to defend the nation.[56] But, as with Federalist No. 70, closer examination of Federalist No. 23 reveals that Hamilton's position is more nuanced than it initially appears.

First, Hamilton may disappoint the strong executive crowd because No. 23 does not speak to executive power specifically but, instead, addresses the need for the federal government *as a whole*—Congress and the president together—to possess all the power necessary to provide for national defense.[57] When Hamilton argued that it was necessary to provide the federal government with the broad powers needed to defend the nation, he was arguing that it was important to reject the system created by the Articles of Confederation because it failed to give the federal government the power it needed.[58] The federal government as a whole must be assigned the power needed to carry out important responsibilities such as defending the nation. These powers would be plenary in the sense that they would be completely assigned to the federal government, but they would be limited in the sense that the federal government would have only the power necessary to carry out its enumerated functions: "Shall the Union be constituted the guardian of the common safety? Are fleets and armies and revenues necessary to this purpose? The government of the Union must be empowered to pass all laws, and to make all regulations which have relation to them [i.e., to the specific powers assigned to Congress of raising fleets and armies and revenues]."[59]

It may be possible to identify some central themes when we consider what the Framers intended with regard to executive power. They wanted to cure the defects of the Articles of Confederation, which failed to provide for any executive branch at all, without re-creating a monarchy. They wanted to ensure that each branch of the federal government had the power necessary to carry out its responsibilities, which, for the president, would mean the power to defend the nation against sudden attack. As part of the constitutional system of checks and balances, the Framers divided

Locke's federative powers between the president and Congress, and they tried to ensure that power would not be concentrated in any one branch.

These are general principles. How can we begin to apply them in order to develop specific theories of emergency presidential power? As a starting point, some, like Fisher, emphasize that the Constitution represents a break with the British model, reflecting the Framers' decision to share the war powers and power over foreign affairs between the president and Congress. Others, like Yoo, conclude that the president has the authority to act unilaterally in these areas, arguing that these are matters of "executive power" uniquely suited to the executive branch. Yoo's argument looks to specific language in the Constitution. Article II begins by stating that "The executive Power shall be vested in a President of the United States of America." "Executive power" is not expressly defined in the Constitution, but advocates for broad presidential power note the contrast between this "vesting" clause in Article II and the vesting clause in Article I, which states that "All legislative Powers *herein granted* shall be vested in a Congress of the United States" (emphasis added). They reason that the Framers chose their words carefully, limiting Congress's authority to the express and implied powers granted by the Constitution. By choosing to omit this limiting language in Article II, they argue, the Framers meant to assign the president all the power that *inherently* belongs to the executive of any nation. In this view, some power is inherently, by its very nature, "executive" — regardless of what the Constitution says in express or implied terms.

Critics of this approach point out that Article II goes on to list specific powers after the vesting clause; for instance, the president is to be "Commander in Chief of the Army and Navy" and is given power to grant pardons, make treaties (with the advice and consent of the Senate, and with a two-thirds vote), appoint Supreme Court justices (again, with the advice and consent of the Senate, though a two-thirds vote is not required), and ask for written opinions from any of the Cabinet secretaries[60] on any subject relating to their duties. As Supreme Court Justice Robert H. Jackson put it in 1952, if the Framers simply meant to assign the president *all* of the "executive power," without limitation, then "it is difficult to see why the forefathers bothered to add several specific items, including some trifling ones."[61]

Advocates of broad presidential power emphasize that war power and power over foreign affairs are uniquely "executive" functions necessarily committed to presidential discretion. They argue that Congress's formal power to declare war is distinguished from the president's substantive power to "make war," noting that the Constitutional Convention amended an original draft of the Constitution giving to Congress the power to make war, changing the word "make" to "declare" in the final version. In this view, "declaring" war is little more than a formality. Others take a different view of the significance of the changed language, pointing to records from the Constitutional Convention indicating that the change was intended only to "leav[e] to the Executive the power to repel sudden attacks."[62] This debate will be taken up in more detail in chapter 9.

Advocates of broad presidential power also argue that direction of foreign affairs is a uniquely executive function, citing a speech the future Supreme Court Chief Justice John Marshall made in 1800 when he was a member of the U.S. House of Representatives. Marshall, who was defending President John Adams against charges that Adams had improperly delivered a criminal suspect to Great Britain pursuant to an extradition treaty, described the president as "the sole organ of the nation in its external relations, and its sole representative with foreign nations."[63] Marshall was not suggesting, however, that the president had sole authority over foreign affairs, only that the president is the sole organ of the U.S. government when it comes to implementing treaties duly approved by the Senate.[64] However, a Supreme Court opinion written more than one hundred years later cited Marshall's remarks to support a view of broad presidential power in the area of foreign affairs.[65] In the court's 1936 *Curtiss-Wright* decision, Justice Sutherland quoted Marshall's sole organ statement to support the conclusion that the president has extremely broad, even "plenary and exclusive power . . . in the field of international relations—a power which does not require as a basis for its exercise an act of Congress, but which, of course, like every other governmental power, must be exercised in subordination to the applicable provisions of the Constitution."[66] In other words, Justice Sutherland asserted, when it comes to foreign affairs, the president has unilateral authority and need not seek approval from Congress.

Although Sutherland's discussion of plenary presidential authority in the field of foreign affairs was dicta, a part of the opinion not necessary for the court to reach its ultimate result, his statement has been, as we will see, cited by subsequent advocates of broad presidential power. Critics of the sole organ doctrine charge that Justice Sutherland took Marshall's words out of context, "implying a scope of presidential power that Marshall never embraced."[67] We will take up the sole organ doctrine again in chapter 5.

An important problem in considering emergency presidential power is how to assess the various arguments advanced on the subject. The starting point for analyzing different theories of presidential power is the Constitution itself. However, as noted, the Constitution does not always provide clear answers to specific questions, and it does not come with explicit instructions telling us—or the president, Congress, and the courts—how it should be interpreted. We have begun to explore other interpretive approaches (apart from a literal interpretation of the Constitution) by discussing some ways to consider what the Framers intended. In addition, scholars, judges, presidential advisers, members of Congress, and presidents themselves can turn to court precedent as well as to presidential and congressional practice to determine the scope and limits of emergency presidential power. Once the Constitution was ratified and George Washington took office as the nation's first president, the contours of emergency power were shaped in part by what presidents did in practice and how Congress and the Supreme Court responded. Debate over what presidential power would mean in practice began with the first president, as we discuss in the next chapter.

2

PRESIDENTIAL POWER

IN THE YOUNG REPUBLIC

WASHINGTON'S NEUTRALITY
PROCLAMATION, A "HALF-WAR"
WITH FRANCE, AND THE ALIEN
AND SEDITION ACTS

In the 1790s, a new nation began to develop the meaning of the Constitution in practice, filling in gaps and attempting to resolve ambiguities. The nation's first president tested the limits of his power in the context of foreign affairs and matters of war and peace but ultimately recognized that Congress shared power in these areas. In 1793, with Great Britain and France at war, it was not clear whether the United States was obligated to assist France pursuant to a treaty signed in 1778.[1] Secretary of the Treasury Alexander Hamilton urged Washington to suspend the treaty, arguing that this was justified by the French Revolution; the French government that had entered into the treaty with the United States no longer existed.[2] Secretary of State Thomas Jefferson argued that the United States should respect its treaty obligations to France.[3] President Washington, who was concerned that private citizens might take actions that would bring the United States into the war between Great Britain and France, issued a proclamation on April 22, 1793, declaring that the United States would remain neutral and requiring U.S. citizens to stay out of the conflict.[4] After consulting his cabinet, Washington decided to proceed unilaterally, rather than call Congress into special session to consider the question.[5]

This was an example of emergency presidential power: Washington was claiming the independent authority to take action he considered justified by national security concerns. The problem, of course, was that by declaring neutrality, Washington could effectively preempt Congress's authority to decide whether to make war.[6] When critics questioned Washington's authority to issue the proclamation, Hamilton used the pseudonym "Pacificus" to write essays in defense of the president's unilateral action.[7] Hamilton reasoned that *some* branch of the federal government must have the power to interpret treaties and declare neutrality when it was appropriate to do so. Logically, he said, it did not make sense for the judiciary or the legislature to do this. The judiciary does play a role in interpreting treaties, but only when a case is brought before a court asking it to resolve a specific dispute. Congress, Hamilton asserted, has no constitutional power to make or interpret treaties, and it "is not the *organ* of intercourse between the United States and foreign nations." Therefore, by process of elimination, the power of interpreting treaties and declaring neutrality must belong to the executive branch.[8]

Hamilton further supported his conclusion by arguing that these duties were part of the executive power assigned to the president by the Constitution.[9] Contrasting the language of the Vesting Clause in Article I with that in Article II,[10] Hamilton concluded that since the executive power was vested in a president without limitation, the president possessed *all* power that could be described as "executive"—unless the Constitution specifically said otherwise: "the *executive power* of the nation is vested in the President; subject only to the *exceptions* and *qualifications* which are expressed in the [Constitution]." For instance, since the Constitution specifically assigns Congress the power to declare war, that is not part of the executive power belonging to the president. However, since the power to interpret treaties and to declare neutrality is not specifically assigned to another branch of government, it properly belongs to the president as part of the constitutional grant of executive power.[11]

Hamilton observed that it was not unprecedented for the president to exercise some implied executive power; Washington had already done so by removing federal officeholders from office, though the Constitution does not expressly grant the president such removal power. However, Hamilton understood that the president does not exercise power in a vacuum. A declaration of peace must be considered in the context of Congress's power to declare war. Since the president is charged with executing the law, it is his duty to enforce a state of peace when, in his view, a treaty requires it. Hamilton did not claim that by "declaring peace"

Washington had preempted Congress's power to declare war. Congress remains "free to perform its duties," including deciding to declare war; however, since the president may act first, as Washington did here, he can "establish an antecedent state of things, which ought to weigh in the legislative decisions."[12]

Hamilton's view did not necessarily seem incompatible with Madison's view of checks and balances. For Hamilton, the president did not operate in an independent bubble of authority. Executive power was sometimes divided, with Congress possessing concurrent authority, for instance, to determine whether a treaty requires the country to go to war—a power overlapping with the president's duty to determine whether the same treaty requires the nation to remain at peace. Accordingly, even when executive power is assigned to the president, Congress may not be precluded from acting, though, in Hamilton's view, it ought to take previous presidential action into account in making its decisions.[13] Still, Hamilton's position did not satisfy Jefferson, who urged Madison to "take up your pen . . . and cut [Hamilton] to pieces in the face of the public."[14]

Jefferson believed that Hamilton's construction of executive power went too far, that declaring peace was beyond the president's purview.[15] Madison shared Jefferson's concerns, worrying that Hamilton would give to the president "[a]n assumption of prerogatives clearly not found in the Constitution [and] having the appearance of being copied from a Monarchical model."[16] Madison believed that Hamilton was improperly writing Congress out of the equation, as it alone possessed the power to declare war and because the Senate shared with the president the power to make peace, through the Senate's responsibility to approve treaties by a two-thirds majority.[17] However, Madison ultimately found it difficult to complete the task Jefferson urged on him.[18] Madison mustered his responses to Hamilton in a series of essays written under the pen name "Helvidius." Madison argued that Hamilton took an overly broad view of executive power that was more closely aligned with the British model than with the U.S. Constitution, though Madison observed that even Locke had concluded that the executive and federative powers were distinct.[19] Madison suggested that Locke, living under a monarch, saw a need to assign federative powers to the king but that the Framers, who rejected the British model of broad executive power and prerogative, had decided differently; under the Constitution, powers over war and foreign affairs were not fully invested in the president.

Madison then took what might be called a formalistic approach to defining the separation of powers, insisting that the power to make treaties is a legislative power because it involves lawmaking. The president's duty is merely to carry out treaties, like other laws.[20] Madison might have been better served to apply the definition of separation of powers he had given in the Federalist Papers—that it did not aim to place each branch of government in a hermetically sealed compartment but, rather, sought to assign overlapping powers, a system of checks and balances designed to achieve the ultimate goal of preventing the concentration of power in any one branch.[21] In fact, this seemed to be Madison's real objection to Hamilton's definition of executive power—not some formalistic concern that executive power would intrude on the legislative sphere but a fear that Hamilton's model would simply concentrate too much power in the hands of the president, raising concerns of "tyranny."[22] Madison believed that allowing the president to interpret treaties and declare neutrality would be incompatible with his responsibility as commander in chief: "Those who are to *conduct a war* cannot in the nature of things, be proper or safe judges, whether *a war ought* to be *commenced, continued,* or *concluded.*"[23]

Though Hamilton's defense of Washington's actions raised concerns for Jefferson and Madison about unbridled executive power, in practice, the proclamation was not as sweeping as it seemed. In order for the proclamation to be enforced against U.S. citizens who violated its terms, statutory authorization proved necessary. The executive branch was forced to abandon prosecutions when jurors rejected the notion of convicting citizens for a crime created by executive proclamation instead of statute.[24] Faced with the problem of an unenforceable proclamation, Washington turned to Congress, asking for authority to prosecute violators of neutrality and conceding that the legislative branch could, at its discretion, either ratify or reject his initial decision to proclaim neutrality. In 1794, Congress passed legislation generally affirming Washington's neutrality proclamation and giving him the statutory authorization to prosecute citizens who threatened to entangle the United States in the European war.[25]

The question of war power presented other challenges. The Framers of the Constitution were familiar with the concepts of "perfect" and "imperfect" war. The first was a formally declared general war, the second a more limited war, not formally declared, typically involving self-defense. The Supreme Court recognized this distinction as well but concluded that since "the whole powers of war [were] . . . vested in Congress [by the Constitution]. . . . Congress may authorize general hostilities . . . or partial hostilities."[26]

War between Great Britain and France and the question of whether the new United States would enter into that conflict led to additional developments regarding the interaction between executive and legislative powers. The Alien and Sedition Acts were enacted in 1798, amid fears that the new United States would be drawn into a war with France and that the excesses of France's Reign of Terror would be repeated in the United States by Americans sympathetic to the French Revolution. France had allied with the colonies during the American Revolution, but, after the United States gained independence, tensions developed between the new nation and France. There were also long-standing tensions between Britain and France that, as noted, had developed into open warfare, and the United States was affected by this, as well. When the United States entered into a treaty with Britain that resolved Americans' anger aroused by British seizures of American ships, France saw that as a sign that the United States was becoming too friendly with Britain for its taste. France responded by raiding American ships. When the Adams administration attempted to engage in diplomacy with France, the French suggested that the United States would have to pay a bribe before discussions could begin—this was the infamous "XYZ affair." (President Adams referred to three French agents who proposed the bribe as X, Y, and Z.) War between the United States and its former ally, France, seemed imminent—in fact, President Adams described these events as "the Half-War with France."[27]

Adams was a Federalist, and his party took an anti-France position, preparing for war and using patriotic feeling to rally support around the president. His opponents, the Democratic-Republicans, led by Vice President Thomas Jefferson,[28] were sympathetic to the French, whom they saw as defenders of democratic government in their war against Britain, which was, of course, still a monarchy. Federalists believed the French revolutionaries were dangerous radicals, especially after the Reign of Terror, during which the Revolutionary government guillotined thousands of political enemies; the Democratic-Republicans believed the Federalists were too cozy with the British and wanted to lead the new United States back toward monarchy and aristocracy.[29]

The Federalists saw the XYZ affair and tensions with France as an opportunity to weaken their political opponents, the Democratic-Republicans, and, in 1798, Federalist members of Congress passed several pieces of legislation toward this end. The centerpieces were the Alien and Sedition Acts[30] and the lesser-known but, in later years, quite important Alien Enemies Act (also known as the Enemy Alien Act).[31]

The Alien Act[32] authorized the president, at any time that the law was in effect, "to order all such aliens [i.e., noncitizens] as he shall judge dangerous to the peace and safety of the United States . . . to depart out of the territory of the United States." In other words, the president was given the sole authority to determine, during peacetime, if a noncitizen was "dangerous" and to order the deportation of such a person. The president's decision could not be challenged in court. Noncitizens who were ordered to leave the country and did not comply could be imprisoned and barred from gaining citizenship in the future. The Sedition Act made it a crime "to print, utter or publish . . . any false, scandalous and malicious writing . . . against the government of the United States [including Congress or the president] . . . with intent to defame [them], or to bring them into contempt or disrepute; or to excite against them the hatred of the good people of the United States, or to stir up sedition [discontent or rebellion] within the United States."[33]

Critics of the Alien Act argued that Congress had improperly delegated to the president its duty to enact clear legislation; instead of defining specific offenses, the act's vague language left it entirely up to the president to determine when noncitizens were dangerous.[34] These critics worried that the act concentrated too much power in the hands of the president, who was authorized to judge whether an individual was dangerous and deport him or her from the country without trial.[35] The Sedition Act was seen as violating the First Amendment's Free Speech Clause by punishing critics of the government because of their viewpoint.

The Alien Act was never enforced, but the Sedition Act was used to prosecute and convict critics of the Adams administration. The Democratic-Republicans protested that both laws were unconstitutional. Jefferson expressed his opposition in a document called the Kentucky Resolutions (his authorship was kept secret, but the resolutions were approved by the Kentucky General Assembly). Jefferson argued that the Constitution gave the federal government limited power, emphasizing the Tenth Amendment, which provides that "the powers not delegated to the United States by the Constitution, nor prohibited by it to the states, are reserved to the states respectively, or to the people." In other words, Jefferson believed the Alien and Sedition Acts were unconstitutional because the Constitution simply did not give the federal government the power granted by these legislative acts. The Federalists responded that (1) noncitizens had no constitutional rights,[36] (2) during time of crisis (again, war with France seemed imminent), government had the right and responsibility to crack down on dissent, (3) each law reflected the government's "right and duty . . . of self-preservation," and (4) if the laws were unconstitutional, courts would refuse to enforce them.[37]

The Alien and Sedition Acts were scheduled to expire within three years and did in fact expire without being renewed (neither law was ever challenged in court; however, the Supreme Court later concluded that "[a]lthough the Sedition Act was never tested in this Court, the attack upon its validity has carried the day in the court of history.").[38] The laws provoked an outcry and backlash against the Federalists, helping lead to Jefferson's election to the presidency in 1800 (as president, Jefferson pardoned those who had been convicted under the Sedition Act). These laws are, in retrospect, seen as a mistake, as an example of the government overreaching during a time of crisis to unnecessarily crack down on dissent and opposition.

However, a third law passed in 1798, the Alien Enemies Act (also called the Enemy Alien Act), remains on the books more than two hundred years later, in essentially the same language used in 1798.[39] The Alien Enemies Act allowed—and still allows—the arrest and deportation of noncitizens when war is declared or the United States is invaded or invasion is threatened.[40] In these circumstances, "natives, citizens, denizens, or subjects of the hostile nation or government" who are male[41] and over the age of fourteen can be "apprehended, restrained, secured and removed as alien enemies."[42] The president is assigned power to determine "the manner and degree of restraint" and can establish other regulations necessary "for the public safety," though noncitizens apprehended under this law are permitted a hearing in court.[43] However, the Supreme Court has ruled that courts may not review the president's determination that a particular noncitizen is dangerous. The court additionally has ruled that the law continues to apply after formal hostilities end.[44]

This is a broad, sweeping law—and, as interpreted by the Supreme Court, it grants the president (or others the president assigns authority to) seemingly unchecked power to designate a noncitizen as an enemy simply by virtue of his or her affiliation with a "hostile nation or government," whether or not the noncitizen has taken any specific action. The Alien Enemies Act has been invoked several times over the years, including during the War of 1812, World War I, and World War II.[45] Its existence and application may have helped strengthen the misimpression that noncitizens are not covered by the constitutional protections contained in the Bill of Rights.

Events in the 1790s suggested that presidents could wield broad power during crisis, though not by completely writing Congress out of the equation. Different observers reach different conclusions as to the historical lessons to be learned. With regard to the Pacificus-Helvidius debate, for example, John Yoo concludes that "[h]istory has looked more favorably on Hamilton's arguments than Madison's." Yoo sees the episode as marking the beginning of the idea that "Presidents . . . would exercise the initiative in foreign affairs."[46] He also suggests that Hamilton's definition of executive power lays the groundwork for the unitary executive theory, which we consider in chapter 9. Louis Fisher does not see Washington's neutrality proclamation as precedent for unilateral presidential action; after all, the proclamation itself needed congressional approval before it could be enforced in practice. For Fisher, the episode shows that Washington recognized the limits of executive power and ultimately deferred to Congress.[47] Similarly, President Adams did not unilaterally seize the power to deport enemy aliens or punish dissenters; these powers were granted him by Congress.[48] As we will see, later presidents acted on their own during war or crisis, sometimes seeking congressional approval, sometimes not.

3

LINCOLN AND
THE WARTIME CONSTITUTION

As the nation moved into the nineteenth century, the scope and limits of emergency presidential power remained uncertain. Adams had exerted extraordinary power during a time of crisis, but he had done so pursuant to specific acts of Congress. Some of his successors further pressed the limits of their authority in the context of national security,[1] acting without authorization from Congress.[2] In 1846, President James Polk, who was seeking to expand U.S. territory, sent troops into "disputed territory along the Texas-Mexico border."[3] Polk justified his action as a defensive measure taken in response to the threat that Mexico might attack Texas.[4] When the U.S. troops—themselves seen as invaders by Mexico—were attacked by Mexican forces, Polk "stampeded Congress into a recognition of a state of war."[5]

Polk seemed to be expanding the idea that the Constitution implicitly provides presidents with the authority to respond quickly to national security threats. His actions pointed out a flaw in the theory of implied emergency presidential powers by demonstrating that the actual existence of an "emergency" could be subjectively determined. Polk's critics argued that his view of presidential power was dangerous. Abraham Lincoln, then a member of the U.S. House of Representatives, argued that Polk's actions in essentially initiating war on his own and later seeking congressional recognition of the established fact of war were reminiscent of the "Kingly oppressions" that drove the Framers to assign war-making power to Congress. Lincoln suggested that Polk's defenders gave the president the power of a monarch that "*no one man*" should possess.[6]

Other early and mid-nineteenth-century presidents looked to specific authorization from Congress before taking action, as Adams had done. For instance, Thomas Jefferson took military measures against the Barbary states in North Africa four decades before Polk's action against Mexico, but Jefferson sought and received explicit congressional authorization.[7] Jefferson accepted a version of unilateral emergency presidential power, though he believed that a president who initially acted on his own to defend the nation would ultimately have to seek approval from Congress; otherwise, such action would be illegitimate.[8] When President James Buchanan, Lincoln's predecessor, believed military action might be necessary to respond to potential threats to American shipping in Central America, he expressly asked Congress for advance authority to deploy military forces, if the circumstances demanded such action. Congress rejected President Buchanan's request, and one senator argued that Buchanan was essentially asking Congress to give him unbounded power to decide when and how war could be waged—an attempt to usurp Congress's constitutional power to declare war.[9]

Despite his criticism of the events leading to the Mexican War, when Lincoln became president he took a position that was, on the surface, closer to Polk's than Buchanan's when it came to presidential power in the context of war or crisis. Of course, there were important differences between Lincoln's and Polk's actions: Polk used a contrived emergency as pretext for sending troops to fight a foreign war aimed at acquiring new territory, while Lincoln was responding to a rebellion that threatened the survival of the Union.[10] In responding to the emergency of secession, President Lincoln did not always wait for congressional authorization. In important ways, he simply acted on his own. However, he sought and gained retroactive approval for most of these actions. Lincoln did break new ground by asserting that the Constitution implicitly gave the president extraordinary power—even the power to set aside individual rights during wartime. But Lincoln could argue that a clear emergency—a civil war that threatened the nation's very survival—justified his extraordinary actions.

Even before Lincoln took office, seven states had already seceded from the Union. After his inauguration in March 1861, Lincoln decided that swift presidential action was necessary. Faced with the crisis of secession, then open warfare, Lincoln decided to take action first, seeking congressional authorization later. In his first few months in office, with Congress in recess, Lincoln took a number of independent actions, some of which involved powers apparently committed to Congress by the Constitution. Lincoln decided to send supplies to the imperiled (and soon-to-fall) Fort Sumter, in Charleston Harbor. Then, after Sumter fell, he called up the militia, called for volunteers to join the regular military, suspended the writ of habeas corpus, prohibited the mailing of "disloyal" publications, authorized the Treasury to transfer money to private individuals who would make purchases for the military, and ordered a naval blockade of the Confederacy.[11]

As the Civil War became a long, drawn-out struggle, Lincoln continued to exert broad, seemingly extraconstitutional presidential power, including the right "to arrest people without warrant, to seize property, to suppress newspapers, [and] to emancipate slaves"—even though Congress never formally declared war.[12] This was an unprecedented expansion of presidential power without clear advance authorization by Congress. Lincoln was criticized, even by some abolitionists, as a tyrant.[13]

How could Lincoln justify these actions, none of which are expressly assigned to the executive branch by the Constitution?[14] Lincoln argued that swift, decisive action was necessary to save the nation. He asked, rhetorically, "[m]ust a government, of necessity, be too *strong* for the liberties of its own people, or too *weak* to maintain its own existence?"[15] For Lincoln, the question answered itself—he would do what he believed was necessary to preserve the Union.[16]

Although Lincoln's choice has obvious pragmatic appeal—especially in hindsight—the Constitution itself does not expressly provide for such power. Many scholars conclude, nonetheless, that emergency action may be justifiable, at least in some circumstances. The idea that a president may exercise power not expressly delegated to the executive by the Constitution traces its origins to "Lockean prerogative," what the political philosopher John Locke described as "[t]h[e] power to act according to discretion, for the publick good, without the prescription of the Law, and sometimes even against it."[17] Locke described this as an emergency power available to the executive when normal processes are too slow to cope with crisis. It allows the executive to act even when the law does not expressly provide authority—or even when the law prohibits action.[18]

Although the Framers did not expressly incorporate Lockean prerogative into the Constitution, they envisioned presidential authority to respond to emergencies that threatened the nation.[19] Most scholars recognize the availability of emergency presidential power, if not as a creature of the Constitution, then at least as a historical reality describing how the presidency has functioned in practice.[20] However, some argue that there is an important difference between the prerogative described by Locke and the extraordinary power Lincoln exercised: the former is an emergency power inherent to all executives, while the latter can be connected to the Constitution, at least as an implied power.[21] The historian Arthur M. Schlesinger Jr. and the political scientist Louis Fisher argue that this is an important distinction and that Lincoln's actions were carefully circumscribed in the sense that he did not claim extraconstitutional authority to act.[22] However, they reach these conclusions in different ways. Schlesinger suggests that Lincoln's actions were justified as implied constitutional powers—in other words, that the Constitution implicitly gave Lincoln the authority to act on his own; Fisher argues that Lincoln recognized he was acting extra-constitutionally and properly deferred to Congress by seeking retroactive approval for his actions.

For Schlesinger, Lincoln's actions can be understood and justified within the bounds of the Constitution by considering two points. First, Lincoln invoked the tradition that the Constitution implicitly assigns the federal government authority to respond to emergencies that threaten the nation. Schlesinger describes this as Lincoln's way of constitutionalizing the Lockean prerogative by asserting that the federal government had an implied right to self-preservation that justified extraordinary presidential action in response to crisis.[23] Second, Schlesinger argues that Lincoln added something to the national self-preservation argument Polk and others had presented in other contexts. Lincoln suggested that the Constitution itself was different in wartime, and he grounded this argument in specific clauses of the Constitution: the presidential oath and the Commander in Chief Clause.[24]

Article II, section 1, of the Constitution requires the president to take the following oath or affirmation before entering office: "I do solemnly swear (or affirm) that I will faithfully execute the Office of President of the United States, and will to the best of my Ability, preserve, protect and defend the Constitution of the United States." Lincoln saw this as a basis for extraordinary presidential power—if the president was sworn to defend the Constitution, "what limits were there on his duty to act if the nation was in danger?"[25] If the federal government had an implicit right to self-preservation, that right could be exercised by the president. With the "government itself go[ing] to pieces," his first responsibility was to preserve the nation.[26]

Lincoln also found a basis for expanded wartime presidential power in the Commander in Chief Clause.[27] Some believed, and some still believe, this clause simply makes the president civilian commander of the military with authority to issue orders to military forces—in fact, the Supreme Court had said as much in *Fleming v. Page*, an 1850 decision.[28] Lincoln, however, concluded that, as commander in chief during wartime, he had "a right to take any measure which may best subdue the enemy."[29]

While Schlesinger suggested that Lincoln's actions could be understood as an exercise of implied constitutional power requiring no endorsement by Congress, others, while still viewing Lincoln's actions as justified, emphasize retroactive congressional approval as an essential step necessary to mark Lincoln's actions with the stamp of legality.[30] Louis Fisher asserts that Lincoln "appreciated that his powers were not indefinite . . . and he took steps to preserve not only the Union, but the Constitution."[31] Though he initially took unilateral action, Lincoln forthrightly made the case to Congress that he had only acted in its place by exercising power assigned to Congress under the Constitution (e.g., the power to suspend habeas corpus).[32] He asked for and received "statutory ratification to legalize what he had done."[33] This allowed Lincoln to preserve the constitutional order even as he preserved the Union by acknowledging when his actions exceeded his power under Article II and relying on Congress to legitimize his acts.[34]

Daniel Farber concludes that, while "some of what Lincoln and his subordinates did exceed[ed] their constitutional authority," these actions were not "a threat to the entire constitutional order [because of] Lincoln's willingness to seek congressional ratification and face the legal consequences if it was not forthcoming."[35] Although Lincoln took sweeping unilateral action, especially at the beginning of the Civil War, he eventually obtained retroactive approval from Congress for most of his actions, as discussed later in this chapter.[36] Farber, Fisher, and other scholars conclude that doing so legitimized Lincoln's actions, demonstrating that he did not hold himself above Congress or the Constitution and did not claim that his power was unchecked. These scholars would caution against resting Lincoln's actions on either inherent or implied presidential power alone, arguing that this creates a template for potentially unrestricted power.[37]

These different viewpoints raise some questions to consider in analyzing Lincoln's actions. Was Lincoln exercising implied constitutional power that simply obviated the need to seek congressional input? In other words, was retroactive congressional approval nice but not absolutely necessary?[38] Or, as Fisher and Farber hold, was it essential for Lincoln to gain retroactive congressional approval for actions that otherwise exceeded his constitutional authority? Can or should either of these rules be applied broadly to other presidents, as well? If a kind of implied or inherent Lockean prerogative exists, how far does the prerogative extend? If, on the other hand, presidents must turn to Congress when they take extraordinary action, does this mean that a president may always legitimize extraconstitutional action by gaining retroactive approval? What would happen if Congress believes the president acted illegally? What role, if any, should the courts play? What happens, or what *should* happen, if a court rules that the president exceeded his or her constitutional authority? As we'll see, this question presented itself at the beginning of the Civil War when the Supreme Court's chief justice disagreed with one of Lincoln's decisions.

Lincoln insisted he was acting constitutionally in setting aside individual rights in a *limited* way—during the temporary emergency posed by the Civil War—and he conceded that his actions might very well be unconstitutional in other times. In essence, Lincoln argued that the president had the right and, indeed, the duty to suspend constitutional protections for the limited purpose of preserving the nation. However, Lincoln's actions threatened to create broader precedent, especially as applied by future presidents in different, perhaps unforeseen circumstances.

Lincoln's defenders (and, of course, there are many) argue that he did only what was necessary to defeat an insurrection and that he carefully preserved constitutional rights and deferred to the other branches of the federal government whenever possible—newspapers were not broadly censored, there was no revival of the Sedition Act from 1798, and expansions of presidential power were designed to last only as long as the rebellion itself.[39] They conclude that Lincoln took unilateral action exceeding his Article II powers only when absolutely necessary and that he demonstrated his commitment to the rule of law under the Constitution by seeking retroactive approval from Congress.[40] One potential problem was that future presidents might exploit Lincoln's actions as precedent for broader uses of presidential power. That is one reason why it is important to consider *why* Lincoln's actions were justified—was he exercising an emergency power that did not require congressional approval, or was it essential that he did make his case to Congress and obtain retroactive approval for his actions?

JUDICIAL DECISIONS INVOLVING LINCOLN'S ASSERTION OF PRESIDENTIAL POWER DURING THE CIVIL WAR

As noted, during his first months in office (with Congress in recess), President Lincoln took several extraordinary and unilateral actions, including suspending habeas corpus, arresting allegedly disloyal individuals, and organizing a naval blockade. It was far from clear that these actions were constitutional, and there was a question as to whether the courts or Congress (or both) would act to rein Lincoln in.[41] As we'll see, the courts, or more specifically, the chief justice of the U.S. Supreme Court, had the first opportunity, with Congress out of session in early 1861.

Lincoln took these actions in the midst of national crisis and insurrection; Confederate forces had attacked Fort Sumter in South Carolina just over a month after the new president was inaugurated. On April 15, 1861, after the fort fell, Lincoln issued a call for troops. Washington itself was threatened—it lay between Virginia, which seceded on April 17, and Maryland, which seemed likely to leave the Union as well.[42]

Troops headed from Massachusetts and Pennsylvania for the capital city had to pass through a railroad station in Baltimore, a city with many pro-secession residents. The troops were met by a mob of thousands of hostile Marylanders. Fighting broke out between soldiers and the crowd, and several people on both sides were killed. With the city of Washington on the verge of being cut off and possibly invaded, Lincoln considered whether to suspend the writ of habeas corpus in an effort to preserve order in Maryland and ensure that federal troops could safely pass through Baltimore on their way to the capital.[43] Habeas corpus (Latin for "You may have the body" or "produce the body") is a civil liberties protection dating back at least to Magna Carta, in 1215. Someone who believes that the government is unlawfully detaining him or her can ask a court to issue a writ of habeas corpus, which requires the government to produce the prisoner in court and explain why the detention is lawful.[44] As we've seen, the protection is referred to in the U.S. Constitution, Article I, section 9, which provides that "[t]he Privilege of the Writ of Habeas Corpus shall not be suspended, unless when in Cases of Rebellion or Invasion the public Safety may require it."

In late April 1861, Lincoln wrote a letter to General Winfield Scott, commanding general of the U.S. Army, instructing Scott that he was "authorized to suspend the writ [of habeas corpus]" "for the public safety" in the course of "suppressing . . . insurrection" in the area between Philadelphia and Washington.[45] In other words, Scott was authorized to arrest and indefinitely detain people he deemed dangerous without permitting them access to a court to challenge their detention. In May 1861, federal troops arrested John Merryman in Cockeysville, Maryland. Merryman, a secessionist and the leader of a militia company training to join the rebellion, was taken from his home and held at Fort McHenry, in Baltimore.[46]

It was certainly not obvious that Lincoln had the constitutional authority to suspend habeas corpus since the Constitution refers to suspension of the writ in Article I, which addresses mainly the powers of Congress. Merryman managed to obtain counsel and sought a writ of habeas corpus from U.S. Supreme Court Chief Justice Roger Taney, sitting as circuit court judge. Taney issued the writ, ordering the Army to produce Merryman in court and provide a legal justification for his detention. The military refused to comply, relying on President Lincoln's instruction to General Scott authorizing him to suspend habeas corpus.[47]

When the military refused to produce Merryman, Taney issued a written opinion (pursuant to the Judiciary Act of 1789, he decided the case himself, without the other members of the court).[48] Taney ruled that the president had acted unconstitutionally in suspending habeas corpus. Taney reasoned that, since the provision for suspending habeas corpus appears in Article I, only Congress may suspend habeas corpus. In addition, Taney concluded that, even if Congress did suspend habeas corpus, a civilian prisoner could not be detained indefinitely and ultimately had the right to a trial in federal court, as long as the federal courts were open and functioning. In other words, the military could not, absent necessity, detain and try a civilian in a military court or tribunal.[49]

The following is excerpted from the *Merryman* decision. Consider how Chief Justice Taney interpreted the scope of the president's war powers in writing his opinion, and notice how sharply critical he is of Lincoln's actions.

Ex parte[50] *Merryman*, 17 F.Cas. 144 (1861)

Before the Chief Justice of the Supreme Court of the United States, at Chambers.

The application in this case for a writ of *habeas corpus* is made to me under the 14th section of the Judiciary Act of 1789, which renders effectual for the citizen the constitutional privilege of the *habeas corpus*. That act gives to the Courts of the United States, as well as to each Justice of the Supreme Court, and to every District Judge, power to grant writs of *habeas corpus* for the purpose of an inquiry into the cause of commitment. . . .

The petition presents the following case: The petitioner resides in Maryland, in Baltimore county. While peaceably in his own house, with his family, it was at two o'clock, on the morning of the 25th of May, 1861, entered by an armed force, professing to act under military orders. He was then compelled to rise from his bed, taken into custody, and conveyed to Fort McHenry, where he is imprisoned by the commanding officer, without warrant from any lawful authority.

The commander of the fort, Gen. George Cadwalader, by whom he is detained in confinement . . . does not deny any of the facts alleged in the petition.

. . . The case, then, is simply this: A military officer residing in Pennsylvania issues an order to arrest a citizen of Maryland, upon vague and indefinite charges, without any proof, so far as appears. Under this order his house is entered in the night; he is seized as a prisoner, and conveyed to Fort McHenry, and there kept in close confinement. And when a *habeas corpus* is served on the commanding officer, requiring him to produce the prisoner before a Justice of the Supreme Court, in order that he may examine into the legality of the imprisonment, the answer of the officer is that he is authorized by the President to suspend the writ of *habeas corpus* at his discretion, and, in the exercise of that discretion, suspends it in this case, and on that ground refuses obedience to the writ.

As the case comes before me, therefore, I understand that the President not only claims the right to suspend the writ of *habeas corpus* himself, at his discretion, but to delegate that discretionary power to a military officer, and to leave it to him to determine whether he will or will not obey judicial process that may be served upon him.

No official notice has been given to the courts of justice, or to the public, by proclamation or otherwise, that the President claimed this power, and had exercised it in the manner stated in the return. And I certainly listened to it with some surprise, for I had supposed it to be one of those points of constitutional law upon which there is no difference of opinion, and that it was admitted on all hands that the privilege of the writ could not be suspended except by act of Congress....

Having, therefore, regarded the question as too plain and too well settled to be open to dispute, if the commanding officer had stated that upon his own responsibility, and in the exercise of his own discretion, he refused obedience to the writ, I should have contented myself with referring to the clause [from Article I, section 9] in the Constitution [and ordering the government to appear in court to justify Merryman's detention].... But being thus officially notified that the privilege of the writ has been suspended under the orders and by the authority of the President, and believing as I do that the President has exercised a power which he does not possess under the Constitution, a proper respect for the high office he fills requires me to state plainly and fully the grounds of my opinion, in order to show that I have not ventured to question the legality of this act without a careful and deliberate examination of the whole subject.

The clause in the Constitution which authorizes the suspension of the privilege of the writ of *habeas corpus* is in the ninth section of the first article.

This article is devoted to the Legislative Department of the United States, and has not the slightest reference to the Executive Department....

... [T]he great importance which the framers of the Constitution attached to the privilege of the writ of *habeas corpus*, to protect the liberty of the citizen, is proved by the fact that its suspension, except in cases of invasion and rebellion, is first in the list of prohibited powers; and even in these cases the power is denied and its exercise prohibited unless the public safety shall require it.[51]

It is the second article of the Constitution that provides for the organization of the Executive Department, and enumerates the powers conferred on it, and prescribes its duties. And if the high power over the liberty of the citizens now claimed was intended to be conferred on the President, it would undoubtedly be found in plain words in this article. But there is not a word in it that can furnish the slightest ground to justify the exercise of the power.

The article begins by declaring that the Executive power shall be vested in a President of the United States of America, to hold his office during the term of four years ... the short term for which he is elected, and the narrow limits to which his power is confined, show the jealousy and apprehensions of future danger which the framers of the Constitution felt in relation to that department of the Government, and how carefully they withheld from it many of the powers belonging to the executive branch of the English Government which were considered as dangerous to the liberty of the subject, and conferred (as that in clear and specific terms) those powers only which were deemed essential to secure the successful operation of the Government.

. . . [The president] is, from necessity, and the nature of his duties, the Commander-in-Chief of the army and navy, and of the militia, when called into actual service. But no appropriation for the support of the army can be made by Congress for a longer term than two years, so that it is in the power of the succeeding House of Representatives to withhold the appropriation for its support, and thus disband it, if, in their judgment, the President used or designed to use it for improper purposes. . . .

So, too, his powers in relation to the civil duties and authority necessarily conferred on him are carefully restricted, as well as those belonging to his military character. He cannot . . . make a treaty with a foreign nation or Indian tribe without the advice and consent of the Senate. . . . He is not empowered to arrest any one charged with an offence against the United States, and whom he may, from the evidence before him, believe to be guilty; nor can he authorize any officer, civil or military, to exercise this power, for the fifth article of the amendments to the Constitution expressly provides that no person "shall be deprived of life, liberty, or property without due process of law;" that is, judicial process. And even if the privilege of the writ of *habeas corpus* was suspended by act of Congress, and a party not subject to the rules and articles of war was afterwards arrested and imprisoned by regular judicial process, he could not be detained in prison or brought to trial before a military tribunal, for the article in the Amendments to the Constitution immediately following the one above referred to—that is, the sixth article [Amendment]—provides that, "In all criminal prosecutions, the accused shall enjoy the right to a speedy and public trial by an impartial jury of the State and district wherein the crime shall have been committed, which district shall have been previously ascertained by law; and to be informed of the nature and cause of the accusation; to be confronted with the witnesses against him; to have compulsory process for obtaining witnesses in his favor, and to have the assistance of counsel for his defence."

And the only power, therefore, which the President possesses, where the "life, liberty, or property" of a private citizen is concerned, is the power and duty prescribed in the third section of the second article, which requires "that he shall take care that the laws be faithfully executed." He is not authorized to execute them himself, or through agents or officers, civil or military, appointed by himself, but he is to take care that they be faithfully carried into execution as they are expounded and adjudged by the coordinate branch of the Government to which that duty is assigned by the Constitution. It is thus made his duty to come in aid of the judicial authority, if it shall be resisted by a force too strong to be overcome without the assistance of the Executive arm. But in exercising this power, he acts in subordination to judicial authority, assisting it to execute its process and enforce its judgments.

With such provisions in the Constitution, expressed in language too clear to be misunderstood by any one, I can see no ground whatever for supposing that the President, in any emergency or in any state of things, can authorize the suspension of the privilege of the writ of *habeas corpus*, or arrest a citizen, except in aid of the judicial power. He certainly does not faithfully execute the laws if he takes upon himself legislative power by suspending the writ of *habeas corpus* and the judicial power, also, by arresting and imprisoning a person without due process of law. Nor can any argument be drawn from ... the necessities of government for self-defense, in times of tumult and danger. The Government of the United States is one of delegated and limited powers....

The right of the subject to the benefit of the writ of *habeas corpus,* it must be recollected, was one of the great points in controversy during the long struggle in England between arbitrary government and free institutions, and must therefore have strongly attracted the attention of statesmen engaged in framing a new and, as they supposed, a freer government than the one which they had thrown off by the Revolution. For, from the earliest history of the common law, if a person was imprisoned, no matter by what authority, he had a right to the writ of *habeas corpus*, to bring his case before the King's Bench, and, if no specific offence was charged against him in the warrant of commitment, he was entitled to be forthwith discharged....

Blackstone, in his *Commentaries on the laws of England* (3d vol., 133, 134,) says:

"... the glory of the English law consists in clearly defining the times, the causes, and the extent, when, wherefore, and to what degree the imprisonment of the subject may be lawful. This it is which induces the absolute necessity of expressing upon every commitment [i.e., imprisonment] the reason for which it is made, that the court upon a habeas corpus may examine into its validity, and, according to the circumstances of the case, may discharge, admit to bail, or remand the prisoner...."...

[T]he military authority in this case has gone far beyond the mere suspension of the privilege of the writ of *habeas corpus*. It has, by force of arms, thrust aside the judicial authorities and officers to whom the Constitution has confided the power and duty of interpreting and administering the laws, and substituted a military government in its place, to be administered and executed by military officers. For at the time these proceedings were had against John Merryman, the District Judge of Maryland, the commissioner appointed under the act of Congress, the District

Attorney and the Marshal, all resided in the city of Baltimore, a few miles only from the home of the prisoner. Up to that time there had never been the slightest resistance or obstruction to the process of any Court or judicial officer of the United States in Maryland, except by the military authority. And if a military officer, or any other person, had reason to believe that the prisoner had committed any offence against the laws of the United States, it was his duty to give information of the fact and the evidence to support it to the District Attorney, and it would then have become the duty of that officer to bring the matter before the District Judge or Commissioner, and if there was sufficient legal evidence to justify his arrest, the Judge or Commissioner would have issued his warrant to the Marshal to arrest him, and, upon the hearing of the party, would have held him to bail, or committed him for trial, according to the character of the offense as it appeared in the testimony, or would have discharged him immediately if there was not sufficient evidence to support the accusation. There was no danger of any obstruction or resistance to the action of the civil authorities, and therefore no reason whatever for the inter-position of the military. . . .

The Constitution provides . . . that "no person shall be deprived of life, liberty, or property, without due process of law." It declares that "the right of the people to be secure in their persons, houses, papers, and effects against unreasonable searches and seizures shall not be violated, and no warrant shall issue but upon probable cause, supported by oath or affirmation, and particularly describing the place to be searched and the persons or things to be seized." It provides that the party accused shall be entitled to a speedy trial in a court of justice.

And these great and fundamental laws, which Congress itself could not suspend, have been disregarded and suspended, like the writ of *habeas corpus*, by a military order, supported by force of arms. Such is the case now before me; and I can only say that if the authority which the Constitution has confided to the judiciary department and judicial officers may thus upon any pretext or under any circum-stances be usurped by the military power at its discretion, the people of the United States are no longer living under a Government of laws, but every citizen holds life, liberty, and property at the will and pleasure of the army officer in whose military district he may happen to be found.

In such a case my duty was too plain to be mistaken. I have exercised all the power which the Constitution and laws confer on me, but that power has been resisted by a force too strong for me to overcome. It is possible that the officer who has incurred this grave responsibility may have misunderstood his instructions, and exceeded the authority intended to be given him. I shall, therefore, order all the proceedings in this case, with my opinion, to be filed and recorded in the Circuit Court of the United States for the District of Maryland, and direct the clerk to transmit a copy, under seal, to the President of the United States. It will then remain for that high officer, in fulfilment of his constitutional obligation to "take care that the laws be faithfully executed," to determine what measures he will take to cause the civil process of the United States to be respected and enforced.

Chief Justice Taney's opinion was a flat denunciation of Lincoln's actions as unconstitutional, an affront to fundamental, hallowed protections of individual rights. Taney concluded that the Constitution assigned Congress, not the president, the power to suspend *habeas corpus*, and he suggested Lincoln was acting more like a monarch than a president—the last thing the Framers of the Constitution could have intended.[52] In fact, Taney seemed to leave no room for any presidential authority beyond the plain text of the Constitution. One scholar quips that, in *Merryman*, "Taney systematically reduced the president's constitutional powers to Lilliputian proportions."[53] In addition, Taney's opinion leaves out context. His opinion does not describe the rebellion and suggests that normal, peacetime circumstances prevailed.

As Taney noted, however, there were practical limits to his own power as a judge—his decision would have force only if the president respected and obeyed it.[54] As it turned out, Lincoln essentially ignored *Merryman*.[55] This was certainly not surprising—while Taney's opinion studiously ignored the crisis the nation faced, Lincoln could not. The two men, who were political adversaries, had very different views about secession. Taney believed states had a constitutional right to leave the union, and he advocated a "peaceful separation."[56] Lincoln's priority was taking action he believed necessary to maintain the Union.[57] In addition, Taney was the author of the *Dred Scott*[58] decision, which was one of the sparks that helped ignite the Civil War. Many northerners viewed Taney's decision in the *Dred Scott* case "as a partisan and unconscionable defense of slavery."[59] The opinion "squander[ed] his judicial reputation."[60] It is not surprising that Lincoln (who, as a Senate candidate in 1858, had criticized Taney's decision in *Dred Scott*) did not treat *Merryman* with the degree of respect normally afforded to judicial decisions.

Farber asserts that "[o]ne goal of the [Civil] [W]ar . . . was to establish the primacy of the rule of law."[61] The rule of law depends on, among other things, the idea that the law is supreme—even elected officials must defer to it, and no person (or, in the context of the Civil War, no individual state or collection of states) is above the law.[62] The seceding Confederate states insisted that they had the final say in interpreting the meaning of the

Constitution, and Lincoln, of course, rejected that view. It is therefore paradoxical, to put it mildly, that Lincoln, at the outset of that war, cast doubt on the supremacy of the law as interpreted by the Supreme Court's chief justice. Although Taney wrote for himself, not for the entire Supreme Court (he was sitting as a circuit court judge), Lincoln was coming close to denying the authority of the court to set limits on presidential power as defined by the Constitution.[63] There are possible ways to resolve this paradox, as Lincoln himself suggested.[64] However, this and other actions Lincoln took "seemed to be tearing gaping holes in" the rule of law.[65]

Although Lincoln did not defer to the chief justice's opinion in *Merryman*, he did respond to Taney's criticism. When Congress returned to session in July 1861, Lincoln asked it to retroactively approve his decision to suspend habeas corpus as well as other measures, conceding that his actions might not have been "strictly legal" but arguing that they were justified by "public necessity" and were actions he "believed" to be within Congress's power to authorize.[66] In other words, Lincoln had essentially acted in Congress's place to take action constitutionally available to the federal government as a whole and necessary to respond to the rebellion. In his address to Congress, Lincoln supplied the context missing from Taney's opinion, explaining the situation he confronted as a newly inaugurated president dealing with rebellion. Though Lincoln was deferential to Congress, he parenthetically noted that the Constitution does not expressly assign to Congress *alone* the power to suspend habeas corpus; perhaps the power was shared with the president.[67] Excerpts from Lincoln's July 4, 1861, address to Congress follow:

President Lincoln's Message to Congress in Special Session, July 4, 1861

Fellow-citizens of the Senate and House of Representatives:

Having been convened on an extraordinary occasion, as authorized by the Constitution, your attention is not called to any ordinary subject of legislation.

At the beginning of the present Presidential term, four months ago, the functions of the Federal Government were found to be generally suspended within the several States of South Carolina, Georgia, Alabama, Mississippi, Louisiana, and Florida, excepting only those of the Post Office Department.

Within these States, all the Forts, Arsenals, Dock-yards, Customhouses, and the like, including the movable and stationary property in, and about them, had been seized, and were held in open hostility to this Government, excepting only Forts Pickens, Taylor, and Jefferson, on, and near the Florida coast, and Fort Sumter, in Charleston harbor, South Carolina. . . .

The Forts remaining in the possession of the Federal government, in, and near, these States, were either besieged or menaced by warlike preparations; and especially Fort Sumter was nearly surrounded by well-protected hostile batteries, with guns equal in quality to the best of its own, and outnumbering the latter as perhaps ten to one. A disproportionate share of the Federal muskets and rifles, had somehow found their way into these States, and had been seized, to be used against the government. . . . The Navy was scattered in distant seas; leaving but a very small part of it within the immediate reach of the government. Officers of the Federal Army and Navy, had resigned in great numbers; and, of those resigning, a large proportion had taken up arms against the government. Simultaneously, and in connection, with all this, the purpose to sever the Federal Union, was openly avowed. . . .

Finding this condition of things, and believing it to be an imperative duty upon the incoming Executive, to prevent, if possible, the consummation of such attempt to destroy the Federal Union, a choice of means to that end became indispensable. This choice was made; and was declared in the Inaugural address. The policy chosen looked to the exhaustion of all peaceful measures, before a resort to any stronger ones. . . .

In precaution against [the exhaustion of provisions at Fort Sumter], the government had, a few days before, commenced preparing an expedition, as well adapted as might be, to relieve Fort Sumter . . . it was also resolved to notify the Governor of South Carolina, that he might ex[pect] an attempt would be made to provision the Fort; and that, if the attempt should not be resisted, there would be no effort to throw in men, arms, or ammunition, without further notice, or in case of an attack upon the Fort. This notice was accordingly given; whereupon the Fort was attacked, and bombarded to its fall, without even awaiting the arrival of the provisioning expedition. . . .

By the affair at Fort Sumter . . . the assailants of the Government, began the conflict of arms, without a gun in sight, or in expectancy, to return their fire, save only the few in the Fort, sent to that harbor, years before, for their own protection, and still ready to give that protection, in whatever [way] was lawful. In this act, discarding all else, they have forced upon the country, the distinct issue: "Immediate dissolution, or blood."

And this issue embraces more than the fate of these United States. It presents to the whole family of man, the question, whether a constitutional republic, or a democracy—a government of the people, by the same people—can, or cannot, maintain its territorial integrity, against its own domestic foes. It presents the question, whether discontented individuals, too few in numbers to control administration, according to organic law, in any case, can always, upon the pretences made in this case, or on any other pretences, or arbitrarily, without any pretence, break up their government, and thus practically put an end to free government upon the earth. It forces us to ask: "Is there, in all republics, this inherent, and fatal weakness?" "Must a government, of necessity, be too strong for the liberties of its own people, or too weak to maintain its own existence?"

So viewing the issue, no choice was left but to call out the war power of the Government; and so to resist force, employed for its destruction, by force, for its preservation. . . .

Recurring to the action of the government, it may be stated that, at first, a call was made for 75,000 militia; and rapidly following this a proclamation was issued for closing the ports of the insurrectionary districts by proceedings in the nature of blockade. So far all was believed to be strictly legal. At this point the insurrectionists announced their purpose to enter upon the practice of privateering.

Other calls were made for volunteers, to serve three years, unless sooner discharged; and also for large additions to the regular Army and Navy. These measures, whether strictly legal or not, were ventured upon, under what appeared to be a popular demand, and a public necessity; trusting, then as now, that Congress would readily ratify them. It is believed that nothing has been done beyond the constitutional competency of Congress.

Soon after the first call for militia, it was considered a duty to authorize the Commanding General, in proper cases, according to his discretion, to suspend the privilege of the writ of habeas corpus; or, in other words, to arrest, and detain, without resort to the ordinary processes and forms of law, such individuals as he might deem dangerous to the public safety. This authority has purposely been exercised but very sparingly. Nevertheless, the legality and propriety of what has been done under it, are questioned; and the attention of the country has been called to the proposition that one who is sworn to "take care that the laws be faithfully executed," should not himself violate them. Of course some consideration was given to the questions of power and propriety before this matter was acted upon. The whole of the laws which were required to be faithfully executed were being resisted and failing of execution in nearly one-third of the States. Must they be allowed to finally fail of execution, even had it been perfectly clear that by the use of the means necessary to their execution some single law, made in such extreme tenderness of the citizen's liberty that practically it relieves more of the guilty than of the innocent, should to a very limited extent, be violated? To state the question more directly, are all the laws, but one, to go unexecuted, and the government itself go to pieces, lest that one be violated? Even in such a case, would not the official oath be broken if the government should be overthrown when it was believed that disregarding the single law would tend to preserve it? But it was not believed that this question was presented. It was not believed that any law was violated. The provision of the Constitution that "the privilege of the writ of habeas corpus shall not be suspended unless when, in cases of rebellion or invasion, the public safety may require it," is equivalent to a provision—is a provision—that such privilege may be suspended when, in cases of rebellion, or invasion, the public safety does require it. It was decided that we have a case of rebellion, and that the public safety does require the qualified suspension of the privilege of the writ which was authorized to be made. Now it is insisted that Congress, and not the Executive, is vested with this power; but the Constitution itself is silent as to which or who is to exercise the power; and as the provision was plainly made for a dangerous emergency, it cannot be believed the framers of the instrument intended, that in every case, the danger should run its course, until Congress could be called together, the very assembling of which might be prevented, as was intended in this case, by the rebellion.

No more extended argument is now offered; as an opinion, at some length, will probably be presented by the Attorney-General. Whether there shall be any legislation upon the subject, and if any, what, is submitted entirely to the better judgment of Congress.

Congress retroactively approved most of Lincoln's actions, although it did not immediately endorse Lincoln's decision to suspend habeas corpus.[68] However, in 1863—six months after Lincoln had, once again, unilaterally acted to suspend habeas corpus (this time in order to enforce the military draft)—Congress passed the Habeas Corpus Act of 1863, retroactively approving Lincoln's decisions to suspend habeas and authorizing him to do so at any time during "the present rebellion."[69] It is estimated that thousands of people were imprisoned by the military and held indefinitely without trial during the Civil War.[70] As we'll discuss in the next chapter, others were tried by military tribunals.[71]

Although Lincoln has been accused of acting as a dictator, both by some of his contemporaries and by later critics, most modern observers conclude that these charges go too far and find Lincoln's actions to be justified.[72] As noted, some argue that Lincoln's unilateral actions were redeemed by retroactive congressional approval.[73] Farber points out that Lincoln stood for re-election in 1864 and stood a real chance of losing to the Democratic nominee, General George McClellan.[74]

One problem we face today in evaluating Lincoln's actions is that it is difficult to criticize a president who saved the Union and began the process of emancipation. As Secretary of War Edwin Stanton said when Lincoln died, "now he belongs to the ages."[75] Nearly 150 years later, that pronouncement rings true. Lincoln is a literally larger-than-life figure, towering over visitors to his monument on the National Mall. Twenty-first-century observers may hesitate to second-guess his decisions, taken to save the country during a time of unquestionable national emergency. There may be concerns about tarnishing Lincoln's legacy by suggesting that he overstepped his bounds in some areas.

For these reasons, there may be a desire to place Lincoln in a special category—the Supreme Court itself recognized this in the *Ex parte Milligan* case, decided just one year after Lincoln died.[76] Though the *Milligan* Court effectively issued a posthumous rebuke to Lincoln, it was careful to explain that it was doing so only in order to make clear that there were limits on presidential power that were necessary to rein in future presidents who might be "[w]icked men, ambitious of power, with hatred of liberty and contempt of law . . . fill[ing] the place once occupied by Washington and Lincoln."[77]

The Civil War itself is (one hopes) a unique event in American history. Lincoln concluded that it was an emergency that called for strong, decisive presidential action to deal with the existential crisis posed by the Civil War. Lincoln also believed that the Civil War put the Constitution itself on trial.[78] The questions for us today are what guidelines, if any, his actions may provide for the exercise of presidential power in modern circumstances. Was the Civil War a unique crisis, justifying extraordinary executive action only in very limited circumstances (and even then perhaps requiring retroactive approval by Congress), or can it serve as broader precedent providing justification for unilateral presidential action in other contexts? To put it another way, if some degree of implied prerogative exists that allows the president to take emergency actions, how far does the prerogative extend, and how, if at all, can it be limited?

Ross J. Corbett observes that "[p]rerogative clearly sits uncomfortably with constitutionalism."[79] The obvious danger is dictatorship: a president claiming power to act unilaterally in the name of the public good may see no limits to the prerogative. Few people today would question Lincoln's conclusion that the United States faced a national emergency during the Civil War.[80] But what happens when the emergency is less clear or more open to debate? What if a president falsely claims emergency as a pretext for expanded power? What if a well-intentioned president simply makes a mistake and the perceived emergency is not genuine?[81] What if the emergency stretches on indefinitely? A power conceived as extraordinary and limited to emergencies may become commonplace and routine. Even if the crisis is genuine and finite, how, exactly, is emergency power to be defined? May the president take any and all actions he or she deems necessary? Are there any limits? Is it necessary and, if so, is it sufficient to require presidents who take unilateral action to seek retroactive approval from Congress? Will Congress have the ability, in practice, to rescind a decision to commit the nation to military action?

Locke acknowledged the dangers of prerogative but offered no legal safeguard, concluding that, if the executive overstepped its bounds, "the people have no remedy in this, as in all other cases where they have no judge on earth, but to appeal to Heaven."[82] By that, Locke meant revolution— the people would judge the use of prerogative and would overthrow a ruler who offended Heaven; that is the laws of nature.[83] Of course, the Constitution does provide for terrestrial judges through Article III, and that branch of government sometimes sees fit to check executive power with the tools of the legal system.[84] In fact, after the Civil War had ended and after Lincoln's assassination, the Supreme Court issued a decision that can be seen as a rebuke of expanded presidential power, as discussed in the next chapter.

Although Chief Justice Taney ruled against the Lincoln administration's exercise of wartime powers in the *Merryman* case, Lincoln managed to avoid a ruling by the entire Supreme Court during the Civil War that would have admonished him for his actions. However, in a 5–4 decision handed down in 1863, a divided court did address one aspect of emergency presidential power.[85] In the *Prize Cases*, the court ruled that the president had acted within his constitutional authority when he ordered a blockade of the Confederacy in 1861 while Congress was out of session. Since a blockade is generally recognized as an act of war, it was argued that Lincoln could not take such action until Congress authorized it. The question had practical significance for the owners of several ships captured after Lincoln ordered the blockade in April 1861 but before Congress ratified it in July 1861; if Lincoln's initial action was illegal, then the ships and their property would have to be returned to their owners. However, as Farber notes, the broader point resolved in the *Prize Cases* was that all nine justices agreed Lincoln had the authority to use military force in response to the rebellion.[86] This was a ratification of the theory that presidents have implied constitutional power to wage at least defensive war, using military force to repel invasion or suppress insurrection before Congress has time to act.[87] An excerpt from the *Prize Cases* follows:

The Prize Cases, 67 U.S. 635 (1863)

Justice Grier, majority opinion.

... Had the President a right to institute a blockade of ports in possession of persons in armed rebellion against the Government, on the principles of international law, as known and acknowledged among civilized States? ...

That a blockade *de facto* actually existed, and was formally declared and notified by the President on the 27th and 30th of April, 1861, is an admitted fact in these cases ...

Let us enquire whether, at the time this blockade was instituted, a state of war existed which would justify a resort to these means of subduing the hostile force.

War has been well defined to be, "That state in which a nation prosecutes its right by force."

The parties belligerent in a public war are independent nations. But it is not necessary, to constitute war, that both parties should be acknowledged as independent nations or sovereign States. A war may exist where one of the belligerents claims sovereign rights as against the other. ...

As a civil war is never publicly proclaimed, *eo nomine*,[88] against insurgents, its actual existence is a fact in our domestic history which the Court is bound to notice and to know.

The true test of its existence, as found in the writings of the sages of the common law, may be thus summarily stated:

When the regular course of justice is interrupted by revolt, rebellion, or insurrection, so that the Courts of Justice cannot be kept open, *civil war exists*, and hostilities may be prosecuted on the same footing as if those opposing the Government were foreign enemies invading the land.

By the Constitution, Congress alone has the power to declare a national or foreign war. It cannot declare war against a State, or any number of States, by virtue of any clause in the Constitution. The Constitution confers on the President the whole Executive power. He is bound to take care that the laws be faithfully executed. He is Commander-in-chief of the Army and Navy of the United States, and of the militia of the several States when called into the actual service of the United States. He has no power to initiate or declare a war either against a foreign nation or a domestic State. But, by the Acts of Congress of February 28th, 1795, and 3d of March, 1807, he is authorized to called out the militia and use the military and naval forces of the United States in case of invasion by foreign nations and to suppress insurrection against the government of a State or of the United States.

If a war be made by invasion of a foreign nation, the President is not only authorized but bound to resist force by force. He does not initiate the war, but is bound to accept the challenge without waiting for any special legislative authority. And whether the hostile party be a foreign invader or States organized in rebellion, it is nonetheless a war although the declaration of it be "unilateral." ...

...The President was bound to meet [the Civil War] in the shape it presented itself, without waiting for Congress to baptize it with a name; and no name given to it by him or them could change the fact. ...

Whether the President, in fulfilling his duties as Commander-in-chief in suppressing an insurrection, has met with such armed hostile resistance and a civil war of such alarming proportions as will compel him to accord to them the character of belligerents is a question to be decided by him, and this Court must be governed by the decisions and acts of the political department of the Government to which this power was entrusted. "He must determine what degree of force the crisis demands." The proclamation of blockade is itself official and conclusive evidence to the Court that a state of war existed which demanded and authorized a recourse to such a measure under the circumstances peculiar to the case....

If it were necessary to the technical existence of a war that it should have a legislative sanction, we find it in almost every act passed at the extraordinary session of the Legislature of 1861, which was wholly employed in enacting laws to enable the Government to prosecute the war with vigor and efficiency. And finally, in 1861, we find Congress ... in anticipation of such astute objections, passing an act

> approving, legalizing, and making valid all the acts, proclamations, and orders of the President, &c., as if they had been *issued and done under the previous express authority* and direction of the Congress of the United States.

Without admitting that such an act was necessary under the circumstances, it is plain that, if the President had in any manner assumed powers which it was necessary should have the authority or sanction of Congress, that ... this ratification has operated to perfectly cure the defect....

The objection made to this act of ratification, that it is *ex post facto* and therefore unconstitutional and void, might possibly have some weight on the trial of an indictment in a criminal Court. But precedents from that source cannot be received as authoritative in a tribunal administering public and international law.

On this first question, therefore, we are of the opinion that the President had a right, *jure belli*, to institute a blockade of ports in possession of the States in rebellion which neutrals are bound to regard.

Advocates of broad presidential power look to the *Prize Cases* for precedential support, but there may be limits to the decision's value. The decision involved extraordinary circumstances—rebellious states were engaged in military action against the federal government. Lincoln was, in the court's words, simply "resist[ing] force by force"—not initiating offensive military action.[89] Justice Grier's majority opinion emphasized that the president had "no power to initiate or declare a war either against a foreign nation or a domestic State."[90] In addition, Justice Grier relied at least in part on prior statutory authorization for Lincoln's actions.[91] Also, once again, Congress had retroactively approved Lincoln's decision, as Justice Grier noted. It can be argued that the *Prize Cases* may be read only as providing support for "an emergency response to attack, pending submission for approval to Congress."[92] Others, however, read the *Prize Cases* as recognizing broader authority for the president to take unilateral, independent actions he or she deems necessary to protect national security.[93] We will return to this debate over the significance of the *Prize Cases* when we discuss presidential power in the context of the war on terror.

4

SETTING LIMITS
ON WARTIME POWER?

THE *EX PARTE MILLIGAN* DECISION

In the *Prize Cases*, the Supreme Court recognized some degree of implied emergency presidential power, but it did not describe this as an unlimited source of power. In the *Ex parte Milligan* case, decided in 1866, one year after the Civil War ended, the court made clear what some of the limits were.[1] Lambdin Milligan had been arrested by the U.S. military in 1864 and charged, along with several codefendants, with conspiring to lead an armed uprising aimed at seizing more arms, freeing Confederate prisoners of war, and kidnapping the governor of Indiana.[2] Milligan, a U.S. citizen from Indiana, was tried by a military commission, convicted, and sentenced to be hanged.[3]

Milligan, a lawyer and politician who opposed the war and had passionately criticized the Lincoln administration, believed that he had been improperly tried before a military commission in Indiana instead of before a civilian court. The military commission did not afford Milligan procedural rights he would have received in civilian court—for instance, the right to insist on a unanimous verdict by a civilian jury (only a two-thirds majority was required for a death sentence before the military commission).[4] After his conviction and sentencing, Milligan filed a petition for a writ of habeas corpus, arguing that he could not be tried by a military court because he was a civilian and Indiana was not a theater of war. In 1866, his petition reached the Supreme Court, where the U.S. government argued that the findings of a military commission, operating under martial law—that is, when normal constitutional protections are suspended and the military enforces the law—could be reviewed only by military authorities, not by civilian courts.[5] The government asserted that protections in the Bill of Rights were "peace provisions" that could be set aside during war, when "the safety of the people becomes the supreme law."[6] That was essentially a description of prerogative—executive power to do what is necessary to protect the people even if not expressly authorized by the law. The following is excerpted from the Supreme Court's decision in *Ex parte Milligan*.

Ex parte Milligan, 71 U.S. 2 (1866)

Mr. Justice DAVIS delivered the opinion of the court.

On the 10th day of May, 1865, Lambdin P. Milligan presented a petition to the Circuit Court of the United States for the District of Indiana to be discharged from an alleged unlawful imprisonment. The case made by the petition is this: Milligan is a citizen of the United States; has lived for twenty years in Indiana, and, at the time of the grievances complained of, was not, and never had been, in the military or naval service of the United States. On the 5th day of October, 1864, while at home, he was arrested by order of General Alvin P. Hovey, commanding the military district of Indiana, and has ever since been kept in close confinement.

On the 21st day of October, 1864, he was brought before a military commission, convened at Indianapolis by order of General Hovey, tried on certain charges and specifications, found guilty, and sentenced to be hanged, and the sentence ordered to be executed on Friday, the 19th day of May, 1865....

Milligan insists that said military commission had no jurisdiction to try him upon the charges preferred, or upon any charges whatever, because he was a citizen of the United States and the State of Indiana, and had not been, since the commencement of the late Rebellion, a resident of any of the States whose citizens were arrayed against the government, and that the right of trial by jury was guaranteed to him by the Constitution of the United States....

The opinions of the judges of the Circuit Court were [divided] on three questions, which are certified to the Supreme Court:

1st. "On the facts stated in [Milligan's] petition and exhibits, ought a writ of habeas corpus to be issued?"

2d. "On the facts stated in said petition and exhibits, ought the said Lambdin P. Milligan to be discharged from custody as in said petition prayed?"

3d. "Whether, upon the facts stated in said petition and exhibits, the military commission mentioned therein had jurisdiction legally to try and sentence said Milligan in manner and form as in said petition and exhibits is stated?"

The importance of the main question presented by this record cannot be overstated, for it involves the very framework of the government and the fundamental principles of American liberty.

During the late wicked Rebellion, the temper of the times did not allow that calmness in deliberation and discussion so necessary to a correct conclusion of a purely judicial question. *Then,* considerations of safety were mingled with the exercise of power, and feelings and interests prevailed which are happily terminated. *Now* that the public safety is assured, this question, as well as all others, can be discussed and decided without passion or the admixture of any element not required to form a legal judgment. . . .

. . . Milligan claimed his discharge from custody by virtue of the act of Congress "relating to habeas corpus, and regulating judicial proceedings in certain cases," approved March 3d, 1863.[7] . . .

In interpreting a law, the motives which must have operated with the legislature in passing it are proper to be considered. This law was passed in a time of great national peril, when our heritage of free government was in danger.

An armed rebellion against the national authority, of greater proportions than history affords an example of, was raging, and the public safety required that the privilege of the writ of habeas corpus should be suspended. The President had practically suspended it, and detained suspected persons in custody without trial, but his authority to do this was questioned. It was claimed that Congress alone could exercise this power, and that the legislature, and not the President, should judge of the political considerations on which the right to suspend it rested. The privilege of this great writ had never before been withheld from the citizen, and, as the exigence of the times demanded immediate action, it was of the highest importance that the lawfulness of the suspension should be fully established. It was under these circumstances, which were such as to arrest the attention of the country, that this law was passed. The President was authorized by it to suspend the privilege of the writ of habeas corpus whenever, in his judgment, the public safety required, and he did, by proclamation, bearing date the 15th of September, 1863, reciting, among other things, the authority of this statute, suspend it. The suspension of the writ does not authorize the arrest of anyone, but simply denies to one arrested the privilege of this writ in order to obtain his liberty.

It is proper therefore to inquire under what circumstances the courts could rightfully refuse to grant this writ, and when the citizen was at liberty to invoke its aid.

. . . The language used [in the 1863 Habeas Corpus Act] is plain and direct, and the meaning of the Congress cannot be mistaken. The public safety demanded, if the President thought proper to arrest a suspected person, that he should not be required to give the cause of his detention on return to a writ of habeas corpus. But it was not contemplated that such person should be detained in custody beyond a certain fixed period unless certain judicial proceedings, known to the common law, were commenced against him. The Secretaries of State and War were directed [by the act] to furnish to the judges of the courts of the United States a list of the names of all parties, not prisoners of war, resident in their respective jurisdictions, who then were or afterwards should be held in custody by the authority of the President, and who were citizens of states in which the administration of the laws in the Federal tribunals was unimpaired. After the list was furnished, if a grand jury of the district convened and adjourned, and did not indict or present one of the persons thus named, he was entitled to his discharge, and it was the duty of the judge of the court to order him brought before him to be discharged if he desired it. The refusal or omission to furnish the list could not operate to the injury of anyone who was not indicted or presented by the grand jury, for, if twenty days had elapsed from the time of his arrest and the termination of the session of the grand jury, he was equally entitled to his discharge as if the list were furnished [and he had not been indicted]. . . .

[The court then concluded that it had jurisdiction to consider Milligan's petition.]

. . . The controlling question in the case is this: upon the facts stated in Milligan's petition and the exhibits filed, had the military commission mentioned in it jurisdiction legally to try and sentence him? Milligan, not a resident of one of the rebellious states or a prisoner of war, but a citizen of Indiana for twenty years past and never in the military or naval service, is, while at his home, arrested by the military power of the United States, imprisoned, and, on certain criminal charges preferred against him, tried, convicted, and sentenced to be hanged by a military commission, organized under the direction of the military commander of the military district of Indiana. Had this tribunal the legal power and authority to try and punish this man?

No graver question was ever considered by this court, nor one which more nearly concerns the rights of the whole people, for it is the birthright of every American citizen when charged with crime to be tried and punished according to law. . . . The founders of our government . . . secured in a written constitution every right which the people had wrested from power during a contest of ages. By that Constitution and the laws authorized by it, this question must be determined. The provisions of that instrument on the administration of criminal justice are too plain and direct to leave room for misconstruction or doubt of their true meaning. . . . The fourth [amendment] proclaims the right to be secure in person and effects against unreasonable search and seizure, and directs that a judicial warrant shall not issue "without proof of probable cause supported by oath or affirmation." The fifth declares "that no person shall be held to answer for a capital or otherwise infamous crime unless on presentment by a grand jury, except in cases arising in the land or naval forces, or in the militia, when in actual service in time of war or public danger, nor be deprived of life, liberty, or property without due process of law." And the sixth guarantees the right of trial by jury, in such manner and with such regulations that, with upright judges, impartial juries, and an able bar, the innocent will be saved and the guilty punished....

These securities for personal liberty thus embodied were such as wisdom and experience had demonstrated to be necessary for the protection of those accused of crime. And so strong was the sense of the country of their importance, and so jealous were the people that these rights, highly prized, might be denied them by implication, that, when the original Constitution was proposed for adoption, it encountered severe opposition, and, but for the belief that it would be so amended as to embrace them, it would never have been ratified.

The Constitution of the United States is a law for rulers and people, equally in war and in peace, and covers with the shield of its protection all classes of men, at all times and under all circumstances. No doctrine involving more pernicious consequences was ever invented by the wit of man than that any of its provisions can be suspended during any of the great exigencies of government. Such a doctrine leads directly to anarchy or despotism, but the theory of necessity on which it is based is false, for the government, within the Constitution, has all the powers granted to it which are necessary to preserve its existence, as has been happily proved by the result of the great effort to throw off its just authority.

Have any of the rights guaranteed by the Constitution been violated in the case of Milligan?, and, if so, what are they?

Every trial involves the exercise of judicial power, and from what source did the military commission that tried him derive their authority? Certainly no part of judicial power of the country was conferred on them, because the Constitution expressly vests it "in one supreme court and such inferior courts as the Congress may from time to time ordain and establish,"[8] and it is not pretended that the commission was a court ordained and established by Congress. They cannot justify on the mandate of the President, because he is controlled by law, and has his appropriate sphere of duty, which is to execute, not to make, the laws, and there is "no unwritten criminal code to which resort can be had as a source of jurisdiction."

But it is said that the [commission's] jurisdiction is complete under the "laws and usages of war." It can serve no useful purpose to inquire what those laws and usages are, whence they originated, where found, and on whom they operate; they can never be applied to citizens in states which have upheld the authority of the government, and where the courts are open and their process unobstructed. This court has judicial knowledge that, in Indiana, the Federal authority was always un-opposed, and its courts always open to hear criminal accusations and redress grievances, and no usage of war could sanction a military trial there for any offence whatever of a citizen in civil life in nowise connected with the military service. Congress could grant no such power, and, to the honor of our national legislature be it said, it has never been provoked by the state of the country even to attempt its exercise. One of the plainest constitutional provisions was therefore infringed when Milligan was tried by a court not ordained and established by Congress and not composed of judges appointed during good behavior. . . .

Another guarantee of freedom was broken when Milligan was denied a trial by jury. . . . The sixth amendment affirms that, "in all criminal prosecutions, the accused shall enjoy the right to a speedy and public trial by an impartial jury," language broad enough to embrace all persons and cases; but the fifth, recognizing the necessity of an indictment or presentment before anyone can be held to answer for high crimes, "excepts cases arising in the land or naval forces, or in the militia, when in actual service, in time of war or public danger," and the Framers of the Constitution doubtless meant to limit the right of trial by jury in the sixth amendment to those persons who were subject to indictment or presentment in the fifth.

The discipline necessary to the efficiency of the army and navy required other and swifter modes of trial than are furnished by the common law courts, and, in pursuance of the power conferred by the Constitution, Congress has declared the kinds of trial, and the manner in which they shall be conducted, for offences committed while the party is in the military or naval service. Everyone connected with these branches of the public service is amenable to the jurisdiction which Congress has created for their government, and, while thus serving, surrenders his right to be tried by the civil courts. *All other persons,* citizens of states where the courts are open, if charged with crime, are guaranteed the inestimable privilege of trial by jury. This privilege is a vital principle, underlying the whole administration of criminal justice; it is not held by sufferance, and cannot be frittered away on any plea of state or political necessity. When peace prevails, and the authority of the government is undisputed, there is no difficulty of preserving the safeguards of liberty, for the ordinary modes of trial are never neglected, and no one wishes it otherwise; but if society is disturbed by civil commotion—if the passions of men are aroused and the restraints of law weakened, if not disregarded—these safeguards need, and should receive, the watchful care of those intrusted with the guardianship of the Constitution and laws. In no other way can we transmit to posterity unimpaired the blessings of liberty, consecrated by the sacrifices of the Revolution.

It is claimed that martial law covers with its broad mantle the proceedings of this military commission. The proposition is this: that, in a time of war, the commander of an armed force (if, in his opinion, the exigencies of the country demand it, and of which he is to judge) has the power, within the lines of his military district, to suspend all civil rights and their remedies and subject citizens, as well as soldiers to the rule of *his will,* and, in the exercise of his lawful authority, cannot be restrained except by his superior officer or the President of the United States.

If this position is sound to the extent claimed, then, when war exists, foreign or domestic, and the country is subdivided into military departments for mere convenience, the commander of one of them can, if he chooses, within his limits, on the plea of necessity, with the approval of the Executive, substitute military force for and to the exclusion of the laws, and punish all persons as he thinks right and proper, without fixed or certain rules.

. . . [I]f true, republican government is a failure, and there is an end of liberty regulated by law. Martial law established on such a basis destroys every guarantee of the Constitution, and effectually renders the "military independent of and superior to the civil power"—the attempt to do which by the King of Great Britain was deemed by our fathers such an offence that they assigned it to the world as one of the causes which impelled them to declare their independence. Civil liberty and this kind of martial law cannot endure together; the antagonism is irreconcilable, and, in the conflict, one or the other must perish.

This nation, as experience has proved, cannot always remain at peace, and has no right to expect that it will always have wise and humane rulers sincerely attached to the principles of the Constitution. Wicked men, ambitious of power, with hatred of liberty and contempt of law, may fill the place once occupied by Washington and Lincoln, and if this right is conceded, and the calamities of war again befall us, the dangers to human liberty are frightful to contemplate. If our fathers had failed to provide for just such a contingency, they would have been false to the trust reposed in them. They knew—the history of the world told them—the nation they were founding, be its existence short or long, would be involved in war; how often or how long continued human foresight could not tell, and that unlimited power, wherever lodged at such a time, was especially hazardous to freemen. For this and other equally weighty reasons, they secured the inheritance they had fought to maintain by incorporating in a written constitution the safeguards which time had proved were essential to its preservation. Not one of these safeguards can the President or Congress or the Judiciary disturb, except the one concerning the writ of habeas corpus.

It is essential to the safety of every government that, in a great crisis like the one we have just passed through, there should be a power somewhere of suspending the writ of habeas corpus. In every war, there are men of previously good character wicked enough to counsel their fellow-citizens to resist the measures deemed necessary by a good government to sustain its just authority and overthrow its enemies, and their influence may lead to dangerous combinations. In the emergency of the times, an immediate public investigation according to law may not be possible, and yet the [danger] to the country may be too imminent to suffer such persons to go at large. Unquestionably, there is then an exigency which demands that the government, if it should see fit in the exercise of a proper discretion to make arrests, should not be required to produce the persons arrested in answer to a writ of habeas corpus. The Constitution goes no further. It does not say, after a writ of habeas corpus is denied a citizen, that he shall be tried otherwise than by the course of the common law; if it had intended this result, it was easy, by the use of direct words, to have accomplished it. The illustrious men who framed that instrument were guarding the foundations of civil liberty against the abuses of unlimited power; they were full of wisdom, and the lessons of history informed them that a trial by an established court, assisted by an impartial jury, was the only sure way of protecting the citizen against oppression and wrong. Knowing this, they limited the suspension to one great right, and left the rest to remain forever inviolable. But it is insisted that the safety of the country in time of war demands that this broad claim for martial law shall be sustained. If this were true, it could be well said that a country, preserved at the sacrifice of all the cardinal principles of liberty, is not worth the cost of preservation. Happily, it is not so. . . .

. . . [T]here are occasions when martial rule can be properly applied. If, in foreign invasion or civil war, the courts are actually closed, and it is impossible to administer criminal justice according to law, *then*, on the theatre of active military operations, where war really prevails, there is a necessity to furnish a substitute for the civil authority, thus overthrown, to preserve the safety of the army and society, and as no power is left but the military, it is allowed to govern by martial rule until the laws can have their free course. As necessity creates the rule, so it limits its duration, for, if this government is continued *after* the courts are reinstated, it is a gross usurpation of power. Martial rule can never exist where the courts are open and in the proper and unobstructed exercise of their jurisdiction. It is also confined to the locality of actual war. Because, during the late Rebellion, it could have been enforced in Virginia, where the national authority was overturned and the courts driven out, it does not follow that it should obtain in Indiana, where that authority was never disputed and justice was always administered. And so, in the case of a foreign invasion, martial rule may become a necessity in one state when, in another, it would be "mere lawless violence." . . .

To the third question [whether the military commission could legally try and sentence Milligan] . . . an answer in the negative must be returned.

It is proper to say, although Milligan's trial and conviction by a military commission was illegal, yet, if guilty of the crimes imputed to him, and his guilt had been ascertained by an established court and impartial jury, he deserved severe punishment. Open resistance to the measures deemed necessary to subdue a great rebellion, by those who enjoy the protection of government, and have not the excuse even of prejudice of section to plead in their favor, is wicked; but that resistance becomes an enormous crime when it assumes the form of a secret political organization, armed to oppose the laws, and seeks by stealthy means to introduce the enemies of the country into peaceful communities, there to light the torch of civil war and thus overthrow the power of the United States. Conspiracies like these, at such a juncture, are extremely perilous, and those concerned in them are dangerous enemies to their country, and should receive the heaviest penalties of the law as an example to deter others from similar criminal conduct. It is said the severity of the laws caused them; but Congress was obliged to enact severe laws to meet the crisis, and as our highest civil duty is to serve our country when in danger, the late war has proved that rigorous laws, when necessary, will be cheerfully obeyed by a patriotic people, struggling to preserve the rich blessings of a free government.

The two remaining questions in this case [whether a writ of habeas corpus should be issued and whether Milligan should be discharged from custody] . . . must be answered in the affirmative. The suspension of the privilege of the writ of habeas corpus does not suspend the writ itself. The writ issues as a matter of course, and, on the return made to it, the court decides whether the party applying is denied the right of proceeding any further with it.

If the military trial of Milligan was contrary to law, then he was entitled, on the facts stated in his petition, to be discharged from custody. . . . Milligan avers he was a citizen of Indiana, not in the military or naval service, and was detained in close confinement, by order of the President, from the 5th day of October, 1864, until the 2d day of January, 1865, when the Circuit Court for the District of Indiana, with a grand jury, convened in session at Indianapolis, and afterwards, on the 27th day of the same month, adjourned without finding an indictment or presentment against him. If these averments were true (and their truth is conceded for the purposes of this case), the court was required to liberate him on taking certain oaths prescribed by the law, and entering into recognizance for his good behavior.

But it is insisted that Milligan was a prisoner of war, and therefore excluded from the privileges of the statute. It is not easy to see how he can be treated as a prisoner of war when he lived in Indiana for the past twenty years, was arrested there, and had not been, during the late troubles, a resident of any of the states in rebellion. If in Indiana he conspired with bad men to assist the enemy, he is punishable for it in the courts of Indiana; but, when tried for the offence, he cannot plead the rights of war, for he was not engaged in legal acts of hostility against the government, and only such persons, when captured, are prisoners of war. If he cannot enjoy the immunities attaching to the character of a prisoner of war, how can he be subject to their pains and penalties?

This case, as well as the kindred cases of Bowles and Horsey, were disposed of at the last term, and the proper orders were entered of record. There is therefore no additional entry required.

On one level, the decision in *Milligan* reads like a ringing endorsement of civil liberties and a rejection of presidential prerogative. The court acknowledged that Congress had taken the extraordinary step of authorizing the president to suspend habeas corpus (after the president had already done so, on his own initiative) and agreed that Congress's action was justified by the "armed rebellion." However, the court made clear that even this extraordinary act did not grant the president or the military unlimited authority; the court ruled that civilians like Milligan had a constitutional right to a jury trial in a civilian court as long as such courts were operating, as they were in Indiana at all times. When Congress suspends access to the writ of habeas corpus, the military may detain suspects for a finite period of time, not indefinitely, and, as long as civilian courts are operating, the suspect (if a civilian and a citizen) must ultimately be turned over to the civilian justice system. In fact, five justices concluded that, even if Congress had expressly authorized trial by military commission, it still would not have been constitutionally permissible under the circumstances.[9]

In an often-cited passage, Justice Davis's majority opinion rejected the idea of implied emergency presidential power, declaring that:

> No doctrine involving more pernicious consequences was ever invented by the wit of man than that any of its provisions can be suspended during any of the great exigencies of government. Such a doctrine leads directly to anarchy or despotism, but the theory of necessity on which it is based is false, for the government, within the Constitution, has all the powers granted to it which are necessary to preserve its existence, as has been happily proved by the result of the great effort to throw off its just authority.

Of course, Davis's opinion glossed over what had actually happened during the Civil War—Lincoln had never limited himself to the plain text of the Constitution in claiming power necessary to preserve the Union. As discussed, there are arguable justifications for Lincoln's actions, but the court's opinion in *Milligan* seems to embrace the fiction that the Union was saved without any resort to implied emergency presidential power.

This observation helps expose another layer in *Milligan*: describing it simply as a rebuke of presidential power depends on evaluating the decision within a vacuum, cut off from some of the ways in which power was actually exercised during the war. The court itself conceded that its decision was possible only *after* the war ended.[10] As Justice Davis wrote: "[d]uring the late wicked Rebellion, the temper of the times did not allow that calmness in deliberation and discussion so necessary to a correct conclusion of a purely judicial question." The court was able to put aside "passion" only once the war was over. In fact, during the war, military courts in the North convicted and sentenced civilians without intervention by the Supreme

Court.[11] One notable case involved Clement Vallandigham, a Democratic politician who advocated for peace with the South. After Vallandigham gave a speech in 1863 denouncing the war as "unnecessary" and urging voters to (peacefully, by election) depose Lincoln, whom he denounced as a monarch, he was charged with violating a military order prohibiting "the habit of declaring sympathies for the enemy." A military commission convicted him and sentenced him to prison for the remainder of the war.[12] Like Milligan three years later, Vallandigham turned to the Supreme Court for recourse—but, in 1863, as armies fought, the court declined to hear Vallandigham's case, concluding that it lacked jurisdiction to review the military commission's proceedings.[13]

Although Lincoln publicly argued that military arrests were necessary in the context of the Civil War, he ordered Vallandigham's release and exile to the Confederacy (though Vallandigham managed to return to the North and run an unsuccessful gubernatorial campaign in Ohio).[14] But, especially when considered alongside *Milligan*, the court's refusal to review the merits of Vallandigham's case indicated that the court, like Lincoln, saw a need for different rules during wartime. Vallandigham, like Milligan, was a citizen of a northern state and a civilian. Like Milligan, Vallandigham was tried in an area where the civilian courts were open and functioning. The only apparent way to distinguish the two cases, as the court itself seemed to concede in *Milligan*, was that Vallandigham's case came before the court during the war whereas Milligan's was on the docket after the war had ended.

Despite the court's strong language to the contrary in *Milligan*, its action—or inaction—in *Vallandigham* seemed like an implicit acknowledgment that different rules applied during wartime. The court was unable or, perhaps, unwilling to rein in presidential power *during* the war.[15] One can argue that Lincoln effectively created precedent for emergency authority through his actions.[16] By defying Chief Justice Taney's decision in *Merryman* and by later gaining retroactive approval from Congress for his decision to suspend habeas corpus, Lincoln demonstrated that a president could, at least in some circumstances, take extraconstitutional action without paying a penalty (especially if Congress retroactively supported his actions).

Lincoln's actions, as well as action (and inaction) by Congress and the Supreme Court, leave a number of questions to be answered. Did Lincoln successfully constitutionalize the Lockean prerogative, carving out a sphere of emergency presidential power? Or, were his actions legitimate only because Congress ratified them? Can the *Prize Cases* be cited to justify broad presidential control over the use of military force, or is the decision's applicability limited to the use of defensive force to respond to insurrection or invasion? Did the court effectively set limits on presidential power in the postwar *Milligan* case, or did its actions, and inaction, during the war say otherwise? Was the Civil War itself simply a unique event that cannot be readily analogized to other crises? As we'll see, supporters and critics of emergency presidential power reach different conclusions, but debate continues even as presidents decide how to respond to the threat posed by terrorism in the twenty-first century.

After the Civil War, the Supreme Court and Congress showed signs that they were concerned about reining in emergency presidential power. As we saw, the court rejected (though only after the war ended) Lincoln's view of a wartime constitution in the *Milligan* case. In the 1870s, President Grant acted without congressional authorization in ordering the navy to defend Santo Domingo[17] (which Grant wanted to make part of the United States) against attack from Haiti. This was similar to the action President Polk had taken in sending troops to defend Texas against what he claimed was a threat from Mexico. This time, however, Congress did not rubber-stamp the president's actions; instead, it rejected Grant's proposal to annex Santo Domingo and forced Grant to rescind his order to the navy.[18] After the explosion of the USS *Maine* in Havana harbor, in 1898, President McKinley sought congressional approval for military action and received it, ultimately in the form of a declaration of war.[19]

During World War I, President Woodrow Wilson generally sought congressional approval for his actions and did not assert claims of unilateral emergency presidential power. U.S. entry into the war was marked by a formal congressional declaration of war, and Congress passed laws giving Wilson authority to suppress dissent and opposition to the war at home. The Espionage Act, enacted in June 1917, prohibited any attempt to "interfere with the operation or success of the military or naval forces of the United States" or "to cause insubordination" in the armed forces or to "willfully obstruct" military recruiting or enlistment.[20] The Sedition Act, a 1918 amendment to the original Espionage Act, outlawed the speaking, writing, or publishing of anything disloyal to the government, flag, or armed services of the United States.[21] Violations of either law could result in a prison sentence of up to twenty years.

Although the language in the original Espionage Act could have been seen mainly as an effort to target dangerous spies or saboteurs, the Wilson administration enforced both Acts to clamp down on dissent—in other words, speech in and of itself, not necessarily linked to action. More than two thousand people were prosecuted under the Espionage Act between 1917 and 1921, and more than a thousand were convicted, but none of these convictions involved spying or sabotage; instead, prosecutions targeted Americans on the political left.[22]

The Supreme Court upheld the constitutionality of the Espionage Act as enforced by the Wilson administration.[23] However, Justice Brandeis's dissent in *Milwaukee Social Democratic Pub. Co.* pointed to a potential problem: even if the executive branch exercised power pursuant to congressional authorization, the executive branch could overstep its bounds by misinterpreting and/or overreading the authority granted by Congress. Justice Brandeis concluded that Congress, under the Espionage Act, simply had not granted Postmaster General Albert Burleson the power to deny second-class mail rates[24] in the future to a Socialist newspaper on the basis of previously published editorials that criticized the war and the military draft.[25] Brandeis's opinion, though a dissent, made an important point. Even when presidents act or purport to act pursuant to congressional authorization, there are limits on their power. Congress cannot authorize the president to take action that would violate the Bill of Rights or another part of the Constitution.[26] It will be useful to keep this in mind when we consider claims of presidential power that rest on purported congressional authorization—most notably, when Presidents Bush and Obama cited congressional authorization to justify actions taken after the September 11, 2001, terrorist attacks.[27]

Even after World War I ended, the clampdown on dissent continued, but this time the executive branch claimed unilateral authority to wield emergency presidential power. In the wake of the Russian Revolution of 1917, many Americans worried that communism would come to the United States. Attorney General Mitchell A. Palmer specifically predicted that the feared revolution would come to the United States on May 1, 1920, unless preemptive action was taken to rein in radicalism. Palmer argued that if Congress would not provide legislative authorization, then the executive branch should act on its own.[28] In 1919 and 1920, the Justice Department conducted the so-called Palmer raids, which resulted in the roundup and detention of thousands of suspected radicals, many of whom were deported.[29] Federal courts halted some of the deportation proceedings, warning against the use of arbitrary, unchecked government power and reminding officials that the Bill of Rights protects citizens as well as noncitizens against the deprivation without due process.[30] Assistant Secretary of Labor Louis F. Post also objected to Palmer's action, and Attorney General Palmer was ultimately discredited.[31] While federal courts acted to rein in Palmer's actions, when similarly unsupported accusations led to a much broader roundup during World War II, this time of Japanese Americans, citizens and noncitizens alike, the Supreme Court failed to act as a check on arbitrary power, as we'll see in chapter 6.

5

EXPANDED PRESIDENTIAL POWER
DURING WORLD WAR II

NAZI SABOTEURS AND MILITARY
COMMISSIONS

World War II presented another crisis—not internal rebellion but external danger—that, like the Civil War, directly threatened the nation.[1] President Franklin D. Roosevelt, like Lincoln before him, claimed that this emergency justified independent presidential action. Though he often worked with Congress, he also acted unilaterally to respond to threats posed by Nazi Germany and Imperial Japan.

The United States formally entered World War II after Japan attacked the U.S. Pacific fleet at Pearl Harbor, in Hawaii (then a U.S. territory), on December 7, 1941. The nation was stunned by the sudden attack, and President Roosevelt immediately asked Congress to declare war against Japan, which Congress did, on December 8, 1941. A few days later, Roosevelt asked Congress to declare war against Germany and Italy, which Congress did on December 11.[2]

Even before Pearl Harbor, however, Roosevelt had cited national emergency as a basis for taking unilateral action in anticipation of war. After Germany invaded Poland in September 1939, Roosevelt declared a state of limited emergency. Most of Europe quickly fell to the Nazis. By mid-1940, Germany seemed poised to invade Britain, and Nazi control of Europe seemed certain to pose a threat to the United States. British prime minister Winston Churchill, as well as the British king, asked Roosevelt to send help—in the form of naval destroyers. Before France's surrender, it had also asked the United States for destroyers. Roosevelt declined France's request and hesitated with the British, each time saying he could not act without Congress's authorization and was not confident he could gain it. Congress in fact passed a law in June 1940 prohibiting the transfer of military equipment "essential to the defense of the United States" unless approved by the chief of naval operations or the chief of staff of the army.[3]

Nonetheless, Roosevelt ultimately decided, in late summer of 1940, that he would exchange fifty destroyers for ninety-nine-year leases on British naval bases in the Caribbean and in Newfoundland.[4] Attorney General (and future Supreme Court justice) Robert Jackson wrote an opinion concluding that the president had broad power to act independently with regard to foreign policy, basing this conclusion in part on a 1936 Supreme Court decision[5] suggesting in dicta that the president had broad authority to conduct foreign relations and did not always need congressional authorization before acting in this area. Jackson also cited the Commander in Chief Clause of the Constitution, as well as acts of Congress that arguably provided authority for the exchange, as providing additional support for Roosevelt to act.[6] Of course, Congress seemed to have set limits on presidential power in this area through the June 1940 law prohibiting the transfer of military equipment absent approval by military officials.[7] Roosevelt argued that, if he had gone to Congress before making the deal, speedy action would have been impossible.[8] Roosevelt justified his decision to make the exchange with Britain in the name of national security, saying that "[p]reparation for defense is an inalienable prerogative of a sovereign state."[9] Few would disagree with that statement; the question, however, was whether Roosevelt was justified in acting on his own in making such preparation. One critic called Attorney General Jackson's opinion "an endorsement of unrestrained autocracy in the field of [U.S.] foreign relations."[10]

Roosevelt and Attorney General Jackson were making arguments similar to those Lincoln had made to defend his actions early in the Civil War. Like Lincoln, Roosevelt argued that his actions were necessary to defend the nation, insisting when he announced the transfer of destroyers to Britain that "[u]nder present circumstances, this exercise of sovereign right is essential to the maintenance of our peace and safety."[11] Jackson also echoed Lincoln by invoking the Commander in Chief Clause as at least a partial basis for presidential action; however he, and Roosevelt, did not claim any authority to take action prohibited by statute.[12] Jackson added an argument that would not have been available for Lincoln in the context of responding to domestic insurrection: the Supreme Court's 1936 *Curtiss-Wright* decision, which seemed at first glance to support broader presidential authority in the area of foreign relations.[13]

In *Curtiss-Wright*, the court had stated as dicta that the president possesses "plenary and exclusive power . . . as the sole organ of the federal government in the field of international relations."[14] As such, the court said, the president could take unilateral action in this area without approval by Congress. The "sole organ" concept comes from a speech John Marshall gave in 1800 as a member of the U.S. House of Representatives, before he began serving as chief justice of the Supreme Court. Marshall, defending President John Adams's actions in carrying out the extradition of a criminal suspect under a treaty with the British, reasoned that:

> [t]he president is the sole organ of the nation in its external relations, and its sole representative with foreign nations. Of consequence, the demand of a foreign nation can only be made on him. He possesses the whole executive power. He holds and directs the force of the nation. Of consequence, any act to be performed by the force of the nation is to be performed through him. He is charged to execute the laws. A treaty is declared to be a law. He must then execute a treaty, where he, and he alone, possesses the means of executing it.[15]

Although Marshall used the seemingly expansive term "sole organ" in describing the president, it is clear from both the plain words of his statement and the context that he did not mean to assign the president plenary control over foreign affairs. Marshall's point was that Adams was the sole organ of the government in carrying out the treaty, not that he possessed exclusive power to act.[16] However, the court, writing more than one hundred years later in the *Curtiss-Wright* case, misconstrued his words, insisting that Marshall's speech referred to:

> the very delicate, plenary and exclusive power of the President as the sole organ of the federal government in the field of international relations—a power which does not require as a basis for its exercise an act of Congress, but which, of course, like every other governmental power, must be exercised in subordination to the applicable provisions of the Constitution.[17]

In advising Roosevelt, Jackson did not push *Curtiss-Wright* to the limits of its logic: he did not argue that presidential power regarding foreign affairs was plenary and could be exercised without Congress's authorization.[18] However, by citing *Curtiss-Wright*, he was strengthening the authority of a court opinion that depended on a misconception of history. As we'll see, other presidential advisers have made similar or even broader use of *Curtiss-Wright* and the sole organ theory.

While Roosevelt might be criticized for acting unilaterally in making the initial decision to lend destroyers to Britain, like Lincoln he did obtain retroactive congressional approval for his action. In March 1941, Congress passed the Lend-Lease Act, providing express authority for the president to transfer "defense articles" to other countries when he deemed this vital to the defense of the United States.[19] Roosevelt took other independent action before Pearl Harbor, including declaring a state of unlimited national emergency in May 1941 and asserting that it was necessary to prepare American defenses against aggression in the Western Hemisphere. Roosevelt used his declaration as a basis for sending troops to Iceland. Senator Robert Taft denounced this action, charging that the president had "no legal or constitutional right to send American troops to Iceland" on his own initiative and that doing so undermined Congress's sole authority to declare war. Roosevelt justified his actions as an effort to effectuate Congress's intent, as expressed in statutes like the Lend-Lease Act, to aid countries fighting against Hitler as a way to protect the United States, and Congress did not act to rein in the president with regard to his decision to send troops to Iceland.[20]

Roosevelt's actions before Pearl Harbor were justified by a potential threat to national security. That potential threat was realized by the attack on Pearl Harbor on December 7, 1941—though it came from Japan, not Germany.[21] The United States had sustained a direct attack, and additional attacks seemed imminent.[22] By early 1942, German submarines were operating off the east coast of the United States, sinking ships and sometimes coming within a mile of the shore, close enough to observe American civilians in waterfront homes.[23] There were concerns about sabotage by enemy agents, and, in fact, two groups of German saboteurs did land, one on Long Island and one in Florida, in 1942. The two separate teams planned to destroy factories, railroads, bridges, and other strategic targets within the United States. The saboteurs had all lived in the United States—in fact, at least one was a naturalized U.S. citizen.[24] All eight would-be saboteurs were arrested within two weeks of the landings; the leader of the group that landed on Long Island turned himself in to the FBI and gave information that led to the capture of all the others, from both teams.[25]

The FBI agents who interrogated the would-be saboteurs initially anticipated that the eight prisoners would be indicted and tried in civil court. However, the Roosevelt administration decided to try the men through a military tribunal,[26] pursuant to orders issued by the president.

The administration preferred a military tribunal for multiple reasons. First, press coverage had praised the FBI for capturing the saboteurs on its own, rather than as the result of one man turning himself in and helping to track down the others; a public trial in civil court could be embarrassing and could also provide the Germans with the real story, perhaps encouraging them to try additional landings. Second, Attorney General Francis Biddle (Jackson's successor), as well as other government lawyers, believed it would be difficult to obtain lengthy prison sentences for the saboteurs in civil court, because the charges would likely involve only attempted sabotage (fortunately, the saboteurs had been stopped, or had abandoned their mission, before they could actually carry out their plans). Government lawyers concluded that civil courts might be able to impose prison sentences of only two years. Finally, creating a military tribunal was an attractive option because the tribunal, unlike a civil court or court-martial, could move quickly, follow improvised rules that favored the government, impose a death sentence, and conduct its proceedings in secret, without review by any civil court.[27]

The rules for establishing and conducting proceedings before a military tribunal were not clear; the Constitution does not specifically address the use of military tribunals, although they have been used in certain circumstances since the Revolutionary War.[28] Roosevelt's advisers concluded that the Germans could be tried before either a court-martial or a military tribunal but that a court-martial would have to follow statutory procedures enacted by Congress under the Articles of War,[29] whereas a military tribunal might not be required to follow the same rules (though "it ha[d] been the practice for military commissions to follow the composition and procedure of courts-martial").[30] The Roosevelt administration saw an opportunity here; if the rules for military tribunals were unclear and did not necessarily track the rules for courts-martial, then they had leeway to shape the rules to their purposes.

President Roosevelt made clear that he wanted a military tribunal created that would hold secret proceedings not subject to review by any court and that would sentence the saboteurs to death as an "almost obligatory" judgment. On July 2, 1942, he issued a proclamation establishing a military tribunal to try the Germans.[31] Roosevelt claimed authority to do so "as President of the United States of America and Commander in Chief of the Army and Navy of the United States, by virtue of the authority vested in me by the Constitution and the statutes of the United States."[32]

As provided by Roosevelt's proclamation, the tribunal would consist of seven military generals appointed by the president, with military lawyers assigned to represent the Germans. Attorney General Biddle and Judge

Advocate General Myron Cramer were assigned as prosecutors in the trial. The tribunal would try the saboteurs for violations of the uncodified "law of war" in addition to statutory offenses defined by Congress for use in civil courts and courts-martial.[33] While statutory law is specifically defined by Congress, the law of war is less certain, based on international custom and practice. The tribunal could try the Germans for a broader range of offenses than would be available in a court-martial proceeding and could sentence the men to death (a punishment not available under existing statute for sabotage in time of war) by a two-thirds vote (the Articles of War required a unanimous vote for the death penalty in cases where it was available). Roosevelt also authorized the tribunal to develop its own rules for conducting proceedings; in other words, the tribunal would not have to follow rules of evidence and procedure that applied in civil courts and courts-martial. Roosevelt's proclamation denied the men access to any civil court (i.e., it foreclosed habeas corpus or other review by a court). The proclamation provided that the only appeal of the tribunal's judgment would be directly to the president; by contrast, the Articles of War provided for review of military court decisions by the Judge Advocate General's office.[34]

There were several potential flaws associated with President Roosevelt's chosen course of action. First, the proclamation essentially shut the legislative and judicial branches out of the process—the president "appointed the tribunal, selected the judges, prosecutors and defense counsel, and served as the final reviewing authority."[35] The president created the rules the tribunal would follow—or, for the most part, gave the tribunal authority to create its own rules. This produced conflict with Article 38 of the Articles of War, which gave the president authority to make procedural rules for military tribunals, provided that (1) "in so far as [the president] shall deem practicable, [the tribunals should] apply the rules of evidence generally recognized in the trial of criminal cases in the district courts of the United States"; (2) "nothing contrary to or inconsistent with these articles shall be so prescribed"; and (3) "that all rules made in pursuance of this article shall be laid before the Congress annually."[36] Roosevelt provided no explanation as to why it was not practicable to follow the rules of evidence used in civilian courts, some of the rules he expressly prescribed were inconsistent with the Articles of War, and the rules the tribunal followed were not laid before Congress. Roosevelt's order authorized the tribunal to consider charges based on violations of the hazy, uncodified laws of war, a decision that seemed to intrude on Congress's constitutionally assigned authority to "define and punish . . . Offenses against the Law of Nations" under

Article I, section 8, of the Constitution. Roosevelt effectively attempted to suspend habeas corpus for the saboteurs, denying them access to the courts, although Congress had not authorized any suspension—recall Lincoln's similar decision, which was challenged in the *Merryman* case. Finally, Roosevelt's proclamation authorized punishment for the Germans that did not exist at the time they landed in the United States: he authorized the death penalty *after* the men were captured, which seemed to conflict with the Ex Post Facto Clause of Article I, section 9, of the Constitution.[37]

Pursuant to Roosevelt's orders, the tribunal began closed proceedings on July 8, 1942. The Germans were charged with four crimes relating to espionage and sabotage, including violations of the laws of war, the Articles of War, and conspiracy. The tribunal announced that it would essentially decide rules of procedure as the trial went forward, rather than stating them in advance; as questions came up, the tribunal would advise counsel what rules applied. One of the prosecutors agreed that the tribunal had authority "to do anything it pleases; there is no dispute about that." As Louis Fisher observes, "defense counsel did not know the rules in advance. They discovered them as the trial progressed."[38]

The German saboteurs were assigned experienced military lawyers, and their counsel charged that the proceedings before the tribunal violated the Constitution because (1) the civil courts were open and functioning[39] and (2) President Roosevelt was acting contrary to the Articles of War as enacted by Congress.[40] Prosecutors argued that *Milligan* did not apply because the Germans, unlike Milligan, were enemy aliens[41] who landed behind American defenses out of uniform (i.e., as spies bent on sabotage). They further argued that violations of the laws of war could properly be tried before the tribunal as opposed to a civil court.[42]

When lawyers for the defendants were unable to convince the tribunal of the force of their argument, they tried to take their case directly to the president, requesting a meeting with Roosevelt to discuss their concerns.[43] When Roosevelt declined the meeting, the defense lawyers sought to present their arguments to the Supreme Court on a petition for a writ of habeas corpus. The Court, which was on summer recess, convened to hold emergency oral argument on July 29, 1942.[44]

The Supreme Court was asked to decide whether the German saboteurs should have access to the civil courts; the court was not ruling on the ultimate question of guilt or innocence. The court was, to a large extent, operating in the dark and was under a great deal of pressure to support the president's position. On the first point, since the tribunal's proceedings were secret, the court did not know exactly what rules the tribunal was using and how it was operating. On the second point, the court was deciding this case as World War II raged.[45] It faced pressure from the public, from the president, and even internally from some of its own members. Two justices worked closely with the Roosevelt administration—Justice James Byrnes was a "de facto member of the [Roosevelt] administration" who advised the attorney general on legislation and executive orders, while Justice Felix Frankfurter had met with the secretary of war to discuss the saboteurs' case before it reached the Supreme Court.[46]

Defense attorneys urged the court to uphold central principles of constitutional democracy, even—or especially—when tested during wartime. The defense argued that any crimes alleged against the Germans had to proceed from statutes passed by Congress, not from the murky "law of war," and that any alleged statutory violations could be tried in civil courts. Roosevelt lacked authority to issue the proclamation, the defense maintained, and it was up to Congress "to define the law of war and to say what constitutes a criminal offense." Similarly, Congress, not the president, possessed authority to suspend habeas corpus and deny the defendants access to civil courts. Defense attorneys further argued that the president had intruded on Congress's power by (a) authorizing imposition of a death sentence by a two-thirds vote (not a unanimous vote as required by the Articles of War); (b) bypassing the review process under the Articles of War and giving himself final authority to review the tribunal's decisions; and (c) giving the tribunal authority to make up procedural rules on the fly. In addition, they noted that Roosevelt's proclamation was issued *after* the men had committed the alleged offenses and created new offenses and penalties that did not previously exist, in violation of the Constitution's Ex Post Facto Clause, which bars punishment for an act that was not illegal when it was carried out. Prosecutors argued that the Germans could be denied access to the courts because they were "enemies of the United States" and, as such, could lawfully be held in custody by the military—in other words, habeas corpus rights did not apply to the saboteurs. They also suggested that the president was operating in an area where executive authority could not be limited by Congress or the courts, asserting that "[t]he President's power over enemies who enter this country in time of war, as armed invaders intending to commit hostile acts, must be absolute." However, prosecutors backed off this point when challenged during oral argument, and the court avoided dealing with the question of whether absolute presidential power existed in this area.[47]

The court reached a speedy decision, issuing a brief per curiam opinion the day after oral argument concluded.[48] The court denied the Germans' petition without providing reasoning or explanation, paving the way for the tribunal's proceedings to continue, and promising to provide a full written opinion later.[49]

By the time Chief Justice Stone began preparing the promised written opinion, six of the eight saboteurs had been convicted by the tribunal and executed.[50] Stone was concerned that the president had violated the Articles of War. He recognized, however, that he and the rest of the court were effectively boxed in: if the court's written opinion expressed any doubt about the president's actions and the tribunal's legitimacy, that would suggest that six men had been executed on the strength of a conviction obtained through an illegitimate body. Moreover, Stone believed the ultimate opinion had to be unanimous—even a concurring opinion would be a problem under the circumstances. As a clerk for one of the justices who decided the case later said, "[The court] sent the [saboteurs] to their deaths some months before Chief Justice Stone was able to get out an opinion telling why."[51]

When Stone circulated a draft opinion, it was not immediately clear that he would win the support of all the justices; at least one concurring opinion was also prepared. In an effort to shore up unqualified support for Stone's opinion, Justice Frankfurter wrote a memorandum to his colleagues urging them to defer to the president as a matter of patriotism. Frankfurter suggested that his colleagues not engage in "abstract constitutional discussions" and allow any potentially troubling precedent to be sorted out "during peacetime." His memorandum imagined a conversation with the saboteurs,[52] in which Frankfurter accused the Germans of having a "helluva cheek to ask for a writ that would take you out of the hands of the Military Commission." Frankfurter urged his colleagues not to let the dead Germans create a "bitter conflict" between different branches of the government after the saboteurs' bodies were "rotting in lime."[53]

Ultimately, the court did issue a unanimous opinion, with no separate concurrences (though the opinion did note some disagreement among the justices as to whether Congress intended for the Articles of War to govern the tribunal's proceedings—some justices thought Congress did intend this but did not bar the president or the tribunal from following different procedures, whereas others concluded that Congress simply did not intend for the Articles of War to apply to a proceeding involving enemy invaders).[54] Excerpts from the court's opinion in *Ex parte Quirin* follow— notice how the court distinguishes *Milligan*, how the court describes the war powers of Congress and the president, and what the court says about unilateral presidential power to decide what to do with the enemy saboteurs.

Ex parte Quirin, 317 U.S. I (1942)

Per curiam opinion issued July 31, 1942; opinion of the Court by Chief Justice Stone issued October 29, 1942.

The question for decision is whether the detention of petitioners by respondent for trial by Military Commission, appointed by Order of the President of July 2, 1942, on charges preferred against them purporting to set out their violations of the law of war and of the Articles of War, is in conformity to the laws and Constitution of the United States.

After denial of their applications by the District Court, petitioners asked leave to file petitions for habeas corpus in this Court. In view of the public importance of the questions raised by their petitions and of the duty which rests on the courts, in time of war as well as in time of peace, to preserve unimpaired the constitutional safeguards of civil liberty, and because, in our opinion, the public interest required that we consider and decide those questions without any avoidable delay, we directed that petitioners' applications be set down for full oral argument at a special term of this Court, convened on July 29, 1942.

On July 31, 1942, after hearing argument of counsel and after full consideration of all questions raised, this Court affirmed the orders of the District Court and denied petitioners' applications for leave to file petitions for habeas corpus. By per curiam opinion, we announced the decision of the Court, and that the full opinion [i.e., the opinion excerpted here] in the causes would be prepared and filed with the Clerk....

All the petitioners were born in Germany; all have lived in the United States. All returned to Germany between 1933 and 1941. All except petitioner Haupt are admittedly citizens of the German Reich, with which the United States is at war. Haupt came to this country with his parents when he was five years old; it is contended that he became a citizen of the United States by virtue of the naturalization of his parents during his minority, and that he has not since lost his citizenship.

After the declaration of war between the United States and the German Reich, petitioners received training at a sabotage school near Berlin, Germany, where they were instructed in the use of explosives and in methods of secret writing. Thereafter petitioners, with a German citizen, Dasch, proceeded from Germany to a seaport in Occupied France, where petitioners Burger, Heinck and Quirin, together with Dasch, boarded a German submarine which proceeded across the Atlantic to Amagansett Beach on Long Island, New York. The four were there landed from the submarine in the hours of darkness, on or about June 13, 1942, carrying with them a supply of explosives, fuses, and incendiary and timing devices. While landing, they wore German Marine Infantry uniforms or parts of uniforms. Immediately after landing, they buried their uniforms and the other articles mentioned and proceeded in civilian dress to New York City.

The remaining four petitioners at the same French port boarded another German submarine, which carried them across the Atlantic to Ponte Vedra Beach, Florida. On or about June 17, 1942, they came ashore during the hours of darkness, wearing caps of the German Marine Infantry and carrying with them a supply of explosives, fuses, and incendiary and timing devices. They immediately buried their caps and the other articles mentioned, and proceeded in civilian dress to Jacksonville, Florida, and thence to various points in the United States. All were taken into custody in New York or Chicago by agents of the Federal Bureau of Investigation. All had received instructions in Germany from an officer of the German High Command to destroy war industries and war facilities in the United States, for which they or their relatives in Germany were to receive salary payments from the German Government. They also had been paid by the German Government during their course of training at the sabotage school, and had received substantial sums in United States currency, which were in their possession when arrested. . . .

The President, as President and Commander in Chief of the Army and Navy, by Order of July 2, 1942, appointed a Military Commission and directed it to try petitioners for offenses against the law of war and the Articles of War, and prescribed regulations for the procedure on the trial. . . . On the same day, by Proclamation, the President declared that "all persons who are subjects, citizens or residents of any nation at war with the United States or who give obedience to or act under the direction of any such nation, and who during time of war enter or attempt to enter the United States . . . through coastal or boundary defenses, and are charged with committing or attempting or preparing to commit sabotage, espionage, hostile or warlike acts, or violations of the law of war, shall be subject to the law of war and to the jurisdiction of military tribunals."

The Proclamation also stated . . . that all such persons were denied access to the [civil] courts. Pursuant to direction of the Attorney General, the Federal Bureau of Investigation surrendered custody of petitioners to respondent, Provost Marshal of the Military District of Washington, who was directed by the Secretary of War to receive and keep them in custody, and who thereafter held petitioners for trial before the Commission.

On July 3, 1942, the Judge Advocate General's Department of the Army prepared and lodged with the Commission the following charges against petitioners, supported by specifications:

1. Violation of the law of war.
2. Violation of Article 81 of the Articles of War,[55] defining the offense of relieving or attempting to relieve, or corresponding with or giving intelligence to, the enemy.

3. Violation of Article 82, defining the offense of spying.
4. Conspiracy to commit the offenses alleged in charges 1, 2 and 3.

The Commission met on July 8, 1942, and proceeded with the trial, which continued in progress while the causes were pending in this Court.... It is conceded that, ever since petitioners' arrest, the state and federal courts in Florida, New York, and the District of Columbia, and in the states in which each of the petitioners was arrested or detained, have been open and functioning normally.

... Petitioners' main contention is that the President is without any statutory or constitutional authority to order the petitioners to be tried by military tribunal for offenses with which they are charged; that, in consequence, they are entitled to be tried in the civil courts with the safeguards, including trial by jury, which the Fifth and Sixth Amendments guarantee to all persons charged in such courts with criminal offenses....

The Government challenges each of these propositions. But regardless of their merits, it also insists that petitioners must be denied access to the courts, both because they are enemy aliens or have entered our territory as enemy belligerents, and because the President's Proclamation undertakes in terms to deny such access to the class of persons defined by the Proclamation, which aptly describes the character and conduct of petitioners. It is urged that, if they are enemy aliens or if the Proclamation has force, no court may afford the petitioners a hearing. But there is certainly nothing in the Proclamation to preclude access to the courts for determining its applicability to the particular case. And neither the Proclamation nor the fact that they are enemy aliens forecloses consideration by the courts of petitioners' contentions that the Constitution and laws of the United States constitutionally enacted forbid their trial by military commission. As announced in our per curiam opinion, we have resolved those questions by our conclusion that the Commission has jurisdiction to try the charge preferred against petitioners. There is therefore no occasion to decide contentions of the parties unrelated to this issue. We pass at once to the consideration of the basis of the Commission's authority.

We are not here concerned with any question of the guilt or innocence of petitioners. Constitutional safeguards for the protection of all who are charged with offenses are not to be disregarded in order to inflict merited punishment on some who are guilty. ... But the detention and trial of petitioners—ordered by the President in the declared exercise of his powers as Commander in Chief of the Army in time of war and of grave public danger—are not to be set aside by the courts without the clear conviction that they are in conflict with the Constitution or laws of Congress constitutionally enacted.

Congress and the President, like the courts, possess no power not derived from the Constitution. But one of the objects of the Constitution, as declared by its preamble, is to "provide for the common defence." As a means to that end, the Constitution gives to Congress the power to "provide for the common Defence," Art. I, § 8, cl. I; "To raise and support Armies," "To provide and maintain a Navy," Art. I, § 8, cl. 12, 13, and "To make Rules for the Government and Regulation of the land and naval Forces," Art. I, § 8, cl. 14. Congress is given authority "To declare War, grant Letters of Marque and Reprisal, and make Rules concerning Captures on Land and Water," Art. I, § 8, cl. 11, and "To define and punish Piracies and Felonies committed on the high Seas, and Offences against the Law of Nations," Art. I, § 8, cl. 10....

The Constitution confers on the President the "executive Power," Art. II, § 1, cl. 1, and imposes on him the duty to "take Care that the Laws be faithfully executed." Art. II, § 3. It makes him the Commander in Chief of the Army and Navy, Art. II, § 2, cl. 1, and empowers him to appoint and commission officers of the United States. Art. II, § 3, cl. 1.

The Constitution thus invests the President, as Commander in Chief, with the power to wage war which Congress has declared, and to carry into effect all laws passed by Congress for the conduct of war and for the government and regulation of the Armed Forces, and all laws defining and punishing offenses against the law of nations, including those which pertain to the conduct of war.

By the Articles of War, Congress has provided rules for the government of the Army. It has provided for the trial and punishment, by courts martial, of violations of the Articles by members of the armed forces and by specified classes of persons associated or serving with the Army. But the Articles also recognize the "military commission" appointed by military command as an appropriate tribunal for the trial and punishment of offenses against the law of war not ordinarily tried by court martial and authorize the President, with certain limitations, to prescribe the procedure for military commissions. Articles 81 and 82 authorize trial, either by court martial or military commission, of those charged with relieving, harboring or corresponding with the enemy and those charged with spying....

From the very beginning of its history, this Court has recognized and applied the law of war as including that part of the law of nations which prescribes, for the conduct of war, the status, rights and duties of enemy nations, as well as of enemy individuals. By the Articles of War ... Congress has explicitly provided, so far as it may constitutionally do so, that military tribunals shall have jurisdiction to try offenders or offenses against the law of war in appropriate cases. Congress ... has thus exercised its authority to define and punish offenses against the law of nations by sanctioning, within constitutional limitations, the jurisdiction of military commissions to try persons for offenses which, according to the rules and precepts of the law of nations, and more particularly the law of war, are cognizable by such tribunals. And the President, as Commander in Chief, by his Proclamation in time of war, has invoked that law. By his Order creating the present Commission, he has undertaken to exercise the authority conferred upon him by Congress, and also such authority as the Constitution itself gives the Commander in Chief, to direct the performance of those functions which may constitutionally be performed by the military arm of the nation in time of war.

. . . It is unnecessary for present purposes to determine to what extent the President as Commander in Chief has constitutional power to create military commissions without the support of Congressional legislation. For here, Congress has authorized trial of offenses against the law of war before such commissions. We are concerned only with the question whether it is within the constitutional power of the National Government to place petitioners upon trial before a military commission for the offenses with which they are charged. We must therefore first inquire whether any of the acts charged is an offense against the law of war cognizable before a military tribunal, and, if so, whether the Constitution prohibits the trial. . . .

It is no objection that Congress, in providing for the trial of such offenses, has not itself undertaken to codify that branch of international law or to mark its precise boundaries, or to enumerate or define by statute all the acts which that law condemns. . . . Congress has incorporated by reference, as within the jurisdiction of military commissions, all offenses which are defined as such by the law of war . . . and which may constitutionally be included within that jurisdiction. Congress had the choice of crystallizing in permanent form and in minute detail every offense against the law of war, or of adopting the system of common law applied by military tribunals so far as it should be recognized and deemed applicable by the courts. It chose the latter course.

By universal agreement and practice, the law of war draws a distinction between the armed forces and the peaceful populations of belligerent nations, and also between those who are lawful and unlawful combatants. Lawful combatants are subject to capture and detention as prisoners of war by opposing military forces. Unlawful combatants are likewise subject to capture and detention, but, in addition, they are subject to trial and punishment by military tribunals for acts which render their belligerency unlawful. The spy who secretly and without uniform passes the military lines of a belligerent in time of war, seeking to gather military information and communicate it to the enemy, or an enemy combatant who without uniform comes secretly through the lines for the purpose of waging war by destruction of life or property, are familiar examples of belligerents who are generally deemed not to be entitled to the status of prisoners of war, but to be offenders against the law of war subject to trial and punishment by military tribunals. . . . Such was the practice of our own military authorities before the adoption of the Constitution, and during the Mexican and Civil Wars. . . .

Specification I of the first charge is sufficient to charge all the petitioners with the offense of unlawful belligerency, trial of which is within the jurisdiction of the

Commission, and the admitted facts affirmatively show that the charge is not merely colorable or without foundation.

Specification I states that petitioners,

"being enemies of the United States and acting for . . . the German Reich, a belligerent enemy nation, secretly and covertly passed, in civilian dress, contrary to the law of war, through the military and naval lines and defenses of the United States . . . and went behind such lines, contrary to the law of war, in civilian dress . . . for the purpose of committing . . . hostile acts, and, in particular, to destroy certain war industries, war utilities and war materials within the United States."

This specification so plainly alleges violation of the law of war as to require but brief discussion of petitioners' contentions. As we have seen, entry upon our territory in time of war by enemy belligerents, including those acting under the direction of the armed forces of the enemy, for the purpose of destroying property used or useful in prosecuting the war, is a hostile and warlike act. It subjects those who participate in it without uniform to the punishment prescribed by the law of war for unlawful belligerents. . . .

Citizenship in the United States of an enemy belligerent does not relieve him from the consequences of a belligerency which is unlawful because in violation of the law of war. Citizens who associate themselves with the military arm of the enemy government, and, with its aid, guidance and direction, enter this country bent on hostile acts, are enemy belligerents within the meaning of the Hague Convention and the law of war. . . .

But petitioners insist that, even if the offenses with which they are charged are offenses against the law of war, their trial is subject to the requirement of the Fifth Amendment that no person shall be held to answer for a capital or otherwise in-famous crime unless on a presentment or indictment of a grand jury, and that such trials by Article III, § 2, and the Sixth Amendment must be by jury in a civil court. . . .

Presentment by a grand jury and trial by a jury of the [area] where the crime was committed were, at the time of the adoption of the Constitution, familiar parts of the machinery for criminal trials in the civil courts. But they were procedures unknown to military tribunals, which are not courts in the sense of the Judiciary Article, and which, in the natural course of events, are usually called upon to function under conditions precluding resort to such procedures. As this Court has often recognized, it was not the purpose or effect of § 2 of Article III, read in the light of the common law, to enlarge the then existing right to a jury trial. The object was to preserve unimpaired trial by jury in all those cases in which it had been recognized by the common law and in all cases of a like nature as they might arise in the future, but not to bring within the sweep of the guaranty those cases in which it was then well understood that a jury trial could not be demanded as of right. . . .

We cannot say that Congress, in preparing the Fifth and Sixth Amendments, intended to extend trial by jury to the cases of alien or citizen offenders against the law of war otherwise triable by military commission, while withholding it from members of our own armed forces charged with infractions of the Articles of War punishable by death.... We conclude that the Fifth and Sixth Amendments did not restrict whatever authority was conferred by the Constitution to try offenses against the law of war by military commission, and that petitioners, charged with such an offense not required to be tried by jury at common law, were lawfully placed on trial by the Commission without a jury.

Petitioners, and especially petitioner Haupt, stress the pronouncement of this Court in the *Milligan* case that the law of war "can never be applied to citizens in states which have upheld the authority of the government, and where the courts are open, and their process unobstructed."

Elsewhere in its opinion [in *Milligan*], the Court was at pains to point out that Milligan, a citizen twenty years resident in Indiana, who had never been a resident of any of the states in rebellion, was not an enemy belligerent either entitled to the status of a prisoner of war or subject to the penalties imposed upon unlawful belligerents. We construe the Court's statement as to the inapplicability of the law of war to Milligan's case as having particular reference to the facts before it. From them, the Court concluded that Milligan, not being a part of or associated with the armed forces of the enemy, was a nonbelligerent, not subject to the law of war save as—in circumstances found not there to be present, and not involved here— martial law might be constitutionally established.

The Court's opinion [in *Milligan*] is inapplicable to the case presented by the present record. We have no occasion now to define with meticulous care the ultimate boundaries of the jurisdiction of military tribunals to try persons according to the law of war. It is enough that petitioners here, upon the conceded facts, were plainly within those boundaries, and were held in good faith for trial by military commission, charged with being enemies who, with the purpose of destroying war materials and utilities, entered, or after entry remained in, our territory without uniform—an offense against the law of war. We hold only that those particular acts constitute an offense against the law of war which the Constitution authorizes to be tried by military commission....

There remains the contention that the President's Order of July 2, 1942, so far as it lays down the procedure to be followed on the trial before the Commission and on the review of its findings and sentence, and the procedure in fact followed by the Commission, are in conflict with Articles of War [as drafted by Congress]....

Petitioners do not argue, and we do not consider, the question whether the President is compelled by the Articles of War to afford unlawful enemy belligerents a trial before subjecting them to disciplinary measures. Their contention is that, if Congress has authorized their trial by military commission upon the charges preferred—violations of the law of war and the 81st and 82nd Articles of War—it has by the Articles of War prescribed the procedure by which the trial is to be conducted....

We need not inquire whether Congress may restrict the power of the Commander in Chief to deal with enemy belligerents. For the Court is unanimous in its conclusion that the Articles in question could not at any stage of the proceedings afford any basis for issuing the writ. But a majority of the full Court are not agreed on the appropriate grounds for decision. Some members of the Court are of opinion that Congress did not intend the Articles of War to govern a Presidential military commission convened for the determination of questions relating to admitted enemy invaders, and that the context of the Articles makes clear that they should not be construed to apply in that class of cases. Others are of the view that—even though this trial is subject to whatever provisions of the Articles of War Congress has in terms made applicable to "commissions"—the particular Articles in question, rightly construed, do not foreclose the procedure prescribed by the President or that shown to have been employed by the Commission, in a trial of offenses against the law of war and the 81st and 82nd Articles of War, by a military commission appointed by the President. [In other words, all the justices agreed that the president did not have to order military commissions to follow the same procedures used by courts-martial.]

Accordingly, we conclude that Charge I, on which petitioners were detained for trial by the Military Commission, alleged an offense which the President is authorized to order tried by military commission; that his Order convening the Commission was a lawful order, and that the Commission was lawfully constituted; that the petitioners were held in lawful custody, and did not show cause for their discharge. It follows that the orders of the District Court should be affirmed, and that leave to file petitions for habeas corpus in this Court should be denied.

In discussing early American views of presidential prerogative, Arthur M. Schlesinger Jr. summarizes the opinion of one member of the first Congress this way: "the legal order would be better preserved if departures from it were frankly identified as such than if they were anointed with a factitious legality and thereby enable to serve as constitutional precedents for future action."[56] The court's decision in *Quirin* would have disappointed this early congressman. In *Quirin*, the court approved a framework for presidential action that was based on the fiction that the president and Congress were acting in concert. In reality, Roosevelt had shut Congress— and the courts—out of the process by establishing an insular tribunal that could make its own rules and answered only to the president. But the court's decision threatened to create precedent for similar presidential initiative in the future.

Perhaps the *Quirin* decision proved the wisdom of what the court had said more than seventy-five years earlier in *Milligan*: it is difficult for the court to make dispassionate decisions on the exercise of emergency presidential power in the midst of war or crisis. But, where the court avoided issuing a decision that affirmatively endorsed presidential use and control of military tribunals during the Civil War, *Quirin* entered the books as possible precedent to be cited by future presidents. The question is, what does it stand for, and, given the context in which it was decided, should the decision in *Quirin* be confidently relied on by modern presidents and their advisers?

Over the years, *Quirin* has become an arguably discredited opinion (though some advocates attempted to restore it to prominence in the months following the September 11, 2001, attacks, as we'll see). Criticism has focused on five points: (1) that the military tribunal should have followed rules Congress enacted in the Articles of War for use by courts-martial and that the tribunal acted illegitimately by essentially making up its rules as it went along; (2) that Congress, not the president or the tribunal, has the constitutional authority and duty to define violations of the laws of war by statute; (3) that it was inappropriate for the president to review the tribunal's judgment on the merits, especially when it was clear that he had a predetermined wish as to the outcome; (4) that the Supreme Court, under external and internal pressure, entered a hasty per curiam opinion allowing the tribunal to proceed that led to an awkward post hoc justification in a written opinion filed months after six of the saboteurs had been executed; and (5) that the court was unable to review the tribunal's legitimacy because it didn't even know precisely what rules the tribunal followed in its secret proceedings. Louis Fisher describes the saboteur proceedings as "an unwise and ill-conceived concentration of power in the executive branch."[57] Supreme Court Justice Antonin Scalia calls the decision "not this Court's finest hour."[58]

Even if *Quirin* is cited by modern presidents, lawyers, or judges, the question is, as noted, what exactly does it stand for? Though Roosevelt really did act independently in creating and defining the tribunal, the court's opinion set aside those facts and declined to endorse any conception of unilateral presidential authority. Despite the reality of how the tribunal actually operated, one could read *Quirin* as standing only for the proposition that the president may order trial before military tribunals when authorized to do so and under rules prescribed by Congress.

Even Justice Frankfurter, who took such an active role in urging his colleagues to line up behind the president, later expressed regret about at least some aspects of the case, admitting, when the court, years later, considered hearing oral argument during a special summer session, that "the *Quirin* experience was not a happy precedent."[59] However, while Frankfurter's internal memo to his colleagues has been subject to criticism, his imagined conversation with the dead German saboteurs hits on a complicated point. As Frankfurter suggested, no one in the United States was likely to mourn the executed saboteurs. If the justices were forced to choose sides between Roosevelt and the defendants, it was not hard to predict what they would do. But critics of these events are not apologists for Nazi Germany—rather, they are echoing the words of defense counsel Kenneth Royall, who of course wanted the United States to win the war but hoped that the country did not "want to win it by throwing away everything we are fighting for, because we will have a mighty empty victory if we destroy the genuineness and truth of democratic government and fair administration of the law."[60]

6

THE INTERNMENT
OF JAPANESE AMERICANS
DURING WORLD WAR II

As Americans on the East Coast worried about landings by German saboteurs, Americans on the West Coast worried about a possible invasion and wondered whether they had to fear Japanese Americans who might ally with the invading enemy. Elected officials, including Earl Warren, who was then California's attorney general, began speaking of "relocating" people of Japanese descent into the interior of the country, where they could not assist potential invaders.[1]

While the threat of Japanese attack and perhaps even invasion was based in part on the reality of the attack on Pearl Harbor,[2] concerns about Japanese Americans were based on generalized fears, not specific proof. As David Cole notes, "there was never any evidence to support the concern that the Japanese [Americans] living [in the United States] posed a threat."[3] In fact, like other Americans, Japanese Americans rushed to enlist in the U.S. military after Pearl Harbor.[4] However, longstanding prejudice ultimately led to the internment of more than 100,000 Japanese Americans.

In order to understand how and why Japanese Americans on the west coast were interned during World War II, it is important to understand the history that predates the war. When Japanese immigrants first came to the United States in the late nineteenth century, they did not face the full fury of nativist prejudices—partly, perhaps, because they were confused with Chinese immigrants, who had preceded Japanese immigrants to the United States and were initially the focus of ugly prejudice and stereotyping that described them as a "yellow peril" bent on overrunning the West Coast.[5] However, by the turn of the century, anti-immigrant activists were making room for animus directed specifically against Japanese Americans. Nativists claimed that newcomers from Japan would accept low wages that would drive down the income of white Americans, and they suggested that Japanese American men might deflower Caucasian women and girls.[6] By the 1890s, the derogatory term "Jap" was used to describe Japanese Americans, and, by the 1920s, a survey of California high school students and college freshmen found more distaste for Japanese than Chinese immigrants, with Japanese Americans seen as "dishonest, tricky and treacherous."[7]

As Japan emerged as a world power in the early twentieth century, fear of and prejudice against Japanese Americans intensified and found expression in the law.[8] In 1906, the San Francisco school board required Japanese American students to attend a segregated school previously used for Chinese Americans. In 1907, President Theodore Roosevelt convinced the school board to reconsider its decision[9] in exchange for his negotiation of a so-called Gentleman's Agreement with Japan that limited further immigration to the United States. In 1913, California lawmakers enacted the Alien Land Act, which prohibited first-generation Japanese Americans or "Issei" born outside the United States from purchasing additional land.[10] Many had already established successful farms in California and were seen as threats to white farmers. Eleven years later, Congress passed the Immigration Restriction Act of 1924. While the "Gentleman's Agreement" had slowed immigration,[11] the Immigration Restriction Act "completely barred further Japanese immigration."[12]

For years before the 1924 Act was passed, opponents of Japanese immigration had claimed that Japanese Americans were simply too different from Caucasian Americans to be assimilated into the American population.[13] In fact, Japanese Americans, especially the Nisei generation born in the United States and recognized as citizens by the Fourteenth Amendment, were often eager to assimilate. Japanese Americans who knew only the United States as their country "were almost wholly America-oriented" and formed quintessentially American organizations like the Japanese American Young Republicans, Young Democrats, and American Legions posts, as well as the prominent Japanese American Citizens League,[14] though, at the same time, they frequently encountered racism and prejudice.[15] Many of the Issei had more difficulty assimilating, but these difficulties cannot be separated from the context of racism and laws that denied the Issei the opportunity to seek citizenship. Although some of the Issei, even teenagers and adults, were willing to attend grade school in order to learn English and joined Christian churches or "Americanized Buddhist churches,"[16] they frequently experienced "cultural isolation" as "membership in a broad spectrum of Americanizing institutions was denied to them."[17]

It was against this backdrop of forced racial isolation, widespread prejudice, and de jure discrimination that the U.S. government developed its plan for removing Japanese Americans from their homes on the West Coast and holding them in detention camps during World War II.[18] Congress ratified the president's plan, which was implemented by the military, so this is not an example of unilateral emergency presidential power. However, it is important to understand the justifications offered for mass internment, as they help us to see how emergency presidential power can present problems even when the president acts with Congress.

Even before Japan's December 7, 1941, attack on Pearl Harbor, the U.S. government had made contingency plans to intern noncitizens in the event of war with Japan, Germany, and Italy.[19] After the attack, the Immigration and Naturalization Service's general counsel drafted a proclamation for President Roosevelt authorizing "summary apprehension" of any Japanese American who was not a U.S. citizen.[20] A few days later, Secretary of War Henry Stimson classified the West Coast and several western states as a zone placed under military control, subject to the command of Lieutenant General John DeWitt. However, there was no immediate decision to round up Japanese Americans on the West Coast. In fact, Peter Irons remarks that "the initial reaction [on the West Coast] . . . was one of tolerance and understanding [toward Japanese Americans]."[21] That changed by the time the new year arrived as "the tide of public opinion abruptly shifted."[22] Leaders began to demand that Japanese Americans on the West Coast be removed from their homes and held in camps. Secretary of the Navy Frank Knox falsely claimed that Japanese Americans were responsible for the attack on Pearl Harbor.[23] A Los Angeles newscaster, John Hughes, urged Attorney General Francis Biddle to intern Japanese Americans, citizens and noncitizens alike, and other members of the press joined Hughes's call.[24] Congressman Leland Ford (R-CA) also called for Japanese Americans to be "placed in inland concentration camps."[25]

On February 19, 1942—more than two months after the attack on Pearl Harbor—President Roosevelt signed Executive Order 9066,[26] authorizing the secretary of war or military commanders to designate "military areas" from which "any persons may be excluded." Persons "excluded" from such areas were to be transported elsewhere and euphemistically provided "other accommodations as may be necessary." Ultimately, that meant detention camps encircled by barbed wire and watched over by armed guards.[27] Roosevelt justified the executive order on the basis of "the authority vested in [him] as President of the United States, and Commander in Chief of the Army and Navy." The order explained that these actions were necessary "to [protect] against espionage and . . . sabotage to national defense material." The executive order did not specify that it was to be applied to Japanese Americans (it did not identify any specific group), but it was used mainly to relocate and incarcerate Japanese Americans, both citizens and noncitizens.[28] In March 1942, Congress passed a law ratifying Roosevelt's actions by providing that anyone resisting relocation or other instructions issued pursuant to the executive order could be imprisoned.[29]

On March 2, 1942, acting pursuant to Executive Order 9066, General DeWitt designated the western parts of California, Oregon, and Washington State, as well as part of Arizona, as "military exclusion areas," and provided that all persons of Japanese descent were slated for removal from these areas.[30] On March 24, 1942, a curfew was instituted for Japanese Americans on the West Coast.[31] Mass removal and relocation of Japanese Americans from the West Coast also began in March, although the removal process was not completed until the end of October 1942.[32] More than 110,000 Japanese Americans, many of them children and almost two-thirds of them American citizens born in the United States, were incarcerated for up to four years in ten camps located mainly in western states.[33] There was no proof that any of the incarcerated people were involved in espionage or sabotage, and no specific charges were ever brought against any of them.[34]

Although most Japanese Americans obeyed the military orders, respected the curfew, and reported for internment,[35] some of them protested these actions as violations of their constitutional rights and initiated legal challenges to the curfew and detention. Gordon Hirabayashi refused to obey the curfew and was arrested, tried, and sentenced to imprisonment. Hirabayashi, a twenty-four-year-old college student who was born in Seattle and had never visited Japan, was also convicted for failing to obey a relocation order. He challenged his conviction, and his case reached the U.S. Supreme Court. The court, ruling only on the question of the constitutionality of the curfew as applied to Japanese Americans who were U.S. citizens,[36] unanimously upheld Hirabayashi's conviction, although three justices wrote concurring opinions.

Chief Justice Stone's opinion for the court identified as the central question "whether, acting in cooperation, Congress and the Executive have constitutional authority to impose the curfew restriction here complained of."[37] He reasoned that the two branches, acting together, possess the complete war power of the national government, which had been defined as "the power to wage war successfully."[38] This power, Stone explained, was "not restricted to the winning of victories in the field and the repulse of enemy forces."[39] It included "every phase of the national defense"; since the Constitution assigns the war power to the executive and Congress, the court must extend the other branches "a wide scope for the exercise of judgment and discretion" in identifying and defending against potential threats to the nation.[40]

In this case, decided in June 1943, the court concluded it was essential to take context into account. In early 1942, when the president and Congress authorized the military to determine who could be subject to curfew, Japan was winning victories against the United States and its allies throughout the Pacific. Under these circumstances, "[t]hat reasonably prudent men charged with the responsibility of our national defense had ample ground for concluding that they must face the danger of invasion, take measures against it, and, in making the choice of measures, consider our internal situation, cannot be doubted."[41] It was reasonable, the court said, for the U.S. government to take actions designed to protect against sabotage and espionage, including by ordering the curfew.

Moreover, the court found, it was reasonable for the government to determine that only Japanese Americans who were U.S. citizens, in addition to noncitizens of Japanese, German, or Italian descent, should be subject to the curfew. The court cited statements by the chairman of the Senate Military Affairs Committee during debate over the legislation ratifying President Roosevelt's executive order. The chairman said it was reasonable to focus attention on Japanese Americans because there was "suspected widespread fifth-column activity among Japanese" in the United States, and such suspicions were linked to "the system of dual citizenship which Japan deemed applicable to American-born Japanese, and in the propaganda disseminated by Japanese consuls, Buddhist priests and other leaders, among American-born children of Japanese."[42] The court added:

> There is support for the view that social, economic and political conditions which have prevailed since the close of the last century, when the Japanese began to come to this country in substantial numbers, have intensified their solidarity and have in large measure prevented their assimilation as an integral part of the white population. . . . Congress and the Executive, including the military commander, could have attributed special significance, in its bearing on the loyalties of persons of Japanese descent, to the maintenance by Japan of its system of dual citizenship. Children born in the United States of Japanese alien parents, and especially those children born before December 1, 1924, are, under many circumstances, deemed, by Japanese law, to be citizens of Japan. The association of influential Japanese residents with Japanese Consulates has been deemed a ready means for the dissemination of propaganda and for the maintenance

of the influence of the Japanese Government with the Japanese population in this country. As a result of all these conditions affecting the life of the Japanese, both aliens and citizens, in the Pacific Coast area, there has been relatively little social intercourse between them and the white population. The restrictions, both practical and legal, affecting the privileges and opportunities afforded to persons of Japanese extraction residing in the United States have been sources of irritation, and may well have tended to increase their isolation, and in many instances their attachments to Japan and its institutions. Viewing these data in all their aspects, Congress and the Executive could reasonably have concluded that these conditions have encouraged the continued attachment of members of this group to Japan and Japanese institutions.[43]

The court acknowledged that the curfew order "necessarily involves some infringement of individual liberty, just as does the police establishment of fire lines during a fire, or the confinement of people to their houses during an air raid alarm—neither of which could be thought to be an infringement of constitutional right."[44] It rejected Hirabayashi's argument that the curfew unconstitutionally deprived him and other U.S. citizens of Japanese ancestry of the equal protection of the laws by arbitrarily discriminating against them.[45] The court conceded that "[d]istinctions between citizens solely because of their ancestry are by their very nature odious to a free people whose institutions are founded upon the doctrine of equality."[46] Indeed, it acknowledged, in normal times it would be inappropriate to make distinctions between U.S. citizens on the basis of race or ancestry alone. However, during wartime and facing the threat of invasion, Congress and the executive were justified in giving the military authority to do what was necessary to defend the nation and, in doing so, were justified in singling out Japanese American U.S. citizens for discriminatory treatment.[47] Again, context was key to the court: if Congress and the executive wanted to protect the West Coast against sabotage in areas believed to be threatened by Japanese invasion or attack, they were justified in subjecting only Japanese Americans to the curfew, especially in light of the "facts and circumstances with respect to the American citizens of Japanese ancestry residing on the Pacific Coast which support the judgment of the war-waging branches of the Government that some restrictive measure was urgent."[48] Relatedly, the court concluded, "we cannot reject as unfounded the judgment of the military authorities and of Congress that there were disloyal members of that population, whose number and strength could not be precisely and quickly ascertained."[49] The court refused to "close our eyes to the fact, demonstrated by experience, that, in time of war, residents having ethnic affiliations with an invading enemy may be a greater source of danger than those of a different ancestry."[50]

Three justices wrote concurring opinions in *Hirabayashi* emphasizing that their conclusions were limited to the specific facts of this case: a decision to impose a curfew under emergency, wartime circumstances. They cautioned that the government's actions came very close to unconstitutional discrimination, in violation of the Fifth Amendment. Justice Frank Murphy wrote in his concurring opinion: "Under the curfew order here challenged, no less than 70,000 American citizens have been placed under a special ban and deprived of their liberty because of their particular racial inheritance. In this sense, it bears a melancholy resemblance to the treatment accorded to members of the Jewish race in Germany and in other parts of Europe. The result is the creation in this country of two classes of citizens for the purposes of a critical and perilous hour—to sanction discrimination between groups of United States citizens on the basis of ancestry. In my opinion, this goes to the very brink of constitutional power."[51]

Chief Justice Stone's majority opinion for the Court in *Hirabayashi* accepted spurious generalizations and stereotypes as the basis for the government's decision to apply the curfew only to U.S. citizens who were Japanese Americans. Stone noted the failure of Japanese Americans to assimilate but failed to consider the reasons why assimilation was often difficult. He solemnly noted Japan's system of dual citizenship for children born in the United States to Japanese immigrants but did not make clear that people like Gordon Hirabayashi never sought dual citizenship—this was a status conferred unilaterally by the Japanese government. Stone suggested that anti-American propaganda *might* spread among Japanese Americans but identified no evidence that any such propaganda actually had spread. Above all, he omitted important context that helped explain the long history of suspicion against Japanese Americans that predated Pearl Harbor, a history rooted in prejudice and racial fears. The closest he came to confronting this history is when he allowed that "[t]he restrictions, both practical and legal, affecting the privileges and opportunities afforded to persons of Japanese extraction residing in the United States have been sources of irritation, and may well have tended to increase their isolation, and in many instances their attachments to Japan and its institutions." However, rather than taking this as a reason to be skeptical of claims that Japanese Americans, as a group, were potentially dangerous, Stone—and the rest of the court—deferred to the Senate Military Affairs Committee chairman who charged that there was "suspected widespread fifth-column activity among Japanese" in the United States.

If the court had looked a bit further into the legislative record, it would have found evidence of clear racial animus. Congressman John Rankin (D-MS) urged that every Japanese American in the United States be put "in concentration camps and ship[ped] back to Asia" arguing that "[t]his is a race war, as far as the Pacific side of this conflict is concerned. . . . The white man's civilization has come into conflict with Japanese barbarism. . . . One of them must be destroyed." His advice with regard to Japanese Americans was "Let's get rid of them now!"[52] Senator Tom Stewart (D-TN) sponsored legislation to intern all Japanese Americans, declaring that "[a] Jap is a Jap anywhere you find him."[53] General DeWitt, the officer who issued the curfew and internment orders, had similar views. He agreed that "[a] Jap is a Jap"[54]—in other words, anyone of Japanese descent was a member of "an enemy race," and, accordingly, all of the more than 110,000 Japanese Americans living on the West Coast of the United States were "potential enemies."[55]

The point of targeting Japanese Americans for first curfew and then internment was purportedly to protect against sabotage and espionage. However, as even General DeWitt conceded, there was no evidence of any sabotage carried out by Japanese Americans—bizarrely, DeWitt claimed this as a reason for concern, charging in his final report on internment that "[t]he very fact that no sabotage has taken place is a disturbing and confirming indication that such action will be taken."[56] Concerns about espionage were exaggerated. In March 1941, months before Pearl Harbor, Lieutenant Commander Kenneth D. Ringle of the Office of Naval Intelligence had helped break up a spy ring operating out of the Japanese consulate in Los Angeles. Although the ring seemed to have included some Japanese Americans, Ringle concluded that broader concerns about widespread disloyalty were unjustified.[57] In a January 1942 report, he warned that "the entire 'Japanese Problem' has been magnified out of its true proportion . . . [and] should be handled on the basis of the *individual* [i.e., through individual hearings] regardless of citizenship, and *not* on a racial basis."[58]

Though he conceded that at least "some" Japanese Americans were "believed" to be loyal, General DeWitt concluded it was simply not possible to separate loyal Japanese Americans from the disloyal "with any degree of safety."[59] In *Hirabayashi*, the court had decided that urgency justified applying the curfew to *all* Japanese American citizens if there was concern that some of them might be disloyal. By December 1944, when the court decided *Korematsu*, more than 110,000 Japanese Americans had been removed from their homes and placed in internment camps. In *Korematsu*, the court had to decide whether the rationale put forward in *Hirabayashi*—that there wasn't time to separate the loyal from the disloyal—justified its decision.

The government supported its decision by pointing to the results of questionnaires given to Japanese Americans after they were brought to the camps. One question asked: "Are you willing to serve in the armed forces of the United States on combat duty, wherever ordered?" Another asked: "Will you swear unqualified allegiance to the United States of America and faithfully defend the United States from any or all attack by foreign or domestic forces, and forswear any form of allegiance or obedience to the Japanese emperor, or to any other foreign government, power, or organization?"[60] The questions often seemed confusing, deceptive, or both. Some detainees believed that if they answered "yes" to each question, they would be released from the camp with no home to return to and nowhere to go.[61] Some, especially the American-born Nisei, saw the second question as a trap: how could you "forswear" or renounce allegiance to Japan without admitting you had once been loyal to a country you had never even known?[62] Women and men who were not of draft age were not sure how to answer the question about military service. There were concerns that families would be broken up if they did not provide uniform answers.[63] Many Japanese Americans understandably resented being asked these questions by a government that had placed them in an internment camp. In the end, though, the vast majority of Japanese Americans who completed the questionnaires answered "yes" to each question.[64]

On December 18, 1944, the Supreme Court handed down its decision in *Korematsu v. United States*. By this time, the war was going much better for the United States and its allies than it had been in early 1942. In the South Pacific, U.S. and allied forces were island hopping their way toward Japan. In Europe, Allied troops were headed for Berlin. In a 6–3 decision, the court concluded that necessity properly supported internment, relying on justifications similar to those cited in *Hirabayashi*: there was not time to separate the loyal from the disloyal; the decision was motivated by military necessity, not racial animus; and the court must be careful not to second-guess decisions regarding national defense made by Congress and the executive. Excerpts from the Supreme Court's decision in *Korematsu* follow. Consider how the Supreme Court relies on answers to the questionnaires mentioned earlier as evidence that at least some Japanese Americans were disloyal, and notice how Justice Murphy, in dissent, responds to the majority's conclusion that urgency justified the mass internment and why he concludes that racism was the real reason for this action. In reading Justice Jackson's opinion, consider why one observer concluded that his dissent "did little more for [Japanese Americans] than his brethren of the majority."[65]

Korematsu v. United States, 323 U.S. 214 (1944)

Majority opinion by Justice Black.

The petitioner, an American citizen of Japanese descent, was convicted in a federal district court for remaining in San Leandro, California, a "Military Area," contrary to Civilian Exclusion Order No. 34 of the Commanding General of the Western Command, U.S. Army, which directed that, after May 9, 1942, all persons of Japanese ancestry should be excluded from that area. No question was raised as to petitioner's loyalty to the United States . . . the importance of the constitutional question involved caused us to grant certiorari.

It should be noted, to begin with, that all legal restrictions which curtail the civil rights of a single racial group are immediately suspect. That is not to say that all such restrictions are unconstitutional. It is to say that courts must subject them to the most rigid scrutiny. Pressing public necessity may sometimes justify the existence of such restrictions; racial antagonism never can.

In the instant case, prosecution of the petitioner was begun by information charging violation of an Act of Congress, of March 21, 1942, . . . which the petitioner knowingly and admittedly violated, was one of a number of military orders and proclamations, all of which were substantially based upon Executive Order No. 9066. . . .

One of the series of orders and proclamations, a curfew order, which, like the exclusion order here, was promulgated pursuant to Executive Order 9066, subjected all persons of Japanese ancestry in prescribed West Coast military areas to remain in their residences from 8 p.m. to 6 a.m. As is the case with the exclusion order here, that prior curfew order was designed as a "protection against espionage and against sabotage." In *Hirabayashi v. United States*, we sustained a conviction obtained for violation of the curfew order. The Hirabayashi conviction and this one thus rest on the same 1942 Congressional Act and the same basic executive and military orders, all of which orders were aimed at the twin dangers of espionage and sabotage.

. . . We upheld the curfew order as an exercise of the power of the government to take steps necessary to prevent espionage and sabotage in an area threatened by Japanese attack.

In the light of the principles we announced in the *Hirabayashi* case, we are unable to conclude that it was beyond the war power of Congress and the Executive to exclude those of Japanese ancestry from the West Coast war area at the time

---

they did. True, exclusion from the area in which one's home is located is a far greater deprivation than constant confinement to the home from 8 p.m. to 6 a.m. Nothing short of apprehension by the proper military authorities of the gravest imminent danger to the public safety can constitutionally justify either. But exclusion from a threatened area, no less than curfew, has a definite and close relationship to the prevention of espionage and sabotage. The military authorities, charged with the primary responsibility of defending our shores, concluded that curfew provided inadequate protection and ordered exclusion. They did so, as pointed out in our *Hirabayashi* opinion, in accordance with Congressional authority to the military to say who should, and who should not, remain in the threatened areas.

In this case, the petitioner challenges the assumptions upon which we rested our conclusions in the *Hirabayashi* case. He also urges that, by May, 1942, when Order No. 34 was promulgated, all danger of Japanese invasion of the West Coast had disappeared. After careful consideration of these contentions, we are compelled to reject them.

. . . Like curfew, exclusion of those of Japanese origin was deemed necessary because of the presence of an unascertained number of disloyal members of the group, most of whom we have no doubt were loyal to this country. It was because we could not reject the finding of the military authorities that it was impossible to bring about an immediate segregation of the disloyal from the loyal that we sustained the validity of the curfew order as applying to the whole group. In the instant case, temporary exclusion of the entire group was rested by the military on the same ground. The judgment that exclusion of the whole group was, for the same reason, a military imperative answers the contention that the exclusion was in the nature of group punishment based on antagonism to those of Japanese origin. That there were members of the group who retained loyalties to Japan has been confirmed by investigations made subsequent to the exclusion. Approximately five thousand American citizens of Japanese ancestry refused to swear unqualified allegiance to the United States and to renounce allegiance to the Japanese Emperor, and several thousand evacuees requested repatriation to Japan.

We uphold the exclusion order as of the time it was made and when the petitioner violated it. In doing so, we are not unmindful of the hardships imposed by it upon a large group of American citizens. But hardships are part of war, and war is an aggregation of hardships. All citizens alike, both in and out of uniform, feel the impact of war in greater or lesser measure. Citizenship has its responsibilities, as well as its privileges, and, in time of war, the burden is always heavier. Compulsory exclusion of large groups of citizens from their homes, except under circumstances of direst emergency and peril, is inconsistent with our basic governmental institutions. But when, under conditions of modern warfare, our shores are threatened by hostile forces, the power to protect must be commensurate with the threatened danger. . . .

It is said that we are dealing here with the case of imprisonment of a citizen in a concentration camp solely because of his ancestry, without evidence or inquiry concerning his loyalty and good disposition towards the United States. Our task would be simple, our duty clear, were this a case involving the imprisonment of a loyal citizen in a concentration camp because of racial prejudice. Regardless of the true nature of the assembly and relocation centers—and we deem it unjustifiable to call them concentration camps, with all the ugly connotations that term implies—we are dealing specifically with nothing but an exclusion order. To cast this case into outlines of racial prejudice, without reference to the real military dangers which were presented, merely confuses the issue. Korematsu was not excluded from the Military Area because of hostility to him or his race. He was excluded because we are at war with the Japanese Empire, because the properly constituted military authorities feared an invasion of our West Coast and felt constrained to take proper security measures, because they decided that the military urgency of the situation demanded that all citizens of Japanese ancestry be segregated from the West Coast temporarily, and, finally, because Congress, reposing its confidence in this time of war in our military leaders—as inevitably it must—determined that they should have the power to do just this. There was evidence of disloyalty on the part of some, the military authorities considered that the need for action was great, and time was short. We cannot—by availing ourselves of the calm perspective of hindsight—now say that, at that time, these actions were unjustified.

———

Justice Murphy, dissenting.

This exclusion of "all persons of Japanese ancestry, both alien and non-alien," from the Pacific Coast area on a plea of military necessity in the absence of martial law ought not to be approved. Such exclusion goes over "the very brink of constitutional power," and falls into the ugly abyss of racism.

In dealing with matters relating to the prosecution and progress of a war, we must accord great respect and consideration to the judgments of the military authorities who are on the scene and who have full knowledge of the military facts. The scope of their discretion must, as a matter of necessity and common sense, be wide. And their judgments ought not to be overruled lightly by those whose training and duties ill-equip them to deal intelligently with matters so vital to the physical security of the nation.

At the same time, however, it is essential that there be definite limits to military discretion, especially where martial law has not been declared. Individuals must not be left impoverished of their constitutional rights on a plea of military necessity that has neither substance nor support. Thus, like other claims conflicting with the asserted constitutional rights of the individual, the military claim must subject itself to the judicial process of having its reasonableness determined and its conflicts with other interests reconciled.

The judicial test of whether the Government, on a plea of military necessity, can validly deprive an individual of any of his constitutional rights is whether the deprivation is reasonably related to a public danger that is so "immediate, imminent, and impending" as not to admit of delay and not to permit the intervention of ordinary constitutional processes to alleviate the danger. Civilian Exclusion Order No. 34, banishing from a prescribed area of the Pacific Coast "all persons of Japanese ancestry, both alien and non-alien," clearly does not meet that test. Being an obvious racial discrimination, the order deprives all those within its scope of the equal protection of the laws as guaranteed by the Fifth Amendment. It further deprives these individuals of their constitutional rights to live and work where they will, to establish a home where they choose and to move about freely. In excommunicating them without benefit of hearings, this order also deprives them of all their constitutional rights to procedural due process. Yet no reasonable relation to an "immediate, imminent, and impending" public danger is evident to support this racial restriction, which is one of the most sweeping and complete deprivations of constitutional rights in the history of this nation in the absence of martial law.

It must be conceded that the military and naval situation in the spring of 1942 was such as to generate a very real fear of invasion of the Pacific Coast, accompanied by fears of sabotage and espionage in that area.... In adjudging the military action taken in light of the then apparent dangers, we must not erect too high or too meticulous standards; it is necessary only that the action have some reasonable relation to the removal of the dangers of invasion, sabotage and espionage. But the exclusion, either temporarily or permanently, of all persons with Japanese blood in their veins has no such reasonable relation. And that relation is lacking because the exclusion order necessarily must rely for its reasonableness upon the assumption that all persons of Japanese ancestry may have a dangerous tendency to commit sabotage and espionage and to aid our Japanese enemy in other ways. It is difficult to believe that reason, logic, or experience could be marshalled in support of such an assumption.

That this forced exclusion was the result in good measure of this erroneous assumption of racial guilt, rather than *bona fide* military necessity is evidenced by the Commanding General's Final Report on the evacuation from the Pacific Coast area. In it, he refers to all individuals of Japanese descent as "subversive," as belonging to "an enemy race" whose "racial strains are undiluted," and as constituting "over 112,000 potential enemies ... at large today" along the Pacific Coast. In support of this blanket condemnation of all persons of Japanese descent, however, no reliable evidence is cited to show that such individuals were generally disloyal, or had generally so conducted themselves in this area as to constitute a special menace to defense installations or war industries, or had otherwise, by their behavior, furnished reasonable ground for their exclusion as a group.

Justification for the exclusion is sought, instead, mainly upon questionable racial and sociological grounds not ordinarily within the realm of expert military judgment.... Individuals of Japanese ancestry are condemned because they are said to be "a large, unassimilated, tightly knit racial group, bound to an enemy nation by strong ties of race, culture, custom and religion." They are claimed to be given to "emperor worshipping ceremonies," and to "dual citizenship." Japanese language schools and allegedly pro-Japanese organizations are cited as evidence of possible group disloyalty.... It is intimated that many of these individuals deliberately resided "adjacent to strategic points," thus enabling them "to carry into execution a tremendous program of sabotage on a mass scale should any considerable number of them have been inclined to do so." ...

The main reasons relied upon by those responsible for the forced evacuation, therefore, do not prove a reasonable relation between the group characteristics of Japanese Americans and the dangers of invasion, sabotage and espionage. The reasons appear, instead, to be largely an accumulation of much of the misinformation, half-truths and insinuations that for years have been directed against Japanese Americans by people with racial and economic prejudices—the same people who have been among the foremost advocates of the evacuation. A military judgment based upon such racial and sociological considerations is not entitled to the great weight ordinarily given the judgments based upon strictly military considerations....

The military necessity which is essential to the validity of the evacuation order thus resolves itself into a few intimations that certain individuals actively aided the enemy, from which it is inferred that the entire group of Japanese Americans could not be trusted to be or remain loyal to the United States. No one denies, of course, that there were some disloyal persons of Japanese descent on the Pacific Coast who did all in their power to aid their ancestral land. Similar disloyal activities have been engaged in by many persons of German, Italian and even more pioneer stock in our country. But to infer that examples of individual disloyalty prove group disloyalty and justify discriminatory action against the entire group is to deny that, under our system of law, individual guilt is the sole basis for deprivation of rights. Moreover, this inference, which is at the very heart of the evacuation orders, has been used in support of the abhorrent and despicable treatment of minority groups by the dictatorial tyrannies which this nation is now pledged to destroy. To give constitutional sanction to that inference in this case, however well intentioned may have been the military command on the Pacific Coast, is to adopt one of the cruelest of the rationales used by our enemies to destroy the dignity of the individual and to encourage and open the door to discriminatory actions against other minority groups in the passions of tomorrow.

No adequate reason is given for the failure to treat these Japanese Americans on an individual basis by holding investigations and hearings to separate the loyal from the disloyal, as was done in the case of persons of German and Italian ancestry. It is asserted merely that the loyalties of this group "were unknown and time was of the essence." Yet nearly four months elapsed after Pearl Harbor before the first exclusion order was issued; nearly eight months went by until the last order was issued, and the last of these "subversive" persons was not actually removed until almost eleven months had elapsed. Leisure and deliberation seem to have been more of the essence than speed. And the fact that conditions were not such as to warrant a declaration of martial law adds strength to the belief that the factors of time and military necessity were not as urgent as they have been represented to be.

...Nor is there any denial of the fact that not one person of Japanese ancestry was accused or convicted of espionage or sabotage after Pearl Harbor while they were still free....It seems incredible that, under these circumstances, it would have been impossible to hold loyalty hearings for the mere 112,000 persons involved—or at least for the 70,000 American citizens—especially when a large part of this number represented children and elderly men and women. Any inconvenience that may have accompanied an attempt to conform to procedural due process cannot be said to justify violations of constitutional rights of individuals.

I dissent, therefore, from this legalization of racism. Racial discrimination in any form and in any degree has no justifiable part whatever in our democratic way of life. It is unattractive in any setting, but it is utterly revolting among a free people who have embraced the principles set forth in the Constitution of the United States. All residents of this nation are kin in some way by blood or culture to a foreign land. Yet they are primarily and necessarily a part of the new and distinct civilization of the United States. They must, accordingly, be treated at all times as the heirs of the American experiment, and as entitled to all the rights and freedoms guaranteed by the Constitution.

———

Justice Jackson, dissenting.

Korematsu was born on our soil, of parents born in Japan. The Constitution makes him a citizen of the United States by nativity, and a citizen of California by residence. No claim is made that he is not loyal to this country. There is no suggestion that, apart from the matter involved here, he is not law-abiding and well disposed. Korematsu, however, has been convicted of an act not commonly a crime. It consists merely of being present in the state whereof he is a citizen, near the place where he was born, and where all his life he has lived.

Even more unusual is the series of military orders which made this conduct a crime. They forbid such a one to remain, and they also forbid him to leave. They were so drawn that the only way Korematsu could avoid violation was to give himself up to the military authority. This meant submission to custody, examination, and transportation out of the territory, to be followed by indeterminate confinement in detention camps.

A citizen's presence in the locality, however, was made a crime only if his parents were of Japanese birth....

Now, if any fundamental assumption underlies our system, it is that guilt is personal and not inheritable. Even if all of one's antecedents had been convicted of treason, the Constitution forbids its penalties to be visited upon him, for it provides that "no attainder of treason shall work corruption of blood, or forfeiture except during the life of the person attainted." But here is an attempt to make an otherwise innocent act a crime merely because this prisoner is the son of parents as to whom he had no choice, and belongs to a race from which there is no way to resign. If Congress, in peacetime legislation, should enact such a criminal law, I should suppose this Court would refuse to enforce it.

But the "law" which this prisoner is convicted of disregarding is not found in an act of Congress, but in a military order. Neither the Act of Congress nor the Executive Order of the President, nor both together, would afford a basis for this conviction. It rests on the orders of General DeWitt. And it is said that, if the military commander had reasonable military grounds for promulgating the orders, they are constitutional, and become law, and the Court is required to enforce them. There are several reasons why I cannot subscribe to this doctrine.

It would be impracticable and dangerous idealism to expect or insist that each specific military command in an area of probable operations will conform to conventional tests of constitutionality. When an area is so beset that it must be put under military control at all, the paramount consideration is that its measures be successful, rather than legal. The armed services must protect a society, not merely its Constitution. The very essence of the military job is to marshal physical force, to remove every obstacle to its effectiveness, to give it every strategic advantage. Defense measures will not, and often should not, be held within the limits that bind civil authority in peace. No court can require such a commander in such circumstances to act as a reasonable man; he may be unreasonably cautious and exacting. Perhaps he should be. But a commander, in temporarily focusing the life of a community on defense, is carrying out a military program; he is not making law in the sense the courts know the term. He issues orders, and they may have a certain authority as military commands, although they may be very bad as constitutional law.

But if we cannot confine military expedients by the Constitution, neither would I distort the Constitution to approve all that the military may deem expedient. That is what the Court appears to be doing, whether consciously or not. I cannot say, from any evidence before me, that the orders of General DeWitt were not reasonably expedient military precautions, nor could I say that they were. But even if they were permissible military procedures, I deny that it follows that they are constitutional. If, as the Court holds, it does follow, then we may as well say that any military order will be constitutional, and have done with it.

The limitation under which courts always will labor in examining the necessity for a military order are illustrated by this case. How does the Court know that these orders have a reasonable basis in necessity? No evidence whatever on that subject has been taken by this or any other court. There is sharp controversy as to the credibility of the DeWitt report. So the Court, having no real evidence before it, has no choice but to accept General DeWitt's own unsworn, self-serving statement, untested by any cross-examination, that what he did was reasonable. And thus it will always be when courts try to look into the reasonableness of a military order.

In the very nature of things, military decisions are not susceptible of intelligent judicial appraisal. They do not pretend to rest on evidence, but are made on information that often would not be admissible and on assumptions that could not be proved. Information in support of an order could not be disclosed to courts without danger that it would reach the enemy. Neither can courts act on communications made in confidence. Hence, courts can never have any real alternative to accepting the mere declaration of the authority that issued the order that it was reasonably necessary from a military viewpoint.

... [A] judicial construction of the due process clause that will sustain this order is a far more subtle blow to liberty than the promulgation of the order itself. A military order, however unconstitutional, is not apt to last longer than the military emergency. Even during that period, a succeeding commander may revoke it all. But once a judicial opinion rationalizes such an order to show that it conforms to the Constitution, or rather rationalizes the Constitution to show that the Constitution sanctions such an order, the Court for all time has validated the principle of racial discrimination in criminal procedure and of transplanting American citizens. The principle then lies about like a loaded weapon, ready for the hand of any authority that can bring forward a plausible claim of an urgent need. Every repetition imbeds that principle more deeply in our law and thinking and expands it to new purposes. ... A military commander may overstep the bounds of constitutionality, and it is an incident. But if we review and approve, that passing incident becomes the doctrine of the Constitution. There it has a generative power of its own, and all that it creates will be in its own image. Nothing better illustrates this danger than does the Court's opinion in this case.

It argues that we are bound to uphold the conviction of Korematsu because we upheld one in *Hirabayashi* ... when we sustained these orders insofar as they applied a curfew requirement to a citizen of Japanese ancestry. I think we should learn something from that experience.

In that case, we were urged to consider only the curfew feature, that being all that technically was involved, because it was the only count necessary to sustain

Hirabayashi's conviction and sentence. We yielded, and the Chief Justice guarded the opinion as carefully as language will do. He said:

"Our investigation here does not go beyond the inquiry whether, in the light of all the relevant circumstances preceding and attending their promulgation, the challenged orders and statute *afforded a reasonable basis for the action taken in imposing the curfew...."* ... However, in spite of our limiting words, we did validate a discrimination on the basis of ancestry for mild and temporary deprivation of liberty. Now the principle of racial discrimination is pushed from support of mild measures to very harsh ones, and from temporary deprivations to indeterminate ones. And the precedent which it is said requires us to do so is *Hirabayashi.* The Court is now saying that, in *Hirabayashi,* we did decide the very things we there said we were not deciding. Because we said that these citizens could be made to stay in their homes during the hours of dark, it is said we must require them to leave home entirely, and if that, we are told they may also be taken into custody for deportation, and, if that, it is argued, they may also be held for some undetermined time in detention camps. How far the principle of this case would be extended before plausible reasons would play out, I do not know.

I should hold that a civil court cannot be made to enforce an order which violates constitutional limitations even if it is a reasonable exercise of military authority. The courts can exercise only the judicial power, can apply only law, and must abide by the Constitution, or they cease to be civil courts and become instruments of military policy.

Of course, the existence of a military power resting on force, so vagrant, so centralized, so necessarily heedless of the individual, is an inherent threat to liberty. But I would not lead people to rely on this Court for a review that seems to me wholly delusive. The military reasonableness of these orders can only be determined by military superiors. If the people ever let command of the war power fall into irresponsible and unscrupulous hands, the courts wield no power equal to its restraint. The chief restraint upon those who command the physical forces of the country, in the future as in the past, must be their responsibility to the political judgments of their contemporaries and to the moral judgments of history.

... I do not suggest that the courts should have attempted to interfere with the Army in carrying out its task. But I do not think they may be asked to execute a military expedient that has no place in law under the Constitution. I would reverse the judgment and discharge the prisoner.

While the court unanimously upheld the military order subjecting Japanese American citizens to a curfew in *Hirabayashi*, the court was divided 6–3 in *Korematsu* on the question of whether internment was constitutional.

In his dissent, Justice Murphy flatly condemned the forced relocation and detention of Japanese Americans as motivated by racism. Justice Jackson warned that the court was establishing dangerous precedent by ratifying the military's judgment that detention was justified.[66] The *Korematsu* decision is generally seen as a horrendous error by the court,[67] though it has never been overruled.[68] However, some observers have continued to suggest that internment of Japanese Americans may have been justified, at least to some extent. In a 1998 book, William Rehnquist, then chief justice of the Supreme Court, considered the fact that Americans of German or Italian descent were treated differently from Japanese Americans during World War II. Rehnquist conceded that making distinctions between members of these groups who were citizens "might not be permissible" but suggested there might have been sufficient reason to treat Japanese American resident "aliens" (i.e., noncitizens lawfully in the country) differently from German or Italian aliens.[69]

David Cole disagrees with Rehnquist, arguing that "it was as wrong to intern the Japanese nationals [i.e., non-U.S. citizens] without individualized determinations [of wrongdoing] as it was to intern the U.S. citizens of Japanese descent."[70] The questions for us today are whether the president, Congress, the Supreme Court, and/or the military might implement and ratify the detention of American citizens[71] or residents in the context of a different emergency (or, as Justice Jackson noted in his dissent, whether the court would have any ability to stop the other branches from taking such action). Is there reason to be concerned today that the court might be unable, unwilling, or both to prevent detentions in the name of national emergency, whether real or exaggerated? Justice Jackson suggests that the best hope for preventing arbitrary detentions in the future lies in the political sphere, writing: "The chief restraint upon those who command the physical forces of the country, in the future as in the past, must be their responsibility to the political judgments of their contemporaries and to the moral judgments of history." What did he mean by that? Is that the best or only way to protect against a repeat of the World War II internments? What other steps could be taken?

7

THE *YOUNGSTOWN* STEEL SEIZURE CASE

THE COURT SETS LIMITS ON PRESIDENTIAL POWER

D uring World War II, Roosevelt sometimes initially acted unilaterally on the basis of implied emergency power but was ultimately able to win support from the other branches of government. However, that support was sometimes purchased with counterfeit currency—in *Quirin*, the fiction that Roosevelt had acted in concert with Congress in setting up a military tribunal, in *Hirabayashi* and *Korematsu*, the false representation that military necessity justified mass internment of Japanese Americans.

In the years after World War II, President Truman tested the limits of emergency presidential power during the Cold War. As it had during the Civil War and World War II, the nation again faced imminent danger—this time, the apocalyptic threat of nuclear war. But there were differences. Unlike previous crises cited as a basis for emergency presidential action, the Cold War dragged on—ultimately for decades. Where Lincoln's and Roosevelt's expanded powers might at least be confined to a finite period of time, expanded presidential power in the context of the Cold War threatened to last indefinitely as the sense of emergency became permanent.

The United States and the Soviet Union, allies for most of World War II, became rivals when the war ended. The United States declared itself opposed to the spread of communism, and Truman took this as a basis for presidential action. When communist North Korean forces invaded South Korea in 1950, Truman committed American military forces to support

South Korea, informing congressional leaders only after the decision had been made.[1] Truman justified his decision by citing his authority as commander in chief and "the traditional power of the President to use the armed forces of the United States without consulting Congress."[2] His supporters defended Truman's decision as necessitated by emergency, and Truman did not initially face much criticism from Congress, though he did not seek even retroactive approval for his actions.[3] However, Truman ultimately ran into a roadblock from the court when he tried to exert presidential power to respond to a domestic crisis related to the fighting in Korea.

The Supreme Court did not rule on the constitutionality of Truman's decision to send troops to Korea, but it did hand down a decision during the Korean War that addressed, at least in part, the question of emergency presidential power. The case, *Youngstown Sheet & Tube Co. v. Sawyer*, grew out of a labor dispute between the United Steelworkers union and steel companies.[4] The union sought wage and benefit increases for its members, which the companies refused to provide unless the government permitted price increases.[5] With the government unwilling to allow a price increase, contract negotiations stalled at the end of 1951. Government efforts to broker a compromise were unsuccessful. In April 1952, the United Steelworkers union announced that it planned to begin a nationwide strike against the steel industry.[6]

As steel companies prepared to close their operations, Truman issued an executive order authorizing Secretary of Commerce Charles Sawyer to seize and operate most of the nation's steel mills in order to ensure that the factories would keep operating and producing military material for the troops in Korea. Truman justified his action on the basis of the president's "very great inherent power to meet great national emergencies." Truman informed Congress that he did not believe its approval was necessary but that, if it wanted, Congress could reject his decision. Congress took no action in response to Truman's executive order.[7]

Truman was not the first president to take control of businesses during wartime; Wilson and Roosevelt had done so during the World Wars. Truman's predecessors had sometimes relied on congressional authorization for their actions, though they also pointed to constitutional authority for independent presidential action. For instance, when Roosevelt issued an executive order in June 1941 authorizing seizure of the North American Aviation plant, a factory that made military airplanes, then Attorney General Jackson did not cite any specific authorization by Congress but argued that Roosevelt's action was justified by the Commander in Chief and Take Care Clauses of Article II. Jackson said that, as commander in chief, the president could act to ensure that the military was supplied and that, pursuant to the Take Care Clause, the president had the duty to execute laws enacted to provide equipment for the military, including taking action to keep the airplane factory running. However, Jackson linked his argument at least tangentially to congressional authorization, reasoning that Congress had expressly authorized the president to purchase supplies for the military, the government had subsequently entered into contracts with the manufacturer, and a failure to seize the factory would frustrate Congress's intent. Later in the war, Roosevelt authorized seizure of property belonging to Montgomery Ward & Co., a retail business, when the company refused a government order to recognize a union and engage in collective bargaining. Roosevelt and his advisers again cited the president's power as commander in chief but also pointed to specific statutory authority—the War Labor Disputes Act, which authorized the president to seize companies in certain industries that were unable to resolve labor disputes. However, retail sales was not an industry specifically included in the law, and a federal district court did not find merit in either the president's statutory or constitutional justifications. An appellate court overruled the district court decision but did not address the constitutional issue; it concluded that Montgomery Ward's activities were covered by the statute.[8]

So, while Truman could point to the recent example of Roosevelt's actions in seizing businesses during World War II, his strongest justification would likely rely on at least some statutory rationale, some suggestion that seizure of the steel factories at least arguably had been authorized by Congress. Here, Truman faced a problem. While laws enacted during World War II, such as the War Labor Disputes Act cited in the Montgomery Ward case, expressly provided presidential authority to take control of industry needed for the war effort, a law passed after World War II declined to provide such authority.[9] The 1947 Taft-Hartley Act addressed the question of labor disputes in defense-related industries but did *not* provide for presidential seizure authority. Instead, Taft-Hartley empowered courts to issue injunctions prohibiting strikes in such industries for eighty days if the president followed certain procedures prior to asking for an injunction. Legislative efforts to insert a provision allowing for emergency seizure powers failed.[10]

When the steel companies sued to regain control of their factories, government lawyers defending Truman's actions argued that there was a constitutional basis for independent presidential action.[11] In making their case to the district court during oral argument, Department of Justice lawyers took the position that emergency presidential power is essentially unlimited—apart from the checks of impeachment by Congress and removal from office by voters. Judicial review was eliminated from the equation—it is up to the president to identify an emergency and, having done so, to take whatever actions he or she deems necessary. For the Department of Justice lawyers, broad presidential power was confirmed by Article II's Vesting Clause, which, in contrast with the analogous provision in Article I, assigns executive power to the president without any limiting language.[12] The government lawyers also cited past presidential action as precedent.[13]

The government's argument boiled down to the claim "that in an emergency the executive had the responsibility to protect the national security and that any action the President took in that respect was legal."[14] This was essentially a restatement of Lockean prerogative—an argument that the president had authority to act for the public good, even if not expressly authorized by law, checked only by the people themselves or their elected representatives in Congress.[15] A government lawyer cited the *Merryman* case, suggesting that the courts have no power to block presidential action under these circumstances.[16] Responding to criticism from the press and even his own allies in Congress, President Truman attempted to distance himself from the argument that the courts had no role to play in reviewing his action, conceding that it was appropriate for the courts to review his decision, though lawyers presenting his case may have suggested otherwise.[17] However, in a public letter explaining his views, he did not back away from the core theory that, as president, he possessed emergency power to seize the steel mills and in fact had a "duty [as] the President under the Constitution to preserve the safety of the nation."[18] Truman's attempt to moderate the government's position still amounted to a modified version of Lockean prerogative that was reviewable by the courts.

Judge David A. Pine of the District Court for the District of Columbia was taken aback by the implications of the position articulated by the Department of Justice at oral argument and issued an opinion rejecting this formulation of emergency power and the somewhat scaled-back version described by Truman in his public letter. Judge Pine emphasized that the Constitution does not assign the president unlimited emergency power and concluded that past examples of unilateral presidential action could not justify President Truman's action if the past actions were themselves unconstitutional.[19]

The case then moved to the Supreme Court, which ruled 6–3 in favor of the steel companies. Justice Black wrote the majority opinion, but each of the other five justices voting with the majority wrote separate opinions.[20] Although the court concluded that President Truman's specific action in seizing the steel mills lacked constitutional support and made clear that there must be limits on presidential power, it is well worth noting that seven justices—four who voted with the majority and three who dissented—also endorsed at least *some* level of unilateral emergency presidential power.[21] Given the variety of views expressed by the justices who voted with the majority, it is perhaps not surprising that Justice Jackson's concurring opinion, rather than Justice Black's majority opinion, has become the most influential one in this case. Excerpts from opinions in the case follow.

Youngstown Sheet & Tube Co. v. Sawyer, 343 U.S. 579 (1952)

Majority opinion by Justice Black.

We are asked to decide whether the President was acting within his constitutional power when he issued an order directing the Secretary of Commerce to take possession of and operate most of the Nation's steel mills....The Government's position is that the order was made on findings of the President that his action was necessary to avert a national catastrophe which would inevitably result from a stoppage of steel production, and that, in meeting this grave emergency, the President was acting within the aggregate of his constitutional powers as the Nation's Chief Executive and the Commander in Chief of the Armed Forces of the United States....

On April 4, 1952, the [United Steelworkers] Union gave notice of a nationwide strike called to begin at 12:01 a.m. April 9. The indispensability of steel as a component of substantially all weapons and other war materials led the President to believe that the proposed work stoppage would immediately jeopardize our national defense and that governmental seizure of the steel mills was necessary in order to assure the continued availability of steel. Reciting these considerations for his action, the President, a few hours before the strike was to begin, issued Executive Order 10340. . . . The order directed the Secretary of Commerce to take possession of most of the steel mills and keep them running. The Secretary immediately issued his own possessory orders, calling upon the presidents of the various seized companies to serve as operating managers for the United States. They were directed to carry on their activities in accordance with regulations and directions of the Secretary. The next morning the President sent a message to Congress reporting his action. Twelve days later, he sent a second message. Congress has taken no action.

Obeying the Secretary's orders under protest, the companies brought proceedings against him in the District Court. Their complaints charged that the seizure was not authorized by an act of Congress or by any constitutional provisions ... the United States asserted that a strike disrupting steel production for even a brief period would so endanger the wellbeing and safety of the Nation that the President had "inherent power" to do what he had done—power "supported by the Constitution, by historical precedent, and by court decisions." . . . Holding against the Government on all points, the District Court . . . issued a preliminary injunction restraining the Secretary from "continuing the seizure and possession of the plants . . ." . . . Deeming it best that the issues raised be promptly decided by this Court, we granted certiorari . . .

[One of] two crucial issues ha[s] developed . . . is the seizure order within the constitutional power of the President? . . . We shall . . . consider and determine that question now . . . The President's power, if any, to issue the order must stem either from an act of Congress or from the Constitution itself. There is no statute that expressly authorizes the President to take possession of property as he did here. Nor is there any act of Congress to which our attention has been directed from which such a power can fairly be implied. Indeed, we do not understand the Government to rely on statutory authorization for this seizure. . . .

Moreover, the use of the seizure technique to solve labor disputes in order to prevent work stoppages was not only unauthorized by any congressional enactment; prior to this controversy, Congress had refused to adopt that method of settling labor disputes. When the Taft-Hartley Act was under consideration in 1947, Congress rejected an amendment which would have authorized such governmental seizures in cases of emergency. . . .

It is clear that, if the President had authority to issue the order he did, it must be found in some provision of the Constitution. And it is not claimed that express constitutional language grants this power to the President. The contention is that presidential power should be implied from the aggregate of his powers under the Constitution. Particular reliance is placed on provisions in Article II which say that "The executive Power shall be vested in a President . . ."; that "he shall take Care that the Laws be faithfully executed," and that he "shall be Commander in Chief of the Army and Navy of the United States."

The order cannot properly be sustained as an exercise of the President's military power as Commander in Chief of the Armed Forces. The Government attempts to do so by citing a number of cases upholding broad powers in military commanders engaged in day-to-day fighting in a theater of war. Such cases need not concern us here. Even though "theater of war" be an expanding concept, we cannot with faithfulness to our constitutional system hold that the Commander in Chief of the Armed Forces has the ultimate power as such to take possession of private property in order to keep labor disputes from stopping production. This is a job for the Nation's lawmakers, not for its military authorities.

Nor can the seizure order be sustained because of the several constitutional provisions that grant executive power to the President. In the framework of our Constitution, the President's power to see that the laws are faithfully executed refutes the idea that he is to be a lawmaker. The Constitution limits his functions in the lawmaking process to the recommending of laws he thinks wise and the vetoing of laws he thinks bad. And the Constitution is neither silent nor equivocal about who shall make laws which the President is to execute. The first section of the first article says that "All legislative Powers herein granted shall be vested in a Congress of the United States...." After granting many powers to the Congress, Article I goes on to provide that Congress may "make all Laws which shall be necessary and proper for carrying into Execution the foregoing Powers, and all other Powers vested by this Constitution in the Government of the United States, or in any Department or Officer thereof."

The President's order does not direct that a congressional policy be executed in a manner prescribed by Congress—it directs that a presidential policy be executed in a manner prescribed by the President. The preamble of the order itself, like that of many statutes, sets out reasons why the President believes certain policies should be adopted, proclaims these policies as rules of conduct to be followed, and again, like a statute, authorizes a government official to promulgate additional rules and regulations consistent with the policy proclaimed and needed to carry that policy into execution. The power of Congress to adopt such public policies as those proclaimed by the order is beyond question. It can authorize the taking of private property for public use. It can make laws regulating the relationships between employers and employees, prescribing rules designed to settle labor disputes, and fixing wages and working conditions in certain fields of our economy. The Constitution does not subject this lawmaking power of Congress to presidential or military supervision or control.

It is said that other Presidents, without congressional authority, have taken possession of private business enterprises in order to settle labor disputes. But even if this be true, Congress has not thereby lost its exclusive constitutional authority to make laws necessary and proper....

The Founders of this Nation entrusted the lawmaking power to the Congress alone in both good and bad times. It would do no good to recall the historical events, the fears of power, and the hopes for freedom that lay behind their choice. Such a review would but confirm our holding that this seizure order cannot stand.

The judgment of the District Court is *Affirmed.*

———

Justice Jackson, concurring.

That comprehensive and undefined presidential powers hold both practical advantages and grave dangers for the country will impress anyone who has served as legal adviser to a President in time of transition and public anxiety.[22] While an interval of detached reflection may temper teachings of that experience, they probably are a more realistic influence on my views than the conventional materials of judicial decision which seem unduly to accentuate doctrine and legal fiction. But, as we approach the question of presidential power, we half overcome mental hazards by recognizing them. The opinions of judges, no less than executives and publicists, often suffer the infirmity of confusing the issue of a power's validity with the cause it is invoked to promote, of confounding the permanent executive office with its temporary occupant. The tendency is strong to emphasize transient results upon policies—such as wages or stabilization—and lose sight of enduring consequences upon the balanced power structure of our Republic.

A judge, like an executive adviser, may be surprised at the poverty of really useful and unambiguous authority applicable to concrete problems of executive power as they actually present themselves. Just what our forefathers did envision, or would have envisioned had they foreseen modern conditions, must be divined from materials almost as enigmatic as the dreams Joseph was called upon to interpret for Pharaoh. A century and a half of partisan debate and scholarly speculation yields no net result, but only supplies more or less apt quotations from respected sources on each side of any question. They largely cancel each other. And court decisions are indecisive because of the judicial practice of dealing with the largest questions in the most narrow way.

The actual art of governing under our Constitution does not, and cannot, conform to judicial definitions of the power of any of its branches based on isolated clauses, or even single Articles torn from context. While the Constitution diffuses power the better to secure liberty, it also contemplates that practice will integrate the dispersed powers into a workable government. It enjoins upon its branches separateness but interdependence, autonomy but reciprocity. Presidential powers are not fixed but fluctuate depending upon their disjunction or conjunction with those of Congress. We may well begin by a somewhat over-simplified grouping of practical situations in which a President may doubt, or others may challenge, his powers, and by distinguishing roughly the legal consequences of this factor of relativity.

1. When the President acts pursuant to an express or implied authorization of Congress, his authority is at its maximum, for it includes all that he possesses in his own right plus all that Congress can delegate. In these circumstances, and in these only, may he be said (for what it may be worth) to personify the federal sovereignty. If his act is held unconstitutional under these circumstances, it usually means that the Federal Government, as an undivided whole, lacks power. A seizure executed by the President pursuant to an Act of Congress would be supported by the strongest of presumptions and the widest latitude of judicial interpretation, and the burden of persuasion would rest heavily upon any who might attack it.

2. When the President acts in absence of either a congressional grant or denial of authority, he can only rely upon his own independent powers, but there is a zone

of twilight in which he and Congress may have concurrent authority, or in which its distribution is uncertain. Therefore, congressional inertia, indifference or quiescence may sometimes, at least, as a practical matter, enable, if not invite, measures on independent presidential responsibility. In this area, any actual test of power is likely to depend on the imperatives of events and contemporary imponderables, rather than on abstract theories of law.

3. When the President takes measures incompatible with the expressed or implied will of Congress, his power is at its lowest ebb, for then he can rely only upon his own constitutional powers minus any constitutional powers of Congress over the matter. Courts can sustain exclusive presidential control in such a case only by disabling the Congress from acting upon the subject. Presidential claim to a power at once so conclusive and preclusive must be scrutinized with caution, for what is at stake is the equilibrium established by our constitutional system.

Into which of these classifications does this executive seizure of the steel industry fit? It is eliminated from the first by admission, for it is conceded that no congressional authorization exists for this seizure....

... It seems clearly eliminated from th[e] [second] class, because Congress has not left seizure of private property an open field, but has covered it by three statutory policies inconsistent with this seizure....

This leaves the current seizure to be justified only by the severe tests under the third grouping, where it can be supported only by any remainder of executive power after subtraction of such powers as Congress may have over the subject. In short, we can sustain the President only by holding that seizure of such strike-bound industries is within his domain and beyond control by Congress. Thus, this Court's first review of such seizures occurs under circumstances which leave presidential power most vulnerable to attack and in the least favorable of possible constitutional postures.

... [T]he executive branch, like the Federal Government as a whole, possesses only delegated powers. The purpose of the Constitution was not only to grant power, but to keep it from getting out of hand. However, because the President does not enjoy unmentioned powers does not mean that the mentioned ones should be narrowed by a niggardly construction. Some clauses could be made almost unworkable, as well as immutable, by refusal to indulge some latitude of interpretation for changing times. I have heretofore, and do now, give to the enumerated powers the scope and elasticity afforded by what seem to be reasonable, practical implications, instead of the rigidity dictated by a doctrinaire textualism.

The Solicitor General seeks the power of seizure in three clauses of the Executive Article, the first reading, "The executive Power shall be vested in a President of the United States of America." Lest I be thought to exaggerate, I quote the interpretation which his brief puts upon it: "In our view, this clause constitutes a grant of all the executive powers of which the Government is capable." If that be true, it is difficult to see why the forefathers bothered to add several specific items, including some trifling ones.

The example of such unlimited executive power that must have most impressed the forefathers was the prerogative exercised by George III, and the description of its evils in the Declaration of Independence leads me to doubt that they were creating their new Executive in his image.... And, if we seek instruction from our own times, we can match it only from the executive powers in those governments we disparagingly describe as totalitarian. I cannot accept the view that this clause is a grant in bulk of all conceivable executive power, but regard it as an allocation to the presidential office of the generic powers thereafter stated.

The clause on which the Government next relies is that "The President shall be Commander in Chief of the Army and Navy of the United States...." These cryptic words have given rise to some of the most persistent controversies in our constitutional history. Of course, they imply something more than an empty title. But just what authority goes with the name has plagued presidential advisers who would not waive or narrow it by nonassertion, yet cannot say where it begins or ends. It undoubtedly puts the Nation's armed forces under presidential command. Hence, this loose appellation is sometimes advanced as support for any presidential action, internal or external, involving use of force, the idea being that it vests power to do anything, anywhere, that can be done with an army or navy.

That seems to be the logic of an argument tendered at our bar—that the President having, on his own responsibility, sent American troops abroad derives from that act "affirmative power" to seize the means of producing a supply of steel for them.... Thus, it is said, he has invested himself with "war powers."

I cannot foresee all that it might entail if the Court should indorse this argument. Nothing in our Constitution is plainer than that declaration of a war is entrusted only to Congress. Of course, a state of war may, in fact, exist without a formal declaration. But no doctrine that the Court could promulgate would seem to me more sinister and alarming than that a President whose conduct of foreign affairs is so largely uncontrolled, and often even is unknown, can vastly enlarge his mastery over the internal affairs of the country by his own commitment of the Nation's armed forces to some foreign venture....

I do not, however, find it necessary or appropriate to consider the legal status of the Korean enterprise to discountenance argument based on it.

Assuming that we are in a war *de facto*, whether it is or is not a war *de jure*, does that empower the Commander in Chief to seize industries he thinks necessary to supply our army? The Constitution expressly places in Congress power "to raise and *support* Armies" and "to *provide* and *maintain* a Navy." (Emphasis supplied.) This certainly lays upon Congress primary responsibility for supplying the armed forces. Congress alone controls the raising of revenues and their appropriation, and may determine in what manner and by what means they shall be spent for military and naval procurement....

There are indications that the Constitution did not contemplate that the title Commander in Chief *of the Army and Navy* will constitute him also Commander in Chief of the country, its industries and its inhabitants. He has no monopoly of "war powers," whatever they are. While Congress cannot deprive the President of the command of the army and navy, only Congress can provide him an army or navy to command. It is also empowered to make rules for the "Government and Regulation of land and naval Forces," by which it may, to some unknown extent, impinge upon even command functions.

That military powers of the Commander in Chief were not to supersede representative government of internal affairs seems obvious from the Constitution and from elementary American history. Time out of mind, and even now, in many parts of the world, a military commander can seize private housing to shelter his troops. Not so, however, in the United States, for the Third Amendment says,

"No Soldier shall, in time of peace be quartered in any house, without the consent of the Owner, nor in time of war, but in a manner to be prescribed by law."

Thus, even in war time, his seizure of needed military housing must be authorized by Congress. It also was expressly left to Congress to "provide for calling forth the Militia to execute the Laws of the Union, suppress Insurrections and repel Invasions. . . ." Such a limitation on the command power, written at a time when the militia, rather than a standing army, was contemplated as the military weapon of the Republic, underscores the Constitution's policy that Congress, not the Executive, should control utilization of the war power as an instrument of domestic policy. Congress, fulfilling that function, has authorized the President to use the army to enforce certain civil rights. On the other hand, Congress has forbidden him to use the army for the purpose of executing general laws except when expressly authorized by the Constitution or by Act of Congress.

. . . [A]dvice to the President in specific matters usually has carried overtones that powers, even under this head, are measured by the command functions usual to the topmost officer of the army and navy. Even then, heed has been taken of any efforts of Congress to negative his authority.

We should not use this occasion to circumscribe, much less to contract, the lawful role of the President as Commander in Chief. I should indulge the widest latitude of interpretation to sustain his exclusive function to command the instruments of national force, at least when turned against the outside world for the security of our society. But, when it is turned inward not because of rebellion, but because of a lawful economic struggle between industry and labor, it should have no such indulgence. His command power is not such an absolute as might be implied from that office in a militaristic system, but is subject to limitations consistent with a constitutional Republic whose law and policymaking branch is a representative Congress. The purpose of lodging dual titles in one man was to insure that the civilian would control the military, not to enable the military to subordinate the presidential office. No penance would ever expiate the sin against free government of holding that a President can escape control of executive powers by law through assuming his military role. What the power of command may include I do not try to envision, but I think it is not a military prerogative, without support of law, to seize persons or property because they are important or even essential for the military and naval establishment.

The third clause in which the Solicitor General finds seizure powers is that "he shall take Care that the Laws be faithfully executed." That authority must be matched against words of the Fifth Amendment that "No person shall be . . . deprived of life, liberty or property, without due process of law." One gives a governmental authority that reaches so far as there is law, the other gives a private right that authority shall go no farther. These signify about all there is of the principle that ours is a government of laws, not of men, and that we submit ourselves to rulers only if under rules.

The Solicitor General lastly grounds support of the seizure upon nebulous, inherent powers never expressly granted, but said to have accrued to the office from the customs and claims of preceding administrations. The plea is for a resulting power to deal with a crisis or an emergency according to the necessities of the case, the unarticulated assumption being that necessity knows no law.

Loose and irresponsible use of adjectives colors all nonlegal and much legal discussion of presidential powers. "Inherent" powers, "implied" powers, "incidental" powers, "plenary" powers, "war" powers and "emergency" powers are used, often interchangeably and without fixed or ascertainable meanings.

The vagueness and generality of the clauses that set forth presidential powers afford a plausible basis for pressures within and without an administration for presidential action beyond that supported by those whose responsibility it is to defend his actions in court. The claim of inherent and unrestricted presidential powers has long been a persuasive dialectical weapon in political controversy. . . . But prudence has counseled that actual reliance on such nebulous claims stop short of provoking a judicial test.

The Solicitor General, acknowledging that Congress has never authorized the seizure here, says practice of prior Presidents has authorized it. He seeks color of legality from claimed executive precedents. . . .

The appeal, however, that we declare the existence of inherent powers *ex necessitate* [necessitated by the circumstances] to meet an emergency asks us to do what many think would be wise, although it is something the forefathers omitted. They knew what emergencies were, knew the pressures they engender for authoritative action, knew, too, how they afford a ready pretext for usurpation. We may also suspect that they suspected that emergency powers would tend to kindle emergencies. Aside from suspension of the privilege of the writ of habeas corpus in time of rebellion or invasion, when the public safety may require it, they made no express provision for exercise of extraordinary authority because of a crisis. I do not think we rightfully may so amend their work, and, if we could, I am not convinced it would be wise to do so, although many modern nations have forthrightly recognized that war and economic crises may upset the normal balance between liberty and authority. ...

Germany, after the First World War, framed the Weimar Constitution, designed to secure her liberties in the Western tradition. However, the President of the Republic, without concurrence of the Reichstag, was empowered temporarily to suspend any or all individual rights if public safety and order were seriously disturbed or endangered. This proved a temptation to every government, whatever its shade of opinion, and, in 13 years, suspension of rights was invoked on more than 250 occasions. Finally, Hitler persuaded President Von Hindenberg [sic] to suspend all such rights, and they were never restored. ...

This contemporary foreign experience ... suggests that emergency powers are consistent with free government only when their control is lodged elsewhere than in the Executive who exercises them. That is the safeguard that would be nullified by our adoption of the "inherent powers" formula. Nothing in my experience convinces me that such risks are warranted by any real necessity. ...

In the practical working of our Government, we already have evolved a technique within the framework of the Constitution by which normal executive powers may be considerably expanded to meet an emergency. Congress may and has granted extraordinary authorities which lie dormant in normal times but may be called into play by the Executive in war or upon proclamation of a national emergency. ... Under this procedure, we retain Government by law—special, temporary law, perhaps, but law nonetheless. The public may know the extent and limitations of the powers that can be asserted, and persons affected may be informed from the statute of their rights and duties.

In view of the ease, expedition and safety with which Congress can grant and has granted large emergency powers, certainly ample to embrace this crisis, I am quite unimpressed with the argument that we should affirm possession of them without statute. Such power either has no beginning or it has no end. If it exists, it need submit to no legal restraint. I am not alarmed that it would plunge us straightway into dictatorship, but it is at least a step in that wrong direction.

As to whether there is imperative necessity for such powers, it is relevant to note the gap that exists between the President's paper powers and his real powers. The Constitution does not disclose the measure of the actual controls wielded by the modern presidential office. That instrument must be understood as an Eighteenth-Century sketch of a government hoped for, not as a blueprint of the Government that is. Vast accretions of federal power, eroded from that reserved by the States, have magnified the scope of presidential activity. Subtle shifts take place in the centers of real power that do not show on the face of the Constitution.

Executive power has the advantage of concentration in a single head in whose choice the whole Nation has a part, making him the focus of public hopes and expectations. In drama, magnitude and finality, his decisions so far overshadow any others that, almost alone, he fills the public eye and ear. No other personality in public life can begin to compete with him in access to the public mind through modern methods of communications. By his prestige as head of state and his influence upon public opinion, he exerts a leverage upon those who are supposed to check and balance his power which often cancels their effectiveness.

Moreover, rise of the party system has made a significant extraconstitutional supplement to real executive power. No appraisal of his necessities is realistic which overlooks that he heads a political system, as well as a legal system. Party loyalties and interests, sometimes more binding than law, extend his effective control into branches of government other than his own, and he often may win, as a political leader, what he cannot command under the Constitution....

But I have no illusion that any decision by this Court can keep power in the hands of Congress if it is not wise and timely in meeting its problems. A crisis that challenges the President equally, or perhaps primarily, challenges Congress.... We may say that power to legislate for emergencies belongs in the hands of Congress, but only Congress itself can prevent power from slipping through its fingers.

The essence of our free Government is "leave to live by no man's leave, underneath the law"—to be governed by those impersonal forces which we call law. Our Government is fashioned to fulfill this concept so far as humanly possible. The Executive, except for recommendation and veto, has no legislative power. The executive action we have here originates in the individual will of the President, and represents an exercise of authority without law. No one, perhaps not even the President, knows the limits of the power he may seek to exert in this instance, and the parties affected cannot learn the limit of their rights. We do not know today what powers over labor or property would be claimed to flow from Government possession if we should legalize it, what rights to compensation would be claimed or recognized, or on what contingency it would end. With all its defects, delays and inconveniences, men have discovered no technique for long preserving free government except that the Executive be under the law, and that the law be made by parliamentary deliberations.

Such institutions may be destined to pass away. But it is the duty of the Court to be last, not first, to give them up.

As Louis Fisher observes, the court's decision in *Youngstown* "explicitly rejects the President's reliance on 'inherent' powers" and emphasizes "that the President operates within a constitutional structure and is subject to congressional and judicial restraints."[23] Maeva Marcus writes that the *Youngstown* decision "helped redress the balance of power among the three branches of government and breathed new life into the proposition that the President, like every citizen, is 'under the law.'"[24] As noted, Justice Jackson's concurring opinion has had more influence than the majority opinion in *Youngstown*.[25] One reason why Jackson's opinion has been influential is that his now-famous tripartite framework seems to provide a pathway through the uncertain thicket of presidential power.[26] On closer inspection, though, the tripartite framework does not yield precise answers to specific questions of presidential power—at best, it provides guidelines, starting points for analysis.[27]

One thing Jackson does make clear, however, is that there must be *some* limits on presidential power. Jackson is especially skeptical of emergency presidential powers, saying this is something the Framers had good reason to leave out of the Constitution and warning that the use of such powers can be incredibly dangerous. Jackson, who had been chief prosecutor at the post–World War II Nuremberg trials, reminds us that Hitler used emergency power as a path to dictatorship. However, like Taney in *Merryman*, Jackson acknowledges that there are practical limits to the court's ability to rein in presidential power.[28] Jackson sees Congress as an important check—perhaps more important than the court. He has "no illusion that any decision by this Court can keep power in the hands of Congress if it is not wise and timely in meeting its problems."[29]

While Jackson's opinion can be seen as an important reminder that there are at least some limits on presidential power, he also acknowledges that it is impossible to precisely define the scope of such power solely on the basis of the text of the Constitution or the intention of its Framers—in reality, presidential power has exceeded what Jackson referred to as the office's "paper power," the limited powers expressly assigned by Article II. An advocate for broad presidential power might especially find hope in Jackson's words about foreign affairs: "I should indulge the widest latitude of interpretation to sustain [the president's] exclusive function to command the instruments of national force, at least when turned against the outside world for the security of our society."[30] Jackson distinguishes such actions from domestic action, concluding that presidential power is much more limited when directed internally. However, as we will see, the line between the foreign and domestic sphere can be blurred, especially in the context of the war on terror, and Jackson's opinion might ironically be cited to justify broad presidential power, at least when it can be linked in some way to foreign affairs.

On one level, Jackson's opinion can be seen simply as an endorsement or summary of past practice: presidents are best advised to act in concert with Congress, and the court is most comfortable in approving presidential action when it is endorsed by Congress.[31] Bellia argues that Jackson was attempting to provide guidance to presidential advisers—his opinion makes mention of his own service in this capacity.[32] In this view, Jackson was informing presidential advisers how to avoid constitutional disputes and suggesting that the president would be best served to act with either express or implied congressional authorization.[33] He may also have been defending the advice he had previously given to President Roosevelt when he was serving as attorney general—recall that his memoranda regarding the transfer of destroyers to Britain and seizure of the North American Aviation plant relied at least tangentially on statutory authority.[34]

Jackson's concurring opinion in *Youngstown* suggests guideposts that could be used to define the limits of presidential power. However, it also leaves important questions unresolved, especially the question of presidential power in the context of foreign affairs. Jackson also suggests limits on the power of the court itself to act as a check: constitutional provisions are vague, and the realities of governing, especially in the context of modern emergencies, have given the president de facto powers not imagined by the Framers. While Jackson may have hoped that his opinion would help guide presidential advisers away from the shoals of constitutional controversy, as we will see, subsequent advisers have sometimes ignored Jackson's guidelines, though perhaps at their own peril.

8

NIXON, WATERGATE, AND A BID FOR
UNBRIDLED PRESIDENTIAL POWER

In the *Youngstown* case, decided in 1952, Justice Jackson's concurring opinion made clear that there were limits on presidential power, even in wartime, and especially when turned inward (i.e., when applied within the United States). He was skeptical of recognizing any emergency presidential power that had not been authorized by Congress.

Despite Jackson's cautionary note, presidential power expanded in the 1950s and 1960s in the context of a seemingly unending crisis—the struggle against communism. President Truman sent troops to Korea without congressional approval. President Lyndon Johnson gained a congressional resolution to support military escalation in Vietnam, but that resolution was gained under false pretenses.[1] Congress frequently deferred to presidential decisions made against the backdrop of the Cold War with the Soviet Union.[2]

Johnson's successor, Richard Nixon, brought the theory and practice of emergency presidential power to new heights. Ultimately, he advanced a definition of power that threatened to upend the constitutional structure by placing the president beyond challenge or restraint. In place of the constitutional system of checks and balances, there would simply be Nixon himself, a presidential center of power that could not be questioned. Nixon imagined a constitutional landscape where he, as president, represented the popular will. His view of presidential power rested on the "implicit belief that opposition to the president was anti-democratic and the preserve of an unrepresentative elite."[3] In this framework, his political antagonists did not simply oppose him—they opposed the popular will itself. Where Alexander Hamilton defended the idea of judicial review as a way for judges to vindicate the popular will, as expressed in the Constitution,

Nixon put himself in place of the Constitution. In Nixon's view, his rivals and critics were not merely opponents but enemies who threatened self-government itself by opposing Nixon, the one true representative of the people.[4]

Armed with this worldview, the Nixon administration not surprisingly produced an "enemies list"—composed not of enemy agents bent on attacking the United States but of journalists, actors, union leaders, and members of Congress who were seen as political opponents of the president.[5] The administration's approach refined the theory that expansive presidential power was justified if used to protect the nation and interpreted it to mean that essentially absolute presidential power was justified in protecting the president against political opponents. Nixon White House counsel John Dean circulated a memo entitled "On Screwing Our Political Enemies," which "addressed the matter of how we can use the available federal machinery to screw our political opponents." Toward this end, Nixon ordered that wiretaps be placed on the phones of his "enemies" and that attempts be made to smear the reputations of those who criticized him.[6]

Nixon justified his activities in the name of national security—again, a modified application of the theory that the president can unilaterally exercise emergency power to protect the nation. Nixon saw his domestic critics, including student activists and other left-wing groups, as dangerous. In 1970, Nixon met with the heads of the FBI, CIA, Defense Intelligence Agency, and National Security Agency to discuss improved methods of gathering "more information about the threat of domestic radicalism."[7] The Nixon administration's Huston Plan[8] called for extensive espionage, including warrantless surveillance, burglary, and opening of mail.[9]

The FBI's opposition forced Nixon to rescind the plan but did not stop him from taking other steps against his perceived enemies. Nixon, no longer trusting the FBI, established his own extralegal investigative force, known as the "plumbers," since one of their tasks was to stop "leaks" of sensitive information by government officials to members of the press or others (though their duties went well beyond this).[10]

The plumbers were a secret group, not authorized by or known to Congress. One of their first assignments was to dig up compromising information about Daniel Ellsberg, who had "leaked" the Pentagon Papers to the *New York Times*, exposing what Ellsberg later described as "unconstitutional behavior" by several presidents.[11] For Nixon, the Pentagon Papers "posed a threat to [his] imperial presidency."[12] The documents "vindicated those who questioned the necessity, wisdom, and morality of the ongoing [Vietnam] War that Nixon insisted was vital to America's credibility as a great power."[13] In addition, public release of the Pentagon

Papers "disturbed the secrecy Nixon believed essential in the conduct of foreign affairs."[14] Nixon claimed that gathering information about Ellsberg's motives was of "vital importance to the national security." Some of Nixon's plumbers burglarized the office of Ellsberg's psychiatrist, hoping to find damaging information that could discredit Ellsberg.[15] On another occasion, Nixon ordered a break-in and theft at the Brookings Institute to discover what information the think tank had compiled on the Vietnam War.[16]

The plumbers' other assignments included forging a document designed to suggest that President John F. Kennedy was involved in the assassination of South Vietnam's leader and, most infamously, breaking into the Democratic National Committee's offices at the Watergate in an attempt to set up a wiretap. The Watergate break-in was itself part of a larger strategy to effectively rig the 1972 presidential election—as Senator Sam Ervin (D-NC) put it, Nixon and his plumbers "were trying to steal . . . the right to vote in a free election."[17] Polls in early 1972 showed Nixon trailing Senator Edmund Muskie (D-ME).[18] Nixon and his men used campaign contributions to fund political spying and sabotage, including hiring agents to infiltrate Muskie's campaign, spreading false stories about Muskie, stealing stationery from campaign offices in order to send fraudulent letters and press releases intended to discredit Muskie, disrupting campaign events, and tapping Muskie's and other Democratic candidates' phones.[19] Muskie ultimately withdrew from the race after he was unable to effectively respond to false allegations that he had used a derogatory term to refer to French Canadians in New Hampshire (the false allegations stemmed from a White House staffer's fabricated letter to a New Hampshire newspaper).[20]

Nixon, in effect, justified all these actions in the name of emergency and national security.[21] In this sense, he was arguably expanding on the theory that previous presidents had used to justify emergency presidential power. Of course, "Nixon exceeded all his predecessors" in secretly turning the government into an instrument of personal vendetta.[22] In Nixon's view, "his opponents were the enemies of not only himself but also the popular will, so his intention was to defeat them not debate with them."[23] Nixon's actions exposed glaring flaws in the theory of implied presidential emergency power that had been used in the past. The first problem, of course, is whether the emergency is real and which branch should determine this. Another problem was how much power the president could exercise in the name of national security. Nixon's actions suggested that the president has absolute power—that the president can take any action deemed necessary to protect the nation—and, since Nixon was the only legitimate representative of the popular will, that meant he could do what was necessary to preserve and protect his presidency. As Schlesinger puts it, "the theory of the Presidency [that Nixon] embodied and propagated meant that the President of the United States, on his own personal and secret finding of emergency, had the right to nullify the Constitution and the law."[24]

Nixon and his administration exerted presidential power on a broad scale, including conducting a secret air war in Cambodia in 1969 and 1970 without Congress's knowledge, illegally wiretapping political opponents, engaging in burglary, effectively rigging the 1972 presidential election by engaging in "dirty tricks" to force out a feared opponent, and obstructing justice.[25] As the Watergate burglary and broader abuses of power came to light, Nixon attempted to use one last application of presidential power to save himself. When a Senate investigating committee and special prosecutor asked Nixon to produce secret tapes he had made of Oval Office conversations with administration officials, Nixon refused, arguing that "executive privilege" made those recordings confidential. He ordered Attorney General Elliot Richardson to fire the special prosecutor, Archibald Cox, and to close down the special prosecutor's office in an effort to avoid being compelled to produce the tapes. Although Richardson and Deputy Attorney General William Ruckelshaus refused to fire Cox, Solicitor General Robert Bork agreed to do so.[26] After a public outcry, Nixon was forced to reopen the special prosecutor's office, and Leon Jaworski was named as the new special prosecutor, on October 31, 1973.[27] Jaworski continued to press Cox's subpoena for the White House tapes. When Nixon refused to release additional tapes, Jaworski petitioned the Supreme Court to order production of the tapes.[28]

Nixon effectively forced a constitutional crisis. He claimed that the courts simply had no authority to compel the president to take action, even if that action was production of evidence of a crime. If that were the case, the president would be above the law, as no court would have the authority to regulate the president's behavior. It was a claim of absolute executive power. When the case came before the Supreme Court, eight justices unanimously rejected Nixon's claim.[29] Excerpts from the court's 1974 decision in *U.S. v. Nixon* follow.

United States v. Nixon, 418 U.S. 683 (1974)

Majority opinion by Chief Justice Burger.

This litigation presents for review the denial of a motion, filed in the District Court on behalf of the President of the United States . . . to quash a third-party subpoena *duces tecum*[30] issued by the United States District Court for the District of Columbia. . . . The subpoena directed the President to produce certain tape recordings and documents relating to his conversations with aides and advisers. The court rejected the President's claims of absolute executive privilege. . . . We granted both the United States' petition for certiorari before judgment and also the President's cross-petition for certiorari . . . because of the public importance of the issues presented and the need for their prompt resolution.

On March 1, 1974, a grand jury of the United States District Court for the District of Columbia returned an indictment charging seven named individuals [all aides or advisers to Nixon] with various offenses, including conspiracy to defraud the United States and to obstruct justice. . . . [T]he grand jury named the President, among others, as an unindicted coconspirator. On April 18, 1974, upon motion of the Special Prosecutor, a subpoena *duces tecum* was issued . . . to the President by the United States District Court. . . . This subpoena required the production . . . of certain tapes, memoranda, papers, transcripts, or other writings relating to certain precisely identified meetings between the President and others. . . . On April 30, the President publicly released edited transcripts of 43 conversations; portions of 20 conversations subject to subpoena in the present case were included. On May 1, 1974, the President's counsel filed . . . a motion to quash the subpoena . . .

On May 20, 1974, the District Court denied the motion to quash. . . . It further ordered "the President . . ." to deliver to the District Court, on or before May 31, 1974, the originals of all subpoenaed items. . . . The District Court rejected . . . the contention that the Judiciary was without authority to review an assertion of executive privilege by the President. . . .

The District Court held that the judiciary, not the President, was the final arbiter of a claim of executive privilege. . . .

[W]e turn to the claim that the subpoena should be quashed because it demands "confidential conversations between a President and his close advisors that it would be inconsistent with the public interest to produce." The first contention is a broad claim that the separation of powers doctrine precludes judicial review of a President's claim of privilege. The second contention is that, if he does not prevail on the claim of absolute privilege, the court should hold as a matter of constitutional law that the privilege prevails over the subpoena *duces tecum*.

In the performance of assigned constitutional duties, each branch of the Government must initially interpret the Constitution, and the interpretation of its powers by any branch is due great respect from the others. The President's counsel, as we have noted, reads the Constitution as providing an absolute privilege of confidentiality for all Presidential communications. Many decisions of this Court, however, have unequivocally reaffirmed the holding of [*Marbury v. Madison*] . . . [and] exercises of power by the Executive Branch and the Legislative Branch have been found invalid as in conflict with the Constitution. . . .

Since this Court has consistently exercised the power to construe and delineate claims arising under express powers [assigned by the Constitution to Congress or the President], it must follow that the Court has authority to interpret claims with respect to powers alleged to derive from enumerated powers.

Our system of government "requires that federal courts on occasion interpret the Constitution in a manner at variance with the construction given the document by another branch." . . . Notwithstanding the deference each branch must accord the others, the "judicial Power of the United States" vested in the federal courts by Art. III, § 1, of the Constitution can no more be shared with the Executive Branch than the Chief Executive, for example, can share with the Judiciary the veto power, or the Congress share with the Judiciary the power to override a Presidential veto. Any other conclusion would be contrary to the basic concept of separation of powers and the checks and balances that flow from the scheme of a tripartite government. . . .

We therefore reaffirm that it is the province and duty of this Court "to say what the law is" with respect to the claim of privilege presented in this case [*Marbury v. Madison*]. . . .

In support of his claim of absolute privilege, the President's counsel urges two grounds. . . . The first ground is the valid need for protection of communications between high Government officials and those who advise and assist them in the performance of their manifold duties; the importance of this confidentiality is too plain to require further discussion. Human experience teaches that those who expect public dissemination of their remarks may well temper candor with a concern for appearances and for their own interests to the detriment of the decision-making process. Whatever the nature of the privilege of confidentiality of Presidential communications in the exercise of Art. II powers, the privilege can be said to derive from the supremacy of each branch within its own assigned area of constitutional duties. Certain powers and privileges flow from the nature of enumerated powers; the protection of the confidentiality of Presidential communications has similar [implied] constitutional underpinnings.

The second ground asserted by the President's counsel in support of the claim of absolute privilege rests on the doctrine of separation of powers. Here it is argued that the independence of the Executive Branch within its own sphere . . . insulates a President from a judicial subpoena in an ongoing criminal prosecution, and thereby protects confidential Presidential communications.

However, neither the doctrine of separation of powers nor the need for confidentiality of high-level communications, without more, can sustain an absolute, unqualified Presidential privilege of immunity from judicial process under all circumstances. The President's need for complete candor and objectivity from advisers calls for great deference from the courts. However, when the privilege depends solely on the broad, undifferentiated claim of public interest in the confidentiality of such conversations, a confrontation with other values arises. Absent a claim of need to protect military, diplomatic, or sensitive national security secrets, we find it difficult to accept the argument that even the very important interest in confidentiality of Presidential communications is significantly diminished by production of such material for *in camera* inspection with all the protection that a district court will be obliged to provide.

The impediment that an absolute, unqualified privilege would place in the way of the primary constitutional duty of the Judicial Branch to do justice in criminal prosecutions would plainly conflict with the function of the courts under Art. III. In designing the structure of our Government and dividing and allocating the sovereign power among three co-equal branches, the Framers of the Constitution sought to provide a comprehensive system, but the separate powers were not intended to operate with absolute independence....

To read the Art. II powers of the President as providing an absolute privilege as against a subpoena essential to enforcement of criminal statutes on no more than a generalized claim of the public interest in confidentiality of nonmilitary and non-diplomatic discussions would upset the constitutional balance of "a workable government" and gravely impair the role of the courts under Art. III....

In this case, the President challenges a subpoena served on him ... requiring the production of materials for use in a criminal prosecution; he does so on the claim that he has a privilege against disclosure of confidential communications. He does not place his claim of privilege on the ground they are military or diplomatic secrets. As to these areas of Art. II duties, the courts have traditionally shown the utmost deference to Presidential responsibilities. In *C. & S. Air Lines v. Waterman S.S. Corp.* (1948), dealing with Presidential authority involving foreign policy considerations, the Court said:

> The President, both as Commander-in-Chief and as the Nation's organ for foreign affairs, has available intelligence services whose reports are not and ought not to be published to the world. It would be intolerable that courts, without the relevant information, should review and perhaps nullify actions of the Executive taken on information properly held secret.

In *United States v. Reynolds, 345 U.S. 1* (1953), the Court said:

> It may be possible to satisfy the court, from all the circumstances of the case, that there is a reasonable danger that compulsion of the evidence will expose military matters which, in the interest of national security, should not be divulged. When this is the case, the occasion for the privilege is appropriate, and the court should not

> jeopardize the security which the privilege is meant to protect by
> insisting upon an examination of the evidence, even by the judge
> alone, in chambers.

No case of the Court, however, has extended this high degree of deference to a President's generalized interest in confidentiality....

Enforcement of the subpoena *duces tecum* was stayed pending this Court's resolution of the issues raised by the petitions for certiorari. Those issues now having been disposed of, it is obvious that the District Court has ... a very heavy responsibility to see to it that Presidential conversations, which are either not relevant or not admissible, are accorded that high degree of respect due the President of the United States. Mr. Chief Justice Marshall, sitting as a trial judge in the *Burr* case [1807], was extraordinarily careful to point out that "[i]n no case of this kind would a court be required to proceed against the president as against an ordinary individual."

Marshall's statement cannot be read to mean in any sense that a President is above the law, but relates to the singularly unique role under Art. II of a President's communications and activities, related to the performance of duties under that Article. Moreover, a President's communications and activities encompass a vastly wider range of sensitive material than would be true of any "ordinary individual." It is therefore necessary in the public interest to afford Presidential confidentiality the greatest protection consistent with the fair administration of justice. The need for confidentiality even as to idle conversations with associates in which casual reference might be made concerning political leaders within the country or foreign statesmen is too obvious to call for further treatment....

The Supreme Court's decision in *U.S. v. Nixon* came on July 24, 1974. A few days later, Nixon released the subpoenaed tapes. The recordings that were released included a conversation Nixon had with one of his aides in which Nixon discussed ordering the FBI to stay out of the Watergate investigation.[31] Facing almost certain impeachment and removal from office, Nixon resigned from office on August 9, 1974.[32] The court had stood up to Nixon's assertion of unlimited executive power, but, as we'll see, others believed that Nixon's conception of presidential power was perfectly justified.

9

EMERGENCY PRESIDENTIAL POWER

AT ITS ZENITH

THE BUSH ADMINISTRATION AND
THE UNITARY EXECUTIVE

In the 1970s, especially after Nixon's resignation, Congress passed a number of laws aimed at reining in presidential power, including the War Powers Act, the Foreign Intelligence Surveillance Act,[1] and the Independent Counsel Act.[2] Some saw these as important measures designed to prevent presidential overreaching. Others, including future vice president Dick Cheney, saw them as troubling limitations on presidential power. Cheney, while serving as chief of staff in President Ford's administration, believed that he was witnessing "the nadir of the modern presidency in terms of authority and legitimacy."[3] He believed it was urgent for future presidents to restore the full scope of presidential power that had been reined in after Nixon.

Cheney's views on the appropriate scope of presidential power were expressed in the 1987 minority report of the congressional committees investigating the Iran-Contra affair.[4] The Iran-Contra affair involved the Reagan administration's covert sale of missiles to Iran, a transaction designed to secure the release of American hostages held in Lebanon, and the administration's secret use of money received from these arms sales to support the Contras, who opposed the leftist Sandinista regime in Nicaragua.[5] These actions violated federal statutes.[6] The minority report suggested, however, that the president had "inherent . . . powers" to take these actions, powers that could not be regulated by Congress under the Constitution.[7] Congressional action interfering with "core presidential foreign power functions . . . should be struck down."[8] In fact, statutes encroaching on presidential power were "constitutionally . . . illegitimate."[9] According to the minority report, the Constitution also gave the president "some discretion to use [military] force without a declaration of war"—how far this power extended was determined by practice, not by the text of the Constitution itself.[10]

The ideas expressed in the Iran-Contra minority report ultimately found a home in the George W. Bush administration. Bush's presidency provided the opportunity for Cheney and others to advance the vision of the "unitary executive," the theory that the president is not bound by Congress or the courts in exercising executive power.[11] This was the argument suggested by the 1987 Iran-Contra minority report and was essentially the argument Truman and Nixon had previously made (though in different contexts) and that the court previously rejected in *Youngstown* and *U.S. v. Nixon*. Advocates of the unitary executive theory insist that when the president exercises any of the executive power granted under the Constitution, whether explicitly, implicitly, or inherently, the president has the final word on the scope and limits of that power. They argue that all "executive power" belongs to the president alone—it has a "unitary" aspect in the sense that it resides solely in the hands of the president, unreviewable by the other branches of government. Just as the courts and Congress have their spheres of power, so too does the president, and he or she possesses plenary power within the executive sphere.[12] In this view, the president may even possess independent and unilateral authority to interpret the Constitution in defining the limits of presidential power.[13] As one scholar put it, the unitary executive theory asserts that "presidents have sole and complete control over the executive branch" and that "the other branches of government may not interfere with presidential actions arising from [the president's use of] executive powers."[14]

The unitary executive theory is a way to justify emergency presidential power: the Bush administration applied this theory in the context of the war on terror to justify presidential power used to defend the nation. We'll begin, however, by considering the general formulation of the unitary executive theory before we consider how it has been used to justify specific applications of presidential power.[15] The idea of a unitary executive takes as its starting point Article II of the Constitution, most centrally its Vesting Clause, which provides that "[t]he executive Power shall be vested in a President of the United States of America."[16] Advocates of the unitary executive theory contrast this language with Article I's Vesting Clause, which provides that "[a]ll legislative Powers *herein granted* shall be vested in a Congress of the United States."[17] They reason that the Framers of the

Constitution chose their words carefully and that, therefore, it is significant that they used more limiting language in Article I's Vesting Clause. One consequence, in this view, is that Congress is limited to only those legislative powers described in Article I. By contrast, since Article II's Vesting Clause does not contain limiting language, the executive must be assigned *all* the executive power. This power is "unitary" in the sense that it is assigned solely to the president and is not shared with the other branches of the federal government. Any power that is inherently executive—which most centrally includes power over foreign affairs and the military—belongs to the president.[18]

The unitary executive theory is sometimes also supported by reference to the Oath and Take Care Clauses in Article II of the Constitution.[19] Advocates of the unitary executive conclude that the Oath Clause gives the president independent authority to define and interpret the Constitution, reasoning that if the president is sworn to defend the Constitution, then he or she must reject interpretations of the Constitution that interfere with this duty.[20] The Take Care Clause in Article II, section 3, states that "[the president] shall take Care that the Laws be faithfully executed." One reading of this clause is that the president is required to take care that all laws—including the Constitution itself—be "faithfully executed." This supports the view that the president can independently interpret the Constitution and reject contrary interpretations, even by Congress or the courts. In practice, this view is used to justify the conclusion that the president can set aside laws passed by Congress and disregard court opinions that impermissibly interfere with or incorrectly define executive power. Going a step further, presidents may conclude that their "primary duty is to take care that the nation be preserved, to which the duty to take care that the laws, including the Constitution, be faithfully executed, is subordinate."[21]

Critics respond that this version of the unitary executive theory sets aside the system of checks and balances envisioned by the Constitution's Framers. In fact, Louis Fisher argues, the very idea of "inherent" executive power is extraconstitutional. Unlike express and implied powers, which are derived from the text of the Constitution, inherent powers exist outside of and are not limited by the Constitution.[22] Critics further object that advocates of this version of the unitary executive theory "are reading too much into [Article II's] vesting clause."[23] For one thing, Article II *does* spell out a number of specific powers—for instance, that "[t]he President shall be Commander in Chief of the Army and Navy of the United States, and of the Militia of the several States, when called into the actual Service of the United States" and that the president may grant pardons, make treaties (with the advice and consent of the Senate), and nominate federal judges.[24] As Justice Robert H. Jackson wondered, if it were the case that the Framers intended to assign the president "all the executive powers of which the Government is capable," then "why [would] the forefathers [have] bothered to add several specific items, including some trifling ones[?]"[25] Fisher points out that "Congress is not limited to the express and enumerated powers of Article I."[26] This observation casts doubt on the assertion that there is a crucial significance to the difference in wording between the Vesting Clause of Article II and the Vesting Clause in Article I.

David Gray Adler focuses on "the understanding of the term 'executive power' on the eve of the [Constitutional] Convention." The Framers chose this phrase as a way to reject the idea of royal prerogative that was part of the British system. "Executive" was simply more "republic-friendly" than prerogative, and the phrase "executive power" was meant to convey an idea of limited power, in contrast with the broad prerogative available to the British monarch. Since the Framers envisioned an executive with "confined and defined" powers, Adler observes, it does not make sense to conclude that they intended the Vesting Clause to assign broad, unbounded powers to the president.[27] James Pfiffner similarly challenges the assumptions of advocates of the unitary executive theory as to what the Framers intended. Pfiffner argues that the model of separate but overlapping powers, aimed at avoiding a concentration of power in any one branch, "refute[s] . . . assertions by the Bush administration that the president has exclusive control of the 'unitary executive.'"[28]

Advocates of broad presidential power respond that Pfiffner's concern is precisely what recommends the unitary executive theory: it allows one person—the president—the ability to act quickly and decisively to respond to crisis or emergency.[29] In that sense, it builds on the idea of implied emergency presidential powers. However, critics respond, there is a difference between limited, constrained power to respond to emergencies and unchecked power to set aside provisions of the Constitution and laws passed by Congress in the name of national security.[30] This is especially a concern during the open-ended crisis that is the war on terror.[31]

As we'll see, the unitary executive theory challenges historical applications of emergency presidential power—both in its general scope through the suggestion that the president has inherent power that cannot be reined in by Congress or the courts[32] and in its specific application to justify specific measures taken in recent years, including indefinite detention of suspected terrorists, torture, extraordinary rendition, and warrantless surveillance. This view of emergency presidential power raises a number of questions, including these: (1) can the unitary executive theory be justified by the text of the Constitution? (2) can the unitary executive theory be reconciled with the separation of powers? (3) can the unitary executive theory be justified by historical practice? (4) assuming the president has the authority to exert "executive power" without limitation by other branches of the government, what exactly *is* the "executive power" under the Constitution? (5) what consequences has the unitary executive theory had for conducting the "war on terror"? and (6) what implications does the unitary executive theory have for a constitutional system of government?

The unitary executive theory, as applied in recent years, has been dreamed of for decades, but it really came to prominence after the September 11 attacks. This is part of, perhaps the essence of, what President Bush and Vice President Cheney meant when they said that "everything changed" after September 11, 2001.[33]

DID EVERYTHING REALLY CHANGE
AFTER THE SEPTEMBER 11 ATTACKS?

In some ways, the declaration that "everything changed" after September 11, 2001, is an oversimplification. Of course, Americans are worried about attacks within the United States in a way that they may not have worried before. But it's hard to say that everything changed. Many Americans continue to go to work and to school and to live their daily lives much as they did before the September 11 attacks—especially those who are not serving in the military and do not have family members serving in the military. Certainly, there have also been changes—increased security in many aspects of life, long-term military action abroad, and, most important for our purposes, the reality of increased presidential power.

When advocates of the unitary executive claim that "everything changed" after September 11, they may be right when it comes to presidential power. As we've seen, emergency presidential power is not expressly addressed by the Constitution. As we've also seen, there is a tradition of enhanced presidential power during war or crisis, and past presidents have sometimes wielded extraordinary power, especially in the name of defending the nation against rebellion or invasion. To an extent, the Bush administration simply drew on this historical tradition, and President Bush made that clear by immediately, within days or perhaps even hours of the September 11 attacks, defining the attacks as a declaration of war against the United States, paving the way for emergency action.[34] However, no past president had successfully asserted unilateral authority to define the scope of presidential power and to set aside laws passed by Congress that, in the president's view, impermissibly intruded on executive power.[35] What we will focus on is (1) how the Bush administration and its successor, the Obama administration, have defined emergency presidential power, especially in the context of the ongoing crisis associated with the response to the threat of terrorism; (2) specific presidential actions that have been taken since the September 11, 2001, attacks; and (3) whether these actions can be justified. In short, did the Bush and Obama administrations go beyond the bounds of constitutional authority?

We will begin with the George W. Bush administration. Justifying the traditional idea of enhanced emergency presidential power through the unitary executive doctrine had specific, extraordinary results, as set forth in a number of Bush administration legal memoranda. These memoranda, many of which were not made public until after Bush left office,[36] provide analysis intended to serve as legal justification for specific actions. Many of the memos were prepared by lawyers in the Office of Legal Counsel (OLC), which is part of the Justice Department. The OLC issues legal opinions that are, if accepted by the president, binding on every cabinet department, and it is often asked to resolve disagreements about what the law means.[37] It historically operated independently, as its key role was to issue objective opinions regarding disputes over constitutional interpretation within the executive branch.[38]

After the September 11 attacks, the OLC came under the direction of the Vice President's office and played an important role in drafting secret legal memoranda that were used to justify many of the policies employed in the war on terror.[39] Administration officials believed that gaining legal approval from the OLC for their actions would provide them with immunity from prosecution if their actions were later deemed to be criminal.[40] Several pivotal memos were drafted by John Yoo, a deputy assistant attorney general in the OLC from 2001 to 2003. These memos made assertions and reached conclusions that paved the way for the specific use of presidential power in several contexts, including (1) the detention and trial of suspected terrorists; (2) permissible interrogation methods to be used with suspected terrorists; and (3) warrantless surveillance, as discussed in chapters 10–12.

EXPANDED PRESIDENTIAL POWER
TO MAKE WAR

After the September 11 attacks, the United States prepared for a military response against Afghanistan, where Osama Bin Laden and others involved in the attacks were believed to be located. Congress quickly provided legislative authorization for such actions in the Authorization for the Use of Military Force, or AUMF.[41] However, in an initially classified memorandum dated September 25, 2001, Yoo concluded that the President did not actually need any authorization from Congress in order to take military action to defend the nation, since such decisions "are for the President alone to make."[42]

At first glance, this might look like simply another chapter in the historical tradition of using presidential power to respond independently to an emergency or to a claimed emergency with military action. If, without congressional authorization, President Polk could send troops to Mexico to stop a possible invasion of Texas and if President Lincoln could raise armies and organize a naval blockade of rebellious states, then President Bush, in responding to a terrorist attack against the United States, could also act unilaterally to defend the nation. Indeed, Yoo's memo cited as precedent the *Prize Cases*, which vindicated Lincoln's initially unilateral decision to order a blockade of the Confederacy. But Yoo went further. Where Lincoln had sought retroactive congressional approval for a limited military response targeted at rebellious states,[43] Yoo concluded that the president had plenary power to deploy the military—to wage war against *any* potential threat. Congress's constitutional authority to declare war was merely a formality, as Yoo claimed the Framers themselves understood:[44] the president, as commander in chief, has "sole authority to decide whether to make war."[45]

Since there was no dispute that the AUMF gave President Bush authorization from Congress to attack Afghanistan (an action Bush ordered a few weeks later), why did Yoo describe power for the president that went further, including the authority to order military action against individuals, groups, or states "that cannot be demonstrably linked to the September 11 incidents"?[46] Yoo was advancing the unitary executive theory, asserting that, when the president wields executive power given to him by the Constitution—here, the decision to deploy military force—he does so absolutely, with no need for authorization from another branch of the government.[47] In fact, Yoo asserted, the president can set aside congressional efforts to limit his power in this area as the decision whether to make war is "for the President alone to make."[48] Excerpts from Yoo's September 25, 2001, memo follow:

The President's Constitutional Authority to Conduct Military Operations against Terrorists and Nations Supporting Them

September 25, 2001

Memorandum Opinion for the Deputy Counsel to the President[49]

You have asked for our opinion as to the scope of the President's authority to take military action in response to the terrorist attacks on the United States on

September 11, 2001. We conclude that the President has broad constitutional power to use military force. Congress has acknowledged this inherent executive power in both the War Powers Resolution ... (1973) (the "WPR"), and in the Joint Resolution [i.e., the AUMF] passed by Congress on September 14, 2001. ... Further, the President has the constitutional power not only to retaliate against any person, organization, or State suspected of involvement in terrorist attacks on the United States, but also against foreign States suspected of harboring or supporting such organizations. Finally, the President may deploy military force preemptively against terrorist organizations or the States that harbor or support them, whether or not they can be linked to the specific terrorist incidents of September 11. ...

We conclude that the Constitution vests the President with the plenary authority, as Commander in Chief and the sole organ of the Nation in its foreign relations, to use military force abroad—especially in response to grave national emergencies created by sudden, unforeseen attacks on the people and territory of the United States. ...

Our review establishes that all three branches of the Federal Government—Congress, the Executive, and the Judiciary—agree that the President has broad authority to use military force abroad, including the ability to deter future attacks.

The President's constitutional power to defend the United States and the lives of its people must be understood in light of the Founders' express intention to create a federal government "cloathed with all the powers requisite to [the] complete execution of its trust." The Federalist No. 23. ... Foremost among the objectives committed to that trust by the Constitution is the security of the Nation. ...

We now turn to the more precise question of the President's inherent constitutional powers to use military force. ...

The text, structure and history of the Constitution establish that the Founders entrusted the President with the primary responsibility, and therefore the power, to use military force in situations of emergency. Article II, Section 2 states that the "President shall be Commander in Chief of the Army and Navy of the United States, and of the Militia of the several States, when called into the actual Service of the United States." U.S. Const. art. II, § 2, cl. 1. He is further vested with all of "the executive Power" and the duty to execute the laws. U.S. Const. art. II, § 1. These powers give the President broad constitutional authority to use military force in response to threats to the national security and foreign policy of the United States.

By their terms, these provisions vest full control of the military forces of the United States in the President. The power of the President is at its zenith under the Constitution when the President is directing military operations of the armed forces, because the power of Commander in Chief is assigned solely to the President. It has long been the view of this Office that the Commander-in-Chief Clause is a substantive grant of authority to the President and that the scope of the President's authority to commit the armed forces to combat is very broad. ... The

President's complete discretion in exercising the Commander-in-Chief power has also been recognized by the courts. In the *Prize Cases* ... for example, the Court explained that, whether the President "in fulfilling his duties as Commander in Chief" had met with a situation justifying treating the southern States as belligerents and instituting a blockade, was a question "to be *decided by him*" and which the Court could not question, but must leave to "the political department of the Government to which this power was entrusted."

Some commentators have read the constitutional text differently. They argue that the vesting of the power to declare war gives Congress the sole authority to decide whether to make war. This view misreads the constitutional text and misunderstands the nature of a declaration of war. Declaring war is not tantamount to making war—indeed, the Constitutional Convention specifically amended the working draft of the Constitution that had given Congress the power to make war. An earlier draft of the Constitution had given to Congress the power to "make" war. When it took up this clause on August 17, 1787, the Convention voted to change the clause from "make" to "declare." ... A supporter of the change argued that it would "leav[e] to the Executive the power to repel sudden attacks." ... If the Framers had wanted to require congressional consent before the initiation of military hostilities, they knew how to write such provisions.

Finally, the Framing generation well understood that declarations of war were obsolete.... Instead of serving as an authorization to begin hostilities, a declaration of war was only necessary to "perfect" a conflict under international law.... Given this context, it is clear that Congress's power to declare war does not constrain the President's independent and plenary constitutional authority over the use of military force....

Our reading of the text is reinforced by analysis of the constitutional structure. First, it is clear that the Constitution secures all federal executive power in the President to ensure a unity in purpose and energy in action.... The centralization of authority in the President alone is particularly crucial in matters of national defense, war, and foreign policy ... "[o]f all the cares or concerns of government, the direction of war most peculiarly demands those qualities which distinguish the exercise of power by a single hand." Federalist No. 74....

Second, the Constitution makes clear that the process used for conducting military hostilities is different from other government decision-making. In the area of domestic legislation, the Constitution creates a detailed, finely wrought procedure in which Congress plays the central role. In foreign affairs, however, the Constitution does not establish a mandatory, detailed, Congress-driven procedure for taking action. Rather, the Constitution vests the two branches with different powers—the President as Commander in Chief, Congress with control over funding and declaring war—without requiring that they follow a specific process in making war. By establishing this framework, the Framers expected that the process for war-making would be far more flexible, and capable of quicker, more decisive action, than the legislative process. Thus, the President may use his Commander-in-Chief and executive powers to use military force to protect the Nation, subject to congressional appropriations and control over domestic legislation.

Third, the constitutional structure requires that any ambiguities in the allocation of a power that is executive in nature—such as the power to conduct military hostilities—must be resolved in favor of the executive branch. Article II, section I provides that "[t]he executive Power shall be vested in a President of the United States." . . . By contrast, Article I's Vesting Clause gives Congress only the powers "herein granted." . . . This difference in language indicates that Congress's legislative powers are limited to the list enumerated in Article I, section 8, while the President's powers include inherent executive powers that are unenumerated in the Constitution . . .

There can be little doubt that the decision to deploy military force is "executive" in nature. . . . It calls for action and energy in execution, rather than the deliberate formulation of rules to govern the conduct of private individuals. Moreover, the Framers understood it to be an attribute of the executive. "The direction of war implies the direction of the common strength," wrote Alexander Hamilton, "and the power of directing and employing the common strength forms a usual and essential part in the definition of the executive authority." The Federalist No. 74. . . . As a result, to the extent that the constitutional text does not explicitly allocate the power to initiate military hostilities to a particular branch, the Vesting Clause provides that it remain among the President's unenumerated powers.

Fourth, depriving the President of the power to decide when to use military force would disrupt the basic constitutional framework of foreign relations. From the very beginnings of the Republic, the vesting of the executive, Commander-in-Chief, and treaty powers in the executive branch has been understood to grant the President plenary control over the conduct of foreign relations. . . .

In the relatively few occasions where it has addressed foreign affairs, the Supreme Court has agreed with the executive branch's consistent interpretation. Conducting foreign affairs and protecting the national security are, as the Supreme Court has observed, "'central Presidential domains.'" . . . This foreign affairs power is exclusive: it is "the very delicate, plenary and exclusive power of the President as sole organ of the federal government in the field of international relations—a power which does not require as a basis for its exercise an act of Congress." *United States v. Curtiss-Wright Export Corp.*, 299 U.S. 304, 320 (1936).

Conducting military hostilities is a central tool for the exercise of the President's plenary control over the conduct of foreign policy. There can be no doubt that the use of force protects the Nation's security and helps it achieve its foreign policy goals. Construing the Constitution to grant such power to another branch could prevent the President from exercising his core constitutional responsibilities in foreign affairs....

Attorney General (later Justice) Robert Jackson formulated the classic statement of the executive branch's understanding of the President's military powers in 1941:

> Article II, section 2, of the Constitution provides that the President "shall be Commander in Chief of the Army and Navy of the United States." By virtue of this constitutional office he has supreme command over the land and naval forces of the country and may order them to perform such military duties as, in his opinion, are necessary or appropriate for the defense of the United States. These powers exist in time of peace as well as in time of war....
>
> Thus the President's responsibility as Commander in Chief embraces the authority to command and direct the armed forces in their immediate movements and operations designed to protect the security and effectuate the defense of the United States.... [T]his authority undoubtedly includes the power to dispose of troops and equipment in such manner and on such duties as best to promote the safety of the country. (*Training of British Flying Students in the United States,* 40 Op. Att'y Gen. 58, 61–62 [1941])

Other Attorneys General have defended similar accounts of the President constitutional powers and duties, particularly in times of unforeseen emergencies....

[The OLC] has taken the position in recent Administrations ... that the President may unilaterally deploy military force in order to protect the national security and interests of the United States ... [e.g., in Bosnia, and Haiti]....

> In 1940, after the fall of Denmark to Germany, President Franklin Roosevelt ordered United States troops to occupy Greenland, a Danish possession in the North Atlantic of vital strategic interest to the United States.... Congress was not consulted or even directly informed.... Later, in 1941, the President ordered United States troops to occupy Iceland, an independent nation, pursuant to an agreement between himself and the Prime Minister of Iceland. The President relied upon his authority as Commander in Chief, and notified Congress only after the event.... [quoted from previous Office of Legal Counsel opinion]
>
> From the instructions of President Jefferson's Administration to Commodore Richard Dale in 1801 to 'chastise' Algiers and Tripoli[50] if they continued to attack American shipping, to the present, Presidents have taken military initiatives abroad on the basis of their constitutional authority.... [quoting from previous OLC opinion] ...

Judicial decisions since the beginning of the Republic confirm the President's constitutional power and duty to repel military action against the United States through the use of force, and to take measures to deter the recurrence of an attack. As Justice Joseph Story said long ago, "[i]t may be fit and proper for the government, in the exercise of the high discretion confided to the executive, for great public purposes, to act on a sudden emergency, or to prevent an irreparable mischief, by summary measures, which are not found in the text of the laws." *The Apollon* (1824)....

If the President is confronted with an unforeseen attack on the territory and people of the United States, or other immediate, dangerous threat to American interests and security, the courts have affirmed that it is his constitutional responsibility to respond to that threat with whatever means are necessary, including the use of military force abroad. *See, e.g., Prize Cases* ... ("If a war be made by invasion of a foreign nation, the President is not only authorized but bound to resist force by force ... without waiting for any special legislative authority.")....

The historical practice of all three branches confirms the lessons of the constitutional text and structure. The normative role of historical practice in constitutional law, and especially with regard to separation of powers, is well settled. Both the Supreme Court and the political branches have often recognized that governmental practice plays a highly significant role in establishing the contours of the constitutional separation of powers: "a systematic, unbroken, executive practice, long pursued to the knowledge of the Congress and never before questioned ... may be treated as a gloss on 'executive Power' vested in the President by § 1 of Art. II." *Youngstown Sheet & Tube Co.,* 343 U.S. at 610–11 (Frankfurter, J., concurring)....

The historical record demonstrates that the power to initiate military hostilities, particularly in response to the threat of an armed attack, rests exclusively with the President. As the Supreme Court has observed, "[t]he United States frequently employs Armed Forces outside this country—over 200 times in our history—for the protection of American citizens or national security." *United States v. Verdugo-Urquidez....* On at least 125 such occasions, the President acted without prior express authorization from Congress.... Perhaps the most significant deployment without specific statutory authorization took place at the time of the Korean War, when President Truman, without prior authorization from Congress, deployed United States troops in a war that lasted for over three years and caused over 142,000 American casualties....

Further, when Congress has in fact authorized deployments of troops in hostilities, past Presidents have taken the position that such legislation, although welcome, was not constitutionally necessary....

[W]e think it clear that Congress, in enacting the [AUMF] ... has confirmed that the President has broad constitutional authority to respond, by military means or otherwise, to the incidents of September 11.

First, the findings in the Joint Resolution include an express statement that "the President has authority under the Constitution to take action to deter and prevent acts of international terrorism against the United States." This authority is in addition to the President's authority to respond to *past* acts of terrorism. In including this statement, Congress has provided its explicit agreement with the executive branch's consistent position, as articulated in . . . this memorandum, that the President has the plenary power to use force even before an attack upon the United States actually occurs, against targets and using methods of his own choosing. . . .

The Constitution confides in the President the authority, independent of any statute, to determine when a "national emergency" caused by an attack on the United States exists. Nonetheless, congressional concurrence is welcome in making clear that the branches agree on [the] seriousness of the terrorist threat currently facing the Nation and on the justifiability of a military response.

. . . [I]t should be noted here that the Joint Resolution is somewhat narrower than the President's constitutional authority. The Joint Resolution's authorization to use force is limited only to those individuals, groups, or states that planned, authorized, committed, or aided the attacks, and those nations that harbored them. It does not, therefore, reach other terrorist individuals, groups, or states, which cannot be determined to have links to the September 11 attacks. Nonetheless, the President's broad constitutional power to use military force to defend the Nation . . . would allow the President to take whatever actions he deems appropriate to pre-empt or respond to terrorist threats from new quarters.

Conclusion

In light of the text, plan, and history of the Constitution, its interpretation by both past Administrations and the courts, the longstanding practice of the executive branch, and the express affirmation of the President's constitutional authorities by Congress, we think it beyond question that the President has the plenary constitutional power to take such military actions as he deems necessary and appropriate to respond to the terrorist attacks upon the United States on September 11, 2001. Force can be used both to retaliate for those attacks, and to prevent and deter future assaults on the Nation. Military actions need not be limited to those individuals, groups, or states that participated in the attacks on the World Trade Center and the Pentagon: the Constitution vests the President with the power to strike terrorist groups or organizations that cannot be demonstrably linked to the September 11 incidents, but that, nonetheless, pose a similar threat to the security of the United States and the lives of its people, whether at home or overseas. In both the War Powers Resolution and the Joint Resolution, Congress has recognized the President's authority to use force in circumstances such as those created by the September 11 incidents. Neither statute, however, can place any limits on the

President's determinations as to any terrorist threat, the amount of military force to be used in response, or the method, timing, and nature of the response. These decisions, under our Constitution, are for the President alone to make.

John C. Yoo
Deputy Assistant Attorney General
Office of Legal Counsel

Yoo offers a number of arguments to support his central assertion that the authority to use military force belongs exclusively to the president, including that (1) the Commander in Chief Clause "is a substantive grant of authority to the President" assigning broad control over the military, including authority "to commit the armed forces to combat"; (2) Article I's declare war clause does not give Congress the authority to authorize the use of military force; (3) the Supreme Court has recognized the president as the "sole organ of the federal government in the field of international relations"; and (4) "[on] at least 125 . . . occasions," presidents have acted unilaterally to use military force.

One striking aspect of Yoo's analysis is his decision to disregard contrary authority. Lawyers would say that his analysis reads more like a "brief," meaning a piece of advocacy, than a "memorandum" (despite its title), typically meaning an analysis that takes opposing or conflicting views into account and considers the merits of all views. Some defend Yoo's choice: the law professors Eric A. Posner and Adrian Vermeule have argued that the conception of the Office of Legal Counsel as an objective dispenser of constitutional analysis is misguided as OLC's "jurisprudence has traditionally been pro-executive."[51] Another law professor, Jack Balkin, disagrees, countering that "the purpose of the OLC is [not] to push a particular ideological agenda heedless of any larger responsibilities to the Nation as a whole."[52] Was Yoo right to construct this document as a piece of advocacy, or was he wrong to omit authority that might contradict his conclusions? What factors might have guided Yoo's decision on this point?

If Yoo had considered contrary authority, there would be significant examples to confront. First, on his assertion that the Commander in Chief Clause provides the president with "substantive" authority, meaning something beyond the mere authority to act as civilian commander of the military, recall that Justice Jackson's concurring opinion in *Youngstown* had cautioned that:

These cryptic words [in the Commander in Chief Clause] have given rise to some of the most persistent controversies in our constitutional history. Of course, they imply something more than an empty title. But just what authority goes with the name has plagued presidential advisers who would not waive or narrow it by nonassertion, yet cannot say where it begins or ends. It undoubtedly puts the Nation's armed forces under presidential command. Hence, this loose appellation is sometimes advanced as support for any presidential action, internal or external, involving use of force, the idea being that it vests power to do anything, anywhere, that can be done with an army or navy. . . . I cannot foresee all that it might entail if the Court should indorse this argument. Nothing in our Constitution is plainer than that declaration of a war is entrusted only to Congress. Of course, a state of war may, in fact, exist without a formal declaration. But no doctrine that the Court could promulgate would seem to me more sinister and alarming than that a President whose conduct of foreign affairs is so largely uncontrolled, and often even is unknown, can vastly enlarge his mastery over the internal affairs of the country by his own commitment of the Nation's armed forces to some foreign venture.[53]

Yoo's analysis simply avoids discussion of Jackson's *Youngstown* opinion. That need not be a fatal error—the Supreme Court may make mistakes, too, and perhaps Yoo simply believed Jackson's opinion was not correct or not useful. Moreover, if Yoo had confronted Jackson's concurring opinion in *Youngstown* when discussing the meaning of the Commander in Chief Clause, he could have pointed out that Jackson's analysis emphasizes a distinction between foreign and domestic affairs and asserts that presidential authority to use the military outside the United States is entitled to "the widest latitude of interpretation."[54] However, addressing Jackson's opinion in *Youngstown* would have meant discussing the tripartite framework that emphasizes joint presidential-congressional action as the soundest basis for the exercise of power. Given that Yoo's unitary executive theory emphasizes presidential supremacy, Yoo might have decided that the best choice was simply to leave Jackson's opinion out of his analysis. When Yoo does cite Jackson as an authority, he cites an opinion Jackson wrote as attorney general before he joined the Supreme Court.

Although Yoo does not seek to exploit Jackson's distinction between presidential authority when it comes to foreign affairs as opposed to the domestic sphere, he does cite another source to make this point: the

Supreme Court's 1936 *Curtiss-Wright* opinion and the "sole organ" doctrine. But Yoo fails to note criticism—that language in *Curtiss-Wright* regarding plenary executive control over foreign affairs was merely dicta not having precedential value and that the sole organ doctrine itself depends on a misunderstanding of history. As discussed in chapter 5, the term itself comes from a speech that then-Congressman John Marshall gave in defense of President John Adams's decision to extradite a murder suspect to England pursuant to a treaty. Marshall argued that the president was the sole organ of the nation in carrying out the treaty, as ratified by the Senate. Marshall did not suggest that the president possessed plenary or exclusive power over foreign affairs.[55]

The text of the Constitution seems to offer a substantial obstacle to Yoo's conclusions: how can the president have unilateral authority to deploy military force when Article I assigns Congress the power "[t]o declare war"?[56] Yoo emphasizes debate at the 1787 Convention that produced the Constitution. Originally, Congress was to be assigned the power to "make" war, but this was changed to give Congress the power to "declare" war. Yoo cites this as evidence that the Framers did not mean "to require congressional consent before the initiation of military hostilities [by the president]."[57] However, debate records do not support this conclusion: When James Madison and Elbridge Gerry moved to insert the word "declare" in place of "make," debate records indicate that this change would "leav[e] to the Executive the power to repel sudden attacks." Another delegate commented that this was a useful change as "[t]he Executive sh[oul]d be able to repel and not to commence attacks."[58] Lou Fisher flatly states that it was "never the understanding" that, "although Congress may "declare war," the president is at liberty to "make" war."[59] In fact, "such an interpretation would defeat everything the framers said about Congress being the only political body authorized to take the country from a state of peace to a state of war."[60] M. Andrew Campanelli, Kai Draper, and Jack Stucker agree with Fisher that, "John Yoo's arguments to the contrary notwithstanding, there is compelling evidence that most, if not all, [of the Framers and ratifiers of the Constitution] believed that, in virtue of its Declare War Clause, the Constitution vests the power to create war in Congress alone."[61] The historian Jack Rakove concludes that it is not clear precisely what changing the verb "make" to "declare" meant, but he suggests that it was intended to "preserve the capacity of the president to wage war [in the sense of directing operations] with the essential attributes of energy and dispatch."[62] Other scholars conclude that the Framers meant to provide the president with authority to repel sudden attacks,[63] a point emphasized in the *Prize Cases*[64] (though Yoo cites the *Prize Cases* for the broader proposition that it is the president who decides when and how to use military force).

James Pfiffner concludes that "Yoo's arguments that the framers intended to give the war powers to the executive stretch the text of the Constitution and the deliberations of the framers beyond reasonable interpretations."[65] Pfiffner points to the writings of Jay, Madison, and Hamilton. In Federalist No. 4, Jay warned that it was dangerous to entrust executives with war power, citing the example of "[a]bsolute monarchs [who] will often make war when their nations are to get nothing by it, but for purposes and objects merely personal, such as a thirst for military glory, revenge for personal affronts, ambition, or private compacts to aggrandize or support their particular families or partisans."[66] Madison echoed Jay, describing the danger that the promise of military glory could entice executives to war.[67] In 1793, Madison concluded that "[t]hose who are to *conduct* war cannot, in the nature of things, be proper or safe judges, whether a war ought to be *commenced, continued,* or *concluded.*"[68] Madison's words reflected the Framers' decision to reject the British model and, instead, to divide war power and power over foreign affairs between the president and Congress.[69]

Even Hamilton, whom Yoo cites in his September 25, 2001, memo for the proposition that "energy" is required in an executive who can defend the nation, can be cited to counter Yoo's conclusions. Pfiffner notes that, in 1801, Hamilton explained that, under the Constitution, "[t]he Congress shall have power to declare war, the Plain meaning of which is, that it is in the peculiar and exclusive province of Congress, *when the nation is at peace* to change that state into a state of war."[70] Though, as Yoo notes, Hamilton emphasized the need for an executive who could act to defend the nation, especially during an emergency, in Federalist No. 69, Hamilton also made clear that the president is not a king:

> The President is to be commander-in-chief of the army and navy of the United States. In this respect his authority would be nominally the same with that of the king of Great Britain, but in substance much inferior to it. It would amount to nothing more than the supreme command and direction of the military and naval forces, as first General and admiral of the Confederacy; while that of the British king extends to the *declaring* of war and to the *raising* and *regulating* of fleets and armies—all which, by the Constitution under consideration, would appertain to the legislature.[71]

If Yoo had confronted these opposing points of view, he could, of course, have offered reasons to disagree. One point he might emphasize—and a point he does, in fact, emphasize in his analysis (though not in response to the objections noted in the preceding paragraphs) is the importance of past presidential practice.[72] Yoo claims that "[t]he historical record demonstrates that the power to initiate military hostilities, particularly in response to the threat of an armed attack, rests exclusively with the president."[73] He notes that, "[o]n at least 125 . . . occasions, the President acted without prior express authorization from Congress. . . . Such deployments, based on the President's constitutional authority alone, have occurred since the Administration of George Washington."[74] Yoo singles out President Truman's unilateral decision to deploy U.S. troops in the Korean War as a particular example. However, Louis Fisher describes Truman's decision as a "violation of constitutional and statutory requirements."[75] Truman relied on United Nations Security Council resolutions rather than on congressional authorization as the basis for his actions, but Fisher notes that "UN machinery is not a legal substitute for congressional authority."[76] The Constitution assigns Congress war-making power, and the UN Charter did not and could not override the Constitution.[77] As for Yoo's reference to the more than 125 occasions when presidents have unilaterally ordered the use of military force, Fisher observes that Truman's supporters made a similar argument, but those occasions involved small-scale actions—chasing bandits or cattle rustlers, fighting pirates.[78]

Is Yoo right to cite historic presidential practice as precedent to define the scope of presidential war power? Pfiffner offers this cautionary note: "[d]espite the historical reality that presidents have often dominated national security policy, repeated violation of the provisions of the Constitution do not make them constitutional."[79] Yoo counters that, especially because there are so few Supreme Court decisions defining presidential power, past presidential practice must play an important role "as a source of constitutional meaning."[80] Eric A. Posner and Adrian Vermeule agree that "customary practices are a source of law."[81] Scott M. Matheson Jr., who is a critic of the Bush administration's use of power, also agrees that "[d]uring the course of expounding the Constitution and executive power, longstanding historical practice has been influential in separation of powers disputes."[82] What role should presidential practice play in defining the scope and limits of power? Is Yoo's reliance on specific presidential actions persuasive? For instance, Yoo cites the *Prize Cases* decision and President Clinton's decision to order a cruise missile strike against what he said were Al Qaeda–related facilities in Afghanistan and Sudan after a terrorist attack on U.S. embassies in 1998. Do these examples provide support for Yoo's conclusions about presidential power?

Yoo's September 25, 2001, memo was the first of several that made the case for broad presidential power justified by the unitary executive theory in the context of conducting the "war on terror." His analysis was limited to the decision to use military force abroad to defend the United States. However, the principle of unilateral executive authority was applied to a number of other areas, including the detention of suspected terrorists, which we'll discuss next.

10

DETAINING AND TRYING SUSPECTED TERRORISTS

John Yoo's argument that the president possesses plenary authority to make all decisions regarding the use of military force had consequences that went beyond the immediate decision to send troops to Afghanistan in October 2001. Conducting the "war on terror" also meant detaining suspected terrorists and gathering, through interrogation, information to prevent future attacks. Emergency presidential power might apply in each of these areas, as each involves threats to national security. If, as Yoo concluded, decisions regarding the use of military force were for the president alone, would that mean the president could unilaterally decide what to do in these areas too?

Questions arose as suspected terrorists were captured in Afghanistan and elsewhere: would they receive trials in civilian courts? If not, what procedures would be used? Would they be tried before military tribunals, like the Nazi saboteurs in *Quirin*? If so, what rules would apply? Could they be held indefinitely, without charges, as the CIA interrogated them to gather information that might prevent future terrorist attacks? Who would make these decisions, and what role, if any, would Congress and the courts play?

In past conflicts, distinctions have been made between lawful enemy combatants—soldiers in uniform captured on the battlefield—and unlawful enemy combatants, spies out of uniform, saboteurs, or soldiers in uniform who violated the laws of war (e.g., by mistreating civilians or prisoners of war). The court's decision in *Quirin* discussed this distinction, and the Geneva Conventions adopted after World War II recognized a similar distinction. Traditionally, lawful enemy combatants were prisoners of war (POWs) who could be held for the duration of the conflict and who would be repatriated when hostilities ended. POWs could not be punished or put on trial. Unlawful enemy combatants, by contrast, who had violated the laws of war, could be tried before military tribunals and sentenced to prison or even executed, like the saboteurs in *Quirin*. Of course, as we saw in *Quirin*, there were still questions about how such military trials should take place, who should make the rules, and who defines violations of the laws of war.

The Geneva Conventions adopted in 1949 and ratified by the United States in 1955 provide specific guidance about classifying enemy combatants. Under Article 4 of the Geneva Convention Relative to the Treatment of Prisoners of War (GPW), captured combatants are entitled to prisoner-of-war status if they are members of traditional enemy armed forces or if they are members of "militias and members of other volunteer corps, including those of organized resistance movements" who satisfy four conditions: "(a) That of being commanded by a person responsible for his subordinates; (b) That of having a fixed distinctive sign recognizable at a distance; (c) That of carrying arms openly; (d) That of conducting their operations in accordance with the laws and customs of war."[1] The GPW further provides that "Should any doubt arise as to whether persons, having committed a belligerent act and having fallen into the hands of the enemy, belong to any of the categories enumerated in Article 4, such persons shall enjoy the protection of the present Convention until such time as their status has been determined by a competent tribunal."[2]

Prisoners of war are entitled to specific protections under the GPW, including the right to "humane treat[ment]," protection "against acts of violence or intimidation and against insults and public curiosity," and the right to refuse to respond to questioning and interrogation.[3] Relatedly, "[n]o physical or mental torture, nor any other form of coercion, may be inflicted on prisoners of war to secure from them information of any kind whatever. Prisoners of war who refuse to answer may not be threatened, insulted, or exposed to any unpleasant or disadvantageous treatment of any kind."[4]

The Geneva Conventions also provide protections for captured combatants who do not qualify for POW status. Common Article 3 (so-called because it is included in each of the four Geneva Conventions of 1949), provides as follows:

> In the case of armed conflict not of an international character[5] occurring in the territory of one of the High Contracting Parties, each Party to the conflict shall be bound to apply, as a minimum, the following provisions:

(1) Persons taking no active part in the hostilities, including members of armed forces who have laid down their arms and those placed hors de combat by sickness, wounds, detention, or any other cause, shall in all circumstances be treated humanely, without any adverse distinction founded on race, colour, religion or faith, sex, birth or wealth, or any other similar criteria.

To this end, the following acts are and shall remain prohibited at any time and in any place whatsoever with respect to the above-mentioned persons:

(a) violence to life and person, in particular murder of all kinds, mutilation, cruel treatment and torture;

(b) taking of hostages;

(c) outrages upon personal dignity, in particular humiliating and degrading treatment;

(d) the passing of sentences and the carrying out of executions without previous judgement pronounced by a regularly constituted court, affording all the judicial guarantees which are recognized as indispensable by civilized peoples.

As we'll see, the U.S. Supreme Court ultimately ruled that Common Article 3 applies to suspected terrorists detained and tried by the United States.

The undeclared war on terror presented new problems—it wasn't obvious how to fit prisoners[6] into the traditional enemy combatant framework, which was better suited to traditional wars between nations involving soldiers fighting in uniform on battlefields. Members of Al Qaeda or other terrorist groups do not wear uniforms, they do not fight for a nation, and they generally do not fight on a traditional battlefield. Taliban fighters may more closely match the traditional model, as they fight or fought for the government of Afghanistan. However, the Taliban was not recognized as the official government of Afghanistan by the United Nations, and Taliban fighters do not wear uniforms or other "distinctive signs," often blending in with the civilian population. In addition, even if Taliban fighters or even Al Qaeda members were classified as POWs, they could likely be held for years, even indefinitely, as the undeclared war on terrorism has no foreseeable end date. Finally, classifying prisoners as POWs would interfere with plans to interrogate them and, it was hoped, to gain information that would prevent future terrorist attacks.

The fact that Taliban fighters and members of Al Qaeda do not wear uniforms also creates another problem. In traditional wars, it was (usually) comparatively easy to identify enemy soldiers, as they wore uniforms; even if they didn't (like the saboteurs in *Quirin*), they could usually be identified as agents of an opposing army. Suspected terrorists are much more difficult to classify. Problems may arise as to whether they are combatants at all or, instead, have been misidentified and were not engaged in any belligerent conduct.

One way to resolve the dilemma of what to do with suspected terrorists would have been to place them in the civilian justice system, charging them with statutory crimes and imprisoning them if convicted. In fact, this approach has been used for a number of suspected terrorists, many of whom have been convicted.[7] However, the Bush administration decided that hundreds of prisoners would be held by the military, and the Obama administration has continued that practice, at least for prisoners captured during the Bush years.

The OLC, in another memo—this time, drafted by Yoo's colleague Patrick Philbin—provided legal analysis justifying presidential authority to detain suspected terrorists in the military system. The November 2001 memo concluded that suspected terrorists need not be treated as prisoners of war or given access to civilian courts. The president would have the sole authority to institute procedures for their trial before a military tribunal and could decide to hold them indefinitely without access to civilian courts. As John Yoo had done in his memo, Philbin acknowledged that Congress had passed a law (the Uniform Code of Military Justice) authorizing the president to set up military tribunals—but, even if Congress had not done this, Philbin concluded that the president had the power to take this step unilaterally, with or without Congress's approval. In other words, the president's emergency powers included the authority to create a detention system for suspected terrorists. As with decisions about how to wage war, in Philbin's view, the president's authority to create a system for holding and trying suspected terrorists was final and unreviewable. Excerpts from Philbin's November 2001 memo follow.

Legality of the Use of Military Commissions to Try Terrorists

The President possesses inherent authority under the Constitution, as Chief Executive and Commander in Chief of the Armed Forces of the United States, to establish military commissions to try and punish terrorists captured in connection with the attacks of September 11 or in connection with U.S. military operations in response to those attacks.

November 6, 2001

Memorandum Opinion for the Counsel to the President

You have asked us to consider whether terrorists[8] captured in connection with the attacks of September 11 or in connection with ongoing U.S. operations in response to those attacks could be subject to trial before a military court....

We conclude that under [statutory authority] and his inherent powers as Commander in Chief, the President may establish military commissions to try and punish terrorists apprehended as part of the investigation into, or the military and intelligence operations in response to, the September 11 attacks. The President both has inherent authority as Commander in Chief to convene military commissions and has received authorization from Congress for their use to the full extent permitted by past executive practice.... [W]hether the laws of war apply in this context is a political question for the President to determine in his role as Commander in Chief....

Background

A military commission is a form of military tribunal typically used in three scenarios: (i) to try individuals (usually members of enemy forces) for violations of the laws of war; (ii) as a general court administering justice in occupied territory; and (iii) as a general court in an area where martial law has been declared and the civil courts are closed.... The commission ... consists of a board of officers who sit as adjudicators without a jury. The commission's decision is subject to review by the convening authority and is not subject to direct judicial review.

Military commissions have been used throughout U.S. history to prosecute violators of the laws of war.... Military commissions have tried offenders drawn from the ranks of aliens and citizens alike charged with war crimes arising as early as the Revolutionary War, the Mexican-American War, and the Civil War, and as recently as World War II....

Military commissions are not courts within Article III of the Constitution, nor are they subject to the jury trial requirements of the Fifth and Sixth Amendments of the Constitution.... Unlike Article III courts, the powers of military commissions are derived not from statute, but from the laws of war.... That is, their authority derives from the Constitution's vesting of the power of Commander in Chief in the President....

The Uniform Code of Military Justice (UCMJ) expressly addresses the use of military commissions in article 21[9] ... that provision contains an explicit congressional authorization for military commissions ... [but] even if Congress had not sanctioned the use of military commissions to try all offenses against the laws of war, the President, exercising his authority as Commander in Chief, could order the creation of military commissions to try such offenses....

The history of the provision [in the UCMJ regarding military commissions] also makes it abundantly clear that its purpose was to express congressional approval for the traditional use of military commissions under past practice . . . [T]he fact that military commissions were used long before any reference to them appeared in the Articles of War demonstrates that the President has authority as Commander in Chief to create them without authorization (and free from any restriction) of Congress. . . . The statute, in other words, simply endorses and incorporates by reference executive branch practice. . . .

Indeed, if [the UCMJ] were read as restricting the use of military commissions and prohibiting practices traditionally followed, it would infringe on the President's express constitutional powers as Commander in Chief. . . .

The congressional sanction for the use of military commissions is a permissible exercise of Congress's powers under the Constitution. . . . Or, to be more precise, it is permissible at least so long as any congressional regulations do not interfere with the President's authority as Commander in Chief. . . .

The congressional authorization for military commissions in 10 U.S.C. § 821 endorses sufficiently broad jurisdiction for the commissions that there will likely be no need to rely solely on the President's inherent authority as Commander in Chief to convene commissions in the present circumstances. As noted above, Congress has endorsed the pre-existing practice of permitting military commissions to try "all offenses which are defined as such by the law of war." . . . It is important, nevertheless, to note that the President has inherent authority as Commander in Chief to convene such tribunals even without authorization from Congress. . . .

The Commander in Chief Clause . . . vests in the President the full powers necessary to prosecute successfully a military campaign. It has long been understood that the Constitution provides the federal government all powers necessary for the execution of the duties the Constitution describes. . . .

It was well recognized at the time of the Founding, moreover, that one of the powers inherent in military command was the authority to institute tribunals for punishing violations of the laws of war by the enemy. In 1780, during the Revolutionary War, General Washington as Commander in Chief of the Continental Army appointed a "Board of General Officers" to try the British Major André as a spy. . . . At the time, there was no provision in the American Articles of War providing for jurisdiction in a court-martial to try an enemy for the offense of spying.[10] . . . The term "Commander in Chief" was understood in Anglo-American constitutional thought as incorporating the fullest possible range of power available to a military commander. See John Yoo, *The Continuation of Politics by Other Means: The Original Understanding of War Powers*, 84 Calif. L. Rev. 167, 252–54 (1996). In investing the President with full authority as Commander in Chief, the drafters of the Constitution surely intended to give the President the same authority that General

Washington possessed during the Revolutionary War to convene military tribunals to punish offenses against the laws of war. . . .

The history of military commissions bears out this conclusion, because as a matter of practice military commissions have been created under the President's inherent authority as Commander in Chief without any authorization from Congress. . . . [A]fter the outbreak of the Civil War, military commissions were convened to try offenses against the laws of war. . . . It was not until 1863 that military commissions were even mentioned in a statute enacted by Congress. In that year, Congress authorized the use of military commissions to try members of the military for certain offenses committed during time of war. . . . The statute, moreover, did not purport to *create* military commissions. Rather, it acknowledged that they could be used as alternatives to courts martial in some cases.

As explained above, the current provision in section 821 of the UCMJ also does not *create* military commissions or define exhaustively their authority. Instead, its history shows that it was adopted to preserve the jurisdiction of what was recognized as a pre-existing tribunal. . . . Precisely because it confirms that military commissions existed before any express congressional authorization, the history of section 821 also supports the conclusion that the President has constitutional authority to convene commissions even without legislation authorizing them. . . .

An opinion of the Attorney General issued at the end of the Civil War supports the same conclusion. In 1865, Attorney General Speed addressed the use of military commissions to try those accused in the plot to assassinate President Lincoln and explained that even if Congress had not provided for the creation of military commissions, they could be instituted by military commanders as an inherent incident of their authority to wage the military campaign. . . .

The Supreme Court has never squarely addressed the question whether the President may convene military commissions wholly without congressional authorization. In *Quirin*, the Court expressly declined to decide "to what extent the President as Commander in Chief has constitutional power to create military commissions without the support of Congressional legislation." . . . And in later cases the Court has remained uncommitted. . . .

For the reasons outlined above, we conclude that the best understanding of the Constitution is that the President does have the power, as Commander in Chief, to create military commissions to try enemy belligerents for offenses against the laws of war even in the absence of the congressional sanction for their use. . . .

The most likely constitutional issue to be raised concerning military commissions would be an objection to the denial of the rights to trial by jury in criminal cases and grand jury indictment as provided in Article III, Section 2 and the Fifth and Sixth Amendments. Such objections would most likely be raised with respect to military commissions convened within the territorial United States, and we address them in that context. We believe that if a particular use of military commissions to try offenses against the laws of war is constitutionally permissible within the United States, it follows *a fortiori*[11] that such a use is permissible to deal with enemy belligerents overseas, where many constitutional protections would not apply in any event.

It has long been settled that the guarantees to trial by jury in criminal cases contained in the Constitution were not intended to *expand* the rights to these procedures beyond those that existed at common law. . . . Thus, petty offenses triable at common law without a jury may be tried without a jury under the Constitution. . . . The Fifth Amendment right to grand jury indictment similarly arises out of the common law. . . .

At the time of the Founding, it was well settled that offenses under the laws of war were a distinct category of offense, unlike criminal offenses against the civil law, and were subject to trial in military tribunals without the benefits of the procedures of the common law enshrined in the Constitution. The Articles of War of 1776, for example, made it clear that courts-martial could be convened to try offenders under the Articles without a jury or grand jury. . . . Indeed, throughout the Revolutionary War, military tribunals were used to try offenders without a jury. . . . The text of the Constitution itself makes the distinct nature of military tribunals clear, as the Fifth Amendment expressly excludes "cases arising in the land or naval forces" from the guarantee of a grand jury indictment. . . . Precisely because military discipline was viewed as wholly apart from the ordinary criminal law and the provisions in the Constitution relating to it, the Supreme Court has long recognized that military commissions do not exercise judicial power under Article III and are not subject to judicial review. . . . Thus, under the settled understanding that the rights to jury trial and grand jury indictment do not extend beyond the cases where they were available at common law, those rights simply do not extend to trials before military tribunals for offenses against the laws of war. . . .

The Supreme Court endorsed precisely this reasoning to reject constitutional challenges to the use of military commissions to try and execute violators of the laws of war during and after World War II. In *Quirin*, for example, eight German saboteurs were apprehended in the United States by the FBI, turned over to the military, tried by military commission, and sentenced to death. . . .

The Court concluded that there was no constitutional barrier to use of the military commission. As the Court explained, the guarantees in Article III and the Fifth and Sixth Amendments must be understood in light of the common law at the time of the Founding. . . .

The primary support for constitutional arguments to *restrict* the use of military commissions would be based on the Supreme Court's decision in *Ex parte Milligan*. . . . There, the Court held that a military commission could not be used to try a U.S. citizen in the United States for alleged violations of the laws of war, except in areas where martial law has been proclaimed and the civil courts are closed.... In *Milligan* ... the Court rejected the suggestion that the President had full authority to use military commissions to the extent permitted by the "'laws and usages of war.'" In the Court's view, the constitutional guarantees to trial by jury and indictment by grand jury in a capital case could not be denied by resort to a military commission. The Court held open the possibility that military commissions could be used to try citizens if martial law had properly been declared in the area, which could happen in times of invasion when the area in question was actually in the theater of military operations. As the Court put it, the "necessity must be actual and present; the invasion real, such as effectually closes the courts and deposes the civil administration." ...

We believe that the broad pronouncements in *Milligan* do not accurately reflect the requirements of the Constitution and that the case has properly been severely limited by the later decision in *Quirin*.... The [*Quirin*] Court ... ruled that the decision in *Milligan* must be understood "as having particular reference to the facts" of that case.... To explain the limitations on *Milligan*, two scenarios merit consideration here: (1) the use of military commissions to try U.S. citizens seized in the United States, and (2) the use of military commissions to try enemy aliens seized in the United States....

Quirin clearly establishes that U.S. citizens who act as belligerents may be tried by military commission for violations of the law of war ... the constitutional analysis in *Quirin* demonstrates that any person properly charged with a violation of the laws of war, regardless of citizenship or membership in the armed forces (of this country or another power), may be tried by military commission. The critical point for constitutional analysis is that a person properly charged with an offense against the laws of war has no right to an indictment or trial by jury under Article III or the Fifth and Sixth Amendments. Citizenship and membership in the military are not determinative factors for constitutional purposes. A person can properly be chargeable of an offense against the laws of war (such as spying), after all, without being in the armed forces of a belligerent nation. The critical distinction is the nature of the offense....

We caution, however, that applying this standard may raise some ambiguities. The *Milligan* decision holds out at least the possibility that some charges that may be articulated under the law of war (such as the charge of giving aid and comfort to the enemy used in *Milligan*) may not, in some circumstances, amount to acts of belligerency triable by military commission. Exactly which acts place a person in the category of an "enemy belligerent" under *Quirin* thus may be a subject of litigation....

Even if *Milligan* might raise litigation risks for the use of military commissions to try citizens, it should not raise the same difficulties for trying *aliens* charged with violations of the law of war. The *Milligan* Court repeatedly stressed the importance of citizenship in describing Milligan's rights, and even though the Supreme Court has extended many constitutional protections to aliens within the United States, the distinction between the rights of citizens and aliens, especially in times of war, retains vitality today. . . . Since the Alien Enemy Act of 1798 . . . it has been established that in times of declared war, the President may seize enemy aliens and intern or deport them. . . . As the Court in *Eisentrager* explained, since an alien citizen of an enemy nation may constitutionally be deprived of liberty by Executive action solely on the basis of his citizenship during time of war, "no reason is apparent why an alien enemy charged with having committed a crime should have greater immunities from Executive action." . . . As the Court concluded, the "Constitution does not confer a right of personal security or an immunity from military trial and punishment upon an alien enemy engaged in the hostile service of a government at war with the United States." . . . Although there is no "government at war" with the United States in the current scenario, we believe that the same constitutional analysis would surely apply to aliens who have entered the United States to carry on a terrorist war at the behest of any foreign power. . . .

As explained above, [the UCMJ] sanctions the full uses of the military commission established by custom and Executive practice in the United States military. That practice, as noted above, has permitted military commissions to try all offenses against the laws of war. . . . The critical question for determining whether military commissions can properly be used here, therefore, is whether the terrorist attacks have created a situation to which the laws of war apply. That is, are the terrorist acts subject to the laws of war at all, or are they solely criminal matters to be treated under the municipal criminal law of the United States or a particular State?

. . . [I]t would be difficult—or impossible—to articulate any precise multi-pronged legal "test" for determining whether a particular attack or set of circumstances constitutes "war" justifying application of the laws of war—or to use the modern terminology, whether it is an "armed conflict" justifying use of the "laws of armed conflict." As the Supreme Court recognized long ago, determining whether a "war" exists depends largely on pragmatic considerations [citing the *Prize Cases*]. . . . Precisely because it is a question that rests on pragmatic judgments that critically affect the national defense and vital matters of foreign policy, it is a determination that is properly left to the political branches, and particularly to the President . . . the courts should defer to a Presidential determination that the laws of armed conflict apply. . . . The scale of these [terrorist] attacks, the number of deaths they have caused, and the massive military response they have demanded makes it virtually self-evident that the present situation can be treated as an armed conflict subject to the laws of armed conflict. . . .

. . . We stress at the outset that determining that the terrorist attacks can be treated under the rubric of the "laws of war" does *not* mean that terrorists will receive the protections of the Geneva Conventions or the rights that the laws of war accord to lawful combatants. To the contrary, as the U.S. Army Field Manual

The Law of Land Warfare makes clear, persons who do not comply with the conditions prescribed for recognition as lawful combatants (which include wearing a fixed insignia and bearing arms openly) are not entitled to status as prisoners of war and may be punished for hostile acts in violation of the laws of armed conflict. The Supreme Court made the same distinction clear in *Quirin*: "By universal agreement and practice the law of war draws a distinction between . . . those who are lawful and unlawful combatants. . . . Unlawful combatants . . . are subject to trial and punishment by military tribunals for acts which render their belligerency unlawful." 317 U.S. at 30–31. . . .

. . ." [A]ll of the [terrorists'] hostile acts can be treated as violations of the laws of war. It is settled that any violation of the laws of war may be prosecuted as a "war crime." . . . Specific offenses here could include violations of the rule prohibiting "[u]se of civilian clothing by troops to conceal their military character," . . . the rule prohibiting "[f]iring on localities which are undefended and without military significance," . . . and the rule prohibiting deliberate targeting of civilian populations. . . .

/s/

PATRICK F. PHILBIN
Deputy Assistant Attorney General

According to Greek legend, whoever untied the complicated "Gordian knot" would rule all of Asia. It is said that Alexander the Great found a simple though unconventional, way to undo the knot—he used his sword. Philbin took a similar approach to several knotty questions associated with captured suspected terrorists: who decides how and where to try them? If military commissions are used, what rules must they follow? Who defines violations of the laws of war? Philbin suggested that Congress had granted the president authority to make each of these decisions through the Uniform Code of Military Justice, but he offered an alternative way to slice through each problem: the president, as commander in chief, had broad authority to make these decisions, regardless of what Congress or the courts say.

The unitary executive theory simplifies things, but it begs another question: does the Constitution either implicitly or inherently [12] assign the president the broad power Philbin claims? Philbin's argument relies heavily on the Supreme Court's decision in *Quirin*, a decision that has been subject to criticism, as discussed previously—though he acknowledges that *Quirin* did not recognize any unilateral presidential power to create military commissions. Philbin also points to the Major André trial and the trial of Lincoln's accused assassins before military commissions, arguing that these examples support the conclusion that the president may unilaterally convene such tribunals. Louis Fisher points to problems with each as precedent. With regard to Major André, Fisher observes that

> General George Washington did indeed appoint a Board of General Officers to try André as a spy, but anyone with a smattering of American history would know that you cannot derive presidential power from precedents set in 1780. There was no President at the time other than the presiding officer of the Continental Congress. There was not even an executive branch. There was one branch of government: the Continental Congress, exercising legislative, executive, and judicial powers.
>
> The Justice Department [in Philbin's memo] insisted "there was no provision in the American Articles of War providing for the jurisdiction in a court-martial to try an enemy for the offense of spying." [The Justice Department argued, that is, that General Washington acted unilaterally.] That is false. The Continental Congress adopted a resolution in 1776 expressly providing that enemy spies "shall suffer death . . . by sentence of a court martial, or such other punishment as such court martial shall direct," and ordered that the resolution "be printed at the end of the rules and articles of war." The previous year, Congress had made it punishable by court-martial for members of the Continental Army to "hold correspondence with" or "give intelligence" to the enemy. General Washington acted on the basis of legislative authority, not some sort of "inherent" executive authority. . . .[13]

As for the Lincoln conspirators, Fisher notes that "[c]ommentary on these trials has generally criticized the appearance of prejudgment and the spirit of vengeance." Attorney General Speed told President Andrew Johnson that the eight accused conspirators could be tried before a military tribunal for violations of the laws of war, but the opinion provided to Johnson seems to have been provided *after* Johnson had created the tribunal, possibly even after the tribunal had issued its verdicts. Lincoln's first attorney general criticized the military tribunal trial as "unlawful," "a gross blunder," and saw them as "den[ying] the great, fundamental principle, that ours is a government of *Law*." The proceedings suffered from some of the same defects as those described in *Quirin*: an observer at the trial described the tribunal as "a law unto itself. It made its own rules of procedure. It was the sole judge of the law, as well as of the facts." A majority of the tribunal recommended that one conspirator, Mary Surratt, be imprisoned for life, but President Johnson apparently ignored this recommendation, and Surratt was executed.[14]

Philbin's memo concluded that terrorists were not lawful combatants, but it did not make clear how a determination would be made as to whether captured suspected terrorists were, in fact, enemy combatants (lawful or otherwise) at all. In other words, it did not account for the possibility that some prisoners might be innocent. Philbin suggested it would be a good idea to hold prisoners outside the United States, "where many constitutional protections would not apply in any event." He further suggested that there would be a stronger case for trying noncitizens in the military system: U.S. citizens might have a better argument for gaining access to the civilian justice system.

THE ORIGINS OF THE MILITARY DETENTION SYSTEM AND GUANTANAMO

One week after the Philbin memo was completed,[15] President Bush signed the Military Order of November 13, 2001.[16] The president's order built on many of the key assertions made by the November 6 memo: (1) the United States was engaged in "armed conflict" with Al Qaeda; (2) the secretary of defense had authority to detain non-U.S. citizens who the president "had reason to believe" were members of Al Qaeda, had "engaged in, aided or abetted, or conspired to commit, acts of international terrorism," or had harbored a terrorist; (3) such individuals would be detained at "an appropriate location" anywhere in the world, "outside or within the United States"; (4) military commissions trying these individuals could impose the death penalty, life imprisonment, or other sentences by a two-thirds majority of the commission (federal civilian trials require unanimous verdicts); (5) the military commissions had "exclusive jurisdiction," meaning prisoners would have no access to civilian courts; and (6) no time frame was set for trial before the commission—in other words, prisoners could be held indefinitely without trial.[17] Other than providing that conviction and sentencing would require a two-thirds majority of members of the commission and that the commission could consider any evidence that would "have probative value to a reasonable person,"[18] the order did not provide much information about the procedures commissions would follow, noting only that "it is not practicable to apply in military commissions under this order the principles of law and the rules of evidence generally recognized in the trial of criminal cases in the United States district courts."[19] The secretary of defense was authorized to specify additional rules for proceedings before the commissions.[20]

President Bush's order revived the approach used to try the Nazi saboteurs in *Quirin*—though Bush's action went further than what the court had authorized in *Quirin*.[21] First, the court in *Quirin* left open the question of whether a president could order trials before military commissions and authorize procedures for such commissions to follow without congressional authorization. Second, Bush's order applied to a broad range of individuals—not a small, specific group of saboteurs. His order allowed the military to detain and try any and all suspected terrorists without allowing them access to civilian courts. This was essentially a decision to suspend habeas corpus, though, unlike Lincoln, Bush did not formally describe it as such. It also meant prisoners would not be guaranteed protections afforded to civilian defendants under the Constitution and by judicial rules of evidence (for instance, the right to a jury trial, right to a unanimous verdict in federal court, right to cross-examine witnesses, right to review evidence used against them, procedural rules excluding hearsay evidence). Finally, as we'll see, the November 2001 military order paved the way for a detention system. Where the purpose of Roosevelt's 1942 order was to provide a way to try suspected saboteurs, it soon became clear that Bush's order was aimed at creating a detention system that would allow for interrogation of suspected terrorists without providing them access to a court or, as we'll see, a trial or even hearing of any kind.

Bush asserted that he had the authority to detain any non-U.S. citizen[22] if he had "reason to believe" that person was a member of Al Qaeda or otherwise associated with terrorism, even in indirect ways. His order placed captured suspected terrorists in the military commission system, where they would not be entitled to the rights provided in federal civilian court (no specifics were given about what procedures the commissions would use—that was left for the Department of Defense to spell out), and prisoners could be held indefinitely, without trial of any kind (even without trial by a military commission). Finally, his order did not rely on express authorization from Congress, although the order referred to the Authorization for the Use of Military Force and the Uniform Code of Military Justice, in addition to "the authority vested in [Bush] as President and as Commander in Chief of the Armed Forces of the United States by the Constitution."[23]

In March 2002, pursuant to authority provided by the November 2001 military order, the Department of Defense issued Military Commission Order No. 1, which added new procedural rules for trial by commission, including requiring that there be a presumption of innocence and that guilt be proved beyond a reasonable doubt.[24] The March 2002 order further provided protection against self-incrimination and required a unanimous verdict for the death penalty (a two-thirds verdict was sufficient for a finding of guilt and for sentences other than death). Accused persons[25] would be provided with "detailed counsel"—meaning at least one military lawyer. The accused person would also have the ability to retain civilian counsel at his own expense. However, civilian counsel was not guaranteed access to "closed Commission proceedings" or to evidence designated as "protected information" by the Commission. Prosecutors would be military lawyers. Accused persons would have limited ability to call witnesses and obtain evidence.[26]

Adopting language from the November 2001 military order, the March 2002 order provided that the commission could consider any "evidence [that] would have probative value to a reasonable person."[27] Again, that could include hearsay evidence or, conceivably, evidence obtained through coercion or torture. Military commissions would be made up of no fewer than three and no more than seven members, all commissioned officers in the U.S. armed forces to be chosen by the secretary of defense or his designee. The Commission's decision would be reviewed by the secretary of defense and possibly by the president. The order did not provide for any review by a civilian court or any other judicial body (other than the presiding officer, commission members would not necessarily have any judicial training or background). The Commission's presiding officer could bar the accused and any civilian counsel from closed proceedings, for reasons including the protection of classified information, the physical safety of participants in Commission proceedings, or the protection of intelligence sources or "other national security interests." Military defense counsel could not be excluded from closed proceedings but also could not discuss any closed proceedings with the accused or with civilian counsel.[28]

Even before the Department of Defense issued its March 2002 order, the military began implementing President Bush's November 13, 2001, order by rounding up suspected terrorists or suspected members of the Taliban who had been captured in Afghanistan and elsewhere and, beginning in January 2002, sending them to a detention camp at the U.S. naval base in Guantanamo Bay.[29] Guantanamo was chosen because, as Philbin's memo had suggested, it was seen as the "legal equivalent of outer space"—a place where prisoners would have no ground to assert rights.[30] A 1950 Supreme Court decision suggested that noncitizens held outside U.S. territory could not petition U.S. courts for a writ of habeas corpus.[31] Though it was not clear exactly what Guantanamo's status was, the administration believed it could argue that it was not the legal equivalent of U.S. territory. The United States has maintained a base at Guantanamo since 1903, pursuant to an open-ended lease agreement entered into with Cuba after the Spanish-American War. Under the agreement, the United States exercises complete control and jurisdiction over the base, while Cuba maintained ultimate sovereignty over the area (although Cuba has demanded, since the 1959 revolution, that the United States leave).[32]

Although the executive branch orders that paved the way for Guantanamo seemed to aim at establishing a system for putting suspected terrorists on trial before military tribunals, in fact they created a system mainly for detention, not trial.[33] Hundreds of prisoners were held in Guantanamo for years without charges and without access to legal counsel—or, indeed, the outside world.[34] Not all were terrorists, and many were ultimately released,[35] but others remained in Guantanamo.[36] Relatives of the prisoners initiated legal actions challenging the detentions. Two cases—*Rasul et al. v. Bush* and *Hamdi v. Rumsfeld*—reached the Supreme Court and were decided on the same day in 2004. In these cases, the court seemed to rein in the president's claim of absolute authority to designate noncitizens (*Rasul*) and U.S. citizens (*Hamdi*) as enemy combatants and to hold them indefinitely without charges and without access to civilian courts—though important questions were left unresolved, and critics note that neither decision actually ordered the release of any prisoner.

In *Rasul*, a 6–3 majority decided that foreign nationals captured outside the United States and held at Guantanamo could raise habeas challenges to their detention pursuant to the federal habeas corpus statute.[37] Since the Constitution does not expressly spell out the scope or meaning of habeas access to the courts, Congress has enacted statutes, beginning with the Judiciary Act of 1789, that describe the federal courts' habeas jurisdiction. The current statute "grants federal district courts, "within their respective jurisdictions," the authority to hear applications for habeas corpus by any person who claims to be held "in custody in violation of the Constitution or laws or treaties of the United States."[38] The *Rasul* court noted the ancient origins of habeas corpus and described it as "a means of reviewing the legality of Executive detention."[39] It observed that, "[c]onsistent with the historic purpose of the writ, this Court has recognized the federal courts' power to review applications for habeas relief in a wide variety of cases involving Executive detention. . . . The Court has, for example, entertained the habeas petitions of an American citizen who plotted an attack on military installations during the Civil War . . . and of admitted enemy aliens convicted of war crimes during a declared war and held in the United States."[40]

Justice Stevens, writing for the majority,[41] dismissed the Bush administration's argument that it could hold noncitizens at Guantanamo without allowing them access to the courts. The court distinguished the 1950 *Eisentrager* decision, in which it denied habeas access for twenty-one German citizens captured by U.S. forces in China after Germany's surrender and convicted of war crimes by a U.S. military tribunal in China. Unlike the petitioners in *Eisentrager*, the petitioners in *Rasul* were not citizens of a nation at war with the United States, they denied having engaged in hostilities against the United States, they had received no trial of any kind, and they were being held in territory that the United States controlled. It was important to the court that the U.S. exercises "complete jurisdiction and control" over Guantanamo and that the Bush administration conceded that if U.S. citizens were held there, the federal habeas statute (which makes no distinction between citizens and noncitizens) would allow them access to the courts.[42]

Justice Scalia wrote a dissent, joined by Chief Justice Rehnquist and Justice Thomas, calling the majority opinion "judicial adventurism of the worst sort." Justice Scalia charged that the court's decision "ha[d] a potentially harmful effect upon the Nation's conduct of a war."[43] However, *Rasul* did not order the release of any prisoners. The court's decision answered only the limited question of whether prisoners held in U.S. territory or the functional equivalent could file a petition for habeas corpus in federal civilian court, pursuant to statutory law providing for habeas relief.

This was an important threshold statement, as it rejected the president's unlimited authority to detain suspected terrorists indefinitely, denying them access to any kind of hearing and any access to the courts. At the least, the government would be required to provide to a federal court *some* justification for the detention, in responding to the habeas petition. However, *Rasul* did not answer two other questions: (1) precisely what sort of justification would suffice (i.e., what level of proof must the government show?) and (2) "[w]hether and what further proceedings may become necessary after [the government] make their response to the merits of petitioners' claims," as the court put it.[44] In other words, exactly what kind of hearing should take place? Were prisoners entitled to due process under the Constitution—meaning a full opportunity to be heard, to rebut the government's justification, to present evidence? If due process did apply, what kind of hearing must be held—a civilian trial? Or would trial or hearing before a military commission, with reduced procedural safeguards, be enough?

The court addressed some of these questions in *Hamdi v. Rumsfeld*, decided on the same day as *Rasul*. The prisoners in *Rasul* were noncitizens, but *Hamdi* involved a U.S. citizen, which, as Philbin had noted in his

November 2001 memo, might strengthen the argument for providing additional protections not available to noncitizens.[45] Yaser Hamdi was born an American citizen in Louisiana. In 2001, he was seized in Afghanistan by members of the Northern Alliance, military groups opposed to the Taliban. They turned Hamdi over to the United States, and he was held without formal charges and without access to counsel. Initially he was held in Guantanamo, but, once it was discovered that he was a U.S. citizen, he was transferred to naval brigs in Virginia and then in South Carolina. The executive branch claimed Hamdi was too dangerous to be allowed contact even with his family.[46] However, Hamdi's father learned of his son's imprisonment and filed a habeas corpus petition on his son's behalf in June 2002.

When the case reached the Supreme Court, it ruled that Hamdi was entitled to some opportunity to challenge his detention—though perhaps not ultimately in civilian court. Although eight justices believed the executive branch did not have authority to detain Hamdi and hold him indefinitely without hearing, there was disagreement as to what kind of hearing must be provided. Justice O'Connor wrote a plurality opinion concluding that Congress had given the president authority to designate Hamdi as an enemy combatant and detain him but that due process considerations required that Hamdi, as a citizen, be given a hearing before a neutral decision maker where he could challenge his designation as an enemy combatant. Four justices believed that, unless Congress suspended habeas corpus, the executive had only two options: either charge Hamdi and try him in civilian court or release him. However, two of those justices, Souter and Ginsburg, accepted the limited hearing process described in O'Connor's plurality opinion as a compromise, while two others—Scalia and Stevens— dissented because they believed the limited hearing was insufficient and inappropriate. Justice Thomas dissented because he believed the court had no authority to second-guess the president's decision to detain Hamdi. Notice that Justice O'Connor's plurality opinion contains language that seems to be a rejoinder to claims of unlimited presidential power pursuant to the unitary executive doctrine.

Hamdi et al. v. Rumsfeld, 542 U.S. 507 (2004)

Plurality opinion by Justice O'Connor.

At this difficult time in our Nation's history, we are called upon to consider the legality of the Government's detention of a United States citizen on United States soil as an "enemy combatant" and to address the process that is constitutionally owed to one who seeks to challenge his classification as such. . . . We hold that although Congress authorized the detention of combatants in the narrow circumstances alleged here, due process demands that a citizen held in the United States as an enemy combatant be given a meaningful opportunity to contest the factual basis for that detention before a neutral decision-maker.

I

On September 11, 2001, the al Qaeda terrorist network used hijacked commercial airliners to attack prominent targets in the United States. Approximately 3,000 people were killed in those attacks. One week later, in response to these "acts of treacherous violence," Congress passed a resolution authorizing the President to "use all necessary and appropriate force against those nations, organizations, or persons he determines planned, authorized, committed, or aided the terrorist attacks" or "harbored such organizations or persons, in order to prevent any future acts of international terrorism against the United States by such nations, organizations or persons." Authorization for Use of Military Force ("the AUMF"), 115 Stat. 224. Soon thereafter, the President ordered United States Armed Forces to Afghanistan, with a mission to subdue al Qaeda and quell the Taliban regime that was known to support it.

This case arises out of the detention of a man whom the Government alleges took up arms with the Taliban during this conflict. His name is Yaser Esam Hamdi. Born an American citizen in Louisiana in 1980, Hamdi moved with his family to Saudi Arabia as a child. By 2001 . . . he resided in Afghanistan. At some point that year, he was seized by members of the Northern Alliance, a coalition of military groups opposed to the Taliban government, and eventually was turned over to the United States military. The Government asserts that it initially detained and interrogated Hamdi in Afghanistan before transferring him to the United States Naval Base in Guantanamo Bay in January 2002. In April 2002, upon learning that Hamdi is an American citizen, authorities transferred him to a naval brig in Norfolk, Virginia. . . . The Government contends that Hamdi is an "enemy combatant," and that this status justifies holding him in the United States indefinitely—without formal charges or proceedings—unless and until it makes the determination that access to counsel or further process is warranted.

In June 2002, Hamdi's father, Esam Fouad Hamdi, filed the present petition for a writ of habeas corpus. . . . The petition contends that Hamdi's detention was not legally authorized. . . . Hamdi's father has asserted . . . that his son went to Afghanistan to do "relief work," and that he had been in that country less than two months before September 11, 2001, and could not have received military training. The 20-year-old was traveling on his own for the first time, his father says, and "[b]ecause of his lack of experience, he was trapped in Afghanistan once that military campaign began."

The District Court ... appointed the federal public defender as counsel for the petitioners, and ordered that counsel be given access to Hamdi. The United States Court of Appeals for the Fourth Circuit reversed that order, holding that the District Court had failed to extend appropriate deference to the Government's security and intelligence interests. It directed the District Court ... to conduct a deferential inquiry into Hamdi's status. It opined that "if Hamdi is indeed an 'enemy combatant' who was captured during hostilities in Afghanistan, the government's present detention of him is a lawful one."

On remand, the Government filed a response and a motion to dismiss the petition. It attached to its response a declaration from one Michael Mobbs ... who identified himself as Special Advisor to the Under Secretary of Defense for Policy. Mobbs indicated that in this position, he has been "substantially involved with matters related to the detention of enemy combatants in the current war against the al Qaeda terrorists and those who support and harbor them (including the Taliban)." He ... declared that "[b]ased upon my review of relevant records and reports, I am ... familiar with the facts and circumstances related to the capture of ... Hamdi and his detention by U.S. military forces."

Mobbs then set forth what remains the sole evidentiary support that the Government has provided to the courts for Hamdi's detention. The declaration states that Hamdi "traveled to Afghanistan" in July or August 2001, and that he thereafter "affiliated with a Taliban military unit and received weapons training." It asserts that Hamdi "remained with his Taliban unit following the attacks of September 11" and that, during the time when Northern Alliance forces were "engaged in battle with the Taliban," "Hamdi's Taliban unit surrendered" to those forces, after which he "surrender[ed] his Kalishnikov assault rifle" to them. The Mobbs Declaration also states that, because al Qaeda and the Taliban "were and are hostile forces engaged in armed conflict with the armed forces of the United States," "individuals associated with" those groups "were and continue to be enemy combatants." Mobbs states that Hamdi was labeled an enemy combatant "[b]ased upon his interviews and in light of his association with the Taliban." According to the declaration, a series of "U.S. military screening team[s]" determined that Hamdi met "the criteria for enemy combatants," and "a subsequent interview of Hamdi has confirmed that he surrendered and gave his firearm to Northern Alliance forces, which supports his classification as an enemy combatant." ...

The District Court found that the Mobbs Declaration fell "far short" of supporting Hamdi's detention. It criticized the generic and hearsay nature of the affidavit, calling it "little more than the government's 'say-so.'" It ordered the Government to turn over numerous materials for *in camera* review [e.g., copies of Hamdi's statements, notes from interviews with him, a list of his interrogators].... The court indicated that all of these materials were necessary for "meaningful judicial review" of whether Hamdi's detention was legally authorized and whether Hamdi had received sufficient process to satisfy the Due Process Clause of the Constitution and relevant treaties or military regulations.

The Government sought to appeal the production order, and ... [t]he Fourth Circuit reversed ... stress[ing] that, because it was "undisputed that Hamdi was captured in a zone of active combat in a foreign theater of conflict," no factual inquiry or evidentiary hearing allowing Hamdi to be heard or to rebut the Government's assertions was necessary or proper. Concluding that the factual averments in the Mobbs Declaration, "if accurate," provided a sufficient basis upon which to conclude that the President had constitutionally detained Hamdi pursuant to the President's war powers, it ordered the habeas petition dismissed....

On the more global question of whether legal authorization exists for the detention of citizen enemy combatants at all, the Fourth Circuit rejected Hamdi's arguments that 18 U.S.C. § 4001(a)[47] and Article 5 of the Geneva Convention rendered any such detentions unlawful.... We now vacate the judgment below and remand.

II

The threshold question before us is whether the Executive has the authority to detain citizens who qualify as "enemy combatants." There is some debate as to the proper scope of this term, and the Government has never provided any court with the full criteria that it uses in classifying individuals as such. It has made clear, however, that, for purposes of this case, the "enemy combatant" that it is seeking to detain is an individual who, it alleges, was "'part of or supporting forces hostile to the United States or coalition partners'" in Afghanistan and who "'engaged in an armed conflict against the United States'" there. We therefore answer only the narrow question before us: whether the detention of citizens falling within that definition is authorized.

The Government maintains that no explicit congressional authorization is required, because the Executive possesses plenary authority to detain pursuant to Article II of the Constitution. We do not reach the question whether Article II provides such authority, however, because we agree with the Government's alternative position, that Congress has in fact authorized Hamdi's detention, through the AUMF....

[Hamdi] posits that his detention is forbidden by 18 U.S.C. § 4001(a) [which] states that "[n]o citizen shall be imprisoned or otherwise detained by the United States except pursuant to an Act of Congress." Congress passed § 4001(a) in 1971 as part of a bill to repeal the Emergency Detention Act of 1950 ... which provided procedures for executive detention, during times of emergency, of individuals deemed likely to engage in espionage or sabotage. Congress was particularly concerned about the possibility that the Act could be used to reprise the Japanese internment camps of World War II. . . . The Government . . . presses two alternative positions. First, it argues that § 4001(a) . . . applies only to "the control of civilian prisons and related detentions," not to military detentions . . . Second, it maintains that § 4001(a) is satisfied, because Hamdi is being detained "pursuant to an Act of Congress"—the AUMF. . . . [B]ecause we conclude that the Government's second assertion is correct, we do not address the first. . . .

The AUMF authorizes the President to use "all necessary and appropriate force" against "nations, organizations, or persons" associated with the September 11, 2001, terrorist attacks. . . . There can be no doubt that individuals who fought against the United States in Afghanistan as part of the Taliban, an organization known to have supported the al Qaeda terrorist network responsible for those attacks, are individuals Congress sought to target in passing the AUMF. We conclude that detention of individuals falling into the limited category we are considering, for the duration of the particular conflict in which they were captured, is so fundamental and accepted an incident to war as to be an exercise of the "necessary and appropriate force" Congress has authorized the President to use.

The capture and detention of lawful combatants and the capture, detention, and trial of unlawful combatants, by "universal agreement and practice," are "important incident[s] of war." . . . The purpose of detention is to prevent captured individuals from returning to the field of battle and taking up arms once again. . . .

There is no bar to this Nation's holding one of its own citizens as an enemy combatant [citing *Quirin*]. . . .

In light of these principles, it is of no moment that the AUMF does not use specific language of detention. Because detention to prevent a combatant's return to the battlefield is a fundamental incident of waging war, in permitting the use of "necessary and appropriate force," Congress has clearly and unmistakably authorized detention in the narrow circumstances considered here.

Hamdi objects, nevertheless, that Congress has not authorized . . . *indefinite* detention. . . . We take Hamdi's objection to be not to the lack of certainty regarding the date on which the conflict will end, but to the substantial prospect of perpetual detention. We recognize that the national security underpinnings of the "war on terror," although crucially important, are broad and malleable. As the Government concedes, "given its unconventional nature, the current conflict is unlikely to end with a formal cease-fire agreement." . . . The prospect Hamdi raises is therefore not far-fetched. If the Government does not consider this unconventional war won for two generations, and if it maintains during that time that Hamdi might, if released, rejoin forces fighting against the United States, then the position it has taken throughout the litigation of this case suggests that Hamdi's detention could last for the rest of his life. . . .

Hamdi contends that the AUMF does not authorize indefinite or perpetual detention. Certainly, we agree that indefinite detention for the purpose of interrogation is not authorized. Further, we understand Congress' grant of authority for the use of "necessary and appropriate force" to include the authority to detain for the duration of the relevant conflict, and our understanding is based on longstanding law-of-war principles. If the practical circumstances of a given conflict are entirely unlike those of the conflicts that informed the development of the law of war, that understanding may unravel. But that is not the situation we face as of this date. Active combat operations against Taliban fighters apparently are ongoing in Afghanistan. . . . The United States may detain, for the duration of these hostilities, individuals legitimately determined to be Taliban combatants who "engaged in an armed conflict against the United States." . . .

III

Even in cases in which the detention of enemy combatants is legally authorized, there remains the question of what process is constitutionally due to a citizen who disputes his enemy combatant status. Hamdi argues that he is owed a meaningful and timely hearing and that "extra-judicial detention [that] begins and ends with the submission of an affidavit based on third-hand hearsay" does not comport with the Fifth and Fourteenth Amendments. . . . The Government counters that any more process than was provided below would be both unworkable and "constitutionally intolerable." Our resolution of this dispute requires a careful examination both of the writ of habeas corpus, which Hamdi now seeks to employ as a mechanism of judicial review, and of the Due Process Clause, which informs the procedural contours of that mechanism in this instance.

A

Though they reach radically different conclusions on the process that ought to attend the present proceeding, the parties begin on common ground. All agree that, absent suspension, the writ of habeas corpus remains available to every individual detained within the United States. . . . All agree suspension of the writ has not occurred here. Thus, it is undisputed that Hamdi was properly before an Article III court to challenge his detention under 28 U.S.C. § 2241. . . . Further, all agree that § 2241 and its companion provisions provide at least a skeletal outline of the procedures to be afforded a petitioner in federal habeas review. . . .

The simple outline of § 2241 makes clear both that Congress envisioned that habeas petitioners would have some opportunity to present and rebut facts and that courts in cases like this retain some ability to vary the ways in which they do so as mandated by due process. The Government recognizes the basic procedural protections required by the habeas statute . . . but asks us to hold that . . . the presentation of the Mobbs Declaration to the habeas court completed the required factual development. It suggests two separate reasons for its position that no further process is due.

B

First, the Government urges the adoption of the Fourth Circuit's holding below—that because it is "undisputed" that Hamdi's seizure took place in a combat zone, the habeas determination can be made purely as a matter of law, with no further hearing or factfinding necessary. This argument is easily rejected.... [T]he circumstances surrounding Hamdi's seizure cannot in any way be characterized as "undisputed,"... "because Hamdi has not been permitted to speak for himself or even through counsel."... Further, the "facts" that constitute the alleged concession are insufficient to support Hamdi's detention. Under the definition of enemy combatant that we accept today as falling within the scope of Congress' authorization, Hamdi would need to be "part of or supporting forces hostile to the United States or coalition partners" and "engaged in an armed conflict against the United States" to justify his detention in the United States for the duration of the relevant conflict. The habeas petition states only that "[w]hen seized by the United States Government, Mr. Hamdi resided in Afghanistan." An assertion that one *resided* in a country in which combat operations are taking place is not a concession that one was "*captured* in a zone of active combat operations in a foreign theater of war,"... and certainly is not a concession that one was "part of or supporting forces hostile to the United States or coalition partners" and "engaged in an armed conflict against the United States."...

C

The Government's second argument requires closer consideration. This is the argument that further factual exploration is unwarranted and inappropriate in light of the extraordinary constitutional interests at stake. Under the Government's most extreme rendition of this argument, "[r]espect for separation of powers and the limited institutional capabilities of courts in matters of military decision-making in connection with an ongoing conflict" ought to eliminate entirely any individual process, restricting the courts to investigating only whether legal authorization exists for the broader detention scheme.... At most, the Government argues, courts should review its determination that a citizen is an enemy combatant under a very deferential "some evidence" standard.... Under this review, a court would assume the accuracy of the Government's articulated basis for Hamdi's detention, as set forth in the Mobbs Declaration, and assess only whether that articulated basis was a legitimate one....

In response, Hamdi emphasizes that this Court consistently has recognized that an individual challenging his detention may not be held at the will of the Executive without recourse to some proceeding before a neutral tribunal to determine whether the Executive's asserted justifications for that detention have basis in fact and warrant in law. . . . The District Court, agreeing with Hamdi, apparently believed that the appropriate process would approach the process that accompanies a criminal trial. . . . Anything less, it concluded, would not be "meaningful judicial review."

Both of these positions highlight legitimate concerns. And both emphasize the tension that often exists between the autonomy that the Government asserts is necessary in order to pursue effectively a particular goal and the process that a citizen contends he is due before he is deprived of a constitutional right. The ordinary mechanism that we use for balancing such serious competing interests . . . dictates that the process due in any given instance is determined by weighing "the private interest that will be affected by the official action" against the Government's asserted interest . . . and the burdens the Government would face in providing greater process. . . .

1

It is beyond question that substantial interests lie on both sides of the scale in this case. Hamdi's "private interest . . . affected by the official action," is the most elemental of liberty interests—the interest in being free from physical detention by one's own government. . . .

. . . Indeed . . . the risk of erroneous deprivation of a citizen's liberty in the absence of sufficient process here is very real. . . . Moreover, as critical as the Government's interest may be in detaining those who actually pose an immediate threat to the national security of the United States during ongoing international conflict, history and common sense teach us that an unchecked system of detention carries the potential to become a means for oppression and abuse of others who do not present that sort of threat. . . . We reaffirm today the fundamental nature of a citizen's right to be free from involuntary confinement by his own government without due process of law, and we weigh the opposing governmental interests against the curtailment of liberty that such confinement entails.

2

On the other side of the scale are the weighty and sensitive governmental interests in ensuring that those who have in fact fought with the enemy during a war do not return to battle against the United States. . . . Without doubt, our Constitution recognizes that core strategic matters of war-making belong in the hands of those who are best positioned and most politically accountable for making them. . . .

The Government also argues at some length that its interests in reducing the process available to alleged enemy combatants are heightened by the practical difficulties that would accompany a system of trial-like process. In its view, military officers who are engaged in the serious work of waging battle would be unnecessarily and dangerously distracted by litigation half a world away, and discovery into military operations would both intrude on the sensitive secrets of national defense and result in a futile search for evidence buried under the rubble of war. . . .

3

Striking the proper constitutional balance here is of great importance to the Nation during this period of ongoing combat. But it is equally vital that our calculus not give short shrift to the values that this country holds dear or to the privilege that is American citizenship. It is during our most challenging and uncertain moments that our Nation's commitment to due process is most severely tested; and it is in those times that we must preserve our commitment at home to the principles for which we fight abroad. . . .

With due recognition of these competing concerns, we believe that neither the process proposed by the Government nor the process apparently envisioned by the District Court below strikes the proper constitutional balance when a United States citizen is detained in the United States as an enemy combatant. . . .

We therefore hold that a citizen-detainee seeking to challenge his classification as an enemy combatant must receive notice of the factual basis for his classification, and a fair opportunity to rebut the Government's factual assertions before a neutral decision-maker. . . . These essential constitutional promises may not be eroded.

At the same time, the exigencies of the circumstances may demand that, aside from these core elements, enemy combatant proceedings may be tailored to alleviate their uncommon potential to burden the Executive at a time of ongoing military conflict. Hearsay, for example, may need to be accepted as the most reliable available evidence from the Government in such a proceeding. Likewise, the Constitution would not be offended by a presumption in favor of the Government's evidence,[48] so long as that presumption remained a rebuttable one and fair opportunity for rebuttal were provided. Thus, once the Government puts forth credible evidence that the habeas petitioner meets the enemy combatant criteria, the onus could shift to the petitioner to rebut that evidence with more persuasive evidence that he falls outside the criteria. A burden-shifting scheme of this sort would meet the goal of ensuring that the errant tourist, embedded journalist, or local aid worker has a chance to prove military error while giving due regard to the Executive once it has put forth meaningful support for its conclusion that the detainee is in fact an enemy combatant. . . .

We think it unlikely that this basic process will have the dire impact on the central functions of war-making that the Government forecasts. The parties agree that initial captures on the battlefield need not receive the process we have discussed here; that process is due only when the determination is made to *continue* to hold those who have been seized ... arguments that military officers ought not have to wage war under the threat of litigation lose much of their steam when factual disputes at enemy combatant hearings are limited to the alleged combatant's acts. This focus meddles little, if at all, in the strategy or conduct of war, inquiring only into the appropriateness of continuing to detain an individual claimed to have taken up arms against the United States. While we accord the greatest respect and consideration to the judgments of military authorities in matters relating to the actual prosecution of a war, and recognize that the scope of that discretion necessarily is wide, it does not infringe on the core role of the military for the courts to exercise their own time-honored and constitutionally mandated roles of reviewing and resolving claims like those presented here. *Korematsu* v. *United States* ... (Murphy, J., dissenting) ("[L]ike other claims conflicting with the asserted constitutional rights of the individual, the military claim must subject itself to the judicial process of having its reasonableness determined and its conflicts with other interests reconciled")....

In sum, while the full protections that accompany challenges to detentions in other settings may prove unworkable and inappropriate in the enemy combatant setting, the threats to military operations posed by a basic system of independent review are not so weighty as to trump a citizen's core rights to challenge meaning-fully the Government's case and to be heard by an impartial adjudicator.

D

In so holding, we necessarily reject the Government's assertion that separation of powers principles mandate a heavily circumscribed role for the courts in such circumstances. Indeed, the position that the courts must forgo any examination of the individual case and focus exclusively on the legality of the broader detention scheme cannot be mandated by any reasonable view of separation of powers, as this approach serves only to *condense* power into a single branch of government. We have long since made clear that a state of war is not a blank check for the President when it comes to the rights of the Nation's citizens. *Youngstown.* ... Whatever power the United States Constitution envisions for the Executive in its exchanges with other nations or with enemy organizations in times of conflict, it most assuredly envisions a role for all three branches when individual liberties are at stake. ... Likewise, we have made clear that, unless Congress acts to suspend it, the Great Writ of habeas corpus allows the Judicial Branch to play a necessary role in maintaining this delicate balance of governance, serving as an important judicial check on the Executive's discretion in the realm of detentions. ... Thus, while we do not question that our due process assessment must pay keen attention to the particular burdens faced by the Executive in the context of military action, it would turn our system of checks and balances on its head to suggest that a citizen could not make his way to court with a challenge to the factual basis for his detention by his government, simply because the Executive opposes making available such a challenge. Absent suspension of the writ by Congress, a citizen detained as an enemy combatant is entitled to this process.

Because we conclude that due process demands some system for a citizen detainee to refute his classification, the proposed "some evidence" standard is inadequate. Any process in which the Executive's factual assertions go wholly unchallenged or are simply presumed correct without any opportunity for the alleged combatant to demonstrate otherwise falls constitutionally short....This standard ... is ill suited to the situation in which a habeas petitioner has received no prior proceedings before any tribunal and had no prior opportunity to rebut the Executive's factual assertions before a neutral decision-maker.

Today we are faced only with such a case. Aside from unspecified "screening" processes, and military interrogations in which the Government suggests Hamdi could have contested his classification, Hamdi has received no process. An interrogation by one's captor, however effective an intelligence-gathering tool, hardly constitutes a constitutionally adequate factfinding before a neutral decision-maker....Plainly, the "process" Hamdi has received is not that to which he is entitled under the Due Process Clause.

There remains the possibility that the standards we have articulated could be met by an appropriately authorized and properly constituted military tribunal....In the absence of such process, however, a court that receives a petition for a writ of habeas corpus from an alleged enemy combatant must itself ensure that the minimum requirements of due process are achieved....

Justice Souter, with whom Justice Ginsburg joins, concurring in part, dissenting in part, and concurring in the judgment.

...[Hamdi] ...presses the distinct argument that the Government's claim, even if true, would not implicate any authority for holding him that would satisfy [the] ... Non-Detention Act, which bars imprisonment or detention of a citizen "except pursuant to an Act of Congress." The Government responds that Hamdi's incommunicado imprisonment as an enemy combatant seized on the field of battle falls within the President's power as Commander in Chief under the laws and usages of war, and is in any event authorized by two statutes. Accordingly, the Government contends that Hamdi has no basis for any challenge by petition for habeas except to his own status as an enemy combatant; and even that challenge may go no further than to enquire whether "some evidence" supports Hamdi's designation....At the argument of this case, in fact, the Government went further and suggested that as long as a prisoner could challenge his enemy combatant designation when responding to interrogation during incommunicado detention he was accorded sufficient process to support his designation as an enemy combatant.... Since on either view judicial enquiry so limited would be virtually worthless as a way to contest detention, the Government's concession of jurisdiction to hear Hamdi's habeas claim is more theoretical than practical, leaving the assertion of Executive authority close to unconditional.

The plurality rejects any such limit on the exercise of habeas jurisdiction and so far I agree with its opinion. The plurality does, however, accept the Government's position that if Hamdi's designation as an enemy combatant is correct, his detention (at least as to some period) is authorized by ... the [AUMF]. Here, I disagree and respectfully dissent. The Government has failed to demonstrate that the [AUMF] authorizes the detention complained of here even on the facts the Government claims. If the Government raises nothing further than the record now shows, the Non-Detention Act entitles Hamdi to be released....

The threshold issue is how broadly or narrowly to read the Non-Detention Act, the tone of which is severe: "No citizen shall be imprisoned or otherwise detained by the United States except pursuant to an Act of Congress." ... [T]he Act ... superseded a cold-war statute, the Emergency Detention Act of 1950....

The fact that Congress intended to guard against a repetition of the World War II internments when it repealed the 1950 statute ... provides a powerful reason to think that [the Non-Detention Act] was meant to require clear congressional authorization before any citizen can be placed in a cell....

Finally, even if history had spared us the cautionary example of the internments in World War II ... there would be a compelling reason to read [the Non-Detention Act] to demand manifest authority to detain before detention is authorized. The defining character of American constitutional government is its constant tension between security and liberty, serving both by partial helpings of each. In a government of separated powers, deciding finally on what is a reasonable degree of guaranteed liberty whether in peace or war (or some condition in between) is not well entrusted to the Executive Branch of Government, whose particular responsibility is to maintain security. For reasons of inescapable human nature, the branch of the Government asked to counter a serious threat is not the branch on which to rest the Nation's entire reliance in striking the balance between the will to win and the cost in liberty on the way to victory; the responsibility for security will naturally amplify the claim that security legitimately raises. A reasonable balance is more likely to be reached on the judgment of a different branch, just as Madison said in remarking that "the constant aim is to divide and arrange the several offices in such a manner as that each may be a check on the other—that the private interest of every individual may be a sentinel over the public rights." The Federalist No. 51.... Hence the need for an assessment by Congress before citizens are subject to lockup, and likewise the need for a clearly expressed congressional resolution of the competing claims.

Under this principle of reading [the Non-Detention Act] robustly to require a clear statement of authorization to detain, none of the Government's arguments suffices to justify Hamdi's detention....

...[T]here is the Government's claim, accepted by the Court, that the terms of the [AUMF] are adequate to authorize detention of an enemy combatant under the circumstances described....Since the [AUMF] was adopted one week after the attacks of September 11, 2001, it naturally speaks with some generality, but its focus is clear, and that is on the use of military power....[I]t never so much as uses the word detention, and there is no reason to think Congress might have perceived any need to augment Executive power to deal with dangerous citizens within the United States, given the well-stocked statutory arsenal of defined criminal offenses covering the gamut of actions that a citizen sympathetic to terrorists might commit....

It is worth adding a further reason for requiring the Government to bear the burden of clearly justifying its claim to be exercising recognized war powers before declaring [the Non-Detention Act] satisfied. Thirty-eight days after adopting the Force Resolution, Congress passed the ... USA PATRIOT ACT ...; that Act authorized the detention of alien terrorists for no more than seven days in the absence of criminal charges or deportation proceedings.... It is very difficult to believe that the same Congress that carefully circumscribed Executive power over alien terrorists on home soil would not have meant to require the Government to justify clearly its detention of an American citizen held on home soil incommunicado....

[I]it is instructive to recall Justice Jackson's observation that the President is not Commander in Chief of the country, only of the military. Youngstown ... (concurring opinion) ... (Presidential authority is "at its lowest ebb" where the President acts contrary to congressional will). There may be room for one qualification to Justice Jackson's statement, however: in a moment of genuine emergency, when the Government must act with no time for deliberation, the Executive may be able to detain a citizen if there is reason to fear he is an imminent threat to the safety of the Nation and its people....This case, however, does not present that question, because an emergency power of necessity must at least be limited by the emergency; Hamdi has been locked up for over two years....

Whether insisting on the careful scrutiny of emergency claims or on a vigorous reading of [the Non-Detention Act], we are heirs to a tradition given voice 800 years ago by Magna Carta, which, on the barons' insistence, confined executive power by "the law of the land."

Because I find Hamdi's detention forbidden by [the Non-Detention Act] and unauthorized by the [AUMF], I would not reach any questions of what process he may be due in litigating disputed issues in a proceeding under the habeas statute or prior to the habeas enquiry itself. For me, it suffices that the Government has failed to justify holding him in the absence of a further Act of Congress, criminal charges, a showing that the detention conforms to the laws of war, or a demonstration that [the Non-Detention Act] is unconstitutional....

Since this disposition does not command a majority of the Court, however, the need to give practical effect to the conclusions of eight members of the Court rejecting the Government's position calls for me to join with the plurality in ordering remand on terms closest to those I would impose....

It should go without saying that in joining with the plurality to produce a judgment, I do not adopt the plurality's resolution of constitutional issues that I would not reach. It is not that I could disagree with the plurality's determinations ... that someone in Hamdi's position is entitled at a minimum to notice of the Government's claimed factual basis for holding him, and to a fair chance to rebut it before a neutral decision maker, nor, of course, could I disagree with the plurality's affirmation of Hamdi's right to counsel. On the other hand, I do not mean to imply agreement that the Government could claim an evidentiary presumption casting the burden of rebuttal on Hamdi ... or that an opportunity to litigate before a military tribunal might obviate or truncate enquiry by a court on habeas....

Justice Scalia, with whom Justice Stevens joins, dissenting.

...This case brings into conflict the competing demands of national security and our citizens' constitutional right to personal liberty. Although I share the Court's evident unease as it seeks to reconcile the two, I do not agree with its resolution.

Where the Government accuses a citizen of waging war against it, our constitutional tradition has been to prosecute him in federal court for treason or some other crime. Where the exigencies of war prevent that, the Constitution's Suspension Clause ... allows Congress to relax the usual protections temporarily. Absent suspension, however, the Executive's assertion of military exigency has not been thought sufficient to permit detention without charge. No one contends that the [AUMF] ... is an implementation of the Suspension Clause. Accordingly, I would reverse the decision below.

The very core of liberty secured by our Anglo-Saxon system of separated powers has been freedom from indefinite imprisonment at the will of the Executive. Blackstone stated this principle clearly:

> "Of great importance to the public is the preservation of this personal liberty: for if once it were left in the power of any, the highest, magistrate to imprison arbitrarily whomever he or his officers thought proper ... there would soon be an end of all other rights and immunities.... To bereave a man of life, or by violence to

confiscate his estate, without accusation or trial, would be so gross and notorious an act of despotism, as must at once convey the alarm of tyranny throughout the whole kingdom. But confinement of the person, by secretly hurrying him to gaol, where his sufferings are unknown or forgotten; is a less public, a less striking, and therefore a more dangerous engine of arbitrary government. . . .

"To make imprisonment lawful, it must either be, by process from the courts of judicature, or by warrant from some legal officer, having authority to commit to prison; which warrant must be in writing, under the hand and seal of the magistrate, and express the causes of the commitment, in order to be examined into (if necessary) upon a *habeas corpus*. If there be no cause expressed, the gaoler is not bound to detain the prisoner. For the law judges in this respect, . . . that it is unreasonable to send a prisoner, and not to signify withal the crimes alleged against him." . . .

These words were well known to the Founders. Hamilton quoted from this very passage in The Federalist No. 84. . . . The two ideas central to Blackstone's understanding—due process as the right secured, and habeas corpus as the instrument by which due process could be insisted upon by a citizen illegally imprisoned—found expression in the Constitution's Due Process and Suspension Clauses.

The gist of the Due Process Clause, as understood at the founding and since, was to force the Government to follow those common-law procedures traditionally deemed necessary before depriving a person of life, liberty, or property. When a citizen was deprived of liberty because of alleged criminal conduct, those procedures typically required committal by a magistrate followed by indictment and trial. . . .

. . . These due process rights have historically been vindicated by the writ of habeas corpus. In England before the founding, the writ developed into a tool for challenging executive confinement. . . .

The writ of habeas corpus was preserved in the Constitution. . . .

The allegations here, of course, are no ordinary accusations of criminal activity. Yaser Esam Hamdi has been imprisoned because the Government believes he participated in the waging of war against the United States. The relevant question, then, is whether there is a different, special procedure for imprisonment of a citizen accused of wrongdoing *by aiding the enemy in wartime*.

Justice O'Connor, writing for a plurality of this Court, asserts that captured enemy combatants (other than those suspected of war crimes) have traditionally been detained until the cessation of hostilities and then released. That is probably an accurate description of wartime practice with respect to enemy *aliens*. The tradition with respect to American citizens, however, has been quite different. Citizens aiding the enemy have been treated as traitors subject to the criminal process.

... [C]itizens have been charged and tried in Article III courts for acts of war against the United States, even when their noncitizen co-conspirators were not.... During World War II, the famous German saboteurs of *Ex parte Quirin* ... received military process, but the citizens who associated with them (with the exception of one citizen-saboteur, discussed below) were punished under the criminal process....

...The only citizen other than Hamdi known to be imprisoned in connection with military hostilities in Afghanistan against the United States *was* subjected to criminal process and convicted upon a guilty plea. See *United States v. Lindh*....

There are times when military exigency renders resort to the traditional criminal process impracticable. English law accommodated such exigencies by allowing legislative suspension of the writ of habeas corpus for brief periods....

Where the Executive has not pursued the usual course of charge, committal, and conviction, it has historically secured the Legislature's explicit approval of a suspension....

The Suspension Clause was by design a safety valve, the Constitution's only "express provision for exercise of extraordinary authority because of a crisis," *Youngstown* ... (Jackson, J., concurring).... During the Civil War, Congress passed its first Act authorizing Executive suspension of the writ of habeas corpus, see Act of Mar. 3, 1863, 12 Stat. 755, to the relief of those many who thought President Lincoln's unauthorized proclamations of suspension unconstitutional. Later Presidential proclamations of suspension relied upon the congressional authorization....

Writings from the founding generation also suggest that, without exception, the only constitutional alternatives are to charge the crime or suspend the writ....

President Lincoln, when he purported to suspend habeas corpus without congressional authorization during the Civil War, apparently did not doubt that suspension was required if the prisoner was to be held without criminal trial. In his famous message to Congress on July 4, 1861, he argued only that he could suspend the writ, not that even without suspension, his imprisonment of citizens without criminal trial was permitted.

Further evidence comes from this Court's decision in *Ex parte Milligan, supra.* There ... [t]he Court rejected in no uncertain terms the Government's assertion that military jurisdiction was proper "under the 'laws and usages of war'" ...:

> "It can serve no useful purpose to inquire what those laws and
> usages are, whence they originated, where found, and on whom

they operate; they can never be applied to citizens in states which have upheld the authority of the government, and where the courts are open and their process unobstructed."

Milligan is not exactly this case, of course, since the petitioner was threatened with death, not merely imprisonment. But the reasoning and conclusion of *Milligan* logically cover the present case.…

The proposition that the Executive lacks indefinite wartime detention authority over citizens is consistent with the Founders' general mistrust of military power permanently at the Executive's disposal. In the Founders' view, the "blessings of liberty" were threatened by "those military establishments which must gradually poison its very fountain." The Federalist No. 45 … (J. Madison). No fewer than 10 issues of the Federalist were devoted in whole or part to allaying fears of oppression from the proposed Constitution's authorization of standing armies in peacetime. Many safeguards in the Constitution reflect these concerns.… Except for the actual command of military forces, all authorization for their maintenance and all explicit authorization for their use is placed in the control of Congress under Article I, rather than the President under Article II. As Hamilton explained, the President's military authority would be "much inferior" to that of the British King:

> "It would amount to nothing more than the supreme command and direction of the military and naval forces, as first general and admiral of the confederacy: while that of the British king extends to the *declaring* of war, and to the *raising* and *regulating* of fleets and armies; all which, by the constitution under consideration, would appertain to the legislature." The Federalist No. 69.

A view of the Constitution that gives the Executive authority to use military force rather than the force of law against citizens on American soil flies in the face of the mistrust that engendered these provisions.

The Government … places primary reliance upon *Ex parte Quirin*,… [t]he case was not this Court's finest hour. The Court upheld the commission and denied relief in a brief *per curiam* issued the day after oral argument concluded … a week later the Government carried out the commission's death sentence upon six saboteurs.… The Court eventually explained its reasoning in a written opinion issued several months later.

… In *Quirin* it was uncontested that the petitioners were members of enemy forces. They were "*admitted* enemy invaders," … and it was "undisputed" that they had landed in the United States in service of German forces.… But where those jurisdictional facts are *not* conceded—where the petitioner insists that he is *not* a belligerent—*Quirin* left the pre-existing law in place: Absent suspension of the writ, a citizen held where the courts are open is entitled either to criminal trial or to a judicial decree requiring his release.

It follows from what I have said that Hamdi is entitled to a habeas decree requiring his release unless (1) criminal proceedings are promptly brought, or (2) Congress has suspended the writ of habeas corpus. A suspension of the writ could, of course, lay down conditions for continued detention, similar to those that today's opinion prescribes under the Due Process Clause.... But there is a world of difference between the people's representatives' determining the need for that suspension (and prescribing the conditions for it), and this Court's doing so.

The plurality finds justification for Hamdi's imprisonment in the [AUMF]....This is not remotely a congressional suspension of the writ, and no one claims that it is. ... But even if it did, I would not permit it to overcome Hamdi's entitlement to habeas corpus relief. The Suspension Clause of the Constitution, which carefully circumscribes the conditions under which the writ can be withheld, would be a sham if it could be evaded by congressional prescription of requirements *other than the common-law requirement of committal for criminal prosecution* that render the writ, though available, unavailing. If the Suspension Clause does not guarantee the citizen that he will either be tried or released, unless the conditions for suspending the writ exist and the grave action of suspending the writ has been taken; if it merely guarantees the citizen that he will not be detained unless Congress by ordinary legislation says he can be detained; it guarantees him very little indeed....

Several limitations give my views in this matter a relatively narrow compass. They apply only to citizens, accused of being enemy combatants, who are detained within the territorial jurisdiction of a federal court....Where the citizen is captured outside and held outside the United States, the constitutional requirements may be different.... Moreover, even within the United States, the accused citizen-enemy combatant may lawfully be detained once prosecution is in progress or in contemplation....The Government has been notably successful in securing conviction, and hence long-term custody or execution, of those who have waged war against the state.

I frankly do not know whether these tools are sufficient to meet the Government's security needs, including the need to obtain intelligence through interrogation. It is far beyond my competence, or the Court's competence, to determine that. But it is not beyond Congress's. If the situation demands it, the Executive can ask Congress to authorize suspension of the writ—which can be made subject to whatever conditions Congress deems appropriate, including even the procedural novelties invented by the plurality today. To be sure, suspension is limited by the Constitution to cases of rebellion or invasion. But whether the attacks of September 11, 2001, constitute an "invasion," and whether those attacks still justify suspension several years later, are questions for Congress rather than this

Court.... If civil rights are to be curtailed during wartime, it must be done openly and democratically, as the Constitution requires, rather than by silent erosion through an opinion of this Court.

The Founders well understood the difficult tradeoff between safety and freedom.... The Founders warned us about the risk, and equipped us with a Constitution designed to deal with it. Many think it not only inevitable but entirely proper that liberty give way to security in times of national crisis—that, at the extremes of military exigency, *inter arma silent leges.*[49] Whatever the general merits of the view that war silences law or modulates its voice, that view has no place in the interpretation and application of a Constitution designed precisely to confront war and, in a manner that accords with democratic principles, to accommodate it. Because the Court has proceeded to meet the current emergency in a manner the Constitution does not envision, I respectfully dissent.

Justice Thomas, dissenting.

The Executive Branch, acting pursuant to the powers vested in the President by the Constitution and with explicit congressional approval, has determined that Yaser Hamdi is an enemy combatant and should be detained. This detention falls squarely within the Federal Government's war powers, and we lack the expertise and capacity to second-guess that decision. As such, petitioners' habeas challenge should fail, and there is no reason to remand the case.... I do not think that the Federal Government's war powers can be balanced away by this Court. Arguably, Congress could provide for additional procedural protections, but until it does, we have no right to insist upon them. But even if I were to agree with the general approach the plurality takes, I could not accept the particulars. The plurality utterly fails to account for the Government's compelling interests and for our own institutional inability to weigh competing concerns correctly. I respectfully dissent.

In some ways, Justice O'Connor's plurality opinion seems like a straightforward repudiation of the unitary executive doctrine that sets definite limits on emergency presidential power. Justice O'Connor emphatically declared that "a state of war is not a blank check for the President when it comes to the rights of the Nation's citizens." Eight justices made clear that they did not accept the outer limits of unitary executive theory— that the president acts alone, without review by the courts, in exercising executive power. The court did not ratify the government's claim that the president had sole authority to detain citizens who, in the President's view qualify as enemy combatants.[50] However, a plurality of the court decided that Congress had implicitly authorized the president to exercise this authority when it passed the Authorization for Use of Military Force (AUMF).

This could be seen as a return to the approach the court followed in *Youngstown*: the president is well served to act in concert with Congress, rather than taking unilateral action without congressional authorization. Some scholars, however, suggest that the court's decision lacked teeth: after all, the court did not order Rasul's or Hamdi's release and, when discussing what process Hamdi was due, did not even require that he be tried in a civilian court.[51] What chance would Hamdi have for a fair hearing before a military tribunal?[52]

The court's ruling in *Hamdi* did seem to rein in emergency presidential power by requiring that some specific process be afforded to prisoners who are U.S. citizens. Prisoners had to have a chance to show they were wrongly held—perhaps not with the full protection of a jury trial in civilian court but with some meaningful opportunity to rebut the evidence against them. Again, though, there was a limit to the reach of the court's ruling: it left open the possibility that an initial hearing before a military commission, providing limited procedural protections, might be a sufficient basis for holding someone as an enemy combatant (a term the court noted was not clearly defined).[53]

Hamdi himself was released and returned to Saudi Arabia[54] soon after the court's decision, but the question remained: what would the administration do with other prisoners? Following the *Rasul* and *Hamdi* decisions, the administration decided to provide an opportunity for some prisoners held in Guantanamo to challenge their designation as enemy combatants. In a July 2004 memo, the Department of Defense established Combatant Status Review Tribunals or CSRTs.[55] The order applied to foreign nationals held at Guantanamo. CSRTs, composed of three military officers, would determine whether prisoners were enemy combatants, defined in the July 2004 memo as "an individual who was part of or supporting Taliban or Al Qaeda forces or associated forces that have engaged in hostilities against the United States or its coalition partners . . . includ[ing] any person who has committed a belligerent act or has directly supported hostilities in aid of enemy forces." Civilian rules of evidence and procedure would not apply: prisoners would have no right to counsel (they could be assigned a military officer to serve as "personal representative," but personal representatives were instructed to tell CSRT members whatever the prisoner told them), a limited right to call witnesses, and limited ability to examine evidence used against them. The prisoner's innocence would not be presumed: in other words, the burden would be on the prisoner to disprove the government's case. If a CSRT determined that the prisoner was an enemy combatant, the prisoner might then receive a hearing before a military commission or might be held indefinitely.[56] Annual review boards would provide an additional opportunity to determine whether detention of specific prisoners was necessary.

The CSRTs seemed to be developed to as a way for the executive branch to comply with the court's ruling in *Hamdi* that prisoners be given an opportunity to challenge their designation as enemy combatants before a neutral decision maker. However, Joseph Margulies, a lawyer who represented some of the prisoners at Guantanamo, argued that the real purpose of the CSRTs was "to validate a predetermined result."[57] Members of the CSRT would begin proceedings with the assumption that the prisoner was an enemy combatant, that determination having already been made "through multiple levels of review by officers of the Department of Defense."[58] Moreover, the definition of an "enemy combatant" was expanded beyond the definition relied on by the court in *Hamdi*. As defined by the July 2004 Department of Defense memo, it included anyone who "directly supported hostilities in aid of enemy forces."[59] The words "directly supported" were not defined. As applied by CSRTs, they were used to confirm the enemy combatant status of men who were forced to join the Taliban, including one who was conscripted as a cook.[60] The CSRT was required to presume that evidence presented by the military was reliable, and it could rely on secret evidence not shown to the prisoner.[61] Evidence obtained by coercion or torture could be used, and the CSRT could disregard exculpatory evidence.[62] Prisoners could bring in "reasonably available" witnesses and documents to testify, but, in practice, this was not a very meaningful device, as the relevant witnesses were likely to be thousands of miles away and prisoners did not have contact with the world outside Guantanamo.[63] If the CSRT confirmed that a prisoner was an enemy combatant, on the basis of a preponderance of the evidence standard[64] and beginning with the presumption in favor of the government's evidence, the prisoner could be held indefinitely without further hearing, other than periodic review by a Department of Defense annual review board.[65]

Congress seemed to give its backing to the CSRT process. The Detainee Treatment Act of 2005[66] (DTA or 2005 DTA) required the secretary of defense to provide a report describing the procedures CSRTs would use "for determining the status of the detainees held at Guantanamo Bay."[67] The DTA did not comprehensively explain what procedures would have to be followed but did include some basic requirements: (1) there must be a civilian official within the Department of Defense who would act as final reviewing authority within the department regarding CSRT decisions; (2) the procedures must allow some opportunity for periodic review of "any new evidence that may become available relating to the enemy combatant status of a detainee"; and (3) CSRTs would "to the extent practicable, assess (A) whether any statement derived from or relating to such detainee was obtained as a result of coercion; and (B) the probative value (if any) of any such statement."[68] The DTA assumed that CSRTs would determine enemy combatant status on the basis of a preponderance of the evidence standard and could allow a rebuttable presumption in favor of the government's evidence.[69]

The 2005 DTA provided for only very limited judicial review of CSRT decisions: such review would be conducted exclusively by the U.S. Court of Appeals for the District of Columbia Circuit, and the role of the court of appeals in conducting judicial review would be "limited to the consideration of (i) whether the status determination of the Combatant Status Review Tribunal with regard to such alien was consistent with the standards and procedures specified by the Secretary of Defense for Combatant Status Review Tribunals . . . and (ii) to the extent the Constitution and laws of the United States are applicable, whether the use of such standards and procedures to make the determination is consistent with the Constitution and laws of the United States."[70] In other words, the court of appeals, in reviewing CSRT decisions, could consider only (1) whether the CSRT had followed procedures created by the secretary of defense and (2) to the extent that the Constitution and statutory law applied at all (the DTA suggested they might not), whether CSRT procedures were lawful. This did not seem to leave room for the court to consider new evidence,[71] to consider irregularities in a particular proceeding, such as whether a particular prisoner actually had a meaningful opportunity to contest his status designation as an enemy combatant, or even to consider whether the CSRT had reached the right conclusion in any specific case. As noted, no other court could have jurisdiction over claims made by prisoners relating to any aspect of their detention—the DTA expressly provided that, other than the limited court of appeals review just described, "no court, justice, or judge shall have jurisdiction to hear or consider (1) an application for a writ of habeas corpus filed by or on behalf of an alien detained by the Department of Defense at Guantanamo Bay, Cuba."[72]

The Court of Appeals for the District of Columbia Circuit would also have exclusive jurisdiction "to determine the validity of any final decision rendered pursuant to Military Commission Order No. 1, dated August 31, 2005."[73] The court of appeals would be required to review decisions by military tribunals that resulted in the death sentence or a prison term of ten years or more; in all other cases, its review would be discretionary. As with review of CSRT decisions, court of appeals review of decisions by military tribunals would be limited to ensuring that (1) military tribunals followed the procedures created by the secretary of defense; and (2) to the extent that the Constitution and statutory laws applied, that such procedures complied with the law.[74] It seemed that Congress had ratified the CSRT and military tribunal system created by the executive branch; the question remained, though, whether Congress could properly authorize these systems. Did the CSRT and military tribunal systems comply with the law?

One of the first prisoners to appear before a CSRT was Salim Ahmed Hamdan, who was captured in Afghanistan in late 2001 and accused of being Osama Bin Laden's driver, as well as delivering weapons to Al Qaeda members. In October 2004, a CSRT found that Hamdan was indeed an enemy combatant. Charges of conspiracy to aid Al Qaeda were filed against Hamdan, and proceedings began before a military tribunal.[75] Hamdan was assigned military counsel, and his lawyer filed a habeas corpus petition in federal court. In November 2004, a federal district court granted Hamdan's habeas petition, ordering that the military tribunal proceedings be halted. The court ruled that the Geneva Conventions applied to Hamdan. As previously noted, the Geneva Conventions are post–World War II treaties enacted to, among other things, define international standards for treating prisoners of war. The district court concluded that Hamdan was entitled to protection as a prisoner of war under the Geneva Conventions until it was determined that he did not meet the definition of a prisoner of war. The court further held that the military tribunal violated the Geneva Conventions because it could convict Hamdan without giving him access to evidence used against him. A federal court of appeals reversed the district court ruling, saying that the Geneva Conventions did not apply. When the *Hamdan* case reached the U.S. Supreme Court, in 2006, the court determined, in a 5–3 ruling,[76] that the military commission system violated both U.S. military law and the Geneva Conventions. Excerpts from *Hamdan* follow.

Hamdan v. Rumsfeld, 548 U.S. 557 (2006)

Majority opinion by Justice Stevens.

Petitioner Salim Ahmed Hamdan, a Yemeni national, is in custody at an American prison in Guantanamo Bay, Cuba. In November 2001, during hostilities between the United States and the Taliban (which then governed Afghanistan), Hamdan was captured by militia forces and turned over to the U.S. military. In June 2002, he was transported to Guantanamo Bay. Over a year later, the President deemed him eligible for trial by military commission for then-unspecified crimes. After another year had passed, Hamdan was charged with one count of conspiracy "to commit ... offenses triable by military commission."

Hamdan filed petitions for writs of habeas corpus and mandamus to challenge the Executive Branch's intended means of prosecuting this charge. He concedes that a court-martial constituted in accordance with the Uniform Code of Military Justice (UCMJ) ... would have authority to try him. His objection is that the military commission the President has convened lacks such authority, for two principal reasons: First, neither congressional Act nor the common law of war supports trial by this commission for the crime of conspiracy—an offense that, Hamdan says, is not a violation of the law of war. Second, Hamdan contends, the procedures that the President has adopted to try him violate the most basic tenets of military and international law, including the principle that a defendant must be permitted to see and hear the evidence against him.

The District Court granted Hamdan's request for a writ of habeas corpus.... The Court of Appeals for the District of Columbia Circuit reversed.... Recognizing, as we did over a half-century ago, that trial by military commission is an extraordinary measure raising important questions about the balance of powers in our constitutional structure, *Ex parte Quirin*, we granted certiorari....

For the reasons that follow, we conclude that the military commission convened to try Hamdan lacks power to proceed because its structure and procedures violate both the UCMJ and the Geneva Conventions. Four of us also conclude ... that the offense with which Hamdan has been charged is not an "offens[e] that by ... the law of war may be tried by military commissions." ...

I

On September 11, 2001, agents of the al Qaeda terrorist organization hijacked commercial airplanes and attacked the World Trade Center in New York City and the national headquarters of the Department of Defense in Arlington, Virginia. Americans will never forget the devastation wrought by these acts. Nearly 3,000 civilians were killed.

Congress responded by [passing the] ... AUMF.... Acting pursuant to the AUMF, and having determined that the Taliban regime had supported al Qaeda, the President ordered the Armed Forces of the United States to invade Afghanistan. In the ensuing hostilities, hundreds of individuals, Hamdan among them, were captured and eventually detained at Guantanamo Bay.

On November 13, 2001, while the United States was still engaged in active combat with the Taliban, the President issued a comprehensive military order intended to govern the "Detention, Treatment, and Trial of Certain Non-Citizens in the War Against Terrorism." . . . Those subject to the November 13 Order include any noncitizen for whom the President determines "there is reason to believe" that he or she (1) "is or was" a member of al Qaeda or (2) has engaged or participated in terrorist activities aimed at or harmful to the United States. . . . Any such individual "shall, when tried, be tried by military commission for any and all offenses triable by military commission that such individual is alleged to have committed, and may be punished in accordance with the penalties provided under applicable law, including imprisonment or death." . . .

On July 3, 2003, the President announced his determination that Hamdan and five other detainees at Guantanamo Bay were subject to the November 13 Order and thus triable by military commission. In December 2003, military counsel was appointed to represent Hamdan. Two months later, counsel filed demands for charges and for a speedy trial pursuant to Article 10 of the UCMJ. . . . On February 23, 2004, the legal adviser to the Appointing Authority denied the applications, ruling that Hamdan was not entitled to any of the protections of the UCMJ. Not until July 13, 2004, after Hamdan had commenced this action in [a federal district court], did the Government finally charge him with the offense for which, a year earlier, he had been deemed eligible for trial by military commission.

The charging document, which is unsigned, contains 13 numbered paragraphs. The first two paragraphs recite the asserted bases for the military commission's jurisdiction—namely, the November 13 Order and the President's July 3, 2003, declaration that Hamdan is eligible for trial by military commission. The next nine paragraphs, collectively entitled "General Allegations," describe al Qaeda's activities from its inception in 1989 through 2001 and identify Osama bin Laden as the group's leader. Hamdan is not mentioned in these paragraphs.

Only the final two paragraphs, entitled "Charge: Conspiracy," contain allegations against Hamdan. Paragraph 12 charges that "from on or about February 1996 to on or about November 24, 2001," Hamdan "willfully and knowingly joined an enterprise of persons who shared a common criminal purpose and conspired and agreed with [named members of al Qaeda] to commit the following offenses triable by military commission: attacking civilians; attacking civilian objects; murder by an unprivileged belligerent; and terrorism." . . . There is no allegation that Hamdan had any command responsibilities, played a leadership role, or participated in the planning of any activity.

Paragraph 13 lists four "overt acts" that Hamdan is alleged to have committed sometime between 1996 and November 2001 in furtherance of the "enterprise and conspiracy": (1) he acted as Osama bin Laden's "bodyguard and personal driver," "believ[ing]" all the while that bin Laden "and his associates were involved in" terrorist acts prior to and including the attacks of September 11, 2001; (2) he arranged for transportation of, and actually transported, weapons used by al Qaeda members and by bin Laden's bodyguards (Hamdan among them); (3) he "drove or accompanied [O]sama bin Laden to various al Qaida-sponsored training camps, press conferences, or lectures," at which bin Laden encouraged attacks against Americans; and (4) he received weapons training at al Qaeda-sponsored camps....

After this formal charge was filed, the [federal district court] transferred Hamdan's habeas and mandamus petitions to the United States District Court for the District of Columbia. Meanwhile, a Combatant Status Review Tribunal (CSRT) convened pursuant to a military order issued on July 7, 2004, decided that Hamdan's continued detention at Guantanamo Bay was warranted because he was an "enemy combatant." Separately, proceedings before the military commission commenced.

On November 8, 2004, however, the District Court granted Hamdan's petition for habeas corpus and stayed the commission's proceedings. It concluded that the President's authority to establish military commissions extends only to "offenders or offenses triable by military [commission] under the law of war," ... that the law of war includes the Geneva Convention (III) Relative to the Treatment of Prisoners of War, Aug. 12, 1949, ... (Third Geneva Convention); that Hamdan is entitled to the full protections of the Third Geneva Convention until adjudged, in compliance with that treaty, not to be a prisoner of war; and that, whether or not Hamdan is properly classified as a prisoner of war, the military commission convened to try him was established in violation of both the UCMJ and Common Article 3 of the Third Geneva Convention because it had the power to convict based on evidence the accused would never see or hear.

The Court of Appeals for the District of Columbia Circuit ... rejected the District Court's ... conclusion that Hamdan was entitled to relief under the Third Geneva Convention. All three judges agreed that the Geneva Conventions were not "judicially enforceable." ... In other portions of its opinion, the court concluded that our decision in *Quirin* foreclosed any separation-of-powers objection to the military commission's jurisdiction, and held that Hamdan's trial before the contemplated commission would violate neither the UCMJ nor U.S. Armed Forces regulations intended to implement the Geneva Conventions.

On November 7, 2005, we granted certiorari to decide whether the military commission convened to try Hamdan has authority to do so, and whether Hamdan may rely on the Geneva Conventions in these proceedings.

II

On February 13, 2006, the Government filed a motion to dismiss the writ of certiorari. The ground cited for dismissal was the recently enacted Detainee Treatment Act of 2005 (DTA)....

The DTA ... addresses a broad swath of subjects related to detainees. It places restrictions on the treatment and interrogation of detainees in U.S. custody, and it furnishes procedural protections for U.S. personnel accused of engaging in improper interrogation.... It also sets forth certain "procedures for status review of detainees outside the United States."...

The military commission, a tribunal neither mentioned in the Constitution nor created by statute, was born of military necessity.... Though foreshadowed in some respects by earlier tribunals like the Board of General Officers that General Washington convened to try British Major John André for spying during the Revolutionary War, the commission "as such" was inaugurated in 1847.... As commander of occupied Mexican territory, and having available to him no other tribunal, General Winfield Scott that year ordered the establishment of both "'*military commissions*'" to try ordinary crimes committed in the occupied territory and a "*council of war*" to try offenses against the law of war....

When the exigencies of war next gave rise to a need for use of military commissions, during the Civil War, the dual system favored by General Scott was not adopted. Instead, a single tribunal often took jurisdiction over ordinary crimes, war crimes, and breaches of military orders alike.... [E]ach aspect of that seemingly broad jurisdiction was in fact supported by a separate military exigency. Generally, though, the need for military commissions during this period—as during the Mexican War—was driven largely by the then very limited jurisdiction of courts-martial: "The *occasion* for the military commission arises principally from the fact that the jurisdiction of the court-martial proper, in our law, is restricted by statute almost exclusively to members of the military force and to certain specific offences defined in a written code."

Exigency alone, of course, will not justify the establishment and use of penal tribunals not contemplated by Article I, § 8 and Article III, § 1 of the Constitution unless some other part of that document authorizes a response to the felt need.... And that authority, if it exists, can derive only from the powers granted jointly to the President and Congress in time of war....

The Constitution makes the President the "Commander in Chief" of the Armed Forces, Art. II, § 2, cl. 1, but vests in Congress the powers to "declare War . . . and make Rules concerning Captures on Land and Water," . . . to "raise and support Armies," . . . to "define and punish . . . Offences against the Law of Nations," . . . and "To make Rules for the Government and Regulation of the land and naval Forces." . . . The interplay between these powers was described by Chief Justice Chase in the seminal case of *Ex parte Milligan*:

> "The power to make the necessary laws is in Congress; the power to execute in the President. Both powers imply many subordinate and auxiliary powers. Each includes all authorities essential to its due exercise. But neither can the President, in war more than in peace, intrude upon the proper authority of Congress, nor Congress upon the proper authority of the President. ... Congress cannot direct the conduct of campaigns, nor can the President, or any commander under him, without the sanction of Congress, institute

tribunals for the trial and punishment of offences, either of soldiers or civilians, unless in cases of a controlling necessity, which justifies what it compels, or at least insures acts of indemnity from the justice of the legislature."[77]

Whether Chief Justice Chase was correct in suggesting that the President may constitutionally convene military commissions "without the sanction of Congress" in cases of "controlling necessity" is a question this Court has not answered definitively, and need not answer today. For we held in *Quirin* that Congress had, through Article of War 15, sanctioned the use of military commissions in such circumstances. . . .

We have no occasion to revisit *Quirin's* controversial characterization of Article of War 15 as congressional authorization for military commissions. . . . Contrary to the Government's assertion, however, even *Quirin* did not view the authorization as a sweeping mandate for the President to "invoke military commissions when he deems them necessary." . . . Rather, the *Quirin* Court recognized that Congress had simply preserved what power, under the Constitution and the common law of war, the President had had before 1916[78] to convene military commissions—with the express condition that the President and those under his command comply with the law of war. [The Court in *Quirin* concluded] that Congress had authorized military commissions. . . .

The Government would have us dispense with the inquiry that the *Quirin* Court undertook and find in either the AUMF or the DTA specific, overriding authorization for the very commission that has been convened to try Hamdan. Neither of these congressional Acts, however, expands the President's authority to convene military commissions. First, while we assume that the AUMF activated the President's war powers . . . and that those powers include the authority to convene military commissions in appropriate circumstances . . . there is nothing in the text or legislative history of the AUMF even hinting that Congress intended to expand or alter the authorization set forth in . . . the UCMJ.

Likewise, the DTA cannot be read to authorize this commission. Although the DTA, unlike either [the UCMJ] or the AUMF, was enacted after the President had convened Hamdan's commission, it contains no language authorizing that tribunal or any other at Guantanamo Bay. The DTA . . . pointedly reserves judgment on whether "the Constitution and laws of the United States are applicable" in reviewing such decisions [by military commissions] and whether, if they are, the "standards and procedures" used to try Hamdan and other detainees actually violate the "Constitution and laws."

Together, the UCMJ, the AUMF, and the DTA at most acknowledge a general Presidential authority to convene military commissions in circumstances where justified under the "Constitution and laws," including the law of war. Absent a more specific congressional authorization, the task of this Court is, as it was in *Quirin*, to decide whether Hamdan's military commission is so justified. It is to that inquiry we now turn.

V

The common law governing military commissions may be gleaned from past practice and what sparse legal precedent exists. Commissions historically have been used in three situations.... First, they have substituted for civilian courts at times and in places where martial law has been declared. Their use in these circumstances has raised constitutional questions ... but is well recognized. Second, commissions have been established to try civilians "as part of a temporary military government over occupied enemy territory or territory regained from an enemy where civilian government cannot and does not function." ...

The third type of commission, convened as an "incident to the conduct of war" when there is a need "to seize and subject to disciplinary measures those enemies who in their attempt to thwart or impede our military effort have violated the law of war," *Quirin*, has been described as "utterly different" from the other two.... Not only is its jurisdiction limited to offenses cognizable during time of war, but its role is primarily a factfinding one—to determine, typically on the battlefield itself, whether the defendant has violated the law of war. The last time the U.S. Armed Forces used the law-of-war military commission was during World War II. In *Quirin*, this Court sanctioned President Roosevelt's use of such a tribunal to try Nazi saboteurs captured on American soil during the War....

Quirin is the model the Government invokes most frequently to defend the commission convened to try Hamdan. That is both appropriate and unsurprising. Since Guantanamo Bay is neither enemy-occupied territory nor under martial law, the law-of-war commission is the only model available. At the same time, no more robust model of executive power exists; *Quirin* represents the high-water mark of military power to try enemy combatants for war crimes....

The question is whether the preconditions designed to ensure that a military necessity exists to justify the use of this extraordinary tribunal have been satisfied here.

The charge against Hamdan ... alleges a conspiracy extending over a number of years, from 1996 to November 2001. All but two months of that more than 5-year-long period preceded the attacks of September 11, 2001, and the enactment of the AUMF—the Act of Congress on which the Government relies for exercise of its war powers and thus for its authority to convene military commissions. Neither the purported agreement with Osama bin Laden and others to commit war crimes, nor a single overt act, is alleged to have occurred in a theater of war or on any specified date after September 11, 2001. None of the overt acts that Hamdan is alleged to have committed violates the law of war.

These facts alone cast doubt on the legality of the charge and, hence, the commission; [the common law of war provides that, in order to try someone before a military commission] the offense alleged must have been committed both in a theater of war and *during*, not before, the relevant conflict. But the deficiencies in the time and place allegations also underscore—indeed are symptomatic of—the most serious defect of this charge: The offense it alleges is not triable by law-of-war military commission. . . .

There is no suggestion that Congress has, in exercise of its constitutional authority to "define and punish . . . Offences against the Law of Nations," . . . positively identified "conspiracy" as a war crime. . . .

[By contrast] the violation . . . alleged [in *Quirin*] was, by "universal agreement and practice" both in this country and internationally, recognized as an offense against the law of war. . . .

Because the charge does not support the commission's jurisdiction, the commission lacks authority to try Hamdan.

The charge's shortcomings are not merely formal, but are indicative of a broader inability on the Executive's part here to satisfy the most basic precondition—at least in the absence of specific congressional authorization—for establishment of military commissions: military necessity. Hamdan's tribunal was appointed not by a military commander in the field of battle, but by a retired major general stationed away from any active hostilities. . . . Hamdan is charged not with an overt act for which he was caught redhanded in a theater of war and which military efficiency demands be tried expeditiously, but with an *agreement* the inception of which long predated the attacks of September 11, 2001, and the AUMF. That may well be a crime [i.e., triable in civilian court] but it is not an offense that "by the law of war may be tried by military commissio[n]." None of the overt acts alleged to have been committed in furtherance of the agreement is itself a war crime, or even necessarily occurred during time of, or in a theater of, war. Any urgent need for imposition or execution of judgment is utterly belied by the record; Hamdan was arrested in November 2001 and he was not charged until mid-2004. These simply are not the circumstances in which, by any stretch of the historical evidence or this Court's precedents, a military commission established by Executive Order under the authority of Article 21 of the UCMJ may lawfully try a person and subject him to punishment.

VI

Whether or not the Government has charged Hamdan with an offense against the law of war cognizable by military commission, the commission lacks power to proceed. The UCMJ conditions the President's use of military commissions on compliance not only with the American common law of war, but also with the rest of the UCMJ itself, insofar as applicable, and with the "rules and precepts of the law of nations," ... including, *inter alia*, the four Geneva Conventions signed in 1949....The procedures that the Government has decreed will govern Hamdan's trial by commission violate these laws.

A

The commission's procedures are set forth in Commission Order No. 1, which was amended most recently on August 31, 2005 — after Hamdan's trial had already begun. Every commission established pursuant to Commission Order No. 1 must have a presiding officer and at least three other members, all of whom must be commissioned officers. ...The presiding officer's job is to rule on questions of law and other evidentiary ... issues; the other members make findings and, if applicable, sentencing decisions....The accused is entitled to appointed military counsel and may hire civilian counsel at his own expense so long as such counsel is a U.S. citizen with security clearance "at the level SECRET or higher." ...

The accused also is entitled to a copy of the charge(s) against him ... to a presumption of innocence, and to certain other rights typically afforded criminal defendants in civilian courts and courts-martial. ...These rights are subject, however, to one glaring condition: The accused and his civilian counsel may be excluded from, and precluded from ever learning what evidence was presented during, any part of the proceeding that either the Appointing Authority or the presiding officer decides to "close." Grounds for such closure "include the protection of information classified or classifiable ... ; information protected by law or rule from unauthorized disclosure; the physical safety of participants in Commission proceedings, including prospective witnesses; intelligence and law enforcement sources, methods, or activities; and other national security interests." ... Appointed military defense counsel must be privy to these closed sessions, but may, at the presiding officer's discretion, be forbidden to reveal to his or her client what took place therein....

Another striking feature of the rules governing Hamdan's commission is that they permit the admission of any evidence that, in the opinion of the presiding officer, "would have probative value to a reasonable person." ... Under this test, not only is testimonial hearsay and evidence obtained through coercion fully admissible, but neither live testimony nor witnesses' written statements need be sworn. ...Moreover, the accused and his civilian counsel may be denied access to evidence in the form of "protected information" ... so long as the presiding officer concludes that the evidence is "probative" ... and that its admission without the accused's knowledge would not "result in the denial of a full and fair trial." ...

Once all the evidence is in, the commission members (not including the presiding officer) must vote on the accused's guilt. A two-thirds vote will suffice for both a verdict of guilty and for imposition of any sentence not including death (the imposition of which requires a unanimous vote).... Any appeal is taken to a three-member review panel composed of military officers and designated by the Secretary of Defense, only one member of which need have experience as a judge....The review panel is directed to "disregard any variance from procedures specified in this Order or elsewhere that would not materially have affected the outcome of the trial before the Commission."...Once the panel makes its recommendation to the Secretary of Defense, the Secretary can either remand for further proceedings or forward the record to the President with his recommendation as to final disposition....The President then, unless he has delegated the task to the Secretary, makes the "final decision."...He may change the commission's findings or sentence only in a manner favorable to the accused....

B

... Chief among [Hamdan's] particular objections are that he may, under the Commission Order, be convicted based on evidence he has not seen or heard, and that any evidence admitted against him need not comply with the admissibility or relevance rules typically applicable in criminal trials and court-martial proceedings....

One of Hamdan's complaints is that he will be, and *indeed already has been*, excluded from his own trial....

C

...[T]he procedures governing trials by military commission historically have been the same as those governing courts-martial....

...[W]e conclude that the "practicability" determination the President has made is insufficient to justify variances from the [UCMJ's] procedures governing courts-martial....

The President here has determined ...that it is impracticable to apply the rules and principles of law that govern "the trial of criminal cases in the United States district courts,"...to Hamdan's [military] commission. We assume that complete deference is owed that determination. The President has not, however, made a similar official determination that it is impracticable to apply the rules for courts-martial....

Nothing in the record before us demonstrates that it would be impracticable to apply court-martial rules in this case. There is no suggestion, for example, of any logistical difficulty in securing properly sworn and authenticated evidence or in applying the usual principles of relevance and admissibility ... the only reason offered in support of th[e] determination [of impracticability] is the danger posed by international terrorism. Without for one moment underestimating that danger, it is not evident to us why it should require, in the case of Hamdan's trial, any variance from the rules that govern courts-martial.

The absence of any showing of impracticability is particularly disturbing when considered in light of the clear and admitted failure to apply one of the most fundamental protections afforded not just by the Manual for Courts-Martial but also by the UCMJ itself: the right to be present . . . the jettisoning of so basic a right cannot lightly be excused. . . .

Under the circumstances, then, the rules applicable in courts-martial must apply. Since it is undisputed that Commission Order No. 1 deviates in many significant respects from those rules, it necessarily violates Article 36(b) [of the UCMJ]. . . .

The military commission was not born of a desire to dispense a more summary form of justice than is afforded by courts-martial; it developed, rather, as a tribunal of necessity to be employed when courts-martial lacked jurisdiction over either the accused or the subject matter. . . . Exigency lent the commission its legitimacy, but did not further justify the wholesale jettisoning of procedural protections. That history explains why the military commission's procedures typically have been the ones used by courts-martial. . . . Th[e] [UCMJ] not having been complied with here, the rules specified for Hamdan's trial are illegal.

D

The procedures adopted to try Hamdan also violate the Geneva Conventions. . . .

. . . [T]here is at least one provision of the Geneva Conventions that applies here. . . . [Common] Article 3 . . . provides that in a "conflict not of an international character occurring in the territory of one of the High Contracting Parties, each Party to the conflict shall be bound to apply, as a minimum," certain provisions protecting "[p]ersons taking no active part in the hostilities, including members of armed forces who have laid down their arms and those placed *hors de combat* by . . . detention." One such provision prohibits "the passing of sentences and the carrying out of executions without previous judgment pronounced by a regularly constituted court affording all the judicial guarantees which are recognized as indispensable by civilized peoples." . . .

The Court of Appeals thought, and the Government asserts, that Common Article 3 does not apply to Hamdan because the conflict with al Qaeda, being "'international in scope,'" does not qualify as a "'conflict not of an international character.'" . . . That reasoning is erroneous. The term "conflict not of an international character" is used here in contradistinction to a conflict between nations. . . .

Common Article 3, then, is applicable here and, as indicated above, requires that Hamdan be tried by a "regularly constituted court affording all the judicial guarantees which are recognized as indispensable by civilized peoples." . . . While the term "regularly constituted court" is not specifically defined in either Common Article 3 or its accompanying commentary, other sources disclose its core meaning. The commentary accompanying a provision of the Fourth Geneva Convention, for example, defines "'regularly constituted'" tribunals to include "ordinary military courts" and "definitely exclud[e] all special tribunals." ...

As Justice Kennedy explains [in his concurring opinion] ... "[t]he regular military courts in our system are the courts-martial established by congressional statutes." At a minimum, a military commission "can be 'regularly constituted' by the standards of our military justice system only if some practical need explains deviations from court-martial practice." ... no such need has been demonstrated here ...

Inextricably intertwined with the question of [a] regular constitute[ed] [tribunal] is the evaluation of the procedures governing the tribunal and whether they afford "all the judicial guarantees which are recognized as indispensable by civilized peoples." ... Like the phrase "regularly constituted court," this phrase is not defined in the text of the Geneva Conventions. But it must be understood to incorporate at least the barest of those trial protections that have been recognized by customary international law. Many of these are described in Article 75 of Protocol I to the Geneva Conventions of 1949, adopted in 1977. ... Among the rights set forth in Article 75 is the "right to be tried in [one's] presence."

... [A]n accused must, absent disruptive conduct or consent, be present for his trial and must be privy to the evidence against him. ... That the Government has a compelling interest in denying Hamdan access to certain sensitive information is not doubted. ... But, at least absent express statutory provision to the contrary, information used to convict a person of a crime must be disclosed to him. ...

Common Article 3 obviously tolerates a great degree of flexibility in trying individuals captured during armed conflict; its requirements are general ones, crafted to accommodate a wide variety of legal systems. But *requirements* they are nonetheless. The commission that the President has convened to try Hamdan does not meet those requirements.

VII

We have assumed, as we must, that the allegations made in the Government's charge against Hamdan are true. We have assumed, moreover, the truth of the message implicit in that charge—viz., that Hamdan is a dangerous individual whose beliefs, if acted upon, would cause great harm and even death to innocent civilians, and who would act upon those beliefs if given the opportunity. It bears emphasizing that Hamdan does not challenge, and we do not today address, the Government's power to detain him for the duration of active hostilities in order to prevent such harm. But in undertaking to try Hamdan and subject him to criminal punishment, the Executive is bound to comply with the Rule of Law that prevails in this jurisdiction.

The judgment of the Court of Appeals is reversed, and the case is remanded for further proceedings.

Justice Kennedy, concurring in part.

Military Commission Order No. 1 . . . exceeds limits that certain statutes, duly enacted by Congress, have placed on the President's authority to convene military courts. This is not a case, then, where the Executive can assert some unilateral authority to fill a void left by congressional inaction. It is a case where Congress, in the proper exercise of its powers as an independent branch of government, and as part of a long tradition of legislative involvement in matters of military justice, has considered the subject of military tribunals and set limits on the President's authority. . . . Respect for laws derived from the customary operation of the Executive and Legislative Branches gives some assurance of stability in time of crisis. The Constitution is best preserved by reliance on standards tested over time and insulated from the pressures of the moment. . . .

If Congress, after due consideration, deems it appropriate to change the controlling statutes, in conformance with the Constitution and other laws, it has the power and prerogative to do so. . . .

Trial by military commission raises separation-of-powers concerns of the highest order. Located within a single branch, these courts carry the risk that offenses will be defined, prosecuted, and adjudicated by executive officials without independent review. . . . Concentration of power puts personal liberty in peril of arbitrary action by officials, an incursion the Constitution's three-part system is designed to avoid. It is imperative, then, that when military tribunals are established, full and proper authority exists for the Presidential directive.

The proper framework for assessing whether Executive actions are authorized is the three-part scheme used by Justice Jackson in his opinion in *Youngstown Sheet & Tube*. . . . "When the President acts pursuant to an express or implied authorization of Congress, his authority is at its maximum, for it includes all that he possesses in his own right plus all that Congress can delegate." . . . "When the President acts in absence of either a congressional grant or denial of authority, he can only rely upon his own independent powers, but there is a zone of twilight in which he and Congress may have concurrent authority, or in which its distribution is uncertain." . . . And "[w]hen the President takes measures incompatible with the expressed or implied will of Congress, his power is at its lowest ebb."

In this case, as the Court observes, the President has acted in a field with a history of congressional participation and regulation. In the . . . UCMJ . . . Congress has set forth governing principles for military courts. The UCMJ as a whole establishes an intricate system of military justice. It authorizes courts-martial in various forms . . . it regulates the organization and procedure of those courts . . . it defines offenses, and rights for the accused . . . and it provides mechanisms for appellate review . . . the statute further recognizes that special military commissions may be convened to try war crimes. . . . While these laws provide authority for certain forms of military courts, they also impose limitations, at least two of which control this case. If the

President has exceeded these limits, this becomes a case of conflict between Presidential and congressional action—a case within Justice Jackson's third category, not the second or first . . .

[The] structural differences between the military commissions and courts-martial—the concentration of functions, including legal decision-making, in a single executive official; the less rigorous standards for composition of the tribunal; and the creation of special review procedures in place of [courts]—remove safeguards that are important to the fairness of the proceedings and the independence of the court. Congress has prescribed these guarantees for courts-martial; and no evident practical need explains the departures here. For these reasons the commission cannot be considered regularly constituted under United States law and thus does not satisfy Congress' requirement that military commissions conform to the law of war. . . .

. . . [M]oreover, the basic procedures for the commissions deviate from procedures for courts-martial, in violation . . . [of the UCMJ]. . . . [T]he Military Commission Order abandons the detailed Military Rules of Evidence, which are modeled on the Federal Rules of Evidence. . . . Instead, the order imposes just one evidentiary rule: "Evidence shall be admitted if . . . the evidence would have probative value to a reasonable person." . . .

The rule here could permit admission of multiple hearsay and other forms of evidence generally prohibited on grounds of unreliability. Indeed, the commission regulations specifically contemplate admission of unsworn written statements, and they make no provision for exclusion of coerced declarations save those "established to have been made as a result of torture." . . . Besides, even if evidence is deemed nonprobative by the presiding officer at Hamdan's trial, the military-commission members still may view it. In another departure from court-martial practice the military commission members may object to the presiding officer's evidence rulings and determine themselves, by majority vote, whether to admit the evidence.

As the Court explains, the Government has made no demonstration of practical need for these special rules and procedures, either in this particular case or as to the military commissions in general, . . . nor is any such need self-evident. For all the Government's regulations and submissions reveal, it would be feasible for most, if not all, of the conventional military evidence rules and procedures to be followed.

In sum, as presently structured, Hamdan's military commission exceeds the bounds Congress has placed on the President's authority [under] the UCMJ. Because Congress has prescribed these limits, Congress can change them, requiring a new analysis consistent with the Constitution and other governing laws. At this time, however, we must apply the standards Congress has provided. By those standards the military commission is deficient.

In *Hamdan*, five justices concluded that (a) the tribunal trying Hamdan followed rules that violated the Uniform Code of Military Justice and (b) Common Article 3 of the Geneva Conventions applied to trials by military tribunal. Four justices additionally concluded that (1) conspiracy was not an offense triable as a war crime and (2) the specific military tribunal procedures created by the secretary of defense violated Common Article 3 of the Geneva Conventions by excluding Hamdan from his own trial. Justice Kennedy joined Justice Stevens's opinion as to most of its conclusions but did not find it necessary "to address the validity of the conspiracy charge against Hamdan" or to determine whether the military tribunal's specific procedures violated Common Article 3 (though he did agree with Justice Stevens and three other justices that the tribunal failed to comply with Common Article 3 because it was not a "regularly constituted court").

For the moment, at least, the court's decision effectively scuttled the administration's system for trying detainees before military tribunals that did not provide basic procedural protections and dealt another blow to the unitary executive theory.[79] The court emphasized that the president did not have unlimited power to decide how to try detainees—his authority had to stem from an act of Congress. This conclusion rejected the assertion in the November 2001 Philbin memo that, whether or not Congress spoke to the matter, President Bush maintained authority to set up military tribunals to try detainees, at his sole discretion, and subject to rules he made. In *Hamdan*, the court found that the president's military tribunal system conflicted with an act of Congress—the Uniform Code of Military Justice (UCMJ). The tribunals did not follow trial procedures set forth in the UCMJ, and the president did not demonstrate any reason for allowing an exception to these rules on the basis of military necessity. The decision suggested that detainees would have to be tried either before courts-martial or before federal civilian courts—unless Congress revised the UCMJ. The court also rejected the Bush administration's argument that the DTA strictly limited Hamdan's access to judicial review by allowing only very limited review by the Court of Appeals for the D.C. Circuit. On this point, the Supreme Court reasoned that the 2005 DTA, enacted *after* Hamdan's proceedings before the military tribunal had begun, could not apply retroactively to Hamdan.

The court also concluded that the Geneva Conventions applied and that the military tribunals violated Common Article 3 by failing to establish a "regularly constituted court" to try alleged war criminals. Four justices further concluded that the secretary of defense's procedures for military tribunals violated Common Article 3. In a concurring opinion, Justice Kennedy emphasized that, since the president's military commission actually conflicted with an act of Congress (the UCMJ), the president's authority was at its "low ebb" under the *Youngstown Steel* tripartite framework and that the military tribunal system was illegitimate for this reason alone. However, Justice Kennedy's concurring opinion also pointed out a clear way for the executive branch to legitimately use the military commission system it desired: by convincing Congress to expressly grant it such authority.

That's essentially what happened next. Congress held hearings on the military tribunal system, and the Bush administration asked Congress to provide specific authorization for the system that the court had rejected.[80] Military lawyers raised concerns about a tribunal system that deviated from established procedural rules and had failed to convict even a single alleged terrorist.[81] One navy lawyer described the system as "a half hearted and disorganized effort by a skeleton group of inexperienced attorneys to prosecute fairly low-level accused in a process that appears to be rigged."[82]

Despite these criticisms, Congress ultimately passed the Military Commissions Act of 2006. The 2006 MCA "gave the Bush administration most of what it wanted in order to enable it to deal with detainees in ways that had been invalidated by the *Hamdan* ruling."[83] The president was expressly authorized to establish military commissions to try any "alien unlawful enemy combatant."[84] An "unlawful enemy combatant" was defined as "a person who has engaged in hostilities or who has purposefully and materially supported hostilities against the United States or its co-belligerents . . . or a person who [at any time] has been determined to be an unlawful enemy combatant by a Combatant Status Review Tribunal."[85] As a general proposition, the 2006 MCA authorized the secretary of defense to depart from the procedures and rules of evidence used by courts-martial when the secretary determined it was not "practicable" for military commissions to comply with such principles or when compliance would interfere with "military or intelligence activities."[86] This provision gave the secretary of defense leeway to deviate from the rules set forth in the 2006 MCA. Therefore, the rules discussed here should be understood as not fully binding; under the circumstances described in sec. 949a(a) (i.e., when it was not practicable to follow the rules prescribed by Congress or when following these rules would interfere with military or intelligence activities), the secretary of defense could authorize military commissions to follow different rules.

A military judge would be assigned to each commission; other commission members would be commissioned officers of the armed forces on active duty, without any requirement of judicial or legal experience.[87] The accused would be assigned military lawyers as counsel and could retain a civilian lawyer at their own expense.[88] The 2006 MCA endorsed the executive branch's pre-*Hamdan* decision to allow military commissions to consider hearsay evidence, with some limitations.[89] The commission's military judge could determine that hearsay evidence is admissible as long as there is "sufficient basis to find that the evidence is what it claims to be."[90] The evidence could not be "unreliable or lacking in probative value."[91] These provisions allowed the admissibility of evidence that would not be admissible in court-martial proceedings, including, for example, unsigned, unsworn documents attributed to people not available for cross-examination. Statements obtained by torture were not admissible,[92] but statements obtained by coercion short of torture were admissible in some circumstances.[93] Coerced statements obtained before enactment of the 2005 Detainee Treatment Act were admissible if (1) the degree of coercion was disputed and (2) the military judge found that "the totality of the circumstances renders the statement reliable and possessing sufficient probative value" and that "the interests of justice would best be served" by allowing the statement to be used as evidence.[94] Coerced statements obtained after enactment of the 2005 DTA would have to meet the same standards applied to coerced statements obtained before the 2005 DTA and, in addition, could not have been obtained by interrogation methods "amount[ing] to cruel, inhuman, or degrading treatment."[95] That meant, of course, that coerced statements obtained before enactment of the 2005 DTA that were obtained through interrogation methods constituting cruel, inhuman, or degrading treatment could be admissible. Louis Fisher questions whether such evidence could *ever* be "reliable" or have "probative value."[96]

The 2006 MCA provided for circumstances in which the accused could be denied access to evidence used against him (recall that this was a central issue in the *Hamdan* case). Under the 2006 MCA, classified information could be used as evidence but protected from disclosure to the accused "if disclosure would be detrimental to national security."[97] The military judge assigned to the commission was authorized to protect classified information introduced as evidence from disclosure by "delet[ing] specified items of classified information" or substituting information in place of the classified information, for example by providing the accused with a summary of the information.[98] The military judge could also protect from disclosure to the accused the "sources, methods, or activities" that produced classified information introduced as evidence.[99] Louis Fisher argues that the use of classified information under these circumstances undermines other procedural protections extended to the accused, for example by permitting the government to introduce evidence provided by an informant whose identity is kept secret.[100]

The 2006 MCA also assigned the president the authority to "interpret the meaning and application of the Geneva Conventions"[101] (recall that the court relied on its interpretation of the Geneva Conventions in *Hamdan*). In addition, the 2006 MCA provided a definition of "torture" and "cruel or inhuman treatment" under Common Article 3 of the Geneva Conventions, for the purpose of defining offenses in violation of the War Crimes Act (perhaps a bit incongruously, given that the MCA assigned the president the authority to interpret the Geneva Conventions himself).[102] Chapter 11 addresses the question of torture in more detail.

Finally, the 2006 MCA, like the 2005 DTA, strictly limited judicial review of decisions by military tribunals. In *Hamdan*, the court concluded that the DTA's court access provisions could not apply retroactively. The 2006 MCA restated the DTA's court access provisions, making clear they would apply going forward. The Court of Appeals for the District of Columbia Circuit would have exclusive jurisdiction "to determine the validity of a judgment rendered by a military commission."[103] As under the DTA, court of appeals review of decisions by military tribunals would be limited to ensuring that (1) military tribunals followed the procedures prescribed for them[104] and (2) to the extent that the Constitution and statutory laws applied, such procedures complied with the law.[105] The 2006 MCA added one new layer of review: the Supreme Court could review decisions made by the court of appeals.[106] Section 7 of the 2006 MCA, like the 2005 DTA, barred courts from considering a petition for a writ of habeas corpus by an alien enemy combatant.[107] This provision applied to "all cases, without exception, pending on or after the date of the enactment of this Act which relate to any aspect of the detention, transfer, treatment, trial, or conditions of detention of an alien detained by the United States since September 11, 2001."[108]

Congress had now expressly provided the executive branch with the authority to establish and set rules for trial by military commission, with only very limited opportunity for appeal to civilian courts. However, the 2006 MCA itself was challenged in court, and, in 2008, the Supreme Court narrowly ruled, in *Boumediene v. Bush*, that section 7 was unconstitutional. In *Boumediene*, the court focused on section 7 alone and did not address other provisions of the 2006 MCA.[109] As in *Rasul*, petitioners in *Boumediene* were noncitizens held at Guantanamo. In *Rasul*, the court had considered a habeas statute that did not distinguish between citizens and noncitizens. But, since *Rasul*, Congress had passed laws—the 2005 DTA and the 2006 MCA—that attempted to limit noncitizens' access to the courts. The question now was whether Congress could do this by ordinary statute or whether noncitizens held at Guantanamo had a constitutional right to habeas corpus that could not be denied absent a formal suspension of the writ or provision of some adequate substitute for habeas access. In a 5–4 decision, the court ruled that noncitizens held at Guantanamo do have a constitutional right to petition a federal court for a writ of habeas corpus.

Each petitioner in *Boumediene* had appeared before a CSRT, which had found each man to be an enemy combatant. The petitioners had sought a writ of habeas corpus from the U.S. District Court for the District of Columbia and, on appeal, the Court of Appeals for the D.C. Circuit ruled that the 2006 MCA prevented federal courts from considering petitions for the writ. The case was brought before the Supreme Court. As in *Rasul*, the Supreme Court noted the ancient roots of habeas and described it as a fundamental constitutional protection against unlawful restraint, "an essential mechanism in the separation-of-powers scheme" created by the Framers.[110] The court concluded that the Framers' interest in limiting government power in order to protect individual rights extended to noncitizens as well as citizens. The Suspension Clause was designed to ensure that, "except during periods of formal suspension, the Judiciary will have a time-tested device, the writ, to maintain the 'delicate balance of governance' that is itself the surest safeguard of liberty."[111] The fact of U.S. control over Guantanamo defeated the Bush administration's argument that, as territory located outside the United States, the naval base was a place where "the Constitution had no effect."[112] The court considered the implications of this argument—that "it would be possible for the political branches to govern without legal constraint" in territories outside the formal bounds of the United States, though under the government's control—to be dangerous.[113]

As in *Rasul*, the Supreme Court distinguished the facts in *Boumediene* from *Eisentrager*: the petitioners in *Boumediene*, unlike those in *Eisentrager*, contested the claim that they were enemy combatants. Where the Germans in *Eisentrager* received a military trial, the petitioners in *Boumediene* received only a limited CSRT hearing, which failed to afford "a rigorous adversarial process to test the legality of their detention."[114] Though the petitioners in *Boumediene* were "technically outside the sovereign territory of the United States," Guantanamo remains under U.S. control: "[i]n every practical sense Guantanamo is not abroad; it is within the constant jurisdiction of the United States."[115] Accordingly, the court held "that Art. I, § 9, cl. 2, of the Constitution has full effect at Guantanamo Bay."[116] Since Congress had not formally suspended access to habeas corpus, petitioners could be denied access to the writ only if Congress had created an adequate substitute for habeas through the CSRT procedures and the limited court review of CSRT determinations provided in the 2005 DTA.

The court cited several reasons why CSRT hearings could not serve as an adequate and effective substitute for habeas: (1) the "Personal Representative" assigned to the detainee was not his lawyer or even his "advocate"; (2) evidence presented by the government "is accorded a presumption of validity"; (3) a detainee could "present "reasonably available" evidence," but, under the circumstances, "his ability to rebut the Government's evidence against him is limited by the circumstances of his confinement and his lack of counsel"; and (4) hearsay evidence was admissible, so long as the tribunal found it "relevant and helpful."[117] While the DTA and the MCA provided some judicial review of CSRT determinations, the court found that review too limited. The court noted that, in the past, when Congress created substitutes for habeas, it granted courts "broad remedial powers" to ensure that prisoners were not unjustly held. Under the DTA and the MCA, by contrast, the court of appeals had very limited authority. It could not "inquire into the legality of the detention generally but [could] only . . . assess whether the CSRT complied with the 'standards and procedures specified by the Secretary of Defense' and whether those standards and procedures are lawful."[118] In reviewing CSRT determinations, the court of appeals could neither review newly available evidence nor order the release of a prisoner who was unlawfully held. Under these circumstances, judicial review of the CSRT process was not an effective substitute for habeas corpus.

Even if the CSRTs satisfied due process considerations raised in *Hamdi* (which the court did not concede), the *Boumediene* court said that habeas review requires something more—the opportunity to "cu[t] through all forms and g[o] to the very tissue of the structure. It comes in from the outside, not in subordination to the proceedings, and although every form may have been preserved opens the inquiry whether they have been more than an empty shell."[119] The process Congress had created fell short because the CSRT process carried with it a "considerable risk of error" and the court of appeals, being sharply limited in its ability to review CSRT proceedings, simply did not have "the means to correct errors that occurred during the CSRT proceedings."[120] Under the DTA, the court of appeals could not consider new evidence that was unavailable to the government or the prisoner during CSRT proceedings.[121] Given that prisoners who were found to be enemy combatants could be held for "a generation or more," the risk of unjustified detention was "too significant to ignore."[122]

As in prior decisions setting limits on presidential power, the court's decision in *Boumediene* did not order the release of any prisoners: it simply ruled that section 7 of the 2006 MCA was unconstitutional and that noncitizens held at Guantanamo were entitled to seek the writ of habeas corpus from a federal district court. It did not reject the CSRT process, and it cautioned that, "[e]xcept in cases of undue delay, federal courts should refrain from entertaining an enemy combatant's habeas corpus petition at least until after the Department [of Defense], acting via the CSRT, has had a chance to review his status."[123]

By the time the court decided *Boumediene*, some of the prisoners at Guantanamo had been held for nearly seven years without a court hearing of any kind. It is clear that the court found this unacceptable. The court also made clear that it would not be sufficient to hold prisoners in a military detention system that allowed only limited access to federal civilian courts. Prisoners, even noncitizens, have a constitutional right to habeas corpus unless it is suspended by Congress pursuant to the conditions specified in Article I, section 9, of the Constitution. That means they have to have a meaningful opportunity to make their case in court that they are being held unlawfully. Federal courts have the authority to consider their claim of unlawful detention and to order their release, if warranted. The Military Commission Act improperly limited prisoners' access to federal civilian courts through habeas corpus without providing a satisfactory substitute; the limited access to federal civilian court provided by the Detainee Treatment Act of 2005 was insufficient. The court rejected the theory that Guantanamo Bay is a place where the Constitution simply does not apply and emphasized that the American constitutional system depends on a separation of powers. The executive cannot exercise unfettered discretion in detaining suspects in the war on terror indefinitely without hearing of any kind and without meaningful access to the federal civilian courts.

The *Boumediene* decision was seen by some observers[124] as a rebuke to advocates of the unitary executive and as an example of the Supreme Court fulfilling its role as a defender of the Constitution against the other branches of government through judicial review (the court cited *Marbury v. Madison* in rejecting the idea that the president or Congress may "say what the law is"—a direct rejection of the unitary executive theory). The decision made clear that prisoners had to be given meaningful access to civilian courts and that the military commission system, coupled with the Military Commission Act's attempt to cut off habeas corpus, was insufficient. Prisoners had a constitutional right to habeas corpus, so Congress could not overrule the court's decision unless legislators decided that habeas corpus could be suspended pursuant to Article I, section 9 (i.e., because the public safety required suspension because of a "rebellion or invasion," circumstances the court suggested were not present).

However, in some ways, *Boumediene* was a disappointment for those looking to rein in executive power. The Supreme Court had made clear that the president and Congress had crossed constitutional lines, but the court could not order any penalty (the Constitution provides for none, other than impeachment). The result was that the elected branches of government paid no tangible price, despite repeated findings by the court that the president or the president and Congress had gone too far. The executive branch made decisions on the basis of its theory of inherent unilateral emergency power and, for nearly seven years, held prisoners at its discretion, allowing hearings to some, holding others without charges, and releasing still others, seemingly at whim, without allowing prisoners access to the courts. The four court decisions that seemed to set limits on presidential power regarding detention had limited effect, and *Boumediene* itself was decided just a few months before President Bush left office.

In addition, it's worth emphasizing that *Boumediene* was decided by a narrow 5–4 vote. Justice O'Connor, who had written in *Hamdi* that the president did not have a "blank check" in fighting the war on terror, had retired and been replaced by Justice Samuel Alito, who was one of four dissenters in *Boumediene*. Chief Justice Roberts suggested in dissent that *Boumediene* was a political decision, an effort by the court to "shift responsibility for . . . sensitive foreign policy and national security decisions from the elected branches to the Federal Judiciary." Justice Scalia, also dissenting, charged that the majority's decision "will almost certainly cause more Americans to be killed."

At the least, *Boumediene* seemed to make clear that it would not be acceptable to hold prisoners indefinitely without meaningful access to the federal civilian courts. With Bush leaving office just a few months after *Boumediene*, the question of how to follow the decision fell to the Obama administration. Critics of broad presidential power hoped that President Obama would repudiate the previous administration's approach, deciding either to try prisoners in civilian courts or, if there was not evidence to convict them, to release them.[125] As it turned out, the detention system continued under President Obama in essentially the same form, as is discussed in chapter 13.

One of the questions related to Guantanamo was this: why were prisoners held so long without hearing or trial? If these were dangerous terrorists, why not simply prosecute and convict them, sentencing them to long prison terms? The answer was that the Bush administration had other goals that it argued were justified by national security concerns, one of which was "extract[ing] intelligence."[126] In another secret memorandum, government lawyers set forth a rationale for presidential power to order the torture of prisoners in an effort to gain intelligence that could prevent further attacks. One prisoner, Khalid Sheikh Muhammed, the self-described mastermind of the September 11 attacks, was reportedly waterboarded 183 times in one month. The next chapter examines the use of torture in the war on terror.

11

TORTURE IN THE WAR ON TERROR

When U.S. troops began to capture fighters in Afghanistan and when suspected terrorists were handed over to U.S. forces by allies (who often received a bounty), an initial question arose about what to do with the prisoners. As discussed in the previous chapter, the Bush administration sent many of them to Guantanamo Bay, to be held indefinitely without charges or possibly to be tried before military tribunals. One of the reasons for doing this was to extract intelligence from the prisoners—information that could be used to prevent future terrorist attacks.[1] Other suspected terrorists were interrogated in secret prisons around the world. For the U.S. government, in gathering information from these prisoners, "the gloves came off."[2] The government and many in the press have referred to the procedures that were used as "enhanced interrogation techniques." That is an abstract term: to be more specific, some prisoners in Guantanamo, Afghanistan, and elsewhere were waterboarded, deprived of sleep for days, held in coffin-like boxes, or even beaten to death as they hung shackled by their wrists.[3]

Once again, the justification for these tactics in fighting the war on terror began with secret memoranda concluding that the president possessed unilateral power to determine which interrogation methods were justified in the name of national security and defense. In a January 9, 2002, memorandum, John Yoo of the Office of Legal Counsel concluded that the Geneva Conventions, which include prohibitions against torture and cruel or humiliating treatment of prisoners of war, as well as protections even for those not designated as prisoners of war, did not apply to members of Al Qaeda.[4] A January 25, 2002, memorandum to the president signed by Alberto Gonzales, the White House Counsel, cited Yoo's January 9, 2002, memo.[5] The January 25 memo concluded that Al Qaeda and Taliban detainees were not prisoners of war protected by the Geneva Conventions and further suggested that even if the Geneva Conventions were interpreted differently, the president could simply decide, on his own authority, that the Geneva Conventions did not apply.[6] The memo observed that disclaiming the applicability of the Geneva Conventions would give the president "flexibility" in fighting the war on terror, a "new kind of war" that "places a high premium on . . . quickly obtain[ing] information from captured terrorists . . . in order to avoid future atrocities against American civilians."[7] The January 25 memo also asserted that this approach would "[s]ubstantially reduce the threat of domestic criminal prosecution under the War Crimes Act" for interrogators.[8] In other words, the president would be providing protection to interrogators who might worry about facing prosecution for torture.

The January 2002 memos started to clear a path for torture, but some interrogators still had some questions. They remained concerned that they might be criminally prosecuted for torturing detainees.[9] The president's view that their tactics were legal might not be enough. Other laws could define interrogation methods as torture—even if the Geneva Conventions and War Crimes Act did not apply. In 1994, the United States had ratified the UN Convention against Torture and Other Cruel, Inhuman or Degrading Treatment or Punishment (CAT). After the CAT was ratified, Congress passed the federal antitorture statute, which was signed into law by President Clinton.[10] The federal antitorture statute defines torture as "an act committed by a person acting under the color of law specifically intended to inflict severe physical or mental pain or suffering (other than pain or suffering incidental to lawful sanctions) upon another person within his custody or physical control."[11] Violations of the federal antitorture statute can be punished by a prison term of up to twenty years or, if torture results in death, by a life sentence or the death penalty.[12]

Interrogators wanted specific assurances that they would not face prosecution for using interrogation methods that might violate either the War Crimes Act or the federal antitorture statute. They received these assurances in the form of legal opinions from the Office of Legal Counsel.[13] These opinions were viewed as a "get out of jail free card"—a defense against any future prosecution.[14]

In the summer of 2002, the CIA wanted to use specific interrogation methods to extract information from Abu Zubaydah, a prisoner who they believed was a high-level Al Qaeda official.[15] CIA interrogators believed that Zubaydah had information about possible future attacks, including possible attacks planned for the first anniversary of the September 11, 2001, attacks. They wanted to use several interrogation methods to obtain information from Zubaydah, including (1) stress positions designed to produce physical discomfort; (2) "walling" (banging a prisoner into a flexible wall);

(3) sleep deprivation of "not more than eleven days at a time"; (4) placement "in a cramped confinement box with an insect" (interrogators planned to inform Zubaydah, who was afraid of poisonous insects, that the insect could sting him, though it was actually harmless);[16] and (5) waterboarding.

Waterboarding is an interrogation technique with a long history dating back to the fourteenth century. The method was used to extract confessions during the Spanish Inquisition.[17] In more recent times, U.S. courts convicted Japanese soldiers for waterboarding American prisoners of war during World War II.[18] Still more recently, in 1983, a Texas sheriff and his deputies were given prison sentences for waterboarding prisoners.[19] In 2002, the Office of Legal Counsel gave this description of waterboarding, in response to questions from the CIA as to whether using this technique on Abu Zubaydah would be torture:

> In this procedure [waterboarding], the individual is bound securely to an inclined bench . . . [a] cloth is placed over the forehead and eyes. Water is then applied to the cloth . . . [a]s this is done, the cloth is lowered until it covers the nose and mouth. Once the cloth is saturated and completely covers the nose and mouth, air flow is slightly restricted for 20 to 40 seconds due to the presence of the cloth . . . stimulat[ing] increased effort to breathe. This effort plus the cloth produces the perception of "suffocation and incipient panic," i.e. the perception of drowning. . . . This sensation of drowning is immediately relieved by the removal of the cloth. The procedure may then be repeated. . . . You have . . . orally informed us that it is likely that this procedure would not last more than 20 minutes in any one application."[20]

Malcolm Nance, a counterterrorism expert who worked with the U.S. Navy's training program to prepare Navy SEALs to resist torture, disagreed with OLC's conclusion that waterboarding is not torture, and with its description of waterboarding, saying that:

> Waterboarding is a torture technique. Period. There is no way to gloss over it or sugarcoat it. It has no justification outside of its limited role as a training demonstrator.[21] . . .
> Waterboarding is not a simulation. Unless you have been strapped down to the board, have endured the agonizing feeling of the water overpowering your gag reflex, and then feel your throat open and allow pint after pint of water to

involuntarily fill your lungs, you will not know the meaning of the word.

Waterboarding is a controlled drowning that, in the American [training] model, occurs under the watch of a doctor, a psychologist, an interrogator and a trained strap-in/ strap-out team. It does not simulate drowning, as the lungs are actually filling with water. There is no way to simulate that. The victim is drowning. How much the victim is to drown depends on the desired result (in the form of answers to questions shouted into the victim's face) and the obstinacy of the subject. A team doctor watches the quantity of water that is ingested and for the physiological signs which show when the drowning effect goes from painful psychological experience, to horrific suffocating punishment to the final death spiral.

Waterboarding is slow motion suffocation with enough time to contemplate the inevitability of black out and expiration—usually the person goes into hysterics on the board. For the uninitiated, it is horrifying to watch and if it goes wrong, it can lead straight to terminal hypoxia. When done right it is controlled death. Its lack of physical scarring allows the victim to recover and be threaten[ed] with its use again and again.[22]

Sleep deprivation is also an interrogation method with a long history; it was used by the Soviet KGB, the Japanese military during World War II, and the British army during interrogation of suspected IRA members.[23] Menachem Begin, who was prime minister of Israel from 1977 to 1983, had been subjected to sleep deprivation by the KGB years earlier. He describes the experience this way:

In the head of the interrogated prisoner, a haze begins to form. His spirit is wearied to death, his legs are unsteady, and he has one sole desire: to sleep. . . . Anyone who has experienced this desire knows that not even hunger and thirst are comparable with it.

I came across prisoners who signed what they were ordered to sign, only to get what the interrogator promised them.

He did not promise them their liberty; he did not promise them food to sate themselves. He promised them—if they signed—uninterrupted sleep! And, having signed, there was nothing in the world that could move them to risk again such nights and such days.[24]

John Schlapobersky was subjected to sleep deprivation in the 1960s by the apartheid South African government. He describes sleep deprivation as:

> treating [a person] with medication that will make them psychotic. It also demeans the experiences of those who have involuntarily gone through this form of torture. . . . I was kept without sleep for a week in all. I can remember the details of the experience, although it took place 35 years ago. After two nights without sleep, the hallucinations start, and after three nights, people are having dreams while fairly awake, which is a form of psychosis. By the week's end, people lose their orientation in place and time—the people you're speaking to become people from your past; a window might become a view of the sea seen in your younger days. To deprive someone of sleep is to tamper with their equilibrium and their sanity.[25]

U.S. law enforcement authorities have also used sleep deprivation, and the Supreme Court weighed in on the method in a 1944 case called *Ashcraft v. Tennessee*.[26] Police officers had questioned a suspect in a murder case for thirty-six hours continuously without allowing him to sleep. Ultimately, the suspect confessed to being involved in the murder. The Supreme Court ruled, with three justices dissenting, that evidence of the confession was inadmissible in court because it "was not voluntary but compelled," concluding that "[i]t is inconceivable that any court of justice in the land, conducted as our courts are, open to the public, would permit prosecutors serving in relays to keep a defendant witness under continuous cross-examination for thirty-six hours without rest or sleep in an effort to extract a 'voluntary' confession."[27] The court, in a majority opinion written by Justice Black, quoted an American Bar Association report stating that: "It has been known since 1500 at least that deprivation of sleep is the most effective torture and certain to produce any confession desired."[28] Black added:

> The Constitution of the United States stands as a bar against the conviction of any individual in an American court by means of a coerced confession. There have been, and are now, certain foreign nations with governments dedicated to an opposite policy: governments which convict individuals with testimony obtained by police organizations possessed of an unrestrained power to seize persons suspected of crimes against the state, hold them in secret custody, and wring from them confessions by physical or mental torture.

So long as the Constitution remains the basic law of our
Republic, America will not have that kind of government.[29]

In responding to the CIA's question as to whether depriving Abu
Zubaydah of sleep would be torture, the Office of Legal Counsel concluded
that, in some circumstances, "[s]leep deprivation may be used." The OLC
suggested that sleep deprivation would be permissible so long as it was not
used for more than eleven days at a time, provided that personnel with
medical training were available to intervene "in the unlikely event of an
abnormal reaction," and noted that the CIA reported having already kept
Zubaydah awake for seventy-two hours without having caused physical or
mental harm.[30] In fact, in an August 1, 2002, memorandum signed by Jay
Bybee, the OLC approved every specific tactic the CIA proposed for use
with Zubaydah.[31] This memorandum described each of the methods that
the CIA wanted to use on Zubaydah and briefly explained why the OLC
had concluded that none constituted torture in violation of the federal
antitorture law.

In a second OLC memorandum also dated August 1, 2002, John Yoo
provided a more detailed analysis and discussion of the antitorture law.[32]
The Yoo-Bybee memo "served as the legal foundation for the [CIA']s
interrogation program."[33] The Yoo-Bybee memo, which was reportedly
approved by a number of top administration officials, including Vice President Cheney, Attorney General John Ashcroft, Defense Secretary Donald
Rumsfeld, White House counsel Gonzales, CIA director George Tenet,
and others, served as a go-ahead for the use of interrogation methods at
Guantanamo and Abu Ghraib and in secret CIA prisons.[34]

The Yoo-Bybee memo assessed the risk that CIA interrogators could
be prosecuted under the federal antitorture law.[35] Yoo determined that the
interrogators' conduct would be criminal only if it caused suffering "equivalent in intensity to the pain accompanying serious physical injury, such as
organ failure, impairment of bodily function, or even death" or "prolonged
mental harm" lasting "months or years."[36] This assessment meant that
interrogators could beat detainees (within limits), slam them against walls,
place them in a small, unlit confinement box with insects, even waterboard
them. Finally, even if interrogators overstepped the broad limits Yoo set
for them, for instance if they caused long-term mental harm or even killed
a detainee, Yoo concluded they would likely be immune from criminal
prosecution as long as they were acting at the president's direction.[37] Interrogators could also cite necessity or self-defense, arguing that torture was
necessary to protect the nation.[38]

After the OLC issued its two memos, Zubaydah was waterboarded at least eighty-three times in August 2002.[39] It's not clear if any new information was gained. Some of his interrogators later said that Zubaydah had revealed a great deal of information before torture was used and that he revealed no new information after he was waterboarded.[40] Michael Hayden, director of the CIA for two years during the Bush administration, disputed that conclusion, claiming that, after he was waterboarded, Zubaydah revealed the location of another suspected terrorist.[41]

Critics argue that Yoo's conclusions depended on a "disregard [for] basic dictionary definitions" and a resurrection of the Nixonian view of presidential power—if the president does [or authorizes] something, that means it's not illegal.[42] Following are excerpts from the August 1, 2002, Yoo-Bybee memo.

Memorandum for Alberto R. Gonzales

Counsel to the President

Re. Standards of Conduct for Interrogation under 18 U.S.C. §§ 2340–2340A

You have asked for our Office's views regarding the standards of conduct under the Convention Against Torture and Other Cruel, Inhuman and Degrading Treatment or Punishment as implemented by Sections 2340–2340A of title 18 of the United States Code [the antitorture law]. As we understand it, this question has arisen in the context of the conduct of interrogations outside of the United States. We conclude below that Section 2340A proscribes acts inflicting, and that are specifically intended to inflict, severe pain or suffering, whether mental or physical. Those acts must be of an extreme nature to rise to the level of torture within the meaning of Section 2340A and the Convention. We further conclude that certain acts may be cruel, inhuman, or degrading, but still not produce pain and suffering of the requisite intensity to fall within Section 2340A's proscription against torture. We conclude by examining possible defenses that would negate any claim that certain interrogation methods violate the statute.

In Part I, we examine the criminal statute's text and history. We conclude that for an act to constitute torture as defined in Section 2340, it must inflict pain that is difficult to endure. Physical pain amounting to torture must be equivalent in intensity to the pain accompanying serious physical injury, such as organ failure, impairment of bodily function, or even death. For purely mental pain or suffering to amount to torture under Section 2340, it must result in significant psychological harm of significant duration, e.g., lasting for months or even years. . . .

In Part V, we discuss whether Section 2340A may be unconstitutional if applied to interrogations undertaken of enemy combatants pursuant to the President's Commander-in-Chief powers. We find that in the circumstances of the current war against al Qaeda and its allies, prosecution under Section 2340A may be barred because enforcement of the statute would represent an unconstitutional infringement of the President's authority to conduct war. In Part VI, we discuss defenses to an allegation that an interrogation method might violate the statute. We conclude that, under the current circumstances, necessity or self-defense may justify interrogation methods that might violate Section 2340A.

I. 18 U.S.C. §§ 2340–2340A

Section 2340A makes it a criminal offense for any person "outside the United States [to] commit ... or attempt ... to commit torture."[43] ...

A. "Specifically Intended"

To violate Section 2340A, the statute requires that severe pain and suffering must be inflicted with specific intent. ... In order for a defendant to have acted with specific intent, he must expressly intend to achieve the forbidden act. ... Here, because Section 2340 requires that a defendant act with the specific intent to inflict severe pain, the infliction of such pain must be the defendant's precise objective. ... If the defendant acted knowing that severe pain or suffering was reasonably likely to result from his actions, but no more, he would have acted only with general intent. The Supreme Court has used the following example to illustrate the difference between these two mental states:

> [A] person entered a bank and took money from a teller at gunpoint, but deliberately failed to make a quick getaway from the bank in the hope of being arrested so that he would be returned to prison and treated for alcoholism. Though this defendant knowingly engaged in the acts of using force and taking money (satisfying "general intent"), he did not intend permanently to deprive the bank of its possession of the money (failing to satisfy "specific intent").

As a theoretical matter, therefore, knowledge alone that a particular result is certain to occur does not constitute specific intent. ... Thus, even if the defendant knows that severe pain will result from his actions, if causing such harm is not his objective, he lacks the requisite specific intent even though the defendant did not act in good faith. ... [However], when a defendant knows that his actions will produce the prohibited result, a jury will in all likelihood conclude that the defendant acted with specific intent.

Further, a showing that an individual acted with a good faith belief that his conduct would not produce the result that the law prohibits negates specific intent. . . . A good faith belief need not be a reasonable one. . . . Where a defendant holds an unreasonable belief, he will confront the problem of proving to the jury that he actually held that belief. . . .

B. "Severe Pain or Suffering"

The key statutory phrase in the definition of torture is the statement that acts amount to torture if they cause "severe physical or mental pain or suffering." . . . The statute does not, however, define the term "severe." "In the absence of such a definition, we construe a statutory term in accordance with its ordinary or natural meaning." . . . The dictionary defines "severe" as "[u]nsparing in exaction, punishment, or censure" or "[I]nflicting discomfort or pain hard to endure; sharp; afflictive; distressing; violent; extreme; as severe pain, anguish, torture." . . . Thus, the adjective "severe" conveys that the pain or suffering must be of such a high level of intensity that the pain is difficult for the subject to endure.

Congress's use of the phrase "severe pain" elsewhere in the United States Code can shed more light on its meaning. . . . Significantly, the phrase "severe pain" appears in statutes defining an emergency medical condition for the purpose of providing health benefits. . . . These statutes define an emergency condition as one "manifesting itself by acute symptoms of sufficient severity (including severe pain) such that a prudent lay person, who possesses an average knowledge of health and medicine, could reasonably expect the absence of immediate medical attention to result in—placing the health of the individual . . . (i) in serious jeopardy (ii) serious impairment to bodily functions, or (iii) serious dysfunction of any bodily organ or part." . . . Although these statutes address a substantially different subject from Section 2340, they are nonetheless helpful for understanding what constitutes severe physical pain. They treat severe pain as an indicator of ailments that are likely to result in permanent and serious physical damage in the absence of immediate medical treatment. Such damage must rise to the level of death, organ failure, or the permanent impairment of a significant body function. These statutes suggest that "severe pain," as used in Section 2340, must rise to a similarly high level—the level that would ordinarily be associated with a sufficiently serious physical condition or injury such as death, organ failure, or serious impairment of body functions—in order to constitute torture [footnote omitted].

C. "Severe Mental Pain or Suffering"

Section 2340 gives further guidance as to the meaning of "severe mental pain or suffering," as distinguished from severe physical pain and suffering. . . .

1. "PROLONGED MENTAL HARM"

As an initial matter, Section 2340(2) requires that the severe mental pain must be evidenced by "prolonged mental harm." To prolong is to "lengthen in time" or to "extend the duration of, to draw out." Webster's Third New International Dictionary 1815 (1988); Webster's New International Dictionary 1980 (2d ed. 1935). . . . [T]he acts giving rise to the harm must cause some lasting, though not necessarily permanent, damage. For example, the mental strain experienced by an individual during a lengthy and intense interrogation—such as one that state or local police might conduct upon a criminal suspect—would not violate Section 2340(2). On the other hand, the development of a mental disorder such as posttraumatic stress disorder, which can last months or even years, or even chronic depression, which also can last for a considerable period of time if untreated, might satisfy the prolonged harm requirement. . . .

A defendant must specifically intend to cause prolonged mental harm for the defendant to have committed torture. . . .

A defendant could negate a showing of specific intent to cause severe mental pain or suffering by showing that he had acted in good faith that his conduct would not amount to the acts prohibited by the statute. . . .

[Consideration of the legislative history of sections 2340–2340A confirms] that torture is not the mere infliction of pain or suffering on another, but is instead a step well removed. The victim must experience intense pain or suffering of the kind that is equivalent to the pain that would be associated with serious physical injury so severe that death, organ failure, or permanent damage resulting in a loss of significant body function will likely result. If that pain or suffering is psychological, that suffering must result from one of the [four] acts set forth in the statute. In addition, these acts must cause long-term mental harm. Indeed, this view of the criminal act of torture is consistent with the term's common meaning. . . . In short, reading the definition of torture as a whole, it is plain that the term encompasses only extreme acts.

[The memo then considers the text and history of the Convention against Torture or "CAT" and of sections 2340–2340A, which implemented the treaty] . . . CAT . . . distinguishes between torture and other acts of cruel, inhuman, or degrading treatment or punishment. CAT makes clear that torture is at the farthest end of impermissible actions, and that it is distinct and separate from the lower level of "cruel, inhuman, or degrading treatment or punishment."[44] . . .

III. U.S. Judicial Interpretation

There are no reported cases of prosecutions under Section 2340A.[45] . . . Nonetheless, we are not without guidance as to how United States courts would approach the question of what conduct constitutes torture. Civil suits . . . provide insight into what acts U.S. courts would conclude constitute torture under the criminal statute. . . .

. . . Courts appear to look at the entire co[u]rse of conduct rather than any one act. . . . Because of this approach, it is difficult to take a specific act out of context and conclude that the act in isolation would constitute torture. Certain acts do, however, consistently reappear in these cases or are of such a barbaric nature, that it is likely a court would find that allegations of such treatment would constitute torture: (1) severe beatings using instruments such as iron barks [sic—bars], truncheons, and clubs; (2) threats of imminent death, such as mock executions; (3) threats of removing extremities; (4) burning, especially burning with cigarettes; (5) electric shocks to genitalia or threats to do so; (6) rape or sexual assault, or injury to an individual's sexual organs, or threatening to do any of these sorts of acts; and (7) forcing the prisoner to watch the torture of others. . . . While we cannot say with certainty that acts falling short of these seven would not constitute torture under Section 2340, we believe that interrogation techniques would have to be similar to these in their extreme nature and in the type of harm caused to violate the law. . . .

[Decisions in civil] cases . . . are in keeping with the general notion that the term "torture" is reserved for acts of the most extreme nature. . . .

[The memo next discusses decisions applying international law to define torture] . . . both the European Court on Human Rights and the Israeli Supreme Court have recognized a wide array of acts that constitute cruel, inhuman, or degrading treatment or punishment, but do not amount to torture. Thus, they appear to permit, under international law, an aggressive interpretation as to what amounts to torture, leaving that label to be applied only where extreme circumstances exist.

V. The President's Commander-in-Chief Power

Even if an interrogation method arguably were to violate Section 2340A, the statute would be unconstitutional if it impermissibly encroached on the President's constitutional power to conduct a military campaign. As Commander-in-Chief, the President has the constitutional authority to order interrogations of enemy combatants to gain intelligence information concerning the military plans of the enemy. The demands of the Commander-in-Chief power are especially pronounced in the middle of a war in which the nation has already suffered a direct attack. In such a case, the information gained from interrogations may prevent future attacks by foreign enemies. Any effort to apply Section 2340A in a manner that interferes with the President's direction of such core war matters as the detention and interrogation of enemy combatants thus would be unconstitutional.

A. The War with Al Qaeda

At the outset, we should make clear the nature of the threat presently posed to the nation. . . . The situation in which these issues arise is unprecedented in recent American history. Four coordinated terrorist attacks, using hijacked commercial airliners as guided missiles, took place in rapid succession on the morning of September 11, 2001. These attacks were aimed at critical government buildings in the Nation's capital and landmark buildings in its financial center. These events reach a different scale of destructiveness than earlier terrorist episodes, such as the destruction of the Murrah Building in Oklahoma City in 1994. They caused thousands of deaths. Air traffic and communications within the United States were disrupted; national stock exchanges were shut for several days; and damage from the attack has been estimated to run into the tens of billions of dollars. Moreover, these attacks are part of a violent campaign against the United States that is believed to include an unsuccessful attempt to destroy an airliner in December 2001; a suicide bombing attack in Yemen on the U.S.S. *Cole* in 2000; the bombings of the United States Embassies in Kenya and in Tanzania in 1998; a truck bomb attack on a U.S. military housing complex in Saudi Arabia in 1996; an unsuccessful attempt to destroy the World Trade Center in 1993; and the ambush of U.S. servicemen in Somalia in 1993. The United States and its overseas personnel and installations have been attacked as a result of Usama Bin Laden's call for a "jihad against the U.S. government, because the U.S. government is unjust, criminal and tyrannical."

In response, the Government has engaged in a broad effort at home and abroad to counter terrorism. Pursuant to his authorities as Commander-in-Chief, the President in October, 2001, ordered the Armed Forces to attack al Qaeda personnel and assets in Afghanistan, and the Taliban militia that harbored them.... Congress has provided its support for the use of [force] against those linked to the September 11 attacks, and has recognized the President's constitutional power to use force to prevent and deter future attacks both within and outside the United States....

Despite these efforts, numerous upper echelon leaders of al Qaeda and the Taliban, with access to active terrorist cells and other resources, remain at large....

Al Qaeda continues to plan further attacks, such as destroying American civilian airliners and killing American troops, which have fortunately been prevented. It is clear that bin Laden and his organization have conducted several violent attacks on the United States and its nationals, and that they seek to continue to do so. Thus, the capture and interrogation of such individuals is clearly imperative to our national security and defense. Interrogation of captured al Qaeda operatives may provide information concerning the nature of al Qaeda plans and the identities of its personnel, which may prove invaluable in preventing further direct attacks on the United States and its citizens. Given the massive destruction and loss of life caused by the September 11 attacks, it is reasonable to believe that information gained from al Qaeda personnel could prevent attacks of a similar (if not greater) magnitude from occurring in the United States....

B. Interpretation to Avoid Constitutional Problems

As the Supreme Court has recognized, and as we will explain further below, the President enjoys complete discretion in the exercise of his Commander-in-Chief authority and in conducting operations against hostile forces. Because both "[t]he executive power and the command of the military and naval forces is vested in the President," the Supreme Court has unanimously stated that it is "the President alone ... who is constitutionally invested with the entire charge of hostile operations." Hamilton v. Dillin (1874). That authority is at its height in the middle of a war.

In light of the President's complete authority over the conduct of war, without a clear statement otherwise, we will not read a criminal statute as infringing on the President's ultimate authority in these areas....

In order to respect the President's inherent constitutional authority to manage a military campaign against al Qaeda and its allies, Section 2340A must be construed as not applying to interrogations undertaken pursuant to his Commander-in-Chief authority. As our Office has consistently held during this Administration and previous Administrations, Congress lacks authority under Article I to set the terms and conditions under which the President may exercise his authority as Commander in Chief to control the conduct of operations d[u]ring a war.... [T]he President's power to detain and interrogate enemy combatants arises out of his constitutional authority as Commander in Chief.... Congress may no more regulate the President's ability to detain and interrogate enemy combatants than it may regulate his ability to direct troop movements on the battlefield. Accordingly, we ... conclude that [section 2340A] does not apply to the President's detention and interrogation of enemy combatants pursuant to his Commander-in-Chief authority....

C. The Commander-in-Chief Power

It could be argued that Congress enacted 18 U.S.C. § 2340A with full knowledge and consideration of the President's Commander-in-Chief power, and that Congress intended to restrict his discretion in the interrogation of enemy combatants. Even were we to accept this argument, however, we conclude that the Department of Justice could not enforce Section 2340A against federal officials acting pursuant to the President's constitutional authority to wage a military campaign....

The text, structure and history of the Constitution establish that the Founders entrusted the President with the primary responsibility, and therefore the power, to ensure the security of the United States in situations of grave and unforeseen emergencies. The decision to deploy military force in the defense of United States interests is expressly [sic] placed under Presidential authority by the Vesting Clause ... and by the Commander-in-Chief Clause.... This Office has long understood the Commander-in-Chief Clause in particular as an affirmative grant of authority to the President.... The Framers understood the Clause as investing the President with the fullest range of power understood at the time of the ratification of the Constitution as belonging to the military commander. In addition, the structure of the Constitution demonstrates that any power traditionally understood as pertaining to the executive—which includes the conduct of warfare and the defense of the nation—unless expressly assigned in the Constitution to Congress, is vested in the President. Article II, Section 1 makes this clear by stating that the "executive Power shall be vested in a President of the United States of America." That sweeping grant vests in the President an unenumerated "executive power" and contrasts with the specific enumeration of the powers—those "herein"—granted to Congress in Article I. The implications of constitutional text and structure are confirmed by the practical consideration that national security decisions require the unity in purpose and energy in action that characterize the Presidency rather than Congress . . .

The President's complete discretion in exercising the Commander-in-Chief power has been recognized by the courts [citing the *Prize Cases*]. . . .

One of the core functions of the Commander in Chief is that of capturing detaining, and interrogating members of the enemy. . . .

Any effort by Congress to regulate the interrogation of battlefield combatants would violate the Constitution's sole vesting of the Commander-in-Chief authority in the President. There can be little doubt that intelligence operations, such as the detention and interrogation of enemy combatants and leaders, are both necessary and proper for the effective conduct of a military campaign. Indeed, such operations may be of more importance in a war with an international terrorist organization than one with the conventional armed forces of a nation-state. . . . It may be the case that only successful interrogations can provide the information necessary to prevent the success of covert terrorist attacks upon the United States and its citizens. Congress can no more interfere with the President's conduct of the interrogation of enemy combatants than it can dictate strategic or tactical decisions on the battlefield. . . .

VI. Defenses

. . . Even if an interrogation method . . . might arguably cross the line drawn in Section 2340, and application of the statute was not held to be an unconstitutional infringement of the President's Commander-in-Chief authority, we believe that under the current circumstances certain justification defenses might be available that would potentially eliminate criminal liability. Standard criminal law defenses of necessity and self-defense could justify interrogation methods needed to elicit information to prevent a direct and imminent threat to the United States and its citizens.

A. Necessity

We believe that a defense of necessity could be raised, under the current circumstances, to an allegation of a Section 2340A violation. Often referred to as the "choice of evils" defense, necessity has been defined as follows:

> Conduct that the actor believes to be necessary to avoid a harm or evil to himself or to another is justifiable, provided that:
>
> (a) the harm or evil sought to be avoided by such conduct is greater than that sought to be prevented by the law defining the offense charged....

... [T]he necessity defense can justify the intentional killing of one person to save two others because "it is better that two lives be saved and one lost than that two be lost and one saved."...

It appears to us that under the current circumstances the necessity defense could be successfully maintained in response to an allegation of a Section 2340A violation. On September 11, 2001, al Qaeda launched a surprise covert attack on civilian targets in the United States that led to the deaths of thousands and losses in the billions of dollars. According to public and governmental reports, al Qaeda has other sleeper cells within the United States that may be planning similar attacks. Indeed, al Qaeda plans apparently include efforts to develop and deploy chemical, biological and nuclear weapons of mass destruction. Under these circumstances, a detainee may possess information that could enable the United States to prevent attacks that potentially could equal or surpass the September 11 attacks in their magnitude. Clearly, any harm that might occur during an interrogation would pale [in] significance compared to the harm avoided by preventing such an attack, which could take hundreds or thousands of lives.

Under this calculus, two factors will help indicate when the necessity defense could appropriately be invoked. First, the more certain that government officials are that a particular individual has information needed to prevent an attack, the more necessary interrogation will be. Second, the more likely it appears to be that a terrorist attack is likely to occur, and the greater the amount of damage expected from such an attack, the more that an interrogation to get information would become necessary.... While every interrogation that might violate Section 2340A does not trigger a necessity defense, we can say that certain circumstances could support such a defense....

B. Self-Defense

Even if a court were to find that a violation of Section 2340A was not justified by necessity, a defendant could still appropriately raise a claim of self-defense....

The doctrine of self-defense permits the use of force to prevent harm to another person ... [and] "one is justified in using reasonable force in defense of another person, even a stranger, when he reasonably believes that the other is in immediate danger of unlawful bodily harm from his adversary and that the use of such force is necessary to avoid this danger." ... Ultimately, even deadly force is permissible ..."... when the attack of the adversary upon the other person reasonably appears to the defender to be a deadly attack." [memo discusses requirement of "imminent" threat needed to justify self-defense]....

Under the current circumstances, we believe that a defendant accused of violating Section 2340A could have, in certain circumstances, grounds to properly claim the defense of another. The threat of an impending terrorist attack threatens the lives of hundreds if not thousands of American citizens. Whether such a defense will be upheld depends on the specific context within which the interrogation decision is made. If an attack appears increasingly likely, but our intelligence services and armed forces cannot prevent it without the information from the interrogation of a specific individual, then the more likely it will appear that the conduct in question will be seen as necessary. If intelligence and other information support the conclusion that an attack is increasingly certain, then the necessity for the interrogation will be reasonable. The increasing certainty of an attack will also satisfy the imminence requirement....

To be sure, this situation is different from the usual self-defense justification.... Self-defense as usually discussed involves using force against an individual who is about to conduct the attack. In the current circumstances, however, an enemy combatant in detention does not himself present a threat of harm. He is not actually carrying out the attack; rather, he has participated in the planning and preparation for the attack, or merely has knowledge of the attack through his membership in the terrorist organization. Nonetheless, leading scholarly commentators believe that interrogation of such individuals using methods that might violate Section 2340A would be justified under the doctrine of self-defense, because the combatant by aiding and promoting the terrorist plot "has culpably caused the situation where someone might get hurt. If hurting him is the only means to prevent the death or injury of others put at risk by his actions, such torture should be permissible, and on the same basis that self-defense is permissible." ... Thus, some commentators believe that by helping to create the threat of loss of life, terrorists become culpable for the threat even though they do not actually carry out the attack itself. They may be hurt in an interrogation because they are part of the mechanism that has set the attack in motion, ... just as is someone who feeds ammunition or targeting information to an attacker....

Further, we believe that a claim by an individual of the defense of another would be ... supported by the fact that, in this case, the nation itself is under attack and has the right to self-defense....

There can be little doubt that the nation's right to self-defense has been triggered under our law. The Constitution announces that one of its purposes is "to provide for the common defense." ... Article I, § 8 declares that Congress is to exercise its powers to "provide for the common Defence." ... The President has a particular responsibility and power to take steps to defend the nation and its people. ... As Commander-in-Chief and Chief Executive, he may use the armed forces to protect the nation and its people. ... As the Supreme Court observed in The Prize Cases ... in response to an armed attack on the United States "the President is not only authorized but bound to resist force by force ... without waiting for any special legislative authority." The September 11 events were a direct attack on the United States, and as we have explained above, the President has authorized the use of military force with the support of Congress.

... [T]he nation's right to self-defense has been triggered by the events of September 11. If a government defendant were to harm an enemy combatant during an interrogation in a manner that might arguably violate Section 2340A, he would be doing so in order to prevent further attacks on the United States by the al Qaeda terrorist network. In that case, we believe that he could argue that his actions were justified by the executive branch's constitutional authority to protect the nation from attack. This national and international version of the right to self-defense could supplement and bolster the government defendant's individual right.

Conclusion

For the foregoing reasons, we conclude that torture as defined in and proscribed by Sections 2340–2340A, covers only extreme acts. Severe pain is generally of the kind difficult for the victim to endure. Where the pain is physical, it must be of an intensity akin to that which accompanies serious physical injury such as death or organ failure. Severe mental pain requires suffering not just at the moment of infliction but it also requires lasting psychological harm, such as seen in mental disorders like posttraumatic stress disorder. Additionally, such severe mental pain can arise only from the predicate acts listed in Section 2340. Because the acts inflicting torture are extreme, there is significant range of acts that though they might constitute cruel, inhuman, or degrading treatment or punishment fail to rise to the level of torture.

Further, we conclude that under the circumstances of the current war against al Qaeda and its allies, application of Section 2340A to interrogations undertaken pursuant to the President's Commander-in-Chief powers may be unconstitutional. Finally, even if an interrogation method might violate Section 2340A, necessity or self-defense could provide justifications that would eliminate any criminal liability.

Please let us know if we can be of further assistance.

[Signature:] *Jay S. Bybee*
Assistant Attorney General

Critics of the Yoo-Bybee memo may raise various points. First, they might question Yoo's definition of severe physical pain sufficient to qualify as "torture." Yoo's conclusion that severe pain rising to the level of torture must be "equivalent in intensity to the pain accompanying serious physical injury, such as organ failure, impairment of bodily function, or even death" comes from laws "defining an emergency medical condition for the purpose of providing medical benefits."[46] The Department of Justice's Office of Professional Responsibility concluded that these medical benefits statutes were "of no practical value" in interpreting the antitorture law and defining torture.[47] As a separate criticism, the law professors Christopher H. Schroeder and Jack Balkin observe that the memo fails to confront the Supreme Court's *Youngstown* decision and Justice Jackson's concurring opinion that sets forth a framework for analyzing presidential action.[48] Balkin called it "rather embarrassing" that the Yoo-Bybee memo failed to address *Youngstown*. Scott Matheson, at the time a law professor and now a U.S. appellate court judge, criticizes the fact that the Yoo-Bybee memo was kept secret for years.[49] Matheson also describes Yoo's argument that the president could effectively set aside the antitorture law if he concluded it infringed on his constitutional authority under Article II as a "claim of absolute authority [that] cuts so deeply against the grain of the Constitution's separation of powers foundation as to amount to extraconstitutionalism."[50]

Zubaydah was not the only detainee who was waterboarded or otherwise tortured. Khalid Sheikh Mohammed, the self-described planner of the September 11 attacks, was waterboarded 183 times in March 2003.[51] By 2005, the CIA had used "enhanced interrogation techniques" on a total of twenty-eight high-value prisoners.[52] The August 2002 memos influenced interrogation methods in a number of places, including Guantanamo and Abu Ghraib. In October 2002, a CIA lawyer flew to Guantanamo to discuss waterboarding, sleep deprivation, and death threats against detainees there.[53] In December 2002, Secretary of Defense Rumsfeld signed a memorandum order authorizing the use of some of these techniques at Guantanamo, and some of these were used with a prisoner believed to be the planned twentieth 9/11 hijacker.[54] This prisoner was subjected to sleep deprivation, nudity, and prolonged exposure to cold that left him in a "life-threatening situation."[55] Susan Crawford, a Bush administration official involved in reviewing these practices, concluded the detainee had been tortured and, therefore, that his case could not be referred for prosecution.[56] Other detainees at Guantanamo were chained in the fetal position for eighteen hours or more and subjected to extreme temperatures; one was left overnight in an unventilated room where the temperature exceeded 100 degrees Fahrenheit and apparently pulled out his hair during the night.[57]

A copy of the Rumsfeld memo was sent to Afghanistan, where it influenced interrogation tactics.[58] At the Bagram detention camp in Afghanistan, guards and detainees reported "systematic brutality"; some detainees were beaten and hung by their wrists from chains. At least two detainees there were beaten to death.[59] The Rumsfeld memo also made its way to Iraq, where it formed the basis for standard operating procedures.[60] The law professor David Cole says that, in Iraq, "once the line of physical coercion was officially breached, a culture quickly developed that fostered unauthorized abuse. The results were broadcast to the world in June 2004 in a series of photographs of deeply degrading and depraved mistreatment of prisoners at Abu Ghraib."[61]

Sometimes, torture culminated in death. The American Civil Liberties Union conducted a review of autopsy and death reports for detainees who died in custody in Iraq and Afghanistan and concluded that at least eight deaths appeared to have resulted from interrogation techniques.[62] Retired general Barry McCaffrey concluded that "[w]e tortured people unmercifully. We probably murdered dozens of them during the course of that."[63]

The Yoo-Bybee memorandum was written in order to satisfy CIA interrogators that they could use specific interrogation methods without fear of prosecution. By definition, torture is illegal. As we've seen, however, the Bush administration concluded that the techniques they authorized the CIA to use simply did not qualify as torture or, in the alternative, that presidential emergency power permits the president to authorize whatever interrogation methods he believes are necessary to defend the nation.

So far, most interrogators have avoided prosecution, and President Obama has agreed that the Office of Legal Counsel memos provide a legal defense for CIA interrogators, saying that "those who carried out their duties relying in good faith upon legal advice from the Department of Justice . . . will not be subject to prosecution."[64] Attorney General Eric Holder announced an investigation "into whether federal laws were violated in connection with the interrogation of specific detainees at overseas locations."[65] However, given President Obama's assurance to interrogators, it's not clear how they could be prosecuted if they relied on Office of Legal Counsel memos, and, in fact, the Department of Justice announced in August 2012 that it would not prosecute CIA personnel for criminal acts of torture.[66] It is possible that U.S. officials could be prosecuted overseas for approving torture.[67] In fact, an Italian court convicted twenty-three Americans (mainly CIA agents), in absentia, for kidnapping a suspected terrorist and effecting his extraordinary rendition[68] to a country where he was tortured.[69] For now, though, most legal avenues have been closed, and the August 1, 2002, memos can be said to have successfully paved the way for interrogation methods many consider to be torture. Some observers might conclude that this shows that the rule of law simply cannot limit presidential power when it comes to making decisions regarding how to interrogate suspected terrorists. Others could respond that this recent history should prompt a call for new ways to limit presidential power.

12

WARRANTLESS WIRETAPPING

PRESIDENTIAL POWER TO SET ASIDE ACTS OF CONGRESS?

As we have seen, the Nixon administration used warrantless wiretapping as one of its methods for dealing with political enemies within the United States. After President Nixon's resignation, the U.S. Senate voted in 1975 to establish the Church Committee.[1] Headed by Senator Frank Church of Idaho, the committee was tasked with investigating intelligence-gathering abuses by the U.S. government, including but not limited to what had gone on during the Nixon years. The Church Committee investigated and exposed a wide range of abuses that had taken place over the course of several decades, including surveillance programs called "Operation Shamrock" and "Operation Minaret." Operation Shamrock was a thirty-year effort to review telegrams sent from the United States to other countries.[2] At its height, the National Security Agency analyzed as many as 150,000 messages a month. Each night, private telegram companies would secretly provide telegrams to NSA officials. On the basis of information gathered from a review of the telegrams, the NSA compiled a list of "dangerous" Americans (codenamed "Minaret") that included actors, entertainers, political activists, and civil rights leaders.[3]

These programs were terminated after the Church Committee brought them to light, but the Committee was concerned about future warrantless spying on Americans.[4] In the wake of the Church Committee's reports, Congress passed the Foreign Intelligence Surveillance Act or FISA, which was designed to allow the federal government to engage in legitimate intelligence gathering required for national security while preserving individual privacy rights.

FISA, which was signed into law in 1978, provided a specific and "exclusive" framework for foreign intelligence gathering through electronic surveillance and other means,[5] including severe penalties for violations of FISA: any person who engages in electronic surveillance not authorized by the law is guilty of a criminal offense punishable by five years in prison and/or a $10,000 fine for each offense.[6]

In most cases, FISA requires that a warrant be obtained before electronic surveillance can be conducted—with three exceptions. First, no warrant is required when the electronic surveillance is aimed solely at acquiring the contents of communications between "foreign powers";[7] when there is no substantial likelihood the surveillance will acquire the contents of communications involving a U.S. citizen, a lawful U.S. resident, or a U.S. corporation or association; when the surveillance continues for one year or less; and when the attorney general certifies its limited aims.[8] Second, under "an emergency situation" as determined by the attorney general, warrantless emergency surveillance may be conducted for up to seven days, but the attorney general must inform a FISA judge of the decision to authorize emergency warrantless surveillance.[9] Third, the president, through the attorney general, may authorize electronic surveillance within fifteen days of a declaration of war by Congress.[10]

In all other circumstances (including, notably, when electronic surveillance is aimed at a U.S. citizen or legal permanent resident within the United States), a warrant must be obtained. In most cases when the government wants to engage in electronic surveillance, it is required to obtain a warrant from an ordinary federal or state court. Under the Fourth Amendment to the U.S. Constitution, such warrants shall be issued only upon a showing of "probable cause" that criminal activity is occurring. Under FISA, warrants are not obtained from ordinary courts, and a different, lesser, showing of probable cause is required. FISA set up a specialized court, the Foreign Intelligence Surveillance Court (FISC),[11] consisting of eleven federal district court judges around the United States who are designated by the chief justice of the U.S. Supreme Court and authorized to grant orders approving electronic surveillance.[12] FISA judges are authorized to issue orders approving surveillance when there is "probable cause to believe that the target of the surveillance is a foreign power or an agent of a foreign power . . . and each of the facilities or places at which the electronic surveillance is directed is being used, or is about to be used, by a foreign power or an agent of a foreign power."[13] This is a much easier standard for the U.S. government to satisfy than that required when the government seeks a warrant in the course of typical domestic law enforcement: instead of showing probable cause of criminal activity, to obtain a warrant under

FISA the government must show only probable cause to believe that its target is a "foreign power or agent of a foreign power."[14]

FISA essentially created a limited exception to the rules created for domestic surveillance under the Fourth Amendment, allowing the U.S. government to use electronic surveillance to gather foreign intelligence without showing probable cause of specific criminal activity. This exception has been justified on the basis that such intelligence gathering is aimed either at foreign entities or agents of foreign entities, that is, Americans working for foreign governments or organizations, including terrorist organizations. The goal was to ensure that the U.S. government would no longer secretly spy on Americans without a court order, and the National Security Agency, the main agency charged with gathering foreign intelligence (and an agency that had engaged in abuses in the past) developed a "culture of respect for the Fourth Amendment [the text of which] was displayed in large-type posters [at its headquarters]."[15]

After the September 11, 2001, attacks, that culture of respect for the Fourth Amendment was tested. The Bush administration concluded that winning the undeclared "war on terror" would depend on gathering intelligence in order to prevent future attacks. The administration was successful in achieving new power, granted under the Patriot Act,[16] to conduct "roving wiretaps,"[17] meaning that it had authority to engage in surveillance of a particular intelligence target without specifying the particular telephone line, computer, or other device being monitored. This was an express change to existing law and a deviation from the Fourth Amendment requirement that warrants "particularly describe the place to be searched." This change was publicly debated and approved by the Congress.

At the same time, however, the Bush administration was establishing a secret intelligence-gathering program aimed at gaining access to the communications of perhaps millions of Americans.[18] The full scope of the program is still unknown; lawsuits that might bring forth additional information are still pending. However, some information about the surveillance program has been made public—first, through reporting by the *New York Times* in 2005 and later through unclassified government reports. In July 2009, the Offices of Inspectors General for the Departments of Defense and Justice, the CIA, NSA, and the director of National Intelligence issued an unclassified report on the once-secret surveillance program.[19] (A separate classified report was also prepared.) As a whole, the secret program was known as the President's Surveillance Program or "PSP." The portion of the program that has been publicly disclosed was called the Terrorist Surveillance Program or "TSP." The following describes what is known about these activities.[20]

After the September 11, 2001, attacks against the United States, President
Bush authorized the National Security Agency to intercept international
communications in order to gather intelligence that could help prevent
future attacks. This was a classified program, and access was closely guarded:
individuals who knew about the program were "read in," but many intelligence analysts who used information obtained through the program did
not know where the information came from. Most members of Congress
did not know about the program, although the so-called Gang of Eight,
congressional leaders from both parties, received briefings on it.[21] The
program was not initially disclosed to any judges on the FISA court.[22]
Instead, the president asked the attorney general to assess and reauthorize
the program every forty-five days as long as there was "a sufficient factual
basis demonstrating a threat of terrorist attacks in the United States for it
to continue to be reasonable under the standards of the Fourth Amendment
for the President to authorize the warrantless searches involved." The
Department of Justice's Office of Legal Counsel performed this review
after analyzing intelligence gathered by the secret program[23] and then
advised the attorney general whether the program could be reauthorized.
From October 2001 through May 2003, John Yoo wrote the legal memos
used to reauthorize the program. In fact, Yoo was the only OLC lawyer
who knew that the program existed during this time—not even Yoo's boss,
Jay Bybee, was read in to the program. As we'll see, after Yoo left OLC,
other lawyers at OLC who were read in to the program raised concerns
about the program's legality that led to a dramatic confrontation between
the Department of Justice and the White House just months before the
2004 election.

What, exactly, did the TSP involve? After the *New York Times* reported
on this portion of the secret program, in 2005, the Bush administration
acknowledged that it had authorized the interception of international
communications when there was "a reasonable basis to conclude that one
party to the communication is a member of Al-Qaida, affiliated with
Al-Qaida, or a member of an organization affiliated with Al-Qaida." In
other words, if the president concluded that Americans were making phone
calls or sending e-mails to someone outside the United States who the
president reasonably believed was connected with Al Qaeda or an affiliated
organization, the NSA could intercept those communications without
obtaining a warrant.

On the face of it, the TSP directly conflicts with FISA, which does not
permit warrantless surveillance under these circumstances. In fact, Louis
Fisher describes the TSP as "a direct challenge to our system and form of
government."[24] Fisher concludes that, by authorizing surveillance under

the TSP that is prohibited by FISA, the president "claim[ed] the right to ignore statutory law in order to give preference to executive-made law, all done in secret."[25] James Pfiffner agrees with Fisher, asserting that "[w]hat is in question . . . is whether the president has the unilateral authority to ignore the explicit dictates of the law and can undertake secret surveillance within the United States."[26]

How did the administration justify the TSP? Once again, the argument was based on emergency presidential power, as articulated in secret OLC memos. In November 2001, John Yoo wrote an opinion concluding that the PSP, including the TSP, was legally justified. Yoo's opinion asserted that FISA must be read in such a way that it did not interfere with "the President's Article II authorities." He argued that FISA could not "restrict the President's ability to engage in warrantless searches that protect the national security." In authorizing warrantless surveillance, Yoo concluded, the president was limited by Article II and the Fourth Amendment[27] but not necessarily by FISA. Congress could not, he said, limit presidential power unless it included a "clear statement in FISA that it sought to restrict presidential authority to conduct warrantless searches in the national security area."[28]

After Yoo left OLC, other OLC lawyers who saw his memo had "serious concerns" with this analysis. They noted that FISA *does* seem to include a "clear statement" of congressional intent to limit presidential authority to conduct warrantless national security searches—the law creates an exception allowing warrantless searches for fifteen days following a congressional declaration of war. Critics of Yoo's analysis reason that this exception must mean that the president's power to authorize warrantless searches during wartime is otherwise restricted.

Critics of Yoo's analysis also observe that his legal opinions fail to consider Justice Jackson's concurring opinion in *Youngstown Sheet*. As discussed in chapter 7, Jackson's tripartite framework holds that presidential power is at its lowest ebb when the president acts in conflict with Congress's express or implied intent. Applying Jackson's framework to the TSP suggests that the president did not have the power to authorize warrantless surveillance prohibited by FISA.

When Yoo left OLC, in May 2003, another OLC lawyer, Patrick Philbin, was read in to the program so that he could take on Yoo's duties in periodically assessing the legality of the PSP. Philbin asked that OLC's new head, a lawyer named Jack Goldsmith, be read in as well. Goldsmith and Philbin reviewed Yoo's work, and each had concerns about Yoo's written opinions with regard to both legal analysis and factual discussion. They prepared their own analysis. Unlike Yoo, they were not comfortable with asserting that the president could decide to set aside statutory law that, in the administration's view, conflicted with Article II authority. Instead, Goldsmith and Philbin took the 2001 Authorization for the Use of Military Force (AUMF) as the starting point for their analysis. They reasoned that the AUMF reflected Congress's implied intent to authorize at least some warrantless surveillance in connection with the use of force against those who had attacked the United States. If this analysis was correct, it would place the program on stronger ground under the *Youngstown* framework, as the president could claim that he was operating at the maximum extent of his power pursuant to express or implied congressional authorization. However, Goldsmith and Philbin believed that, even under their AUMF-based analysis, some of the surveillance authorized under the PSP was not legally justified. In late 2003, Goldsmith and Philbin discussed their concerns with Attorney General John Ashcroft, and they also raised their concerns with Alberto Gonzales, the White House counsel, and with David Addington, counsel to the vice president. Deputy Attorney General James Comey was also read in to the program and agreed with Goldsmith and Comey that there were problems with Yoo's analysis, especially because Yoo's analysis depended on setting aside an act of Congress.

In early March of 2004, Attorney General Ashcroft was hospitalized, suffering from pancreatitis. With Ashcroft incapacitated, Comey became acting attorney general. On March 6, 2004, Goldsmith and Philbin told Gonzales and Addington that some PSP activities must stop, as they were not legally justified. White House officials disagreed with Goldsmith and Philbin's conclusions. The forty-five-day authorization period was ending, and Gonzales asked Goldsmith to either reauthorize the PSP or, at least, allow a thirty-day temporary reauthorization that would allow Ashcroft to return to duty and reauthorize the program himself. Goldsmith refused, reiterating that parts of the program were not legally justified. White House officials held another meeting, this time with Comey, Goldsmith, and Philbin. Vice President Cheney personally made the case that the PSP should be reauthorized, telling Comey that stopping the program would put thousands of lives at risk. Comey insisted that the program would have to be modified so that he could sign off on the program's legality. The precise modifications Comey asked for remain classified, but, whatever they were, Vice President Cheney did not agree to them.

Instead, Cheney decided to seek approval from congressional leaders. On March 10, 2004, Cheney met with the Gang of Eight, congressional leaders who had previously received briefings about the program.[29] White House counsel Gonzales, who also attended the March 10 meeting, later testified before the Senate Judiciary Committee that the Gang of Eight's "consensus" was that the PSP should continue. However, Senator Jay Rockefeller (D-WV), then Senator Tom Daschle (D-SD), and Representative Nancy Pelosi (D-CA) issued statements indicating that they disagreed with Gonzales and that there was, in fact, no consensus.[30]

At this point, the story takes a bizarre turn. President Bush told Gonzales and White House chief of staff Andrew Card to speak with Attorney General Ashcroft, who was still in the hospital. On March 10, 2004, Card called the hospital and tried to connect Ashcroft with President Bush. Ashcroft's wife said that Ashcroft would not accept the call, and she asked that Ashcroft be left to rest for a day or two. When Card and President Bush persisted, Mrs. Ashcroft spoke with them by phone from the hospital and was told that Card and Gonzales were on their way to meet with Ashcroft on "a matter involving national security."

Deputy Attorney General Comey found out that Card and Gonzales were on their way to see Ashcroft. Comey hurried over to the hospital in an effort to head them off and told his chief of staff to "get as many of my people as possible to the hospital immediately."[31] Comey also called FBI director Robert Mueller and OLC attorney Philbin, asking them both to come to the hospital to "witness [Ashcroft's] condition." Comey also asked Philbin to contact Goldsmith, the head of the OLC.

Comey, Goldsmith, and Philbin beat Gonzales and Card to the hospital. They found Ashcroft in his room, in bad shape, and they told him "not to sign anything." Gonzales and Card arrived a few minutes later. Gonzales told Ashcroft that he had the reauthorization document for the PSP with him and said that the program had to be renewed. Ashcroft refused to do so, citing legal concerns about the PSP and adding that, in any event, his own views did not matter, "because I'm not the attorney general. There [pointing to Comey] is the attorney general." Gonzales and Card left, and a drained Ashcroft sat in a chair, "feeble, barely articulate, clearly stressed."

Later that evening, Card called Comey and told him to come to the White House. Comey said that he would come only with a witness. Joined by Solicitor General Ted Olson, Comey met with Gonzales and Card late in the evening of March 10, 2004. Comey continued to refuse to reauthorize the program without modifications.

The next day, March 11, 2004, President Bush reauthorized the PSP, relying on a certification from White House counsel Gonzales instead of the usual certification by the attorney general. The March 11 reauthorization also departed from past authorizations in that it "explicitly asserted that the President's exercise of his Article II Commander-in-Chief authority displaced any contrary provisions of law, including FISA." After President Bush signed the reauthorization, a number of senior officials, including

Comey, Goldsmith, and FBI director Mueller, prepared to resign. Goldsmith drafted a letter of resignation that cited what he called the "shameful" visit Gonzales and Card had made to Ashcroft in the hospital as one of his reasons for leaving his post. Ashcroft asked Comey to wait to resign until he, Ashcroft, had recovered and could resign with him.

Before these officials carried out their plans to resign, President Bush met with Comey in the White House and told Comey that the program was essential to "save lives." Comey reiterated the legal concerns about the program that he had previously raised with other officials. On March 16, 2004, Comey wrote a memorandum to Gonzales repeating his conclusion that there was no legal basis to support parts of the PSP and that these unjustified surveillance activities should stop immediately, reminding Gonzales that the program depended on "the President's decision to assert his authority to override an otherwise applicable Act of Congress." Gonzales replied in a letter to Comey that stated "Your memo appears to have been based on a misunderstanding of the President's expectations regarding the conduct of the Department of Justice. While the President was, and remains, interested in any thoughts the Department of Justice may have on alternative ways to achieve effectively the goals of the activities authorized by the Presidential authorization of March 11, 2004, the President has addressed definitively for the Executive Branch in the Presidential Authorization the interpretation of the law."

Despite Gonzales's letter, which seemed to dismiss Comey's concerns, on March 17, 2004, President Bush agreed to modify some of the PSP surveillance activities and to discontinue others. Ashcroft, Comey, Goldsmith, and others who had been prepared to resign ended up staying in their jobs. On May 6, 2004, Goldsmith and Comey completed a 108-page memorandum describing the PSP's history and providing legal analysis. The memorandum concluded that the September 2001 AUMF provided legal authority for the PSP.

After some information about the secret surveillance program was made public in 2005, a number of lawsuits were filed against the government and private telecommunications companies claiming violations of FISA. When it amended FISA in 2008, Congress provided retroactive immunity for the private companies and also expanded the president's surveillance authority.[32]

How do we assess the secret surveillance program? Was it legally justified? The program violated the plain language of FISA and the Fourth Amendment to the U.S. Constitution, but the administration concluded that Congress did not have the authority to limit the president's power to gather intelligence in the course of conducting the war on terror and that, therefore, FISA was moot. The administration's conclusion depended on its view that emergency presidential power included the authority to set aside an act of Congress when it interfered with the president's authority to gather intelligence in the course of defending the nation against potential terrorist attacks.

Information about the program was closely guarded, and, for more than a year, the administration relied on the legal opinions of one lawyer within the Justice Department to justify the program's legality. The program arguably allowed some judicial review (in the sense that the presiding FISC judge was advised about it) and limited congressional oversight (in the sense that eight members of Congress were advised about the program). For years, the attorney general provided authorization for the program and, when personnel changes at the Department of Justice led acting Attorney General Comey to refuse reauthorization, top administration officials rushed to a hospital in an attempt to coax approval from an essentially incapacitated John Ashcroft.

As noted, the warrantless surveillance program remained secret until 2005, when reporting by the *New York Times* revealed its existence. The precise scope of the program, what information was gained, how it was used, and whose communications were listened to or read remain unknown as much of the program remains classified. Among the many unanswered questions is: why didn't the administration simply apply for warrants from the FISA court? That court almost never denies an application—and, after the program's existence became public, the administration did apply for and receive warrants to carry out some of the activities that had previously been conducted without a court warrant. Alternatively, why didn't the administration simply ask Congress to revise FISA and authorize the surveillance program? Former FISC presiding judge Lamberth has wondered about this and suggests an answer: "We could have gone to Congress, hat in hand, the judicial branch and the executive together, and gotten any statutory change we wanted in those days [after the September 11 attacks]. . . . And I felt like there was a way the statute could have been tweaked in a way that they [the executive branch] could have lived with. But they wanted to demonstrate that the president's power was supreme, and the judiciary was just a tagalong when necessary, but not appreciated."[33] Judge Lamberth may be right: as it turned out, after the secret surveillance program was revealed publicly, Congress did take action to retroactively ratify some of the activities and to modify FISA to allow additional surveillance, including surveillance targeting non-U.S. persons that can now be conducted without a showing of individualized probable cause and without the executive branch identifying the target of surveillance, even if communications by U.S. persons are intercepted (as long as U.S. persons were not targeted but were communicating with targeted foreign persons).[34]

Were Comey, Goldsmith, Philbin, and others right to raise objections to the secret surveillance program and to refuse to reauthorize it when Attorney General Ashcroft was hospitalized? Although they were prepared to resign if the president did not modify the program, these lawyers ultimately stayed in their positions after President Bush agreed to make some modifications. Was this the right decision? Should they have made their concerns publicly known? To the extent that these lawyers had concerns about the legal justifications John Yoo offered for the program, were those concerns allayed by the May 2004 memo Goldsmith and Comey wrote that focused on the AUMF as authorizing secret warrantless surveillance under the PSP? Was it appropriate for the Bush administration to brief the Gang of Eight about the program, but not other members of Congress? What should members of the Gang of Eight have done if they had concerns about the program's legality?

13

DETENTION AND
MILITARY COMMISSIONS UNDER
THE OBAMA ADMINISTRATION

Critics of the Bush administration's definition and use of emergency presidential power hoped that President Barack Obama would endorse and apply a more limited version of emergency power. These critics saw signs for hope in the context of the detention system at Guantanamo. As one of his first acts in office, President Obama signed an executive order promising to close the detention facilities at Guantanamo "as soon as practicable" and no later than one year from the January 22, 2009, order.[1] The order further provided for "immediate review" of all detentions at Guantanamo Bay, coordinated by the attorney general. The review would determine, as promptly as possible, whether prisoners should be transferred, released, prosecuted in federal civilian court, or handled by "other lawful means." The plan was to identify some prisoners who should be sent to their home countries and other prisoners who would be moved to the United States, where they would be held in preparation for trial before either a regular court-martial or a federal court.[2] However, the January 2010 deadline for closing Guantanamo was not met, and the prison there remained open throughout the president's first term, with no sign of it closing as his second term got underway.

The Obama administration argued that political backlash prevented President Obama from fulfilling the promise made in the January 2009 executive order. This backlash, officials argue, began later in 2009, when the administration announced plans to try some suspected terrorists— including Khalid Sheikh Mohammed, the self-described planner of the September 11 attacks—in federal court. Other prisoners held at Guantanamo would be given military trials.[3] However, some critics warned that it would be dangerous to try Mohammed and other suspected terrorists in New York City, where trial was to be held. Defenders of the decision to try Mohammed in federal court pointed out that other suspected terrorists had been tried and convicted in the same Manhattan courthouse without incident.[4]

Congress ultimately passed legislation preventing the use of federal funds to transfer prisoners at Guantanamo to the United States for any purpose.[5] Although the Obama administration said it would work with Congress to repeal this statutory bar,[6] it backed away from its decision to try Mohammed in federal court, at first saying he would continue to be held in military detention and then announcing he would be tried before a military tribunal. As the Obama administration reconsidered its initial decision, Colonel Jeffrey Colwell remarked that a decision to move Mohammed's trial from civilian court to a military tribunal would be "a sad day for the rule of law," as it would suggest that political calculations were taking precedence over legal considerations.[7]

Even as the Obama administration vacillated over whether to try some prisoners before military or civilian courts, it made clear that other prisoners would simply be held without trial of any kind. Of the approximately 200 prisoners held at Guantanamo in early 2010, the Obama administration indicated that about 40 would be prosecuted in some court, about 110 would be repatriated or transferred to other countries for release, and about 50 who were deemed too difficult to prosecute but too dangerous to release would be imprisoned without trial.[8] In March 2011, President Obama issued Executive Order 13567, entitled "Periodic Review of Individuals Detained at Guantanamo Bay Naval Station Pursuant to the Authorization for the Use of Military Force."[9] Executive Order 13567 describes how prisoners held at Guantanamo as of March 7, 2011, could be subject to "continued law of war detention" if "necessary to protect against a significant threat to the security of the United States." The order defines "law of war detention" as "detention authorized by the Congress under the AUMF, as informed by the laws of war." This presumably meant that the order applied to prisoners who had already been determined to be "enemy combatants" as the Supreme Court described that term in *Hamdi*—in other words, those who were "part of or supporting forces hostile to the United States or coalition partners'" in Afghanistan and who "engaged in an armed conflict against the United States."[10]

Pursuant to the order, prisoners at Guantanamo who were determined to pose a significant threat to U.S. security if released would be provided "periodic review" to reassess their continued detention. The first review would take place within one year of the date of the order. After that, prisoners would receive a full review and hearing every three years, with "file reviews" conducted every six months to determine whether any new information raised a "significant question" as to the justification for the prisoner's continued detention.[11]

The initial review, triennial review, and any interim review warranted by new information, were to take place before a Periodic Review Board (PRB) composed of six "senior officials" appointed by the Departments of State, Defense, Justice, and Homeland Security and by the Offices of the Director of National Intelligence and the chairman of the Joint Chiefs of Staff. The prisoner would be assisted by a government-provided personal representative (not described as a lawyer). The prisoner could also retain private counsel at his own expense. As noted, the ultimate question the PRB was to consider was whether continued detention "is necessary to protect against a significant threat to the security of the United States." Prisoners were permitted to make a statement to the PRB, to introduce relevant information, to answer questions posed by the PRB, and to call witnesses who were "reasonably available and willing to provide information that is relevant and material" to the PRB's ultimate determination.[12]

The secretary of defense was required to provide the PRB with information gathered in the course of reviewing the prisoner's status, including information that might help the prisoner's case. This information was also to be provided to the prisoner's representative or private counsel—however, if necessary to protect national security, the PRB could provide the prisoner's representative or private counsel with a summary of or a substitute for the information provided by the secretary of defense. The summary or substitute was to give the representative or counsel "a meaningful opportunity to assist the [prisoner] during the review process." Hearsay evidence and evidence obtained through coercion or even torture were not ruled out: the PRB was to "consider the reliability of any information provided to it in making its determination." If the PRB could not reach a consensus, a Review Committee made up of the secretary of state, secretary of defense, attorney general, secretary of homeland security, director of national intelligence, and the chairman of the Joint Chiefs of Staff would conduct a review. The PRB process was not designed as a substitute for habeas corpus; prisoners could still file a petition in federal court for the writ.[13]

Critics described the PRB process as upholding a system of preventive detention that allowed prisoners to be held indefinitely without trial on the sole basis of the prediction that they could be dangerous if released. Michael Ratner of the Center for Constitutional Rights described preventive detention as the unconstitutional idea that prisoners can be held because they might be dangerous if released.[14] Indeed, the PRB system did seem to place a prisoner in something like a Catch-22 situation:[15] how could he convince the government he was not dangerous when the fact that he had already been detained for years without charges or trial would logically make him antagonistic toward the United States? The Obama administration would argue that the PRB process applied only to prisoners who had already been determined to be enemy combatants (presumably by a Combatant Status Review Tribunal, or CSRT)[16] and merely offered them an additional opportunity to demonstrate that they should be released. Moreover, prisoners would continue to have access to habeas review by federal courts.[17] However, as of this writing, the Supreme Court has not decided whether the CSRT process itself—or the CSRT process combined with the PRB review—would satisfy the due process requirements outlined in *Hamdi*. Moreover, in *Hamdi*, the court acknowledged that "perpetual detention" of enemy combatants might not be justified.[18] It is possible that, nearly a decade after *Hamdi*, the court might conclude, if asked, that the PRB system creates a system of perpetual detention that is impermissible. This issue may become especially salient if, as expected, U.S. combat operations in Afghanistan conclude at the end of 2014.

In late 2011, Congress passed the National Defense Authorization Act for fiscal year 2012 (2012 NDAA), signed into law by President Obama on December 31, 2011, that essentially ratified the PRB process described in Executive Order 13567.[19] The 2012 NDAA also contained other provisions relevant to the detention system at Guantanamo. First, section 1021 of the act expanded the president's detention authority beyond what had been provided in the 2001 AUMF.[20] The 2001 AUMF provided "[t]hat the President is authorized to use all necessary and appropriate force against those nations, organizations, or persons he determines planned, authorized, committed, or aided the terrorist attacks that occurred on September 11, 2001, or harbored such organizations or persons."[21] The 2012 NDAA reaffirmed that the president retained detention authority under the 2001 AUMF but additionally provided that the president could detain under the law of war "[a] person who was a part of or substantially supported al-Qaeda, the Taliban, or associated forces that are engaged in hostilities against the United States or its coalition partners, including any person who has committed a belligerent act or has directly supported such hostilities in aid of such enemy forces."[22] Such prisoners could be held "under the law of war without trial until the end of the hostilities authorized by the [2001 AUMF]."[23]

What this means, in practice, is that Congress (1) expressly authorized indefinite law of war detention for members of Al Qaeda or the Taliban as the court inferred in *Hamdi* and (2) further authorized indefinite detention for people who "substantially support" Al Qaeda, the Taliban, or "associated forces that are engaged in hostilities against the United States or its coalition partners." Critics argued that this new language created dangerous ambiguities. What does "substantial support" mean? Could a conscripted cook who served Taliban soldiers or members of Al Qaeda be held indefinitely?[24] Critics raised similar questions about the vagueness of the term "associated forces."[25] They also pointed out that the 2012 NDAA did not prohibit indefinite detention for U.S. citizens, though President Obama said that he would not apply the detention authority provided by Congress to U.S. citizens.[26]

Under the 2012 NDAA and the Supreme Court's ruling in *Hamdi*, a prisoner who is determined to be eligible for detention under the law of war would be subject to indefinite detention without trial. Under *Hamdi*, only a limited hearing would be required in order to give the prisoner a meaningful opportunity to challenge the determination that he was an enemy combatant—and such a hearing need not be in civilian court. However, at its discretion, the executive branch could try prisoners held at Guantanamo in court.[27]

As noted, the Obama administration decided to try some of the prisoners held at Guantanamo before military tribunals. These included Khalid Sheikh Mohammed, who was originally slated for trial before a federal court in New York.[28] Since the Supreme Court's 2006 decision in *Hamdan v. Rumsfeld*, the rules for trial by military tribunal have been revised.[29] The Military Commissions Act of 2009 (2009 MCA), enacted as part of the Department of Defense Authorization Act for fiscal year 2010, now governs such trials.[30] In *Hamdan*, the court concluded that the rules used for Salim Hamdan's initial military trial conflicted with statutory law (the Uniform Code of Military Justice) as well as with Common Article 3 of the Geneva Conventions.[31] Specifically, the tribunal was improperly permitted to convict Hamdan on the basis of evidence he could not review, and it was able to consider any evidence that "would have probative value to a reasonable person"—including hearsay evidence or evidence obtained through torture.[32]

Under the 2009 MCA, military tribunals[33] are generally required to follow the procedures and rules of evidence applicable in trials by courts-martial except as otherwise specified in the act and unless, in the view of the secretary of defense, in consultation with the attorney general, exceptions are required by "the unique circumstances of the conduct of military and intelligence operations during hostilities or by other practical need consistent with [the act]."[34] Unless such circumstances apply, the accused person is afforded, at a minimum, certain protections: (1) the right to present evidence in his defense and to cross-examine witnesses; (2) the right to be present during trial, unless that would require the disclosure of information "which could reasonably be expected to cause damage to the national security, including intelligence or law enforcement sources, methods, or activities";[35] (3) the right to be represented by military counsel (and, if the accused pays, by civilian counsel); and (4) the right to have evidence suppressed that is not reliable or probative.[36] Hearsay evidence not admissible before a court-martial may be admissible before a military tribunal in some circumstances if the military judge assigned to the tribunal,[37] after taking into account the relevant circumstances, determines that the evidence is reliable and not otherwise available.[38] Statements made by the accused person in the absence of a Miranda warning may also be admissible.[39] There is a presumption of innocence, and the government must prove guilt beyond reasonable doubt.[40] Statements obtained through torture or cruel or inhuman or degrading treatment are not admissible.[41] Only noncitizen enemy belligerents may be tried before military tribunals.[42] Military tribunal decisions may be appealed to federal civilian courts, including the U.S. Supreme Court.[43]

These rules attempt to remedy the problems the court identified in *Hamdan*, but it remains to be seen whether the 2009 MCA would satisfy the Supreme Court. The *Hamdan* decision rejected the executive branch's rules for military trial. The rules put in place in response to that decision have been created by Congress—but the court could conclude that even rules authorized by Congress conflict with the Constitution and/or the Geneva Conventions. For instance, if evidence obtained through coercion falling short of torture or cruel, inhuman, or degrading treatment is used against a defendant in a military trial, would that violate Common Article 3's requirement that "judgment [be] pronounced by a regularly constituted court, affording all the judicial guarantees which are recognized as indispensable by civilized peoples"? As the government continues to hold military trials under the rules set by the 2009 MCA, there is always the possibility that a defendant will challenge these rules, as Hamdan did, and that the Supreme Court will determine whether Congress's scheme passes muster.

A separate question one might consider is: are military tribunals necessary? Why not simply try suspected terrorists before federal courts?[44] As Attorney General Eric Holder has noted, hundreds of defendants have been tried and convicted in federal court for "terrorism-related offenses"—including Umar Farouk Abdulmutallab (the attempted "Christmas Day bomber"), Faisal Shahzad (the attempted Times Square bomber), and Ahmed Ghailani, convicted for his role in the 1998 U.S. embassy bombings in Africa.[45] As Holder also noted, there are reasons why prosecutors might well prefer to try suspected terrorists in federal courts rather than before military tribunals; for one thing, he observed, "federal prosecutors have a wider range of tools [in federal courts] that can be used to incapacitate suspected terrorists."[46] Military tribunals can consider only violations of the laws of war, whereas civilian courts have jurisdiction over a wider range of offenses.

Military tribunals have been described as creatures of necessity—to be used, for instance, when regular civilian courts are not open or when the military is forced to administer justice in a theater of operations outside the United States. Are military tribunals necessary in the context of the war on terror? Why was the military tribunal system established in the first place to try suspected terrorists? What is the reason, years later, for using these tribunals? Can the military tribunal system be squared with the Constitution and with Common Article 3 of the Geneva Conventions? In *Hamdan*, Justice Kennedy concluded that "[t]he regular military courts in our system are the courts-martial established by congressional statute." Would he and other justices conclude that the new military tribunals— now established by congressional statute but not required to follow the same procedures as courts-martial—are "regularly constituted courts" as contemplated by Common Article 3? Finally, even if military tribunals are legally permissible, are there any practical downsides to using them?[47]

When President Obama took office in 2009, he promised to close Guantanamo and to try at least some of the prisoners held there in federal court. As his second term began in 2013, the prison at Guantanamo remained open, with nearly two hundred prisoners still held there.[48] The administration decided to use military tribunals to try at least some of the prisoners held at Guantanamo. Others have been described as too dangerous to try and too dangerous to release, and these prisoners face the prospect of perpetual detention that Hamdi warned the court about in 2004.[49] The question now is this: what should be done with prisoners still held at Guantanamo? Congress has set limits on the president's ability to bring prisoners to the United States for trial in federal court but has not closed off the possibility of military trial. Are military trials the best decision for some prisoners? Is it legitimate to conclude that some prisoners can be held indefinitely without trial, subject only to limited periodic review? If the executive branch believes that the federal court system is the best place to try some prisoners held at Guantanamo but Congress disagrees, what should the executive do?

14

THE STATE SECRETS PRIVILEGE

EMERGENCY PRESIDENTIAL
POWER BY ANOTHER NAME?

While the George W. Bush administration's use of the state secrets privilege, as discussed in this chapter, and other secretive practices[1] earned Bush the title of "the Secrecy President,"[2] Barack Obama took office in 2009 promising a new era of government transparency[3] and suggesting he would rein in presidential power. However, the new Obama administration also used secrecy as a way to implement a broad vision of emergency presidential power—in some ways, a vision that went beyond what the Bush administration had described.[4] The Obama administration relied on secrecy to seal off controversial decisions, including the decision to order the killing of U.S. citizens without trial or hearing, from review by other branches of government or the public. An important tool it has used to maintain this veil of secrecy is the state secrets privilege, "a common law evidentiary rule that allows the government to withhold information from discovery when disclosure would be inimical to national security."[5]

The state secrets privilege was recognized by the Supreme Court in a 1953 case called *Reynolds v. United States*.[6] In *Reynolds*, a case that received little public attention at the time, the executive branch aimed to "establish an exclusive presidential power: a determination that would be final and conclusive on the legislative and judicial branches."[7] What the executive sought was the power to refuse to disclose material that it deemed protected by the state secrets privilege without making the disputed materials available even for judicial review. The Obama administration has invoked this privilege as a powerful tool designed to seal off executive branch decisions from review and to block litigation aimed at cutting through layers of secrecy to determine whether controversial decisions are constitutionally justified. It has argued for a state secrets privilege that can be used to win dismissal of entire cases, rather than simply protecting confidential information from disclosure during a lawsuit. In order to fully understand the Obama administration's use of the state secrets privilege, it's important to begin with a discussion of the state secrets privilege itself: how the Supreme Court came to recognize this privilege and how it has been used—or, as critics would charge, abused.

In 1948, a U.S. Air Force plane that was testing secret electronic equipment exploded in midair and crashed in Georgia, killing nine men who were aboard, including four civilians. The widows of three of the civilians filed a lawsuit under the Federal Tort Claims Act alleging that their husbands' death had been caused by the government's negligence. In responding to the lawsuit, the U.S. government denied that the government was "in [any] manner responsible for the accident." A federal district court judge ordered the government to produce the accident reports and statements given by survivors of the crash, rejecting the government's claim that "a new kind of [privilege]" protected the documents from disclosure. In response, the government claimed that disclosure of the documents to the judge would make it more difficult to conduct future investigations of crashes and emphasized the "confidential mission" of the plane that had exploded and crashed, arguing that discussing "its mission or information concerning its operation or performance would be prejudicial to th[e] [Air Force] and would not be in the public interest." The government's position was that the executive branch, not the courts, would determine whether it could refuse to disclose secret information. When the district court judge instructed the government to make documents available to him for confidential *in camera*[8] review to determine whether they should be made available in the lawsuit, the government refused.[9]

The district court judge ruled that, since the government refused to produce relevant documents, even for limited *in camera* review, without a "sufficient excuse," the court would have to conclude that the deaths of the civilian employees were caused by the government's negligence. The government had a choice: it could produce the documents or, if it withheld them from even *in camera* review, it would lose the case. Accordingly, on February 20, 1951, the district court judge awarded monetary damages to each of the widows who had brought suit, in a combined amount of $370,000. The government appealed to the Third Circuit Court of Appeals. On appeal, the government argued that the disputed records were "privileged" from disclosure, though it did not specifically invoke the state secrets privilege.

It argued that "access to evidence in a trial would be decided not by the judiciary but by one of the parties to the case: the executive [branch]" insisting that, under British[10] and American precedent, "disclosure by the head of an executive department cannot be coerced." The government "seemed to suggest that access to the accident report, by either plaintiffs or the district judge, might result in some sort of disciplinary proceeding or sanction against witnesses [who had provided information to the government about the accident]." The government also presented a separate argument that executive immunity shielded the documents from production and "that a decision by a department head [here, the secretary of the air force] not to release a document is 'valid and binding' on courts." However, the government also used language in its brief to the Third Circuit that stopped short of demanding "total or blind judicial deference" to executive branch claims. The widows' lawyers, in turn, reminded the court of the importance of "an independent judiciary [that can] determine whether a specific act is within the exclusive authority of the executive branch and thus immune from judicial [interference]" rather than leaving "[t]hat determination . . . to self-serving interpretations of the executive branch."[11]

The Third Circuit sided with the widows, upholding the district court's ruling that the accident report and surviving witness statements should have been produced and were not protected by privilege. In its December 11, 1951, ruling, the Third Circuit rejected the government's suggestion that it could determine, without judicial review, whether it had to disclose documents requested in litigation, reasoning that, if the courts recognized such a "sweeping privilege," the government could shield merely embarrassing documents from disclosure. Citing Edward Livingston and Patrick Henry, the Third Circuit's decision warned that overly broad invocations of government secrecy could be dangerous to the country. The court observed that the government "assert[ed] in effect that the documents sought to be produced contain state secrets of a military [character]" and the court conceded that "[s]tate secrets of a diplomatic or military nature have always been privileged from disclosure in any proceeding." However, the court concluded, *in camera* review would have permitted the district court judge to review the disputed documents without making any privileged information public: if the district court judge confirmed the government's assertion of privilege, then the documents could have been shielded from public disclosure.[12]

As Louis Fisher points out, the Third Circuit's reference to possible "state secrets" at issue in the case "created a major problem when the dispute reached the Supreme Court." The Third Circuit's opinion suggested that the government had claimed that the accident report and witness statements contained "state secrets of a military character." In fact, the government had not said this and had not specifically advanced a claim of privilege based on state secrets. By referring to such a claim, however, the Third Circuit paved the way for the Supreme Court to make this part of the case and to establish precedent for future invocations of such a privilege.[13]

In asking the Supreme Court to review the Third Circuit's decision, "the government for the first time pressed the state secrets privilege in a brief[,]" perhaps recognizing the opportunity presented by the Third Circuit here. The government argued to the Supreme Court that this common-law privilege applied because (1) the plane that exploded and crashed had been carrying out "a highly secret military mission" and (2) disclosure of the plane's "mission or information concerning its operation or performance would be prejudicial to th[e] [air force] and would not be in the public interest." As Fisher points out, "[n]ot a word of this has anything to do with the *contents* of the accident report or the survivors' statements." In fact, if the documents in question had been submitted to the district court judge for *in camera* review, "he would have seen nothing in them that related to military secrets or confidential equipment." However, the Supreme Court justices did not know this, because, like the lower court judges, none of them actually saw the disputed documents and "the government misled the Court on the contents of the accident report." The government suggested to the court that the report might reveal military secrets. In fact, as the families involved in the case learned decades later, none of the disputed documents contained such information. In short, the government's position was that it, rather than the courts, would be "the adjudicator of national security disputes, carefully and judiciously weighing the competing merits of both sides before arriving at a just and balanced verdict." In other words, the courts would play no role in determining whether a state secrets privilege claim was justified; this determination would be made independently, without any outside review, by the executive branch itself.[14]

While the lower courts had rejected the government's position that *in camera* review was inappropriate, the Supreme Court reached a different conclusion.[15] In a 6–3 decision issued March 9, 1953, the court reversed the Third Circuit's ruling in a very short majority opinion written by Chief Justice Vinson.[16] The Supreme Court began its analysis by asserting the existence of a "privilege against revealing military secrets, a privilege which is well established in the law of evidence." The court indicates that this is a basis for protecting "military or state secrets" from disclosure during litigation and that, when the government claims this privilege, courts must rule on the government's claim "without forcing a disclosure of the very thing the privilege is designed to protect." The court cautioned against the danger of "[t]oo much judicial inquiry" and warned that even *in camera* review could "jeopardize . . . [national] security." The court explained that judges reviewing a claim of state secrets privilege should ask how necessary it is for litigants seeking disclosure of the disputed materials to gain access to them. In other words, can the private party seeking information that the government claims is subject to the state secrets privilege advance its claim *only* by gaining access to the disputed materials? This tells the judge how far to go in testing the government's claim—"[w]here there is a strong showing of necessity, the claim of privilege should not be lightly accepted." However, "even the most compelling necessity cannot overcome the claim of privilege if the court is ultimately satisfied that military secrets are at stake." In such a case, where the court is "satisfied that military secrets are at stake," the Supreme Court suggested that a case could be dismissed "without ever reaching the question of evidence." In other words, when a court is "satisfied" that secrets would be revealed if the case proceeded, it must simply dismiss the case without even reviewing the disputed materials to determine whether the claim of privilege is justified.[17]

In *Reynolds* itself, the court concluded that "it should be possible for [plaintiffs] to adduce the essential facts as to causation without resort to material touching upon military secrets." Dismissal of the case was not necessary. The government had offered to make survivors of the crash available for examination, and plaintiffs "should have . . . accepted" this offer in lieu of the accident report or surviving-witness statements. Plaintiffs had argued that the price of governmental privilege should be default—in other words, if the government chose to invoke privilege and deny anyone, even the court, access to the sought-after documents, then plaintiffs should be awarded judgment (as the district court judge had ruled). The Supreme Court, however, rejected this notion, suggesting it had applicability only in the context of criminal cases, where the government could not pursue prosecution without allowing defendant access to relevant documents and information.[18]

The court's logic suffers from some apparent deficiencies. As Louis Fisher observes, "[i]f the government can keep the actual documents from the judge, even for *in camera* inspection, how can the judge 'determine whether the circumstances are appropriate for the claim of privilege?'"[19] How had the Supreme Court determined in this case that (1) the disputed documents were not essential to advancing plaintiffs' claims and (2) the documents themselves contained military or state secrets? None of the justices had actually seen the documents. The Supreme Court's decision simply took the government at its word, "rely[ing] [only] on . . . th[e] claims and assertions [of] executive officials" themselves.[20] The court's decision meant that, in this and other cases, judges and litigants would have no way to know whether the government was actually misrepresenting its claim of privilege. A judge assessing a claim of state secrets privilege would have to "[rule] in the dark."[21]

In fact, it turned out that the Supreme Court had relied on the government's claim at its peril and to the disadvantage of the widows and families whose case was at stake.[22] Decades later, when the accident report and survivors' statements were declassified, they revealed no state secrets; instead, the documents showed that government negligence was indeed to blame for the crash.[23] As lawyers for the families put it in 2003, after the reports had been made publicly available, "in telling the Court otherwise, the Air Force lied."[24]

The court's decision in *Reynolds* "gave a green light to the state secrets privilege, and it has been so used consistently by the Justice Department over the years. . . . In subsequent disputes over access to agency documents, the government [has] regularly cite[d] this decision as legal justification for withholding requested materials."[25] Although invocation of the state secrets privilege does not automatically lead to dismissal of the pending case,[26] in the decades since *Reynolds* was decided, "critics argue that [the state secrets privilege] has morphed into a device by which the federal government maintains nearly total secrecy about its actions."[27] This has been especially true since the September 11, 2001, Al Qaeda attacks against the United States.[28]

The Bush administration invoked the state secrets privilege in responding to lawsuits seeking damages for extraordinary rendition.[29] When Khaled El-Masri, a German citizen of Lebanese descent, filed suit in a U.S. district court claiming[30] he had been transported by CIA agents in early 2004 to a secret prison in Afghanistan known as the "Salt Pit," where he was held for five months, beaten, drugged, and interrogated,[31] the Bush administration claimed that the state secrets privilege required dismissal of the case. El-Masri argued that no state secrets would be revealed by litigating his case because the relevant facts were publicly known and, indeed, the government had acknowledged its use of extraordinary rendition as a general matter.[32] Nevertheless, the U.S. Court of Appeals for the Third Circuit, citing the *Reynolds* decision,[33] agreed with the Bush administration and entirely dismissed El-Masri's claims, concluding that litigation of the case would "require disclosure of information regarding the means and methods by which the CIA gathers intelligence."[34] The "central facts" or "very subject matter" of El-Masri's claims could not move ahead "without threatening disclosure of privileged state secrets."[35]

The Third Circuit also rejected El-Masri's suggestion that it could examine, *in camera*, evidence the government claimed to involve state secrets, making the evidence available only to El-Masri's lawyers rather than to the public at large.[36] Quoting *Reynolds*, the Third Circuit cautioned that "[a] court considering the Executive's assertion of the state secrets privilege . . . must take care not to 'forc[e] a disclosure of the very thing the privilege is designed to protect' by demanding more information than is [necessary]" and noted that, in *Reynolds*, the Supreme Court had made clear that "[w]hen . . . the occasion for the privilege is appropriate, . . . the court should not jeopardize the security which the privilege is meant to protect by insisting upon an examination of the evidence, even by the judge alone, in chambers."[37] The Third Circuit did not acknowledge that, in *Reynolds* itself, the court's reliance on government affidavits and refusal to review disputed documents *in camera* allowed the executive branch to successfully invoke privilege on the basis of misrepresentations to the court.

The Third Circuit concluded that government defendants would not be able to "properly defend themselves without using privileged [evidence]" because the government would have to disclose "the means and methods by which the CIA gathers intelligence."[38] It rejected El Masri's argument that "the state secrets doctrine . . . represent[s] a surrender of judicial control over access to the courts."[39] Although the court had not reviewed the materials that the government claimed were protected by the state secrets privilege, it remained confident that "it is the court, not the Executive, that determines whether the state secrets privilege has been properly invoked."[40] The court relied on a classified declaration submitted by the government and not made available to El Masri that purported to describe "the nature of the information that the Executive seeks to protect and explains why its disclosure would be detrimental to national security."[41]

Similarly, in response to claims brought by Maher Arar, the Bush administration invoked the state secrets privilege.[42] Arar, a dual citizen of Canada and Syria, claimed[43] that U.S. officials had detained him at Kennedy Airport in New York in 2002 when he was traveling home from vacation en route to Canada. U.S. officials delivered him to Jordan, and Jordanian officials delivered him to Syria. He was held in a grave-like cell in Syria for nearly a year, where he was beaten with an electrical cable, threatened with electric shock, and forced to sign a false confession that he had received military training in Afghanistan.[44] In January 2004, Arar filed a lawsuit in a U.S. district court. The government responded by claiming that the state secrets privilege precluded litigation, arguing to the court that allowing Arar's case to proceed would undermine national security by forcing revelation of intelligence-gathering sources and methods.[45] The district court and the court of appeals ultimately decided that it was not necessary to reach the state secrets question, concluding that Arar's case could be dismissed for other reasons.[46]

Although Obama initially suggested that he objected to the Bush administration's secrecy, his own administration did not dramatically change its approach to the state secrets privilege. In fact, one might conclude that the Obama administration relied to a greater extent than the preceding administration on the state secrets privilege in justifying emergency presidential power. Where the Bush administration used the unitary executive theory as a justification for broad, even unbounded, applications of power, the Obama administration used the state secrets privilege to reach the same ends—to insulate emergency presidential power from review—through different means.[47]

From the start, the Obama administration asserted the state secrets privilege as a way to argue that litigation should be dismissed. In February 2009, the Obama administration relied on the state secrets privilege in asking a federal appeals court to uphold dismissal of a lawsuit challenging the CIA's extraordinary rendition program.[48] In April 2009, the Justice Department argued that litigation involving the warrantless wiretapping program discussed in chapter 12 should be dismissed pursuant to the state secrets privilege because allowing the case to proceed "would cause exceptionally grave harm to national security."[49]

Critics noted that, as a presidential candidate, Obama had criticized the Bush administration's use of the state secrets privilege but that, once elected, President Obama was "mimicking [his] predecessor on issues of secrecy."[50] Responding to these criticisms, in September 2009 the Obama administration announced a new policy regarding use of the privilege. In a memorandum,[51] Attorney General Eric Holder explained that the "Department [of Justice] is adopting these policies and procedures to strengthen public confidence that the U.S. Government will invoke the privilege in court only when genuine and significant harm to national defense or foreign relations is at stake and only to the extent necessary to safeguard those interests."[52] According to the memorandum, the Department of Justice would invoke the state secrets privilege in court only "when a government department or agency seeking to assert the privilege makes a sufficient showing that assertion of the privilege is necessary to protect information[,] the unauthorized disclosure of which reasonably could be expected to cause significant harm to the national defense or foreign relations ('national security') of the United States."[53] Before invoking the privilege, the Department of Justice must require government officials to provide specific information, based on their personal knowledge, showing why disclosing the information at issue "can reasonably be expected to cause . . . significant harm to national security."[54] When it does invoke the state secrets privilege, the Department of Justice can do so "only to the extent necessary to protect against the risk of significant harm to national security."[55]

Although the new policy suggested a change, in practice the Obama administration's approach continued to be difficult to distinguish from that of the Bush administration. For one thing, the Obama administration continued to assert the state secrets privilege in a number of cases. In addition, the Obama administration, like the Bush administration, argued that the state secrets privilege would broadly immunize the government from any claim whenever the privilege was invoked. This has meant citing the state secrets privilege as a basis for dismissal, rather than protection of confidential materials, an argument that depends on what some observers describe as a "conflating" of the *Reynolds* holding with an 1876 case called *Totten v. U.S.*[56]

Under *Reynolds*, the Supreme Court did not hold that government invocation of the state secrets privilege automatically results in dismissal of pending litigation. Courts considering state secrets claims are instructed to consider how necessary it is for private litigants seeking disclosure of the disputed materials to gain access to them, and, "[w]here there is a strong showing of necessity, the [government's] claim of privilege should not be lightly accepted." Under *Reynolds*, the court should dismiss the case only if it is "satisfied that military secrets are at stake" and would otherwise be revealed. It may be possible to shield confidential information from disclosure without dismissing the entire case—in fact, that is what the court in *Reynolds* decided with regard to the case before it.[57]

However, critics argue, the scope of the *Reynolds* decision is unjustifiably broadened when it is conflated with the court's decision in *Totten*. In *Totten*, the Supreme Court upheld dismissal of a case seeking compensation claimed by the heir of a Civil War spy who allegedly was owed payment by the U.S. government for his espionage services during the war. The court stated that, "as a general principle . . . public policy forbids the maintenance of any suit in a court of justice, the trial of which would inevitably lead to the disclosure of matters which the law itself regards as confidential." For this reason, a lawsuit seeking damages on the basis of an alleged "contract for secret services with the government" could not continue, as litigation of the case would seek disclosure of a contract that, by its nature, had to be kept secret—the government could not be forced to disclose arrangements it made for espionage.[58] More recently, the Supreme Court has explained that "*Totten* [completely] precludes judicial review in cases . . . where success depends upon the existence of [a] secret espionage relationship with the Government."[59]

Although *Totten*'s specific holding would seem to apply to only a very narrow category of cases that, by the very nature of their resolution, would require the disclosure of state secrets,[60] the Obama administration, like the Bush administration before it, has relied on *Totten* in seeking dismissal of a broader category of cases. For instance, in *Mohamed v. Jeppesen Dataplan Inc.*, a case initiated before Obama took office, the Obama administration pressed for and won a broad recognition of the state secrets privilege that blurred the lines between *Totten* and *Reynolds* to produce a doctrine that promises strengthened protection for government claims of secrecy.[61]

In *Mohamed v. Jeppesen Dataplan, Inc.*, several men who claimed they had been subjected to extraordinary rendition brought suit in federal court against a private company they said had helped transport them to countries where they were tortured. Their complaint included conscience-shocking claims of torture. One man said Americans had delivered him to Egyptian captors who "subjected [him] to electric shock through electrodes attached to his ear lobes, nipples and genitals." Another man described being "transferred to Moroccan security agents" who "cut him with a scalpel all over his body, including on his penis, and poured 'hot stinging liquid' into the open wounds."[62]

Although the government was not named as a defendant in this lawsuit, the Bush administration had intervened in the case and moved to dismiss plaintiffs' claims, citing the state secrets privilege.[63] A federal district court judge accepted the government's argument and dismissed the case before Jeppesen had even responded to the allegations against it. Plaintiffs appealed the decision, and, while the appeal was pending, President Obama succeeded President Bush in office. On appeal, the Obama administration continued to argue that the case should be dismissed, citing the state secrets privilege. A three-judge panel of the U.S. Court of Appeals for the Ninth Circuit disagreed and reversed the district court's decision.[64] The Ninth Circuit panel noted that "Jeppesen, and to a lesser degree the government, argue that *Totten*'s categorical bar prevents litigation of this case because it, like the suit in *Totten*, is predicated on the existence of an alleged secret agreement with the government."[65]

The Ninth Circuit panel rejected this argument, concluding, first, that *Totten* applied only to bar claims resting on alleged secret contracts between *plaintiffs* and the government. If there was a secret arrangement here, it was between Jeppesen and the government.[66] In addition, the Ninth Circuit panel held that Jeppesen and the government were overreading *Totten* to stand for the broad proposition that "the 'very subject matter' of any other kind of lawsuit [can be] a state secret, apart from the limited factual context of *Totten* itself."[67] To the contrary, the Ninth Circuit panel said, *Totten* has narrow application and operates only to bar litigation in cases like *Totten*, where plaintiff's claim depended on proving the existence of a clandestine espionage contract. The government incorrectly suggested that "state secrets form the subject matter of a lawsuit, and therefore require dismissal, any time a complaint contains allegations, the truth or falsity of which has been classified as secret by a government official."[68] The mere fact that litigation contains some allegations that relate to secret government does not warrant application of *Totten* and dismissal of the entire case. If the government's argument prevailed, the Ninth Circuit warned, "the Judiciary [would] effectively cordon off all secret government actions from judicial scrutiny, immunizing the CIA and its partners from the demands and limits of the law."[69] The government's position would run afoul of the separation-of-powers doctrine as it would grant the executive too much power. The courts must play a role in "balancing the need for information in a judicial proceeding and the Executive's Article II prerogatives."[70] The Ninth Circuit said that the *Reynolds* framework allows for this balancing without necessarily requiring dismissal of the case when the government claims state secrets are at issue, while overly broad "application of the winner-takes-all *Totten* rule" would cede too much power to the executive.[71] The best approach, the Ninth Circuit panel concluded, is usually to "excis[e] secret evidence on an item-by-item basis, rather than foreclosing litigation altogether."[72] Outside the "extremely narrow *Totten* context," the state secrets privilege should not be used as a basis for dismissing litigation entirely.[73]

The Ninth Circuit *en banc* agreed to review the panel's decision and, in a 6–5 decision, rejected the panel's conclusions, affirmed the district court's decision, and dismissed plaintiffs' claims on the basis of the state secrets privilege.[74] The *en banc* decision rejected the argument that *Totten* only narrowly applies to cases involving an alleged espionage agreement between plaintiff and the government. Instead, the court said, this is just one example of a case warranting dismissal under the state secrets privilege. In *Mohamed*, some of plaintiffs' claims "*might fall within the Totten* [bar]" because allegations that Jeppesen "conspired with agents of the United States in plaintiffs' forced disappearance, torture and degrading treatment are premised on the existence of an alleged covert relationship between Jeppesen and the government."[75] However, the court noted, plaintiffs' claims that Jeppesen was liable for what it "should have known" about the extraordinary rendition program were "not so obviously tied to proof of a secret agreement between Jeppesen and the government."[76]

The court concluded that it was unnecessary to decide whether the case should be dismissed under *Totten* because it was clear that it should be dismissed under *Reynolds*. The government submitted declarations invoking its state secrets claim; as in *Reynolds* itself, the disputed documents were not submitted to the court for *in camera* review. The government asserted the state secrets privilege operated here to foreclose inquiry into "four categories of evidence . . . (1) information that would tend to confirm or deny whether Jeppesen or any other private entity assisted the CIA with clandestine intelligence activities; (2) information about whether any foreign government cooperated with the CIA in clandestine intelligence activities; (3) information about the scope or operation of the CIA terrorist detention and interrogation program; or (4) any other information concerning CIA clandestine intelligence operations that would tend to reveal intelligence activities, sources, or methods." These were "indisputably matters that the state secrets privilege may [cover]" because disclosure of this information could create a risk that espionage relationships and intelligence sources would be revealed.[77]

The court was deferential to the government's claim, noting that "the [government] certif[ied] at oral argument that its assertion of the state secrets privilege comports with the revised standards set forth in the current administration's September 23, 2009, memorandum, adopted several years after the government first invoked the privilege in this case."[78] The court concluded that "that certification here is consistent with our independent conclusion, having reviewed the government's public and classified declarations, that the government is not invoking the privilege to avoid embarrassment or to escape scrutiny of its recent controversial transfer and interrogation policies, rather than to protect legitimate national security concerns."[79] After reviewing the government's declarations in this case but not any allegedly sensitive material itself, the court concluded that, under *Reynolds*, the case must be dismissed because "there is no feasible way to litigate Jeppesen's alleged liability *without creating an unjustifiable risk of divulging state secrets.*"[80] Plaintiffs claimed that Jeppesen had provided logistical support for the extraordinary rendition program that delivered them to countries where they were tortured. Even though some information about the extraordinary rendition program had been made public, Jeppesen, in the course of defending against plaintiffs' claims, might reveal state secrets. The existence of the extraordinary rendition program was no longer itself a state secret, but just because some information about the program was publicly known did not preclude the possibility that other details might remain state secrets.[81] Further, even if the claims against Jeppesen were baseless, in the course of presenting its defense, Jeppesen would inevitably have to reveal information related to covert operations by the U.S. government; if the claims against Jeppesen were groundless, its defense would reveal how the government "does not conduct covert operations." The district court would be incapable of protecting sensitive information because "[a]dversarial litigation . . . is inherently complex and unpredictable[,]" and it is difficult to separate privileged from nonprivileged information. Methods ordinarily used to shield privileged information from disclosure might not work. The risk that state secrets might be revealed was simply "unjustifiable."[82]

The court insisted it had not conflated *Reynolds* with *Totten*, asserting that "[a] case may fall outside the *Totten* bar and yet it may become clear during the *Reynolds* analysis that dismissal is required at the outset."[83] In this case, the court concluded, "the claims and possible defenses are so infused with state secrets that the risk of disclosing them is both apparent and inevitable. Dismissal under these circumstances, like dismissal under the *Totten* bar, reflects the general principle that 'public policy forbids the maintenance of any suit in a court of justice, the trial of which would inevitably lead to the disclosure of matters which the law itself regards as confidential, and respecting which it will not allow the confidence to be violated.'"[84] Although relief was unavailable to plaintiffs through the courts, plaintiffs might seek "nonjudicial relief," such as a unilateral determination by the executive or legislative branch that plaintiffs were entitled to compensation or apology.[85]

Five judges dissented from the *en banc* decision. Judge Hawkins, writing for the dissenters, criticized the majority's reference to "nonjudicial relief" as evidence that the court had abdicated its role and "disregard[ed] the concept of checks and balances" by permitting the executive branch "to police its own errors and determine the remedy dispensed."[86] The dissenters criticized the majority's deference to the executive branch's claim that state secrets were at stake, reminding that in *Reynolds* itself, it turned out that "avoidance of embarrassment—not preservation of state secrets—appears to have motivated the Executive's invocation of the privilege."[87] The dissenters suggested that, the majority's protestations notwithstanding, the court's decision did conflate *Reynolds* with *Totten* and expanded the evidentiary privilege described in *Reynolds* to permit dismissal of an entire case solely on the basis of "hypothetical claims of privilege that the government ha[d] yet to raise."[88] This threatened to "transform an evidentiary privilege into an immunity doctrine."[89] In other words, instead of using *Reynolds* as a way to shield sensitive information from disclosure, the executive branch was seeking to use *Reynolds* as a way to bar any litigation that raises questions that could potentially touch on confidential matters. The better course, the dissenters argued, would have been to require Jeppesen to answer allegations not enmeshed with claims of privilege, allow Jeppesen to make a claim of privilege only as to specific allegations, and allow the case to "move forward" rather than dismissing it at the outset.[90] Once the case moved forward, the district court could consider whether Jeppesen's defense *actually* threatened to reveal state secrets, rather than assuming that this would necessarily be the case.[91]

The dissenters saw it as a mistake for the majority to discuss *Totten* without making clear that the case did not apply to bar plaintiffs' claims. It was clear *Totten* was "inapplicable," and the majority should have said so, according to the dissenters, rather than leaving this an open question that threatened to expand *Totten*'s reach and use in future cases.[92] The majority's analysis expanded the state secrets privilege in a new way by permitting the government "to prevent parties from litigating the truth or falsity of allegations, or facts, or information simply because the government regards the truth or falsity of the allegations to be secret."[93] The dissenters insisted that the state secrets privilege is "so dangerous as a means of hiding governmental misbehavior under the guise of national security, and so violative of common rights to due process, that courts should confine its application to the narrowest circumstances that still protect the government's essential secrets."[94] The dissenters concluded that dismissal should be a last resort; even in *Reynolds* itself, the Supreme Court did not require dismissal of plaintiffs' claims. In the dissenters' view, plaintiffs in *Mohamed* should have been given the opportunity to advance their claims through the "nonsecret evidence" available to them.[95]

THE OBAMA ADMINISTRATION CITES *JEPPESEN* AS A WAY TO FORECLOSE LITIGATION INVOLVING THE TARGETED KILLING OF A U.S. CITIZEN

The Ninth Circuit issued its *en banc* decision in *Jeppesen* on September 8, 2010.[96] Just a few weeks later, the Obama administration cited that decision in a brief seeking dismissal of a lawsuit seeking to enjoin the government from authorizing the targeted killing of a U.S. citizen without trial or hearing.[97] The lawsuit was *Al-Aulaqi v. Obama*, and it involved the Obama administration's creation of a list of terrorists targeted for "kill or capture." In other words, people on this list were deemed to be so dangerous that they could be targeted for killing if capture was not possible. John Rizzo, former acting general counsel of the CIA, described it as "basically a hit list." Rizzo explained how action would be carried out against those on the list: "The Predator [drone] is the weapon of choice, but it could also be someone putting a bullet in your head."[98]

Controversy over the Obama administration's kill-or-capture list developed when news reports in early 2010 revealed that a U.S. citizen named Anwar al-Aulaqi had been placed on the list. Al-Aulaqi was a Muslim cleric with dual U.S.-Yemeni citizenship (he was born in New Mexico). The U.S. government accused al-Aulaqi of "acting for or on behalf of al-Qa'ida in the Arabian Peninsula (AQAP)" and "providing financial, material or technological support for, or other services to or in support of, acts of terrorism." The government asserted that al-Aulaqi was a leader in AQAP and had taken on an important operational role, including facilitating training camps for terrorists and by helping to plan an attempted bombing of a Northwest Airlines flight from Yemen to Detroit on Christmas Day 2009. In addition, there were news reports that al-Aulaqi had exchanged e-mails with Major Nidal Hasan, who was charged with thirteen counts of murder in the November 2009 Fort Hood shooting. Al-Aulaqi also made public statements calling for "jihad against the west," praising the attempted Christmas Day bombing, and urging others to "follow suit."[99] However, not everyone agreed that al-Aulaqi was, in fact, an important figure at the center of AQAP's operations. Gregory Johnsen called al-Aulaqi "a minor figure in Al Qaeda" and called it "a mistaken assumption" to believe that "killing Mr. Awlaki will make us safer."[100] Johnsen described al-Aulaqi as "a midlevel religious functionary" and "a propaganda threat" because of his U.S. citizenship and ability to speak English but argued that al-Aulaqi had "little standing in the Arab world" and that focusing on him distracted attention from "the real, most dangerous leaders of [AQAP]."[101]

In August 2010, al-Aulaqi's father filed a lawsuit in a U.S. district court alleging that the government did not have legal authority to target his son for killing and to place him on a kill list without "charge, trial or conviction." In responding to the lawsuit, the Obama administration cited the state secrets privilege and the recent *Jeppesen* decision.[102] The administration told the court that it was not necessary to reach the state secrets privilege in this case, as it believed that there were other sufficient reasons to dismiss the lawsuit without reaching the question of whether the privilege applied. However, the government argued, the state secrets privilege provided an independent basis for dismissing the lawsuit in case the court found its other arguments to be unavailing.[103]

The administration's invocation of the state secrets privilege in *Al-Aulaqi* and its citation to *Jeppesen* showed that the government was prepared to expand the *Reynolds* evidentiary privilege into a broader principle of immunity. In other words, the state secrets privilege had become a way to urge courts to dismiss litigation in full when the executive branch argued that "no part of the case can be litigated on the merits without immediately and irreparably risking disclosure of highly sensitive and classified national security information."[104] In *Al-Aulaqi*, the Obama administration argued that "[a]t every turn, litigation of plaintiff's claims would risk or require the disclosure of highly sensitive and properly protected information to respond to allegations regarding purported secret operations and decision criteria."[105] As in *Jeppesen*, in the administration's view it would not make a difference whether some of the facts at issue had already been made public—for instance, the existence of the kill list itself was known to the public. Because state secrets were "intertwined in every step of the case," even in the decision as to whether al-Aulaqi's father had standing to bring the case, there were "inherent risk of disclosures that would harm national security [which] should be apparent from the outset."[106] Resolving whether the government had, in fact, targeted al-Aulaqi (the son) for killing and, if so, whether the government could present its justification for that decision would depend, it was claimed, on evaluation of privileged information.[107] Requiring the government to confirm or deny that it had placed al-Aulaqi on the kill list would be, the administration argued, an "extraordinary" burden, given that al-Aulaqi was "an operational terrorist who remains free to plan attacks against the United States."[108]

The administration's argument was itself quite extraordinary. The government's position amounted to an argument that the president could independently determine whether to target a U.S. citizen for killing without judicial oversight. The existence of the list itself and the reasons the executive branch relied on in placing a citizen on the list were said to be state secrets that could not be reviewed by a judge, even *in camera*.[109] Although the government alleged that al-Aulaqi was a terrorist actively involved in planning attacks against the United States, it refused to provide specific evidence to any court of the threat al-Aulaqi posed.[110]

The district court dismissed *Al-Aulaqi* in December 2010.[111] The court found it unnecessary to rule on the state secrets claim, identifying independent bases for dismissing the lawsuit.[112] However, the court cited the Ninth Circuit's *en banc* decision in *Jeppesen* with approval and endorsed the idea that "in some instances, 'the *Reynolds* privilege converges with the *Totten* bar.'"[113] In other words, under *Reynolds*, dismissal of the entire case is appropriate when "litigating the case to a judgment on the merits would present an unacceptable risk of disclosing state secrets."[114]

In late September 2011, Anwar al-Aulaqi was killed in a U.S. drone strike in Yemen. Another U.S. citizen, Samir Khan, was also killed in the attack, although it is not clear whether he was specifically targeted. Khan's family described the attack as an "assassination" of two U.S. citizens and asked why capture and trial were not possible.[115] Al-Aulaqi's sixteen-year-old son, who was also a U.S. citizen, was killed in a separate attack in Yemen, though it is not clear whether he had been specifically targeted.[116]

On July 18, 2012, the ACLU and the Center for Constitutional Rights filed a lawsuit against the government challenging the killings of Anwar al-Aulaqi, his son Abdulrhman al-Aulaqi, and Samir Khan. The suit claims that these killings "violated the substantive and procedural due process rights of Anwar al-Aulaqi, Samir Khan, and Abdulrahman al-Aulaqi under the Fifth Amendment to the Constitution" as well as their rights "to be free from unreasonable seizures under the Fourth Amendment to the Constitution." In addition, the lawsuit claimed these killings were unconstitutional bills of attainder because the three men were subject to punishment with judicial trial.[117] An attorney for the plaintiffs said they were seeking:

> some kind of accountability, in the most basic sense of the word. The government has killed three of its citizens and we think the government has to account for its actions, first to acknowledge, then to explain. We believe that if you accept that the government has the authority to kill its own citizens without acknowledging its actions, you have set up an authority that will one day be abused. Once you create this power, this power will sit around available to every single future president.[118]

It was expected that the government would invoke the state secrets privilege in arguing for dismissal of the case. Analysis of this claim would proceed in the context of the cases discussed in this chapter. To respond to the merits of the claim, the government would need to answer these questions: how are these killings justified? What authority can the executive branch cite as justification for these killings? What is the source of that authority and what are the limits, if any?

THE TARGETED KILLING OF U.S. CITIZENS: WHAT DOES DUE PROCESS REQUIRE?

The state secrets argument focuses on procedure rather than substance. When a court accepts this argument, especially when it decides that the argument justifies dismissal of the underlying claims, further discussion is short-circuited. It does not matter whether a claim or defense may have merit if the state secrets privilege is used to gain dismissal of the case.

If the Obama administration were to successfully invoke the state secrets privilege as a basis for seeking dismissal of the lawsuit challenging the killings of U.S. citizens, it would not have to offer any separate justification for its actions. If, however, the claims were judged on their merits, the executive branch would have to explain why the targeted killing of U.S. citizens was justified—either as an exercise of unilateral emergency presidential power or because Congress had authorized such action. Either way, argument would center on the Due Process Clause—what process is due before a citizen can be killed? The *Hamdi* case discussed in chapter 10 offers some initial guidelines as to how this argument would play out.

In *Hamdi*, the Supreme Court concluded that due process requires at least a limited hearing in front of a neutral decision maker in order for a U.S. citizen to be detained as an enemy combatant. Justice O'Connor's plurality opinion performed a balancing of competing interests—on the one hand the government's interest in keeping enemy combatants off the battlefield and on the other hand a citizen's interest in freedom from arbitrary imprisonment. She emphasized that, even when congressional authorization is provided to justify detention, a state of war is not a "blank check" for the president and that the judicial branch plays a vital role in maintaining the system of checks and balances under the Constitution and in preventing a concentration of power in the executive branch.

In a March 5, 2012, speech, Attorney General Eric Holder claimed that the Obama administration had learned and applied the lessons of *Hamdi* in deciding when it could authorize the killing of a U.S. citizen who poses an imminent threat of violent attack against the United States.[119] Holder acknowledged that the Fifth Amendment's Due Process Clause is relevant to this decision-making process and explained that, following the *Hamdi* decision, the Obama administration was applying a balancing approach, weighing the government's interest in "counter[ing] threats [to innocent Americans] posed by senior operational leaders of Al Qaeda" against "[a]n individual's interest in making sure that the government does not target him erroneously."[120] However, Holder insisted, due process does not necessarily mean judicial process. In other words, although it is necessary to weigh competing interests before authorizing the killing of a U.S. citizen, satisfying the Due Process Clause does not necessarily require judicial review. The president can determine, on his own, when it is necessary to target a U.S. citizen for killing "who is a senior operational leader of Al Qaeda or associated forces, and who is actively engaged in planning to kill Americans" after the executive branch conducts "a thorough and careful review" aimed at determining (a) that the targeted citizen "poses an imminent threat of violent attack against the United States"; (b) it is not feasible to capture the targeted citizen; and (c) the operation aimed at killing the citizen "would be conducted in a manner consistent with applicable law of war principles." Although Holder described no role for the courts in this process, he indicated that "the Executive Branch regularly informs the appropriate members of Congress about our counterterrorism activities, including the legal framework, and would of course follow the same practice where lethal force is used against U.S. citizens."[121]

In his speech, Holder argued that circumstances weigh in favor of the president making decisions to order the killing of U.S. citizens who are determined to pose an imminent threat to the United States. It is necessary for the United States to have the ability to take quick, decisive action before the potential attack against the United States reaches an "end stage of planning"—delay "would create an unacceptably high risk . . . that Americans would be killed." Moreover, Holder asserted, "[t]he conduct and management of national security operations are core functions of the Executive Branch, as courts have recognized throughout our history." The president, not courts or Congress, is best positioned to make "real-time decisions that balance the need to act" against other factors.[122]

There are at least two ways to respond to Holder's speech. One might conclude that the Obama administration had decided to modulate the Bush administration's definition of executive power by retreating from the unitary executive theory. A few months after taking office, President Obama charged that President George W. Bush's decisions had moved the United States "off course": Obama promised to defend the nation against potential terrorist attacks "with an abiding confidence in the rule of law and due process; in checks and balances and accountability."[123] Defenders of the Obama administration would describe Holder's speech as evidence of delivery on that promise, an explanation of how, exactly, the Obama administration had changed course and implemented a restored commitment to the rule of law. Unlike the Bush administration, they would argue, the Obama administration was presenting its legal arguments openly— Attorney General Holder, in explaining the decision-making process used in targeting a U.S. citizen for killing, said that "it is important to explain these legal principles publicly."[124]

Critics of Holder's speech might respond that, although some of the rhetoric might have changed, the Obama administration's definition of emergency presidential power was essentially the same as the Bush administration's: decisions involving national security are for the president alone to make, especially in the context of responding to potential terrorist threats. Glenn Greenwald argues that the process Holder described in his speech concentrates power in the executive branch, with the president and other executive branch officials acting as "judge . . . jury and . . . executioner all wrapped up in one, acting in total secrecy" without any opportunity for the targeted citizen to respond to accusations used to justify his or her killing.[125] While Holder referred to due process, the process he described includes no role for the judiciary—which runs counter to Justice O'Connor's plurality opinion in *Hamdi*. If, under *Hamdi*, some hearing before a neutral decision maker is required simply to *hold* a citizen as an enemy combatant, how can the president order that a citizen be killed with no hearing at all?[126]

Although Holder declared that the Obama administration had made its legal arguments publicly known, Greenwald notes that an underlying Office of Legal Counsel memorandum used to justify the program Holder discussed was not made public.[127] An unsigned, undated Department of Justice white paper released in February 2013 has reportedly been described by the Obama administration as "a policy document that closely mirrors the arguments of classified memos on targeted killings [prepared] by the Justice Department's Office of Legal Counsel."[128] The white paper describes circumstances in which a U.S. citizen could be killed that closely parallel the framework described by Attorney General Holder in his speech at Northwestern.[129] The white paper claims that the president has authority to order killings under these circumstances because (1) he has a "constitutional responsibility to protect the country" that may be related to "the inherent right of the United States to national self-defense under international law" and (2) the 2001 AUMF authorized the president to use force against Al Qaeda and its associated forces.[130] However, Greenwald would note, even the white paper does not purport to provide the complete legal reasoning relied on by the Obama administration. That reasoning is to be found in an OLC memo or memos that remain undisclosed to the public.

Finally, Greenwald identifies a central problem with the framework Holder (and the white paper) described: if it is for the president to decide when it is necessary to order the killing of a U.S. citizen who is a senior leader of a terrorist group actively engaged in planning to kill Americans, how do we know that the president is right? Holder acknowledged that the targeted individual has an "extraordinarily weighty" interest—that is, the interest in not being targeted erroneously and killed based on a mistake.[131] But, Greenwald argues, Holder's analysis begged the question: how can we be assured that the president won't mistakenly (or, even, intentionally) target an innocent person? Greenwald concludes that Holder's case boiled down to a blunt request: "just trust us" in the executive branch—as well as future presidents who may use these actions as precedent for expanded power.[132]

The Obama administration broke ground by targeting at least three U.S. citizens for killing, but it was not the first to develop a targeted kill list.[133] The George W. Bush administration had identified leaders of terrorist organizations, including Osama Bin Laden, who were targeted for kill or capture.[134] According to reports, the process the Obama administration used began with a "panel of senior government officials" which decided who should be placed on a "kill-or-capture list."[135] Richard Pious notes that the process was "shrouded in secrecy."[136] Indeed, there is no law that authorized the panel to make its decisions, and no public records of its decision-making process were maintained.[137] Attorney General Holder suggested that, when a U.S. citizen was placed on this list, the president ultimately made the decision as to whether killing could be authorized when capture was not feasible.[138] People who were placed on the kill-or-capture list were not informed that they were on the list and were not given an opportunity to challenge the decision.

As discussed, controversy over the Obama administration's kill-or-capture list developed when news reports in early 2010 revealed that Anwar al-Aulaqi had been placed on the list. Shortly after al-Aulaqi was killed, anonymous sources spoke to Charlie Savage, a reporter for the *New York Times*, about the legal justifications for the killing, as provided in a secret June 2010 Office of Legal Counsel memorandum—although they did not make the memorandum itself publicly available. Savage reported that his sources—presumably officials in the Obama administration but referred to only as "people who have read the [memorandum]"—explained that the OLC memo took the September 2001 Authorization for the Use of Military Force or AUMF as the starting point for analysis, concluding that the AUMF provided authority to use force against al-Aulaqi.[139] The memorandum considered the applicability of the Due Process Clause but cited "court cases[140] allowing American citizens who had joined an enemy's forces to be detained or prosecuted in a military court just like noncitizen enemies." The memorandum seemed to suggest that the legal doctrine of necessity—the idea that killing al-Aulaqi was necessary to prevent imminent harm to innocent people—could justify al-Aulaqi's killing.[141] It concluded that an executive order banning assassinations and a federal statute prohibiting the murder of Americans outside the United States did not apply because al-Aulaqi had been targeted as an enemy combatant and, therefore, had been not murdered but simply killed in the course of war.[142]

Critics argue that it is difficult to analyze the legal justifications for al-Aulaqi's killing without seeing the OLC memorandum itself, and they charge that there is no reason to keep legal conclusions secret.[143] Glenn Greenwald notes that David Barron and Martin Lederman, the lawyers identified as the primary drafters of the OLC memo, had sharply criticized the Bush administration for justifying the detention of U.S. citizens without trial by relying on the AUMF.[144] Greenwald argues that it makes no sense to reject detention of U.S. citizens without trial while endorsing the decision to kill a U.S. citizen without a hearing of any sort. Defenders of the Obama administration's decision might point out that, while the 2001 AUMF does not clearly speak to the question of detention—a problem that led four justices in *Hamdi* to part company from the plurality opinion—it does expressly authorize the president "to use all necessary and appropriate force against those nations, organizations, or persons he determines planned, authorized, committed, or aided the terrorist attacks that occurred on September 11, 2001, or harbored such organizations or persons, in order to prevent any future acts of international terrorism against the United States by such nations, organizations or persons." Al-Aulaqi was a leader in Al Qaeda on the Arabian Peninsula. Therefore, as the June 2010 memorandum concluded, Congress had authorized the president to use force to kill al-Aulaqi.[145]

The problem, critics would respond, is that, even assuming one concludes that Congress could authorize the president to order the killing of a U.S. citizen without a judicial hearing or trial, it is far from clear that al-Aulaqi and AQAP are covered by the September 2001 AUMF. AQAP did not exist at the time of the September 11, 2001, attacks against the United States, and al-Aulaqi was not accused of playing any part in those attacks. The 2001 AUMF does not provide authority for the president to take action against Al Qaeda's "associated forces," notwithstanding the Department of Justice white paper's incorrect suggestion to the contrary.[146]

One central question to consider is: *who* should decide whether the president possessed the authority to order al-Aulaqi's killing? Reporting on the 2011 OLC memo, as well as the text of the undated Department of Justice white paper, suggests that OLC lawyers may have concluded that the president had independent authority to order al-Aulaqi's killing, but, as we have seen, not everyone would agree. Who should have the final say on this question? Attorney General Holder argues that it should be and, indeed, must be the president; waiting for judicial review before ordering the killing of dangerous terrorists would cause delays that could allow attacks against the United States to go forward. Glenn Greenwald responds that this approach allows a dangerous concentration of power to accumulate in the executive branch. He argues that history shows that executive branch lawyers appointed by the president will always find ways to justify the president's actions. Unless independent courts review executive branch decisions and the legal justifications offered to support those decisions, presidential power will be unchecked, and each new presidential action and OLC opinion will create precedent for even greater expansions of presidential power.[147]

15

THE OBAMA ADMINISTRATION AND MILITARY ACTION IN LIBYA

In early 2011, the "Arab Spring" brought protest and revolution to countries in North Africa and the Middle East. During the first six weeks of 2011, popular uprisings brought down autocratic rulers in Tunisia and Libya. In February 2011, protests mounted against the Qadhafi regime in Libya. Libyan dictator Muammar Qadhafi dispatched the military to crack down on protesters, but the country quickly became fragmented, with rebels gaining control of significant portions of the country.[1]

Events in Libya created a humanitarian crisis: thousands of refugees fled the country, while those who remained faced bombing and shelling by government forces.[2] On February 26, 2011, the United Nations Security Council adopted a resolution that "condemned the violence and use of force against civilians" by the Qadhafi regime, though it did not call for the use of force by member states in response to Qadhafi's actions.[3]

In the weeks after the UN resolution, fighting continued in Libya. By mid-March, government forces seemed poised to retake Benghazi, a city held by rebel forces. Qadhafi promised to show "no mercy and no pity" as the military took back the city, house by house.[4] On March 17, 2011, the UN Security Council adopted another resolution, this time imposing a no-fly zone for Libyan government forces and authorizing member states to use military force to protect Libyan civilians.[5]

Against this backdrop, President Obama moved toward action, ultimately justifying his decisions on a theory of unilateral emergency presidential power. On March 18, 2011, President Obama called on Qadhafi to end all attacks on civilians and to call back troops that were ready to enter Benghazi. Obama expressed concerns about a potential humanitarian crisis, with the possibility that Qadhafi could kill thousands of civilians.[6] On March 19, 2011, President Obama ordered airstrikes against Libya, asserting that these actions were "authorized by the United Nations Security Council."[7] By the end of March, the Obama administration "had transferred responsibility for the military operations in Libya" to NATO; U.S. forces would play a "supporting role" in NATO's continued efforts in Libya.[8]

The problem, as Louis Fisher notes, is that Congress had not authorized the use of military force, and Libya had neither attacked nor threatened an attack against the United States or U.S. forces.[9] Before he was elected president, candidate Obama conceded that "[t]he President does not have power under the Constitution to unilaterally authorize a military attack in a situation that does not involve stopping an actual or imminent threat to the nation." Though candidate Obama emphasized that the president could act unilaterally "[i]n instances of self-defense," that was an exceptional and limited case, since "[h]istory has shown us time and again . . . that military action is most successful when it is authorized and supported by the Legislative branch. It is always preferable to have informed consent of Congress prior to any military action."[10]

How, then, could President Obama defend his decision to authorize the use of military force in Libya without congressional approval? Once again, the Office of Legal Counsel provided a rationale. In an April 1, 2011, opinion, Principal Deputy Assistant Attorney General Caroline Krass concluded that the president had properly exercised his constitutional power to order military action in Libya without congressional authorization.[11] Basing her analysis mainly on prior OLC opinions and past presidential practice, Krass concluded that the president possessed "independent authority" to take military action when he could "reasonably determine that such use of force [is] in the national interest"—at least when "Congress has not specifically restricted [such authority]."[12] Under the circumstances, the administration argued, Obama reasonably determined that the use of military force in Libya would advance "at least two national interests": (1) the U.S. interest in "security and stability in the Middle East" and (2) "the longstanding U.S. commitment to maintaining the credibility of the United Nations Security Council and the effectiveness of its actions to promote international peace and security."[13]

Note that Krass's analysis included a caveat: the president could independently authorize the use of military force in order to protect important national interests "at least *insofar as Congress has not specifically restricted it.*"[14] The problem is that one can argue Congress *had* specifically restricted the president. The War Powers Resolution of 1973 (WPR) provides in part that:

The constitutional powers of the President as Commander-in-Chief to introduce United States Armed Forces into hostilities, or into situations where imminent involvement in hostilities is clearly indicated by the circumstances, are exercised only pursuant to

(1) a declaration of war,
(2) specific statutory authorization, or
(3) a national emergency created by attack upon the United States, its territories or possessions, or its armed forces.[15]

The language of the WPR seems to limit the president's ability to use force,[16] and scholars have concluded that, indeed, the president may authorize military action without congressional approval only when necessary to repel a sudden attack against the United States or to protect Americans lives overseas.[17] Krass's OLC opinion glides past this obstacle, relegating discussion of this thorny language from the WPR to a footnote and concluding that it merely reflects "a policy statement" by Congress that was not intended to limit presidential action.[18]

Krass's opinion differs in some ways from the Bush-era OLC opinions we considered earlier. For one thing, her opinion was made public immediately. Also, her analysis did not center on the unitary executive theory, which we saw most prominently discussed in John Yoo's opinions. But are these distinctions without a difference? If Krass's opinion reaches the same conclusion as Yoo's—that the president can independently authorize the use of military force—does it matter that she took a different path to reach the same end point? Moreover, it is also worth noting that, although Krass does not rely on inherent presidential power, her analysis has some things in common with Yoo's.

As we saw in chapter 9, Yoo emphasized what he saw as a Hamiltonian view of the presidency—that the Framers wanted an energetic president who, in contrast with Congress, could act quickly to respond to crises, especially in the context of war.[19] Krass's line of argument does not go as far as Yoo's in this regard, but she does conclude that the Constitution designed the president to be capable of quick action in a way that Congress is not, an attribute that positions the president to independently respond to "imminent national security threats and rapidly evolving military and diplomatic circumstances" when Congress cannot act.[20] Like Yoo, Krass emphasizes presidential authority in the areas of "foreign and military affairs, as well as national security."[21] Also like Yoo, she turns to past presidential practice as an important source of precedent. Krass notes that recent presidents independently authorized the use of military force in

Somalia, Bosnia, and Haiti.[22] But the same rejoinder applies to Krass that applied to Yoo: past examples of independent presidential action cannot justify future actions if the past actions were themselves unconstitutional.

However, unlike Yoo, Krass seems to acknowledge Congress's ability to set limits on presidential power to use military force. Krass does not dismiss the WPR, though she does not conclude that it limited Obama's actions in this particular case. In her discussion of the statute, Krass makes reference to limits on independent presidential action—that the president must give a report to Congress[23] within forty-eight hours of "introduc[ing] troops into hostilities" and "generally must terminate such use of force within 60 days (or 90 days for military necessity)."[24] Krass does not suggest that the president could set aside these limits or otherwise conclude that Congress had improperly invaded his constitutional sphere of authority. In fact, and, again, unlike Yoo, she describes the Constitution's Declaration of War Clause as another "possible" limit on presidential power.[25] If the president were to authorize military action rising to the level of a "war," then he could be overstepping his bounds. However, in ordering the use of military force in Libya, Krass concluded that the president had not exceeded his power because the actions in Libya did not "[amount] to a 'war' in the constitutional sense necessitating congressional approval under the Declaration of War Clause."[26] President Obama had authorized a "limited" use of force—"airstrikes and associated support missions" for a "limited mission," not ground troops for an open-ended engagement.[27] Krass concluded that this was not a "war," asserting that war, under the Constitution, requires "prolonged and substantial military engagements, typically involving exposure of U.S. military personnel to significant risk over a substantial period."[28]

Krass's analysis concluded that President Obama possessed constitutional power to authorize military operations in Libya without advance congressional approval, but her opinion suggested that this power was limited. Assuming that Obama's actions were otherwise compatible with the WPR, he would need to seek congressional approval after sixty days.[29] By May 20, 2011, the sixty-day window under the WPR had closed. Krass reportedly advised President Obama that, at this point, he would either have to gain congressional authorization or else "terminate or scale back the mission after May 20."[30] The Pentagon's general counsel, Jeh Johnson, agreed with Krass. However, other government lawyers, including State Department legal adviser Harold H. Koh and White House counsel Robert Bauer, concluded that President Obama could continue the mission without authorization from Congress. They argued that the War Powers Resolution simply did not apply: not only was the mission in Libya not a "war" for constitutional purposes, it did not even rise to the level of "hostilities" for purposes of the WPR.[31] Therefore, the president was justified in acting unilaterally, as this was an area where he was limited neither by the Constitution nor by statutory law.

President Obama decided to follow Koh's and Bauer's advice.[32] When the House of Representatives directed him to submit a report explaining why he had not sought congressional authorization, the Obama administration submitted a document asserting that military action in Libya was justified because "the President had constitutional authority, as Commander in Chief and Chief Executive and pursuant to his foreign affairs powers, to direct such limited military operations abroad."[33] The administration's report adopted Koh's and Bauer's reasoning, asserting that "[t]he President is of the view that the current U.S. military operations in Libya are consistent with the War Powers Resolution and do not under the law require further[34] congressional authorization, because U.S. military operations are distinct from the kind of 'hostilities' contemplated by the Resolution's 60 day termination provision."[35]

Koh expanded on this argument in testimony before the Senate Foreign Relations Committee on June 28, 2011. He argued that the term "hostilities" in the WPR is ambiguous—and, indeed, that Congress intended for the term to be ambiguous so that the president would have room to exercise judgment in unilaterally authorizing military action short of hostilities.[36] Given the WPR's ambiguity, Koh suggested that the meaning of the term "hostilities" has been and should be "determined more by interbranch practice than by a narrow parsing of dictionary definitions."[37] In other words, presidential and congressional interpretation of the term and presidential and congressional action (or inaction)—historical practice—give meaning to the term "hostilities" in the WPR.

Koh concluded that, viewed in the context of historical practice, continued military action in Libya in support of NATO operations did not constitute hostilities under the WPR, for four reasons: (1) the mission was limited—U.S. forces played a "supporting role in a NATO-led multinational civilian protection operation"; (2) U.S. forces had not suffered casualties and were not likely to do so, especially because no U.S. ground troops had been deployed and operations did not involve "active exchanges of fire with hostile forces"; (3) there was a limited risk that military operations would escalate; and (4) the specific operations U.S. military forces were carrying out were limited—mainly "providing intelligence capabilities and refueling assets [to NATO allies]" though also including air strikes "on an as-needed basis" as well as "limited strikes by Predator unmanned aerial vehicles."[38] Koh argued that these actions were in line with or even more narrowly defined than operations authorized by past presidents without congressional approval.[39] Operations in Libya, Koh said, were simply not what Congress, having witnessed "a long, major, and searing war in Vietnam," had in mind when it passed the WPR in 1973.[40]

Koh conceded that Congress could change the dynamic by taking a "clear . . . stance" against continued operations in Libya, and he asked that Congress instead give its imprimatur to these actions through legislation supporting the president's decision. However, he ultimately concluded that operations could continue whether or not Congress endorsed them, since the War Powers Resolution simply did not apply.[41] In the end, he said, this was a question "not . . . of law but of policy."[42] It would be better for the president to have "strong Congressional engagement and support," but it was not essential.[43]

Louis Fisher argues that Koh's analysis is "unpersuasive" and "ignores the political context under which the War Powers Resolution was debated and enacted."[44] One of the specific reasons for passing the WPR related to concerns over President Nixon's decision to order a bombing campaign in Cambodia. Although the Cambodia campaign did not involve ground troops, substantial U.S. casualties, or an exchange of fire with hostile forces, "it was understood by all parties that the bombing constituted hostilities and helped prompt Congress to enact statutory restrictions on presidential power."[45] Moreover, Fisher asserts, as a matter of logic and common sense, Koh's interpretation is strained. Under the Obama administration's analysis, "a nation with superior military force could pulverize another country—including [with] the use of nuclear weapons—and there would be neither hostilities nor war."[46] Finally, Fisher asks, why did President Obama report to Congress within forty-eight hours of beginning operations in Libya in a letter in which he explained that he was doing so "consistent with the War Powers Resolution" if he did not believe that the statute applied?[47]

As noted, in his testimony before the Senate Foreign Relations Committee, State Department legal adviser Koh concluded that ultimately the question as to whether U.S. military operations in Libya would continue was "not one of law but of policy."[48] In other words, Koh suggested, the administration would continue operations if it believed they were necessary and justified—unless Congress expressly said otherwise and instructed the president to stop.[49] Although Congress refused to pass legislation supporting President Obama's decision to use military force in Libya, it also failed to pass legislation that would have limited funding for military operations there.[50] One observer saw a 295–123 vote in the House of Representatives to reject a resolution that would have expressly authorized operations in

Libya as a "symbolic blow" to Obama, while another questioned whether members of the House were merely expressing opposition to this particular president rather than attempting to limit presidential power in general.[51] In the end, though, Congress did not produce legislation expressly rejecting the president's actions.

ASSESSING THE CONSTITUTIONALITY OF PRESIDENT OBAMA'S DECISION TO AUTHORIZE THE USE OF MILITARY FORCE IN LIBYA

As seen, President Obama seemed to have a different view on the scope and limits of presidential power than candidate Obama. Like President George W. Bush, he enlisted government lawyers to justify his actions. How do their arguments hold up?

With regard to the initial decision to use military force in Libya during the sixty-day WPR window, the April 1, 2011, OLC opinion concluded that the president could "reasonably determine" that using force "serve[d] sufficiently important national interests" so long as the military operations he authorized did not rise to the level of a "war."[52] Several objections could be made here: (1) the WPR does not broadly authorize the president to use military force to serve "important national interests"; (2) the phrase "important national interests" is general enough to justify a wide array of potential actions; (3) it is unclear how one assesses whether the president's determination that military force was needed to advance an important national interest was "reasonable"; and (4) it is also unclear how "war" is defined for purposes of the Constitution and whether the OLC was right to conclude that military action in Libya was not a war.

President Obama could respond to these criticisms in several ways. First, he could argue that the WPR does not restrict unilateral presidential action to the sudden-attack scenario—either because Congress did not intend this[53] or because the WPR unconstitutionally sought to limit the president's power in this area. Second, he could respond that concerns about the vagueness of the "important national interests" standard are misplaced. The OLC's April 1, 2011, opinion gives specific examples of such interests, based on past presidential practice and prior OLC opinions.[54] Documenting an important national interest justifying independent presidential action typically means, OLC concluded, demonstrating the existence of a threat to American lives or property, a concern that regional stability would be undermined if the president did not act, and/or a need to act in order to support the credibility and effectiveness of the UN Security Council.[55] Finally, the OLC identified standards to judge whether military action in Libya was a war for purposes of the Constitution and concluded that this test is satisfied "only by prolonged and substantial military engagements, typically involving exposure of U.S. military personnel to significant risk over a substantial period."[56]

With regard to military action after May 20, 2011, when the sixty-day WPR period expired, an additional question is presented: did military operations rise to the level of "hostilities" under the WPR?[57] If not, the president might be able to authorize continuing military operations without seeking congressional approval. In his congressional testimony, State Department legal adviser Koh concluded that the military operations did not constitute "hostilities"—at least not after the United States transferred main responsibility for the operations to NATO. Koh emphasized that U.S. efforts were limited; U.S. forces were supporting NATO-led operations, no U.S. ground troops were deployed, U.S. forces were not exchanging fire with an enemy, U.S. casualties were unlikely, and escalation of U.S. involvement was unlikely.[58] Fisher disagrees, arguing that this analysis ignores the political context of the WPR and depends on a strained definition of "hostilities" that could absurdly define the unilateral use of nuclear weapons as neither hostilities nor war.[59]

Which approach is more persuasive? It depends on how one defines the word "hostilities" under the WPR. In the absence of specific guidance from the statute, one can consider various factors: (1) the context for the WPR and congressional intent in passing the statute; (2) past presidential and congressional practice; (3) pragmatic consideration of the consequences of adopting a specific definition of the word "hostilities"; and (4) case-by-case consideration of the specific facts involved—the nature of the military operations at issue. In considering these various factors, one may also be guided by specific concerns about presidential authority—either the desire to set limits on such authority or the desire to justify presidential action.

Koh focused on past practice, asserting that "whether a particular set of facts constitutes "hostilities" for purposes of the [WPR] has been determined more by interbranch practice than by a narrow parsing of dictionary definitions."[60] Therefore, Obama's decision to continue military operations in Libya could be justified by history—the use of ground troops in Somalia and the Balkans, a larger-scale bombing campaign in Kosovo.[61] Koh's approach emphasized flexibility. He argued that this was, in fact, what Congress intended in passing the WPR and that legislators consciously chose the vague term "hostilities" in order to avoid "straitjacket[ing]" the president, "recogniz[ing] that different situations may call for different responses."[62]

In response, one might argue, as Fisher does, that the Obama administration's interpretation of "hostilities" fails to acknowledge meaningful limits on presidential power.[63] In addition, a critic of the administration's approach could point out that Koh's citation to past presidential practice proves nothing if these past actions were themselves examples of illegitimate use of power. Finally, one could challenge Koh's analysis of the reasons why Congress passed the WPR in the first place. Koh suggested that the goal was to prevent another long war like Vietnam that included "hundreds of thousands of boots on the grounds, secret bombing campaigns, international condemnation, massive casualties, and no clear way out."[64] A critic might respond that Koh's interpretation would mean that the WPR has meaning only when the United States engages in another conflict that is essentially identical to the Vietnam War itself. As Fisher observes, Congress may have meant to do something more than this.[65]

Other factors might guide analysis as well. One could conclude (though the Obama administration did not do so) that the War Powers Resolution is unconstitutional and that Congress simply exceeded its authority in attempting to limit presidential use of military force.[66] President Nixon thought so—he vetoed the WPR, describing it as "unconstitutional and dangerous to the best interests of our Nation."[67] (Congress passed the law over his veto.) John Yoo claimed that Congress may not use the WPR to set a time limit on the president's ability to use military force, though it may try to limit presidential power in other ways—for example, by "cutting off funds for a conflict."[68]

Koh cited "interbranch practice" as the primary factor in determining the scope of the President's authority under the War Powers Resolution.[69] If he's right, what do we make of Congress's response to the Obama administration's actions? Fisher warns that the Obama administration's actions and the legal arguments it offered in defense of those actions threaten to create "precedents [that] are likely to broaden presidential power for future military actions."[70] Is he right? If so, is this a concern?

NOTES

FOREWORD

1. Many of the points raised in the foreword are developed in greater detail in articles and congressional testimony posted on loufisher.org.

INTRODUCTION

1. Daniel Farber, *Lincoln's Constitution* (Chicago: University of Chicago Press, 2003), 127. See also Michael A. Genovese, *The Power of the American Presidency: 1789–2000* (New York: Oxford University Press, 2001), 9–10: "In an effort to understand presidential power, the Constitution is a starting point, but it provides few definitive answers."

2. Farber, *Lincoln's Constitution*, 129.

3. This book does not address presidential power in the context of responding to economic crisis or natural disaster, though these may also be defined as emergencies. The emergency power discussed here is a power claimed when the nation faces a threat or a claimed threat to national security. This is sometimes described as presidential war power, but I use the term "emergency power" to emphasize the frequently recurring argument that broad presidential power is justified by necessity—the need to act promptly and decisively in the face of crisis. See Louis Fisher, *Presidential War Power*, 2nd ed. (Lawrence: University Press of Kansas, 2004). In addition, war is not always identified as a necessary condition for exercising emergency power.

4. Article I, section 9, provides that "[t]he Privilege of the Writ of Habeas Corpus shall not be suspended, unless when in Cases of Rebellion or Invasion the public Safety may require it." See also chapter 3 for additional discussion of this clause. Article I, section 8, also grants Congress other power to respond to emergencies, including the power to declare war and "to [call] forth the militia to execute the laws of the union, suppress insurrections and repel invasions."

5. Farber, *Lincoln's Constitution*, 127. There are exceptions to this general observation. President James Buchanan believed secession was unconstitutional but also believed he had no power to do anything about it. James F. Simon, *Lincoln and Chief Justice Taney: Slavery, Secession and the President's War Powers* (New York: Simon and Schuster, 2006), 173. Buchanan's successor, Abraham Lincoln, took a different view, as discussed in chapters 3 and 4.

6. 5 U.S. 137, 177 (1803). Louis Fisher argues that the Supreme Court does not have the final word on interpreting the Constitution and that judicial review since *Marbury* has been confused with judicial supremacy. See Louis Fisher, *Defending Congress and the Constitution* (Lawrence: University Press of Kansas, 2011). That does not mean that other branches of the federal government or the states may ignore rulings by the court, but it also does not mean that other branches of government are disallowed from offering their own views of constitutional interpretation and taking action to advance those views. For example, Fisher emphasizes Congress's role in shaping constitutional meaning.

7. Presidents may also exercise emergency power granted them by congressional statute. As David Gray Adler observes, "[t]he vague concept of a presidential emergency power . . . may be viewed as either inherent or extraconstitutional, such is the ambiguity of the claim, but what is clear is that Congress may, by statute, vest emergency powers in the president." "The Framers and Executive Prerogative: A Constitutional and Historical Rebuke," *Presidential Studies Quarterly* 42, no. 2 (June 2012): 378, DOI: 10.1111/j.1741-5705.2012.03971.x. Even when presidents act with Congress, however, emergency powers are limited, as discussed, for example, in chapter 6.

8. As Fisher explains, unlike express and implied powers, which are derived from or at least connected to the text of the Constitution, inherent powers exist outside and are not limited by the Constitution. Instead, "[t]hey 'inhere' in the person or in the office." *Defending Congress and the Constitution*, 14–15. Fisher argues that inherent powers "open the door to claims of power that have no limits." Ibid., 15.

9. There may also, as we will see, be disagreement as to when or whether a claimed crisis or emergency actually exists.

10. Alexander Hamilton, John Jay, and James Madison, *The Federalist Papers*, ed. Michael A. Genovese (New York: Palgrave Macmillan, 2009) (hereinafter *The Federalist Papers*), Federalist No. 69 (Hamilton), 193–195.

11. David H. Souter, Harvard Commencement Remarks (May 27, 2010), http://news.harvard.edu/gazette/story/2010/05/text-of-justice-david-souters-speech/.

12. See Clinton Rossiter, *Constitutional Dictatorship: Crisis Government in the Modern Democracies* (Princeton, NJ: Princeton University Press, 1948), describing Lincoln's and Roosevelt's "constitutional dictatorship" as temporary, in contrast with, for example, dictatorships of Stalin and Hitler. A question to consider is whether any dictatorship, even a temporary one, can be constitutional.

1. W. Taylor Reveley III, *War Powers of the President and Congress: Who Holds the Arrows and Olive Branch?* (Charlottesville: University of Virginia Press, 1981), 29.

2. As we'll see, however, President Lincoln suggested that the president might also have temporary power to suspend the writ of habeas corpus, at least when Congress was not able to act, such as when it is not in session. See chapter 3.

3. Stephen I. Vladeck, "Emergency Power and the Militia Acts," *Yale Law Journal* 114 (2004): 149.

4. This is hardly the only time courts have recognized the existence of an implied power or right not expressly identified in the Constitution. Other examples include judicial review, implied congressional powers (such as the power to create a national bank or to subpoena witnesses to testify at congressional hearings), presidential authority to remove department heads from office, the right to privacy, and incorporation of most provisions in the Bill of Rights to apply to the states.

5. Fisher, *Presidential War Power*, 8–9.

6. Max Farrand, ed., *The Records of the Federal Convention of 1787* (New Haven, CT: Yale University Press, 1937), 2:318–319.

7. Louis Fisher, "Abraham Lincoln: Preserving the Union and the Constitution," *Albany Government Law Review* 3 (2010): 503; see also Adler, "The Framers and Executive Prerogative: A Constitutional and Historical Rebuke," 379: "the framers' response to the problem of emergency lay in the doctrine of retroactive ratification. This solution, laid bare, requires a governmental actor who has acted illegally for the purpose of meeting an emergency, to assume the burden of explaining to the lawmaking body why his action was necessary and reasonable."

8. Adler, "The Framers and Executive Prerogative: A Constitutional and Historical Rebuke," 382.

9. Fisher, "Abraham Lincoln: Preserving the Union and the Constitution."

10. See chapter 9 for discussion of the Office of Legal Counsel.

11. See chapter 9 for Yoo's view of debate over the Declare War Clause.

12. Memorandum opinion from John C. Yoo, Deputy Assistant Attorney General, for Timothy Flanigan, Deputy Counsel to the President, *The President's Constitutional Authority to Conduct Military Operations against Terrorists and Nations Supporting Them* (September 25, 2001) (hereinafter September 25, 2001, Yoo memo), http://www.justice.gov/olc/warpowers925.htm.

13. Louis Fisher, "Invoking Inherent Powers: A Primer," *Presidential Studies Quarterly*, 37, no. 1 (March 2007): 2, quoting *Black's Law Dictionary*, sixth edition (1990). David Gray Adler argues that inherent power is not, strictly speaking, extraconstitutional since "[t]he claim of inherent executive power, however

specious it may be, represents an effort to locate within the executive constitutional authority that exceeds the textual grant of enumerated powers, as well as implied authority that flows from that grant, but that, nonetheless, is derived from Article II of the Constitution." "The Framers and Executive Prerogative: A Constitutional and Historical Rebuke," 378. What unites Fisher's and Adler's analyses is the shared criticism that appeals to inherent presidential power conflict with the Framers' intention to subordinate the president to the rule of law. Compare David Gray Adler, "The Steel Seizure Case and Inherent Presidential Power," *Constitutional Commentary* 19 (2002):155, 159: "the Court's repudiation of President Harry Truman's claim of an inherent power to seize the steel mills spoke volumes for its commitment to constitutionalism and the principle of the rule of law" with Louis Fisher, "Restoring the Rule of Law," Statement before the Subcommittee on the Constitution, Senate Committee on the Judiciary (September 16, 2008), 3: "Whenever the executive branch justifies its actions on the basis of 'inherent' powers, the rule of law is jeopardized."

14. *United States v. Curtiss-Wright Corp.*, 299 U.S. 304, 320 (1936).

15. Fisher, "Restoring the Rule of Law," 5–7.

16. Eric A. Posner and Adrian Vermeule, *The Executive Unbound: After the Madisonian Republic* (New York: Oxford University Press, 2011).

17. Adler, "The Steel Seizure Case and Inherent Presidential Power," 155; see also Fisher, "Invoking Inherent Powers: A Primer."

18. Adler, "The Framers and Executive Prerogative: A Constitutional and Historical Rebuke," 378.

19. *Youngstown Sheet & Tube Co. v. Sawyer*, 343 U.S. 579, 635 (1952) (Jackson, J., concurring).

20. September 25, 2001, Yoo memo.

21. A position that Chief Justice Taney took in *Ex parte Merryman*, 17 F.Cas. 144 (1861) as discussed in chapter 3.

22. At present, such authorization does exist through the War Powers Resolution, provided that the president complies with conditions described in the Resolution. See chapter 15 for discussion of the War Powers Resolution.

23. *Youngstown Sheet*, 343 U.S. at 634 (Jackson, J., concurring).

24. Ibid. at 634–635.

25. Jack N. Rakove, *Original Meanings: Politics and Ideas in the Making of the Constitution* (New York: Vintage Books, 1996), 7. In fact, Jackson implicitly acknowledged that it was not impossible to understand what the Framers meant, as much of his concurring opinion in *Youngstown* relies heavily on constitutional text and the Framers' intent. See chapter 7.

26. Ibid.; see also James P. Pfiffner, *Power Play: The Bush Presidency and the Constitution* (Washington, DC: Brookings Institution Press, 2008), 15.

27. Rakove, *Original Meanings*, 10; see also *The Federalist Papers*, 8. (Genovese observes that delegates to the constitutional convention agreed, among other things, that [1] the federal government needed to be stronger, though still limited; [2] the government should not be a monarchy but must adhere to the rule of law;

and [3] separation of powers and checks and balances were important safeguards against tyranny.)

28. Typically referred to as "Montesquieu."

29. John Yoo, *Crisis and Command: The History of Executive Power from George Washington to George W. Bush* (New York: Kaplan, 2009), 3; Pfiffner, *Power Play*, 14.

30. Rakove, *Original Meanings*, 18–19.

31. Christopher H. Pyle and Richard M. Pious, *The Constitution under Siege: Presidential Power versus the Rule of Law* (Durham, NC: Carolina Academic Press, 2010), 52. David Gray Adler defines presidential prerogative "as a claim of authority to act in the absence or violation of law to meet an emergency." "The Framers and Executive Prerogative: A Constitutional and Historical Rebuke," 378.

32. Pyle and Pious, *The Constitution under Siege*, 52–54.

33. Fisher, *Presidential War Power*, 1.

34. John Locke, *Two Treatises of Government*, ed. Peter Laslett (Cambridge: Cambridge University Press, 1988), 2nd Treatise, sections 145–148; see also Rakove, *Original Meanings*, 247.

35. Montesquieu idealized the British system, overlooking the reality that, in practice, Parliament had lost power to the monarch and his ministers by the mid-eighteenth century, when Montesquieu wrote. Rakove, *Original Meanings*, 248.

36. Ibid.

37. Marc W. Kruman, *Between Authority and Liberty: State Constitution Making in Revolutionary America* (Chapel Hill: University of North Carolina Press, 1997). Kruman concludes that the drafters of state constitutions were suspicious of power in all branches of government: the colonists had chafed against parliamentary excesses as well.

38. Rakove, *Original Meanings*, 21, 249–252.

39. Louis Fisher, *The President and Congress: Power and Policy* (New York: Free Press, 1972), 2–27, excerpted in Pyle and Pious, *The Constitution under Siege*, 22–28.

40. Rakove, *Original Meanings*, 254.

41. Some Framers, most notably Alexander Hamilton, praised the model of a limited constitutional monarchy, but not one based on a divine right to rule or broad prerogative. Rakove, *Original Meanings*, 256.

42. Ibid., 259.

43. Ibid., 255–256.

44. Ibid., 268–269.

45. Ibid., 270.

46. *The Federalist Papers*, Federalist No. 70, 199.

47. Ibid. Rome's dictatorship was a temporary one, designed to respond to crisis or emergency.

48. Ibid., 200.

49. Ibid., 202.

50. *The Federalist Papers*, Federalist No. 69, 193–195.

51. *The Federalist Papers*, Federalist No. 4, Library of Congress, http://thomas .loc.gov/home/histdox/fed_04.html.

52. *The Federalist Papers*, Federalist No. 47, 101.

53. *The Federalist Papers*, Federalist No. 48, 108. In fact, Madison was concerned that, in a republican government, the executive would need special protection against the legislative branch: "As the weight of the legislative authority requires that it be thus divided [into two houses], the weakness of the executive may require, on the other hand, that it should be fortified." Ibid., Federalist No. 51, 120.

54. *The Federalist Papers*, Federalist No. 48, 107.

55. *The Federalist Papers*, Federalist No. 23, 61–62.

56. As we will see, supporters of broad executive power turn to Federalist No. 23 for just this purpose. See chapter 9 (discussing September 25, 2001, Yoo memo).

57. *The Federalist Papers*, Federalist No. 23, 62: "Whether there ought to be a *federal government* entrusted with the care of the common defense is a question in the first instance, open for discussion; but the moment it is decided in the affirmative, it will follow that the *government* ought to be clothed with all the powers requisite to complete execution of its trust" (emphasis added).

58. *The Federalist Papers*, Federalist No. 23, 62: "Defective as the present Confederation has been proved to be, this principle [that the federal government needed to have the power necessary to defend the nation] appears to have been fully recognized by the framers of it; though they have not made proper or adequate provision for its exercise. Congress have an unlimited discretion to make requisitions of men and money [from the states]; to govern the army and navy; to direct their operations . . . the intention evidently was that the United States should command whatever resources were by [the states] judged requisite to the 'common defense and general welfare.' It was presumed that a sense of [the states'] true interests, and a regard to the dictates of good faith, would be found sufficient pledges for the punctual performance of the duty of the members to the federal head. The experiment has, however, demonstrated that this expectation was ill-founded and illusory . . . that if we are in earnest about giving the Union energy and duration, we must abandon the vain project of legislating upon the States in their collective capacities . . . the Union must be invested with full power to levy troops; to build and equip fleets; and to raise the revenues which will be required for the formation and support of an army and navy."

59. *The Federalist Papers*, Federalist No. 23, 63.

60. Referred to in Article II of the Constitution as "the principal officer in each of the Executive Departments."

61. *Youngstown*, 343 U.S. at 640–641 (Jackson, J., concurring).

62. Farrand, ed., *The Records of the Federal Convention of 1787*, 2:318–319.

63. Louis Fisher, "Presidential Inherent Power: The Sole Organ Doctrine," *Presidential Studies Quarterly*, 37, no. 1 (March 2007): 140.

64. Ibid.

65. *Curtiss-Wright*, 299 U.S. at 304.

66. *Curtiss-Wright*, 299 U.S. at 320.

67. Fisher, "Presidential Inherent Power: The Sole Organ Doctrine," 148.

CHAPTER 2. PRESIDENTIAL POWER IN THE YOUNG REPUBLIC

1. Yoo, *Crisis and Command*, 84.

2. In fact, its head of state, King Louis XVI, was executed in January 1793.

3. Yoo, *Crisis and Command*, 84–85.

4. Fisher, *Presidential War Power*, 26–27. Washington's proclamation avoided using the word "neutrality," but it is commonly referred to as a proclamation or declaration of neutrality. See Yoo, *Crisis and Command*, 85 ("in order to assuage Jefferson's concerns, the word 'neutrality' was not used"). The proclamation stated that the United States would "adopt and pursue a conduct friendly and impartial toward the belligerent [European] powers." It warned U.S. citizens not to become involved in the conflict between France and Great Britain (or Britain's allies) and provided that citizens who "commit[ed], aid[ed] or abett[ed] hostilities" against any of the European countries involved in the war would not be protected by the United States and would be subject to prosecution. President George Washington, Proclamation of Neutrality, April 22, 1793, in *A Compilation of the Messages and Papers of the Presidents*, ed. James D. Richardson, vol. I, Part I, http://onlinebooks .library.upenn.edu/webbin/metabook?id=mppresidents and http://avalon.law .yale.edu/18th_century/neutra93.asp.

5. Fisher, *Presidential War Power*, 27.

6. Ibid.

7. Alexander Hamilton, *Pacificus No. 1*, June 29, 1793, *The Papers of Alexander Hamilton*, Digital Edition, ed. Harold C. Syrett (Charlottesville: University of Virginia Press, Rotunda, 2011), vol. 15, http://rotunda.upress.virginia.edu/founders /default.xqy?keys=ARHN-print-01-15-02-038.

8. Ibid.

9. Since Article II of the Constitution refers to the "executive power," I will often use that term when discussing emergency presidential power.

10. Article I's Vesting Clause provides that "[a]ll legislative powers herein granted shall be vested in a Congress of the United States." Article II's Vesting Clause provides that "[t]he executive power shall be vested in a President of the United States."

11. Hamilton, *Pacificus No. 1* (emphasis in quoted excerpt is from the original).

12. Ibid.

13. Ibid.

14. Jefferson letter to Madison, July 7, 1793, *The Papers of Thomas Jefferson*, Digital Edition, ed. Barbara B. Oberg and J. Jefferson Looney (Charlottesville: University of Virginia Press, Rotunda, 2008), vol. 26, http://rotunda.upress.virginia .edu/founders/default.xqy?keys=TSJN-print-01-26-02-0391&mode=deref.

Although Hamilton used a pseudonym, Jefferson and Madison knew that he was the author of the Pacificus essays.

15. Jefferson letter to Madison, June 23, 1793, *The Papers of Thomas Jefferson*, vol. 26.

16. Madison letter to Jefferson, June 13, 1793, *The Papers of James Madison*, Digital Edition, ed. J. C. A. Stagg (Charlottesville: University of Virginia Press, Rotunda, 2010), vol. 15, http://rotunda.upress.virginia.edu/founders/default .xqy?keys=JSMN-print-01-15-02-0028.

17. Ibid. ("The right to decide the question whether the duty [and] interest of the U.S. require war or peace under any given circumstances, and whether their disposition be towards the one or the other seems to be essentially [and] exclusively involved in the right vested in the Legislature, of declaring war in time of peace; and in the P[resident]. [and] S[enate] of making peace in time of war.")

18. Madison letter to Jefferson, July 30, 1793, *The Papers of James Madison*, vol. 15. (Madison described the task of replying to Hamilton's *Pacificus* essays as "the most grating one I have ever experienced.")

19. Madison, *Helvidius Number 1*, August 24, 1793, *The Papers of James Madison*, vol. 15.

20. Ibid.

21. Madison, Federalist No. 47, January 30, 1788, *The Papers of James Madison*, vol. 10. In fact, Madison's suggestion that the president's only constitutional duty with regard to treaties is to carry them out ignores Article II's instruction that it is for the president to "make treaties," with the advice and consent of the Senate. Madison took up this problem later in *Helvidius Number 1* but failed to explain how it could be reconciled with his suggestion that the president's power when it comes to treaties is limited to carrying them out. Madison, *Helvidius Number 1*, August 24, 1793, *The Papers of James Madison*, vol. 15.

22. Madison, *Helvidius Number 1*, August 24, 1793, *The Papers of James Madison*, vol. 15.

23. Ibid. (emphasis in original).

24. Fisher, *Presidential War Power*, 28.

25. Ibid.

26. *Talbot v. Seeman*, 5 U.S. 1, 28 (1801). In other early cases, the Supreme Court also affirmed congressional war power. See *Bas v. Tingy*, 4 U.S. 37 (1800) (Chase, J.) ("Congress is empowered to declare a general war, or Congress may wage a limited war; limited in place, in objects and in time"); *Little v. Barreme*, 6 U.S. 170 (1804) (holding that when presidential proclamation made during wartime conflicts with congressional statute, the statute controls).

27. James M. Smith, *Freedom's Fetters: The Alien and Sedition Laws and American Civil Liberties* (Ithaca, NY: Cornell University Press, 1956), 3–7; see also Louis Fisher, *The Constitution and 9/11: Recurring Threats to American Freedoms* (Lawrence: University Press of Kansas, 2008), 72–73.

28. At the time, the vice presidency was awarded to the person who won the

second-highest number of electoral college votes: therefore, the president and the vice president could come from different political parties. This was changed by the Twelfth Amendment, enacted in 1804, which provides that members of the electoral college vote separately for president and vice president, permitting electors to vote for a "ticket" by distinctly identifying their choice for president and vice president.

29. Smith, *Freedom's Fetters*, 8–12.

30. Naturalization Act of 1798, ch. 54, 1 Stat. 566, An Act Concerning Aliens (The Alien Act); The Sedition Act of 1798, ch. 74, 1 Stat. 596.

31. An Act Respecting Alien Enemies (Alien Enemies Act), ch. 66, 1 Stat. 577 (1798).

32. Sometimes referred to as the "Alien Friends Act" to distinguish it from the Alien Enemies Act. See Fisher, *The Constitution and 9/11*, 75–79.

33. David Cole, *Enemy Aliens: Double Standards and Constitutional Freedom in the War on Terrorism* (New York: New Press, 2003), 91–92.

34. Fisher, *The Constitution and 9/11*, 75–77.

35. Ibid. Note that due process and trial rights under the Fifth and Sixth Amendments, like other protections in the Bill of Rights, are not expressly limited to U.S. citizens.

36. Though most constitutional protections, including the Bill of Rights, as noted, are not expressly limited to citizens.

37. Cole, *Enemy Aliens*, 91–92; Fisher, *The Constitution and 9/11*, 75–81; Lawrence Lessig, *The Alien and Sedition Acts of 1798*, December 15, 2004, http://lessig.org/blog/2004/12/the_alien_and_sedition_acts_of.html.

38. *New York Times Co. v. Sullivan*, 376 U.S. 254, 276 (1964).

39. Now codified at 50 U.S.C. §§ 21–24; see also Gerald L. Neuman and Charles F. Hobson, "John Marshall and the Enemy Alien: A Case Missing from the Canon," *The Green Bag*, August 2005, http://www.law.columbia.edu/law_school/communications/reports/winter06/facforum2.

40. The Alien Friends and Sedition Acts applied without a declaration of war or invasion.

41. The law has since been changed to remove the language restricting application to males only. Fisher, *The Constitution and 9/11*, 78.

42. 50 U.S.C. § 21.

43. Ibid.

44. *Ludecke v. Watkins*, 335 U.S. 160 (1948).

45. Smith, *Freedom's Fetters*, 94; see also Cole, *Enemy Aliens*, 91–92.

46. Yoo, *Crisis and Command*, 90–91.

47. Fisher, *Presidential War Power*, 26–28.

48. That doesn't, of course, necessarily mean the laws passed by Congress were themselves constitutional, and, as we will see in other cases as well, it begs the question whether Congress has the authority to delegate or assign certain power to the president.

1. President James Madison is a notable exception. During the War of 1812, Madison did not push the limits of his authority. As Benjamin Wittes and Ritika Singh observe: "Nearly all presidents have neared the limit of their arguable legal powers during a time of conflict and pushed the limit to one degree or another— some presidents have even obliterated it, with varying degrees of grace or infamy. The most fundamental difference between them and Madison is that he did not even approach the limit." "James Madison, Presidential Power and Civil Liberties in the War of 1812," in *What So Proudly We Hailed: Essays on the Contemporary Meaning of the War of 1812*, ed. Pietro S. Novola and Peter J. Kastor (Washington, D.C.: Brookings Institution Press, 2012), 108.

2. Arthur M. Schlesinger Jr., *The Imperial Presidency* (Boston: Houghton Mifflin, 1973), 50–51. Schlesinger notes a number of examples before the Civil War when military action was taken without congressional authorization, especially when the president was acting against "roving bands of stateless and lawless people" as opposed to sovereign states.

3. Fisher, *Presidential War Power*, 41.

4. James K. Polk, "Special Message to Congress on Mexican Relations," May 11, 1846, in Gerhard Peters and John T. Woolley, *The American Presidency Project*, http://www.presidency.ucsb.edu/ws/?pid=67907.

5. Schlesinger, *The Imperial Presidency*, 41.

6. Fisher, *Presidential War Power*, 43–44, quoting *The Collected Works of Abraham Lincoln* (Ann Arbor: University of Michigan Digital Library Production Services, 2001), 1:451–452, http://quod.lib.umich.edu/l/lincoln/lincoln1/1:458?rgn=div1;view=fulltext.

7. Fisher, *Presidential War Power*, 32–36. In fact, Alexander Hamilton criticized Jefferson for being overly deferential to Congress. See ibid., 34–35.

8. Ibid., 36; see also Clement Fatovic, "Constitutionalism and Presidential Prerogative: Jeffersonian and Hamiltonian Perspectives," *American Journal of Political Science* 48, no. 3 (July 2004): 434, and Adler, "The Framers and Executive Prerogative: A Constitutional and Historical Rebuke," 386–387. For example, when war with Great Britain seemed imminent in 1807 but Congress was in recess, Jefferson unilaterally entered into contracts to purchase materials needed to build gunboats and make gunpowder. However, he sought approval from Congress when it reconvened, explaining that he had acted out of necessity, "trust[ing] that the Legislature, feeling the same anxiety for the safety of our country, so materially advanced by this precaution, will approve, when done, what they would have seen so important to be done, if then assembled." David J. Barron and Martin S. Lederman, "The Commander in Chief at the Lowest Ebb—A Constitutional History," *Harvard Law Review* 121 (2008): 941, 974–976.

9. Schlesinger, *The Imperial Presidency*, 56–57.

10. Fisher, "Abraham Lincoln: Preserving the Union and the Constitution," 504: "A close look at Lincoln's actions during the Civil War reveals some similarities

to Polk but also fundamental differences. More so than Polk, Lincoln showed a deeper respect and commitment for popular rule, legislative authority, and constitutional principles."

11. Farber, *Lincoln's Constitution*, 117–118; Fisher, "Abraham Lincoln: Preserving the Union and the Constitution," 521.

12. Schlesinger, *The Imperial Presidency*, 58. A formal declaration of war would have meant recognizing the Confederate states as a sovereign nation with legitimate rights of self-determination, something Lincoln and the United States certainly did not want to do.

13. Farber, *Lincoln's Constitution*, 19–20.

14. Congress had, however, provided statutory authority for Lincoln's decision to call up the militia.

15. Abraham Lincoln, "Special Session Message," July 4, 1861, in Gerhard Peters and John T. Woolley, *The American Presidency Project*, http://www.presidency.ucsb.edu/ws/?pid=69802 (emphasis in original).

16. Fisher, "Abraham Lincoln: Preserving the Union and the Constitution," 521.

17. John Locke, *Two Treatises of Government*, ed. Peter Laslett (Cambridge: Cambridge University Press, 1988), 2nd Treatise, section 160.

18. Ross J. Corbett, *The Lockean Commonwealth* (Albany: State University of New York Press, 2009), 71.

19. Louis Fisher, "Teaching the Presidency: Idealizing a Constitutional Office," *PS: Political Science and Politics* 45, no. 1 (January 2012): 17–31 (quoting from debate at the Constitutional Convention).

20. See, e.g., Farber, *Lincoln's Constitution*, 127 ("Whatever may be said about the legalities, the reality is that presidents generally have not hesitated to do whatever, in their view, needed to be done."). See also Michael A. Genovese, *Presidential Prerogative* (Stanford, CA: Stanford University Press, 2011), 27 ("Nowhere in the Constitution is it specified that the president will have additional powers in times of crisis or emergency. But history has shown us that in times of national crisis, the powers of the president have greatly expanded . . . [t]his historical practice has given the president an enlarged reservoir of power in emergencies . . . [what] constitutional scholar Edward S. Corwin [described] as . . . a constitution broad enough and flexible enough to meet the needs of an emergency situation as defined and measured by the political branches."). See also Sean Mattie, "Prerogative and the Rule of Law in John Locke and the Lincoln Presidency," *Review of Politics* 67, no. 1 (Winter 2005): 80–81, citing Schlesinger, *The Imperial Presidency*, 58–67; see also Robert Scigliano, "The President's 'Prerogative Powers,'" in *Inventing the American Presidency*, ed. Thomas E. Cronin (Lawrence: University Press of Kansas, 1989), 253, and Rossiter, *Constitutional Dictatorship: Crisis Government in the Modern Democracies*, 224–239, and Richard M. Pious, *The American Presidency* (New York: Basic Books, 1979), 47–84.

21. See, e.g., Ross J. Corbett, "The Extraconstitutionality of Lockean Prerogative," *Review of Politics* 68, no. 3 (Summer 2006) for discussion of Lockean prerogative as an extraconstitutional claim to authority.

22. Schlesinger, *The Imperial Presidency*, 60. See also Fisher, *Presidential War Power*, 48.

23. Schlesinger, *The Imperial Presidency*, 60. Other scholars would argue this is a contradiction in terms and that, by definition, Lockean prerogative cannot be "constitutionalized" since it is, by definition, a theory of emergency extraconstitutional power. See, e.g., Corbett, *The Lockean Commonwealth*, 62. In addition, the Framers of the Constitution did not adopt all of Locke's views regarding executive power—instead of following his suggestion that the executive should possess "federative" power over the military and foreign affairs, the Framers divided these powers between the president and Congress. Compare Locke, *Two Treatises of Government*, Second Treatise, sections 146–148 (defining federative power over war and peace and foreign affairs as separate from executive power but concluding that executive and federative powers must be wielded by one person) with U.S. Constitution, Article I, section 8 (assigning various war powers and foreign affairs powers to Congress as a whole or to the Senate). Schlesinger seems to concede that the Lockean prerogative stood in some tension with the Framers' goals as "[t]he idea of prerogative was *not* part of presidential power as defined in the Constitution." *The Imperial Presidency*, 9 (emphasis in original). However, Schlesinger argues, "there is reason to believe that the doctrine that crisis might require the executive to act outside the Constitution in order to save the Constitution remained in the back of [the Framers'] minds." Ibid. David Gray Adler rejects this idea, concluding that "there is nothing in the text of the Constitution, the debates or train of discussion in either the Constitutional Convention or the state ratifying conventions, or in contemporaneous writings for that matter, to support the claim that the president possesses a prerogative power to violate the laws of the nation." "The Framers and Executive Prerogative: A Constitutional and Historical Rebuke," 378. Adler further argues that "an undefined reservoir of discretionary power in the form of Locke's prerogative would have unraveled the carefully crafted design of Article II and repudiated the framers' stated aim of corralling executive power." Ibid., 382.

24. Schlesinger, *The Imperial Presidency*, 60–63; see also Farber, *Lincoln's Constitution*, 154.

25. Schlesinger, *The Imperial Presidency*, 61.

26. Lincoln, "Special Session Message," July 4, 1861.

27. U.S. Const. art. II, § 2.

28. *Fleming v. Page*, 50 U.S. 603, 615 (1850); see also Alexander Hamilton, *The Federalist Papers*, Federalist No. 69: "The President is to be commander-in-chief of the army and navy of the United States. In this respect his authority would be nominally the same with that of the king of Great Britain, but in substance much inferior to it. It would amount to nothing more than the supreme command and direction of the military and naval forces, as first General and admiral of the Confederacy; while that of the British king extends to the *declaring* of war and to the *raising* and *regulating* of fleets and armies—all which, by the Constitution under consideration, would appertain to the legislature."

29. Abraham Lincoln remarks to group of Chicago Christians, September 13, 1862, *Collected Works of Abraham Lincoln*, 5:421, http://quod.lib.umich.edu/l/lincoln /lincoln5/1:933?rgn=div1;view=fulltext; see also Farber, *Lincoln's Constitution*, 154, and Genovese, *The Power of the American Presidency*, 84.

30. Schlesinger suggests that, to the extent that the Framers recognized room for emergency prerogative, presidents who took such action "did so at [their] own peril" and would be answerable to Congress. *The Imperial Presidency*, 9. His discussion of Lincoln, however, creates room for limited unilateral presidential action without such caveats although "the life of the nation had to truly be at stake." Ibid., 66.

31. Fisher, "Abraham Lincoln: Preserving the Union and the Constitution," 521.

32. Barron and Lederman, "The Commander in Chief at the Lowest Ebb," 1000: "Lincoln was arguing that so long as a power resided in the Congress, and Congress was unable to act because it was not in session at a moment of emergency of crisis, the President could, in effect, act [in Congress's place] so as to preserve the nation."

33. Fisher, "Abraham Lincoln: Preserving the Union and the Constitution," 522–528. David Gray Adler agrees with Fisher's view, concluding that "the framers' response to the problem of emergency lay in the doctrine of retroactive ratification." "The Framers and Executive Prerogative: A Constitutional and Historical Rebuke," 379.

34. Fisher, "Abraham Lincoln: Preserving the Union and the Constitution," 532.

35. Farber, *Lincoln's Constitution*, 24, 137–138.

36. Ibid., 138, 141–143.

37. Fisher, *The Constitution and 9/11: Recurring Threats to America's Freedom*, 295.

38. Lincoln himself believed congressional approval was necessary. As discussed in the next chapter, Lincoln, in a July 4, 1861, address, asked Congress to validate his initially unilateral actions, conceding that while some of these actions may not have been "strictly legal . . . nothing has been done beyond the constitutional competency of Congress." *Collected Works of Abraham Lincoln*, 4:421–431, http:// quod.lib.umich.edu/l/lincoln/lincoln5/1:933?rgn=div1;view=fulltext. Louis Fisher observes that this "was an appeal to Congress (and the public) to examine what Lincoln had done under emergency conditions and to independently judge his actions." Fisher, "Abraham Lincoln: Preserving the Union and the Constitution," 525.

39. Schlesinger, *The Imperial Presidency*, 66, 335; see also Eric Foner, ed., *Our Lincoln: New Perspectives on Lincoln and His World* (New York: W. W. Norton, 2008), 60; Farber, *Lincoln's Constitution*, 20.

40. Fisher, "Abraham Lincoln: Preserving the Union and the Constitution," 503.

41. Farber, *Lincoln's Constitution*, 17–18.

42. Ibid., 16.

43. William H. Rehnquist, *All the Laws but One: Civil Liberties in Wartime* (New York: Alfred A. Knopf, 1998), 16–21; see also Farber, *Lincoln's Constitution*, 16–17.

44. Rehnquist, *All the Laws but One*, 36.

45. Ibid., 25; see also Farber, *Lincoln's Constitution*, 158.

46. Rehnquist, *All the Laws but One*, 26; see also Farber, *Lincoln's Constitution*, 17, and Foner, *Our Lincoln*, 38.

47. Foner, *Our Lincoln*, 38; Farber, *Lincoln's Constitution*, 17; Rehnquist, *All the Laws but One*, 32–33; Louis Fisher, *Military Tribunals and Presidential Power: American Revolution to the War on Terrorism* (Lawrence: University Press of Kansas: 2005), 55–56.

48. Historians have raised questions as to whether Chief Justice Taney actually had authority to decide the case. Merryman petitioned Taney under the Judiciary Act of 1789, which authorized any Supreme Court justice or federal judge to exercise original jurisdiction (meaning they could be the first to review the case, rather than reviewing the case on appeal after being decided by another court) in habeas corpus cases brought by federal prisoners. Taney might have struck down this provision of the Judiciary Act as an unconstitutional effort to expand the scope of the Supreme Court's original jurisdiction, as the court had done in *Marbury v. Madison* when presented with a separate section of the Judiciary Act of 1789. If he had done so, Taney would have refused to hear Merryman's petition at all. See Foner, *Our Lincoln*, 38–39.

49. Rehnquist, *All the Laws but One*, 36–37.

50. "Ex parte" means "on behalf of one party alone." When a court decides whether to issue a writ of habeas corpus, requiring the government to appear and justify a detention, the court initially considers whether to issue the writ without hearing from the government. The government has the opportunity to present its case and justify the detention when it appears in court pursuant to the writ.

51. Note that, despite Taney's specific reference to "the liberty of the citizen," Article I, section 9, of the Constitution does not expressly limit habeas protections to U.S. citizens only.

52. Farber, *Lincoln's Constitution*, 158.

53. James F. Simon, *Lincoln and Chief Justice Taney: Slavery, Secession, and the President's War Powers* (New York: Simon and Schuster, 2006), 192–193.

54. Fisher, *Military Tribunals and Presidential Power*, 55–56.

55. Merryman himself was ultimately charged in civil court, freed on bail, and never brought to trial. Fisher, *Military Tribunals and Presidential Power*, 56. Taney helped to make sure that Merryman would never be brought to trial by insisting that he preside at any trial and refusing to allow any other judge to take his place when health problems prevented Taney from presiding. Simon, *Lincoln and Chief Justice Taney*, 197.

56. Simon, *Lincoln and Chief Justice Taney*, 194. Simon suggests that, given these views, Taney should have declined to participate in the *Merryman* case.

57. Ibid., 196–197.

58. *Scott v. Sandford*, 60 U.S. 393 (1857).

59. Simon, *Lincoln and Chief Justice Taney*, 125.

60. Ibid., 126.

61. Farber, *Lincoln's Constitution*, 22.

62. Farber defines the rule of law as additionally depending on (1) comprehensible legal rules that guide individual conduct (as opposed to arbitrary authority); (2) dispute resolution through peaceful means instead of force; and (3) impartial courts that can enforce the law. *Lincoln's Constitution*, 22.

63. Foner, *Our Lincoln*, 41; see also Rehnquist, *All the Laws but One*, 40.

64. For example, Lincoln argued, as noted, that he had the implied constitutional authority and, indeed, the duty to do everything necessary to defend the nation against insurrection; on this reasoning, deferring to Taney was trumped by the necessity of winning the war.

65. Farber, *Lincoln's Constitution*, 22–23.

66. Abraham Lincoln, "Special Session Message," July 4, 1861.

67. Farber, *Lincoln's Constitution*, 158–159.

68. Ibid., 138, 141–143.

69. The 1863 law did not make clear whether Congress recognized any unilateral presidential authority to suspend the writ of habeas corpus. Ibid., 159.

70. Ibid., 144.

71. Ibid., 20.

72. See, e.g., ibid., 115; Schlesinger, *The Imperial Presidency*, 65–67.

73. Fisher, *Presidential War Power*, 48–49; see also Farber, *Lincoln's Constitution*, 24.

74. Farber, *Lincoln's Constitution*, 20.

75. Ibid., 2.

76. *Milligan* is discussed in more detail in the next chapter.

77. 71 U.S. 2, 125 (1866).

78. Farber, *Lincoln's Constitution*, 7.

79. Corbett, *The Lockean Commonwealth*, 62.

80. At the time, however, not everyone agreed, and, as noted, some believed Lincoln had unjustly seized dictatorial powers. Farber, *Lincoln's Constitution*, 19. National emergencies may be easier to judge retrospectively.

81. Genovese, *Presidential Prerogative*, 26.

82. Ibid., 26, quoting Locke, 2nd Treatise, chapter 14.

83. Corbett, *The Lockean Commonwealth*, 93 ("Locke does name the proper judge of prerogative, and it is the people.") and 79 (if prerogative is abused, "the people may limit [the executive's] power"). See also Corbett, "The Extraconstitutionality of Lockean Prerogative," *Review of Politics* 68, no. 3 (Summer 2006) ("Locke established the *people* as the proper judge of prerogative.") (emphasis in original). Corbett concludes that Locke uses "appeal to Heaven" as "euphemism for trial by combat."

84. Congress can also be seen as enforcing limits on emergency presidential power by providing (or denying) retroactive approval.

85. *Prize Cases*, 67 U.S. at 635.

86. Farber, *Lincoln's Constitution*, 141. The dissenting justices, while agreeing with the majority that Lincoln could "meet the adversary upon land and water with all the forces of the government," disagreed that Lincoln had the power to recognize a *legal* state of war. In their view, only Congress could do this (which it did in July 1861—after the ships at issue in the *Prize Cases* had been captured).

87. Ibid., 141–142. As Farber notes, the idea that a president may act unilaterally in responding to an attack was codified into statutory law by the War Powers Resolution of 1973. Ibid., 142. Critics could, of course, argue that the War Powers Resolution is itself unconstitutional in giving the president even this limited power.

88. "By that name."

89. *Prize Cases*, 67 U.S. at 635, 668.

90. Ibid.

91. Stephen I. Vladeck argues that this is the most important part of the opinion and that the Supreme Court only concluded Lincoln had authority to order the blockade because *Congress* had authorized this through the Militia Acts. "Emergency Power and the Militia Acts," 178–180.

92. Thomas H. Lee and Michael D. Ramsey, "Story of the Prize Cases," in *Presidential Power Stories*, ed. Christopher H. Schroeder and Curtis A. Bradley (New York: Foundation Press, 2009), 85; see also Fisher, *Presidential War Power*, 47–48.

93. *Hamdi v. Rumsfeld*, 542 U.S. 507, 581 (2004) (Thomas, J., dissenting).

CHAPTER 4. SETTING LIMITS ON WARTIME POWER?

1. *Ex parte Millligan*, 71 U.S. 2 (1866).

2. Rehnquist, *All the Laws but One*, 75.

3. Fisher, *Military Tribunals and Presidential Power*, 58.

4. Rehnquist, *All the Laws but One*, 85–86.

5. This was an argument that had succeeded several years earlier in the *Vallandigham* case, discussed later in this chapter.

6. Rehnquist, *All the Laws but One*, 104, 121.

7. Note: this act authorized the president to suspend habeas corpus during the rebellion. 12 Stat. 755 (1863).

8. U.S. Const. art. III, § 1.

9. Four justices joined a concurring opinion asserting that Congress could have authorized the military commission if it had determined that such a tribunal was necessary to maintain public safety (for instance, if civilian courts, though operating, were unable to perform all their duties): "We think that Congress had power, though not exercised, to authorize the military commission which was held in Indiana" (71 U.S. at 137).

10. Genovese, *The Power of the American Presidency*, 85: "When the Court handed down its decision [in *Milligan*], the war was over, the danger subsided and

Lincoln, the initiator of Milligan's internment, was dead and buried. The Court's decision did not affect the president who ordered the action, and it did not affect the emergency that the Union faced."

11. The North also held military trials in the South, though this was less controversial because civilian courts were not open in what was enemy territory; the use of military courts in such cases was a matter of necessity. Farber, *Lincoln's Constitution*, 164.

12. Discussion of the *Vallandigham* case is drawn from ibid., 170–174.

13. *Ex parte Vallandigham*, 68 U.S. 243 (1863).

14. Farber, *Lincoln's Constitution*, 171. The Vallandigham prosecution was driven by General Ambrose Burnside. Lincoln thought Burnside had made a mistake in arresting Vallandigham and sent a telegram to Burnside expressing displeasure. However, Lincoln did not criticize the proceedings and in fact defended Vallandigham's prosecution, arguing that Vallandigham's criticisms "damage[d] the military power of the country." Fisher, *Military Tribunals and Presidential Power*, 57–58.

15. Genovese, *The Power of the American Presidency*, 85.

16. Clinton Rossiter, *The Supreme Court and the Commander in Chief* (Ithaca, NY: Cornell University Press, 1976), 39: "the law of the Constitution is what Lincoln did in the crisis, not what the court said later." Quoted in Genovese, *The Power of the American Presidency*, 85.

17. Now the Dominican Republic.

18. Schlesinger, *The Imperial Presidency*, 78.

19. Fisher, *Presidential War Power*, 52–53. However, McKinley provided Congress with incorrect information about the cause of the explosion, stating that it had been caused by a mine in the harbor. Subsequent studies showed the explosion had come from inside the ship—probably from spontaneous combustion of coal that caused an explosion in the ship's powder and ammunition magazines. Louis Fisher, *Destruction of the Maine (1898)*, Law Library of Congress, 2009, http://loc.gov/law/help/usconlaw/pdf/Maine.1898.pdf.

20. 65 Pub. L. No. 24, 40 Stat. 217 (1917).

21. 65 Pub. L. No. 150, 40 Stat. 553 (1918) (repealed 1920).

22. Rehnquist, *All the Laws but One*, 183.

23. See, e.g., *Schenck v. United States*, 249 U.S. 47 (1919); *Milwaukee Social Democratic Pub. Co. v. Burleson*, 255 U.S. 407 (1921).

24. These reduced rates were essential to the commercial viability of the paper.

25. *Milwaukee Social Democratic Pub. Co.*, 255 U.S. at 428–429 (Brandeis, J., dissenting): "[i]t clearly appears that there was no express grant of power [by Congress] to the Postmaster General to deny second-class mail rates to future issues of a newspaper because in his opinion it had systematically violated the Espionage Act in the past; and it seems equally clear that there is no basis for the contention that such power is to be implied."

26. Ibid. at 430.

27. See chapters 9–14.

28. Fisher, *The Constitution and 9/11*, 116.

29. Ibid.

30. Ibid., citing *Ex parte Jackson*, 263 Fed. 110 (D.Mont. 1920) and *Colyer v. Skeffington*, 265 Fed. 17 (D.Mass. 1920).

31. Fisher, *The Constitution and 9/11*, 116–118.

CHAPTER 5. EXPANDED PRESIDENTIAL POWER
DURING WORLD WAR II

1. Schlesinger, *The Imperial Presidency*, 108.

2. Germany and Italy had declared war against the United States earlier the same day.

3. Act of June 28, 1940, ch. 440, § 14(a), 54 Stat. 676, 681. Information in this paragraph is drawn from Fisher, *Presidential War Power*, 75–76; Schlesinger, *The Imperial Presidency*, 105; Yoo, *Crisis and Command*, 298; and Richard M. Pious, "Franklin D. Roosevelt and the Destroyer Deal: Normalizing Prerogative Power," *Presidential Studies Quarterly* 42, no. 1 (March 2012): 190–204, DOI: 10.1111/j.1741-5705.2012.03948.x. In addition to the 1940 law, other laws, including the Neutrality Act of 1937, also set limits on aid to nations at war. Joint Resolution of May 1, 1937, ch. 146, 50 Stat. 121.

4. Pious, "Franklin D. Roosevelt and the Destroyer Deal," 194. Roosevelt later made a similar deal with Mexico, again acting without Congress's initial consent. Ibid., 198.

5. *Curtiss-Wright*, 299 U.S. 304, 319–320 (1936).

6. Fisher, *Presidential War Power*, 76–77; Pious, "Franklin D. Roosevelt and the Destroyer Deal: Normalizing Prerogative Power," 196.

7. Another Roosevelt adviser argued this law did not prevent Roosevelt from transferring destroyers in order to protect American national security and in fact implicitly recognized such authority. Yoo, *Crisis and Command*, 299. Jackson adopted this viewpoint in his memo, concluding that the 1940 law did not prevent the exchange of destroyers for naval bases since the deal would, overall, strengthen U.S. defense. Ibid., 300; Barron and Lederman, "The Commander in Chief at the Lowest Ebb—A Constitutional History," 1045–1046.

8. Pious, "Franklin D. Roosevelt and the Destroyer Deal," 194.

9. Schlesinger, *The Imperial Presidency*, 108.

10. Edward S. Corwin, quoted in Yoo, *Crisis and Command*, 302; see also Fisher, *Presidential War Power*, 77. In contrast, Richard M. Pious defends Roosevelt's decision as "neither dictatorial nor arbitrary." "Franklin D. Roosevelt and the Destroyer Deal: Normalizing Prerogative Power," 200. Pious concludes that "[i]n form Roosevelt acted through his constitutional prerogatives, but in reality he had consulted Congress and obtained its acquiescence and its tacit consent." Before making the deal with the British, Roosevelt consulted with congressional leaders from both parties, who did not indicate any objections. After

the deal was announced, however, other members of Congress called for an investigation, suggesting that the deal was illegal. Congress ultimately took no action to criticize, investigate, or otherwise question Roosevelt's action. Instead, it appropriated money to build U.S. bases on the islands leased to the United States by Britain. It also passed the Lend-Lease Act in March 1941. Ibid., 200–201.

11. Schlesinger, *The Imperial Presidency*, 108.

12. Barron and Lederman, "The Commander in Chief at the Lowest Ebb—A Constitutional History," 1046–1047.

13. Yoo, *Crisis and Command*, 299–300.

14. *Curtiss-Wright*, 299 U.S. 304, 320 (1936).

15. Annals of Congress, 6th Cong., 613 (1800).

16. Fisher, *The Constitution and 9/11*, 295–296; Fisher, *Presidential War Power*, 72.

17. *Curtiss-Wright*, 299 U.S. at 319–320.

18. Schlesinger, *The Imperial Presidency*, 107; Barron and Lederman, "The Commander in Chief at the Lowest Ebb—A Constitutional History," 1045–1047.

19. 55 Stat. 31 (1941).

20. Schlesinger, *The Imperial Presidency*, 111–112. Roosevelt also took unilateral action before Pearl Harbor to aid China in its fight against Japan. Yoo, *Crisis and Command*, 305–306.

21. This is not to say the Roosevelt administration was unaware of the threat Japan posed before December 7, 1941. Yoo, *Crisis and Command*, 289–290.

22. Japan also struck other U.S. bases on December 7–8, 1941, including in the Philippines and on Wake Island and Guam.

23. James T. Cheatham, *The Atlantic Turkey Shoot: U-Boats off the Outer Banks in World War II* (Charlotte, NC: Delmar, 1990), 13.

24. Fisher and Yoo describe two of the saboteurs as U.S. citizens, whereas the Supreme Court identified only one as a citizen. Louis Fisher, *Nazi Saboteurs on Trial: A Military Tribunal and American Law* (Lawrence: University of Kansas Press, 2003), 6–15 (describing Ernest Peter Burger and Herman Haupt as U.S. citizens); Yoo, *Crisis and Command*, 311; *Ex parte Quirin*, 317 U.S. 1 (1942). It may be, though this is not absolutely clear, that the court concluded Burger had lost his U.S. citizenship because he had joined the German military. Fisher, *Nazi Saboteurs on Trial*, 94.

25. Fisher, *Nazi Saboteurs on Trial*, 32–42.

26. The terms "military tribunal" and "military commission" are used as synonyms in this chapter.

27. Fisher, *Nazi Saboteurs on Trial*, 42–47, 50; see also Fisher, *Military Tribunals and Presidential Power*, 95–98.

28. Fisher, *Military Tribunals and Presidential Power*, 9–12.

29. Now the Uniform Code of Military Justice (UCMJ). The UCMJ was enacted in 1950 to modernize the Articles of War. Both the Articles of War and the UCMJ follow most of the same criminal procedures and protections used by civil courts.

30. Fisher, *Nazi Saboteurs on Trial*, 48–49.

31. Franklin D. Roosevelt, "Proclamation 2561—Denying Certain Enemies Access to the Courts," July 2, 1942, in Gerhard Peters and John T. Wooley, *The American Presidency Project*, http://www.presidency.ucsb.edu/ws/?pid=16281.

32. Fisher, *Nazi Saboteurs on Trial*, 49–52. Fisher notes that "Roosevelt was not claiming inherent or exclusive constitutional authority. He acted under a mix of constitutional authority accorded to the President and statutory authority [he claimed was] granted by Congress." Ibid., 51.

33. Roosevelt also issued a military order on July 2, 1942, that referred to the tribunal "trying . . . offenses against both the 'law of war and the Articles of War.'" Ibid., 52. However, Fisher notes, "the order clearly liberated the [tribunal] from some of the restrictions established by Congress in the Articles of War." For instance, Roosevelt authorized the tribunal to make its own rules—it did not have to follow trial procedures created by Congress in the Articles of War. In addition, the tribunal could impose a death sentence based on a two-thirds vote. The Articles of War required a unanimous vote to impose the death penalty. Ibid.

34. Ibid., 50–53.

35. Fisher, *Military Tribunals and Presidential Power*, 124–125.

36. 10 U.S.C. § 1509 (1946) (repealed 1950).

37. Fisher, *Military Tribunals and Presidential Power*, 109, 124–125.

38. Fisher, *Nazi Saboteurs on Trial*, 58; Fisher, *Military Tribunals and Presidential Power*, 101–106.

39. See *Ex parte Milligan*, discussed in chapter 4.

40. Fisher, *Nazi Saboteurs on Trial*, 56.

41. Prosecutors argued that any saboteurs who had U.S. citizenship forfeited it by their association with an enemy of the United States. Ibid., 94.

42. Fisher, *Military Tribunals and Presidential Power*, 97, 102.

43. This was a delicate matter, since the defense attorneys, as military officers, were not sure whether they could act "contrary to the wishes of the Commander in Chief." Fisher, *Nazi Saboteurs on Trial*, 64–67.

44. Ibid., 65–68. There were some procedural oddities in the case: the defense lawyers reached out to justices on the Supreme Court, and the Supreme Court agreed to hear oral argument, before papers were filed in any lower court. A U.S. District Court denied a petition for a writ of habeas corpus the evening before oral argument took place in the Supreme Court, but there was no action taken by the intermediate D.C. Circuit Court of Appeals until after oral argument took place before the high court.

45. Recall the Supreme Court's refusal to exercise jurisdiction over the *Vallandigham* military tribunal case during the Civil War; the *Milligan* ruling came after the war had ended.

46. Ibid., 95–96; see also Yoo, *Crisis and Command*, 314. Justice Murphy, who had served as attorney general in the Roosevelt administration before Jackson, was a member of the military reserves and recused himself from hearing the case. Chief Justice Stone's son served on the defense team, but the prosecution did not object

to Stone's hearing the case. As discussed, Justice Jackson had also previously served as attorney general in the Roosevelt administration.

47. Fisher, *Nazi Saboteurs on Trial*, 88–94; Fisher, *Military Tribunals and Presidential Power*, 108–114.

48. Per curiam means "by the court" as a whole, rather than signed by a specific justice or justices.

49. Fisher, *Nazi Saboteurs on Trial*, 68–69.

50. Ibid., 77–79.

51. Fisher, *Military Tribunals and Presidential Power*, 114–116, 119.

52. Since six of them were now dead, Frankfurter described this as "F.F.'s Soliloquy." Fisher, *Nazi Saboteurs on Trial*, 117–118.

53. Ibid., 117–121.

54. *Ex parte Quirin*, 317 U.S. 1, 47–48 (1942).

55. Enacted by Congress.

56. Schlesinger, *The Imperial Presidency*, 9. The congressman whose views Schlesinger summarized was Alexander White of Virginia.

57. Fisher, *Military Tribunals and Presidential Power*, 121–126.

58. *Hamdi*, 542 U.S. at 507, 569.

59. Fisher, *Military Tribunals and Presidential Power*, 124.

60. Ibid., 114.

CHAPTER 6. THE INTERNMENT OF JAPANESE AMERICANS DURING WORLD WAR II

1. Rehnquist, *All the Laws but One*, 188–189; Fisher, *The Constitution and 9/11*, 144–146.

2. However, it's worth noting that German submarines were more active on the East Coast (as discussed in the previous chapter) than Japanese warships were on the West Coast. A Japanese submarine shelled an oil refinery near Santa Barbara, California, but this took place on February 23, 1942—after President Roosevelt signed the executive order discussed in this chapter. Rehnquist, *All the Laws but One*, 188. In addition, Pearl Harbor is more than two thousand miles from California.

3. David Cole, *Enemy Aliens: Double Standards and Constitutional Freedoms in the War on Terrorism* (New York: New Press, 2003), 97. See also Tetsuden Kashima, *Judgment without Trial: Japanese American Imprisonment during World War II* (Seattle: University of Washington Press, 2003), 20: "No evidence exists that any Issei [first-generation Japanese Americans] or Nisei [second-generation Japanese Americans born in the United States] resident of the United States or its territories ever committed an act of espionage or sabotage on behalf of Japan."

4. Cole, *Enemy Aliens*, 88. The War Department initially decided that persons of Japanese ancestry were generally ineligible for military service (with some exceptions made for interpreters). However, by 1943, Japanese Americans were accepted for service in segregated units that earned high distinction. Perhaps most

notably, members of the 442nd Regimental Combat Team and the 100th Infantry Battalion were highly decorated for their service in North Africa and Europe. Kashima, *Judgment without Trial*, 172–173. General George C. Marshall described these soldiers as "superb," noting that they sustained "terrific casualties" and were known for their "rare courage and tremendous fighting spirit." 442nd Regimental Combat Team Historical Society website, http://www.the442.org.

5. Jacobus tenBroek, Edward N. Barnhart, and Floyd W. Matson, *Prejudice, War and the Constitution* (Berkeley: University of California Press, 1968), 23–25. Significant Japanese immigration to the United States began around 1890. Roger Daniels, *Concentration Camps: North America Japanese in the United States and Canada during World War II* (Malabar, FL: Krieger, 1993), 5.

6. Information in this paragraph is drawn from Peter Irons, *Justice at War: The Story of the Japanese American Internment Cases* (Berkeley: University of California Press, 1983), 9–10.

7. TenBroek, Barnhart, and Matson, *Prejudice, War and the Constitution*, 24–25.

8. Irons, *Justice at War*, 10–12; tenBroek, Barnhart, and Matson, *Prejudice, War and the Constitution*, 25–26.

9. However, Japanese Americans born in the United States continued to attend segregated schools in San Francisco while the Justice Department brought a lawsuit aimed at returning schoolchildren who were Japanese citizens to schools attended by white children. Daniels, *Concentration Camps*, 13–14. Segregation of Japanese Americans lasted for decades in at least some San Francisco schools. John Tateishi, *And Justice for All: An Oral History of the Japanese American Detention Camps* (New York: Random House, 1984), 3–4.

10. In the late nineteenth and early twentieth centuries, Japanese Americans born outside the United States were generally barred from seeking citizenship, though some, especially in Hawaii, were able to skirt naturalization laws barring nonwhite immigrants from gaining U.S. citizenship. Irons, *Justice at War*, 12; see also Daniels, *Concentration Camps*, 19. In 1924, the Supreme Court confirmed that these naturalization laws applied to the Issei and barred them from gaining citizenship. *Ozawa v. United States*, 260 U.S. 178 (1922).

11. It did not stop immigration, however: under the terms of the "Gentleman's Agreement," Japanese Americans who had already come to the United States were permitted to bring their wives to join them in the United States, and many did. Daniels, *Concentration Camps*, 14. Between 1908 and 1924, about 118,000 Japanese immigrants came to the United States, many coming to join husbands in the United States through arranged marriages. Irons, *Justice at War*, 11.

12. Irons, *Justice at War*, 12. The 1924 Immigration Restriction Act, Pub. L. 68–139, 43 Stat. 153, § 13(c), prohibited admission into the United States of any alien ineligible for citizenship, with certain very limited exceptions (e.g., if the would-be immigrant was the wife or unmarried child of an immigrant eligible for admission to the United States). The Supreme Court's 1922 decision in *Ozawa*

held that Congress had properly excluded Japanese American immigrants from obtaining citizenship; therefore, under the terms of the 1924 Act, since Japanese aliens were ineligible for citizenship, no further Japanese immigration into the United States would be permitted. The act was not revised until 1952. "The Immigration Act of 1924," U.S. Department of State, Office of the Historian, http://history.state.gov/milestones/1921–1936/ImmigrationAct.

13. Irons, *Justice at War*, 12–13.

14. The JACL creed, written in 1940, provided: "I am proud that I am an American citizen of Japanese ancestry. . . . I believe in [America's] institutions, ideals and traditions; I glory in her heritage; I boast of her history; I trust in her future. . . . Although some individuals may discriminate against me, I shall never become bitter or lose faith, for I know that such persons are not representative of the majority of the American people. True, I shall do all in my power to discourage such practices, but I shall do it in the American way—above board, in the open, through courts of law, by education, by proving myself to be worthy of equal treatment and consideration. I am firm in my belief that American sportsmanship and attitude of fair play will judge citizenship and patriotism on the basis of action and achievement, and not on the basis of physical characteristics. Because I believe in America, and I trust she believes in me, and because I have received innumerable benefits from her, I pledge myself to do honor to her at all times and all places; to support her constitution; to obey her laws; to respect her flag; to defend her against all enemies, foreign and domestic; to actively assume my duties and obligations as a citizen, cheerfully and without any reservations whatsoever, in the hope that I may become a better American in a greater America." Daniels, *Concentration Camps*, 24–25. The JACL was founded in 1929 and is still an active organization; additional information about the group is available at the Japanese American Citizens League's website, http://www.jacl.org/about/about.htm. The JACL creed was also published in the Congressional Record for May 9, 1941.

15. Daniels, *Concentration Camps*, 23–24: "Outside school . . . the Nisei faced a society that rejected them regardless of their accomplishments. Fully credentialed Nisei education majors, for example, were virtually unemployable as teachers in the very schools in which they had excelled." See also Tateishi, *And Justice for All*, 5 (Mary Tsukamoto, a U.S.-born Japanese American, recalling that boys threw stones at her when she walked home from school and called her and her friends "Japs" and that she was excluded from oratorical contest because of her ancestry); 18 (William Hosokawa, a U.S.-born Japanese American, describing "virulent anti-Orientalism on the West Coast [in the 1930s]"); 60 (Mitsuye Endo, a U.S.-born Japanese American, describing discrimination against Japanese Americans that shut her out of most jobs available in the 1930s); 108 (Mabel Ota, a U.S.-born Japanese American recalling that UCLA did not allow Asian Americans to live in dorms in the 1930s).

16. Irons, *Justice at War*, 13.

17. Daniels, *Concentration Camps*, 22.

18. Most Japanese Americans held in detention camps during World War II lived on the West Coast of the United States, though some Japanese Americans in Alaska and Hawaii were also interned. Kashima, *Judgment without Trial*, 88–93 (Alaska); 67–87 (Hawaii). Japanese Americans in Hawaii were not subject to mass internment: of about 150,000 Japanese Americans living in Hawaii during World War II, about 2,400 were held in camps in Hawaii or on the mainland United States. Kashima concludes that the contrast between the experience of Japanese Americans on the West Coast and that of Japanese Americans in Hawaii can be explained in part by Hawaii's specific "history and relations with this large minority population"—Japanese Americans in Hawaii made up more than one-third of the total population. In addition, he concludes, Japanese American labor in Hawaii was vital to the war effort. Ibid., 86–87; see also Daniels, *Concentration Camps*, 72–73. Finally, Hawaii was different from the West Coast because, while most Japanese Americans in Hawaii were not formally interned, they were subject to martial law for most of the war. Kashima, *Judgment without Trial*, 69.

19. Information in this paragraph is drawn from Irons, *Justice at War*, 5–9.

20. Ibid., 5.

21. Ibid., 6. This is not to say that all was well for Japanese Americans in the initial days and weeks after Pearl Harbor. In December 1941, a number of Japanese Americans were murdered in California and in other parts of the United States, and Japanese businesses were attacked in Stockton, California, where windows were shattered. TenBroek, Barnhart, and Matson, *Prejudice, War and the Constitution*, 72. While newspaper editorials in December 1941 often called for tolerance, "[p]opular anger and apprehension" were already beginning to rise. Ibid.

22. Irons, *Justice at War*, 7. Irons offers two ways to understand why public opinion turned against Japanese Americans on the West Coast. The first is historical racism against Japanese Americans, as discussed earlier in this chapter. The second is the fears that Japan and its allies, Germany and Italy, might conquer the world—and that, in doing so, Japanese troops would commit acts of unspeakable brutality, as had been reported in the Philippines. Ibid., 8. TenBroek, Barnhart, and Matson reached similar conclusions: *Prejudice, War and the Constitution*, 70–73.

23. Daniels, *Concentration Camps*, 35–36.

24. TenBroek, Barnhart, and Matson, *Prejudice, War and the Constitution*, 73–75.

25. Irons, *Justice at War*, 7.

26. 7 Fed. Reg. 1407 (Feb. 19, 1942), http://www.archives.gov/historical-docs /todays-doc/index.html?dod-date=219 or http://historymatters.gmu.edu/d/5154.

27. Daniels, *Concentration Camps*, 105.

28. Mass internment of Italian Americans and German Americans who were not U.S. citizens was considered but rejected. Ibid., 81–82. However, some Italian Americans and German Americans were interned, and, although internment did not occur en masse for these groups, thousands were held in camps. The noncitizens who were detained were provided limited hearings of dubious value. Although only Italian Americans and German Americans who were not U.S. citizens were

held, family members who were U.S. citizens often "voluntarily" decided to join them. See "History: World War II Civil Liberties Violations of German Americans and German Latin Americans by the United States Government," on the German American Internee Coalition website, http://www.gaic.info/ShowPage.php?section=History&page=Wartime_Civil_Liberties_Violations. See also Kashima, *Judgment without Trial*, 130–131.

29. Pub. L. No. 77–503, 56 Stat. 173 (1942).

30. Kashima, *Judgment without Trial*, 132.

31. The curfew also applied to Italian Americans and German Americans who were not U.S. citizens.

32. Irons, *Justice at War*, 73; Daniels, *Concentration Camps*, 104.

33. Daniels, *Concentration Camps*, 104; see also "Children of the Camps: Internment History," PBS website, http://www.pbs.org/childofcamp/history/camps.html.

34. Cole, *Enemy Aliens*, 97.

35. Irons, *Justice at War*, 74.

36. Hirabayahi's sentences for violating the curfew and refusing to report for internment ran concurrently, so the court concluded it was not necessary to address the thornier question of internment in his case. *Hirabayashi v. U.S.*, 320 U.S. 81, 84 (1943).

37. Ibid. at 91–92.

38. Ibid. at 93.

39. Ibid.

40. Ibid.

41. Ibid. at 94.

42. Ibid. at 90–91.

43. Ibid. at 96–98.

44. Ibid. at 99.

45. Ibid. at 100. The court noted that the Fifth Amendment, unlike the Fourteenth Amendment, which expressly applies to the states, includes no Equal Protection Clause but suggested that discrimination by the federal government might violate the Fifth Amendment's Due Process Clause.

46. Ibid.

47. Ibid.

48. Ibid. at 101.

49. Ibid. at 99. The court's conclusion on this point was based at least in part on misleading information presented by the government that incorrectly suggested that more time might have allowed the military to separate loyal from disloyal Japanese Americans. Irons, *Justice at War*, 206–212.

50. *Hirabayashi*, 320 U.S. at 101.

51. Ibid. at 111 (Murphy, J., concurring).

52. TenBroek, Barnhart, and Matson, *Prejudice, War and the Constitution*, 87, quoting Congressional Record, December 15, 1941, 9808, and February 14, 1942, A691–691.

53. TenBroek, Barnhart, and Matson, *Prejudice, War and the Constitution*, 87, quoting Congressional Record, February 26, 1942, 1682–1683.

54. Kashima, *Judgment without Trial*, 133, quoting *San Francisco News*, April 13, 1943.

55. U.S. Army, Western Defense Command and Fourth Army, *Final Report: Japanese Evacuation from the West Coast, 1942* (Washington: General Printing Office, 1943), 34, http://ia600506.us.archive.org/1/items/japaneseevacuatioodewi /japaneseevacuatioodewi.pdf.

56. Ibid.

57. Irons, *Justice at War*, 23; Kashima, *Judgment without Trial*, 36–37.

58. Irons, *Justice at War*, 203, quoting Lieutenant Commander Kenneth D. Ringle, *Report on Japanese Question*, January 26, 1942 (emphasis added), http:// www.history.navy.mil/library/online/jap%20intern.htm.

59. U.S. Army, *Final Report: Japanese Evacuation from the West Coast, 1942*, 9. Peter Irons notes that General DeWitt's original report stated that no amount of time would be sufficient to allow for precise separation of loyal and disloyal Japanese Americans. DeWitt's report was finalized and ready for printing in April 1943, as the government was briefing the *Hirabayashi* case before the Supreme Court. Since the government's argument depended in part on the assertion that there was not time to separate loyal from disloyal Japanese Americans, Assistant Secretary of War John McCloy convinced General DeWitt to allow revision of his report to remove reference to the claim that no amount of time would have been sufficient to separate loyal from disloyal Japanese Americans. With the report changed, the government's brief in *Hirabayashi* "rested on the claim that DeWitt had faced the 'virtually impossible task' of promptly segregating the potentially disloyal from the loyal" and that loyalty hearings would have taken months or years. Compare Irons, *Justice at War*, 206–212, with U.S. Army, *Final Report: Japanese Evacuation*, 9. The court accepted the government's argument, concluding that "we cannot reject as unfounded the judgment of the military authorities and of Congress that there were disloyal members of that population, whose number and strength could not be precisely and quickly ascertained." *Hirabayashi*, 320 U.S. at 99.

60. Daniels, *Concentration Camps*, 113. The questions were numbered 27 and 28 on the questionnaire.

61. Ibid., 115; see also Tateishi, *And Justice for All*, 113.

62. Daniels, *Concentration Camps*, 114.

63. These fears had foundation as those providing "disloyal" answers to the questionnaires were sent to a separate camp at Tule Lake, California. Daniels, *Concentration Camps*, 114.

64. Ibid.

65. Ibid., 139.

66. However, Justice Jackson, like his colleagues in the majority, concluded that the court had "no choice" other than to accept General DeWitt's assertion that the mass internment was reasonable. Louis Fisher responds that "the Court *did* have a choice. It should have said: 'We decide cases based on evidence. You

have provided none and on that ground we invalidate the exclusion order.'"
Defending Congress and the Constitution (Lawrence: University Press of Kansas, 2011), 332.

67. The Civil Liberties Act of 1988, passed by Congress and enacted as law, apologized to Japanese American citizens and resident aliens who were interned in camps during World War II. The act also provided $20,000 in restitution to each internee or his or her descendant. Fred Korematsu was awarded the Presidential Medal of Freedom in 1998. He died in 2005, and a replica of the medal is displayed on his tombstone.

68. Ironically, this decision marked the first time the court employed the doctrine of "strict scrutiny," which has since been used, for example, to place a heavy burden on the government to justify laws based on racial classifications and almost always results in such laws being invalidated. *Korematsu* itself is a rare exception to this rule.

69. Rehnquist, *All the Laws but One*, 210–211.

70. Cole, *Enemy Aliens*, 99.

71. In 1971, Congress passed the Non-Detention Act, signed into law by President Nixon, which provides that "No citizen shall be imprisoned or detained by the United States except pursuant to an Act of Congress." The 1971 Act repealed the Emergency Detention Act of 1950, which authorized detentions of citizens or noncitizens in a time of "internal security emergency." The 1971 Act was also seen as an attempt to prevent a repeat of the mass detentions carried out during World War II. Fisher, *The Constitution and 9/11*, 182–188. However, the Bush administration argued that the Non-Detention Act did not protect U.S. citizens designated as "enemy combatants" from detention. Ibid., 189–190. This issue is discussed in more detail in chapter 10.

CHAPTER 7. THE *YOUNGSTOWN* STEEL SEIZURE CASE

1. Fisher, *Presidential War Power*, 99.

2. Schlesinger, *The Imperial Presidency*, 132.

3. Fisher, *Presidential War Power*, 99–100. Some members of Congress did question Truman's authority to act unilaterally, especially "[a]s military circumstances in Korea worsened," and at least one, Senator Robert Taft (R-OH), flatly charged that the war was illegal. Maeva Marcus, *Truman and the Steel Seizure Case: The Limits of Presidential Power* (Durham, NC: Duke University Press, 1994), 3. On the other hand, some academics, including Schlesinger, endorsed Truman's decision to deploy troops to Korea without congressional approval. Schlesinger argued that Truman's action was justified by historical precedent, including Jefferson's decision to deploy the U.S. Navy against the Barbary pirates. As Louis Fisher observes, Schlesinger's defense of Truman's actions ignored the fact that Jefferson acted pursuant to congressional statute. Schlesinger later admitted that he had engaged in "a flourish of historical documentation and, alas, hyperbole." Fisher, *Presidential War Power*, 103.

4. 343 U.S. 579 (1952), often referred to as the *Steel Seizure* case. See also Marcus, *Truman and the Steel Seizure Case*. Patricia L. Bellia suggests that the *Youngstown* case left open more questions about emergency power than it answered. Patricia L. Bellia, "Story of the *Steel Seizure* Case," in *Presidential Power Stories*, ed. Christopher H. Schroeder and Curtis A. Bradley (New York: Foundation Press, 2009), 234–235, 266.

5. The 1950 Defense Production Act authorized the president to set price limits on goods and services, with a goal of controlling wartime inflation. Ibid., 235.

6. Information in this paragraph is drawn from Marcus, *Truman and the Steel Seizure Case*, 58–82, and Bellia, "Story of the *Steel Seizure* Case," 235–237.

7. Bellia, "Story of the *Steel Seizure* Case," 254–255.

8. Factual information in this paragraph is drawn from ibid., 237–241, 256.

9. The power to seize factories under the War Labor Disputes Act expired in 1947. *Youngstown*, 343 U.S. 579, 599 fn. 1 (1952) (Frankfurter, J., concurring).

10. Bellia, "Story of the *Steel Seizure* Case," 241, 254. The Selective Service Act of 1948 permitted seizure of plants that failed to fill an order for goods required for national defense purposes, and the Defense Production Act of 1950 also authorized the president to seize property in some circumstances; Truman conceded, however, that the conditions necessary for seizure under these laws had not been met. *Youngstown*, 343 U.S. 579, 586; see also 343 U.S. at 664–666 (1952) (Clark, J., concurring) and 343 U.S. at 658 fn. 6 (Burton, J., concurring).

11. Bellia argues that the government made a tactical misstep in the district court by emphasizing independent presidential power rather than focusing on a more narrow argument that the companies' request for a preliminary injunction was not justified by the requisite showing of irreparable harm. Bellia, "Story of the *Steel Seizure* Case," 247–248.

12. Article II's Vesting Clause provides that "*[t]he* executive Power shall be vested in a President of the United States of America" (emphasis added). Article I's Vesting Clause provides that "[a]ll legislative Powers *herein granted* shall be vested in a Congress of the United States" (emphasis added). Department of Justice lawyers argued this was significant as it indicated an intent to limit the legislative powers assigned to Congress to those specifically enumerated in Article I, while the president was assigned *all* "the executive power," without limitation. As Justice Jackson responded, "[i]f that be true, it is difficult to see why the forefathers bothered to add several specific items, including some trifling ones." *Youngstown*, 343 U.S. 579, 640–641 (Jackson, J., concurring).

13. Bellia, "Story of the *Steel Seizure* Case," 251–252, citing transcript of proceedings before district court in *Youngstown*.

14. Marcus, *Truman and the Steel Seizure Case*, 119.

15. In Locke's view, executive prerogative would be checked by the people's right to revolution. The Department of Justice lawyers identified peaceful checks instead but similarly looked to the people (or their elected representatives) as a check on emergency power. Ibid.

16. Ibid.

17. After government lawyers presented the administration's argument to the District Court, the press criticized the Justice Department for "assert[ing] that the President's power was unlimited." Ibid., 125. Members of Congress who had initially defended Truman's actions "took great pains to disassociate themselves from the view that the President's power was unlimited." Ibid.

18. April 27, 1952, letter from President Truman to C. S. Jones, reprinted in *Public Papers of Presidents of the United States, Harry S. Truman, 1945–1953* (Washington, DC: Government Printing Office, 1966), 301. In a supplemental memorandum filed with the court and in proceedings before the Supreme Court, the Department of Justice also attempted to retreat from its position that the courts had no role to play in reviewing emergency action by the president. Bellia, "Story of the *Steel Seizure* Case," 251, 256.

19. Ibid., 251, citing *Youngstown Sheet & Tube Co. v. Sawyer*, 103 F. Supp. 569, 573 (D.D.C. 1952).

20. Justice Clark concurred in the judgment only, meaning that he had reached the same conclusion as Justice Black but disagreed with the majority's reasoning. Four other justices—Jackson, Frankfurter, Burton, and Douglas—wrote concurring opinions that added to the reasoning cited by Justice Black in the majority opinion.

21. Bellia, "Story of the *Steel Seizure* Case," 263–265.

22. As Jackson himself had—he was attorney general from 1940 to 1941.

23. Louis Fisher, foreword to Marcus, *Truman and the Steel Seizure Case*, x. Fisher credited Marcus with making these points clear in her book.

24. Marcus, *Truman and the Steel Seizure Case*, 228. Marcus describes *Youngstown* as putting the brakes on "the trend toward concentration of power in the executive branch." Ibid., 259.

25. Fisher, foreword to *Truman and the Steel Seizure Case*, xii.

26. Bellia, "Story of the *Steel Seizure* Case," 271.

27. Patricia L. Bellia, "Executive Power in *Youngstown*'s Shadows," *Constitutional Commentary* 19 (2002): 87, 91: "Justice Jackson's tripartite framework for evaluating executive action is not a framework at all, nor did he necessarily intend it to be."

28. Though President Truman did not ignore the court's decision in *Youngstown*, as Lincoln had in *Merryman*.

29. *Youngstown*, 343 U.S. at 579, 654 (Jackson, J., concurring).

30. Ibid. at 645.

31. Although the fact that the president acts pursuant to congressional authorization or approval would not automatically legitimize such action: Jackson himself had dissented in *Korematsu*, despite the fact that the president and Congress had acted together to sanction the internment of Japanese Americans.

32. Bellia, "Story of the *Steel Seizure* Case," 275–282.

33. Of course, it may not always be clear when congressional approval (or disapproval) is *implied*. Ibid., 272.

34. Ibid., 276–277.

1. President Johnson claimed that the North Vietnamese attacked American ships twice in the Gulf of Tonkin in August 1964, although there was, in fact, no second attack. Johnson ordered an escalation of U.S. military action in Vietnam, and Congress ratified his action in the Gulf of Tonkin resolution, with Congress acting "particularly on the basis of the claimed second attack." Fisher, *Defending Congress and the Constitution*, 261–262.

2. Iwan Morgan, *Nixon* (New York: Oxford University Press, 2002), 156 ("Increasingly [as the Cold War developed in the 1950s and 1960s] Congress grew to accept its relative impotence in foreign policy as part of the natural order in a dangerous world that necessitated rapid deployment of American power").

3. Ibid., 158.

4. Ibid. ("Nixon's opponents were the entrenched interests of the nation's capital [members of Congress, journalists, federal bureaucrats, and Washington power brokers] while he as president . . . represented the real people in the country beyond").

5. Fred Emery, *Watergate: The Corruption of American Politics and the Fall of Richard Nixon* (New York: Times Books, 1994), 27; Keith W. Olson, *Watergate: The Presidential Scandal That Shook America* (Lawrence: University of Kansas Press, 2003), 30.

6. Schlesinger, *The Imperial Presidency*, 230–232; see also Morgan, *Nixon*, 159–160, 175.

7. Olson, *Watergate*, 16.

8. Named for White House aide Tom Charles Huston.

9. Olson, *Watergate*, 16–17; Morgan, *Nixon*, 175.

10. Olson, *Watergate*, 17–20; Morgan, *Nixon*, 175.

11. Olson, *Watergate*, 17–18. The Pentagon Papers were a secret history of the Vietnam War commissioned by Secretary of Defense Robert S. McNamara. The papers "revealed that four successive presidents [from Truman to Johnson], especially Johnson, had misled and deceived the public about Vietnam." Ibid.

12. Morgan, *Nixon*, 177.

13. Ibid.

14. Olson, *Watergate*, 18.

15. Ibid., 19–20.

16. Emery, *Watergate*, 47–48; Morgan, *Nixon*, 177. Although Nixon ordered the break-in at the Brookings Institute, his order was not carried out. Ken Hughes, "Nixon's Biggest Crime Was Far, Far Worse Than Watergate," History News Network, June 15, 2012, http://hnn.us/articles/nixons-biggest-crime-was-far-far-worse-watergate.

17. Schlesinger, *The Imperial Presidency*, 268–269; see also Morgan, *Nixon*, 179 ("The dirty tricks of the [1972] Nixon campaign . . . went far beyond the customary rough-and-tumble of American elections").

18. Olson, *Watergate*, 26.

19. Ibid., 30–33; see also Morgan, *Nixon*, 179.

20. Carl Bernstein and Bob Woodward, "FBI Finds Nixon Aides Sabotaged Democrats," *Washington Post*, October 10, 1972, http://www.washingtonpost.com/wp-srv/national/longterm/watergate/articles/101072-1.htm; see also Rick Perlstein, *Nixonland: The Rise of a President and the Fracturing of America* (New York: Scribner, 2008), 628–629. Although it is hard to conclusively determine whether the Nixon administration's efforts against Muskie were responsible for forcing him out of the race, Keith W. Olson concludes that it is clear that the Nixon administration sought this very result and that sabotage of Muskie's campaign was funded by Nixon's re-election campaign. Olson, *Watergate*, 33.

21. Olson, *Watergate*, 92, 179.

22. Schlesinger, *The Imperial Presidency*, 264.

23. Morgan, *Nixon*, 158.

24. Schlesinger, *The Imperial Presidency*, 266.

25. Ibid., 379; see also Morgan, *Nixon*, 165, 175–183.

26. Morgan, *Nixon*, 185. These events, which occurred on October 20, 1973, are known as the "Saturday Night Massacre."

27. Ibid.

28. Nixon had turned over a few tapes in November 1973, but none contained any incriminating information, although one tape did contain a mysterious eighteen-and-a-half-minute gap. Ibid., 186.

29. Justice Rehnquist recused himself because he had served in the Office of Legal Counsel in the Nixon administration.

30. A command to produce documents or other materials, as opposed to a subpoena *ad testificandum*, requiring live oral testimony.

31. "Richard M. Nixon: The Watergate Tapes," University of California, Berkeley Library website, http://www.lib.berkeley.edu/MRC/watergate.html (see June 23, 1972, recording and transcripts); see also Olson, *Watergate*, 155–159.

32. Senator Barry Goldwater (R-AZ) told Nixon's chief of staff, Alexander Haig, that there were only twelve votes for Nixon in the Senate—he would have needed thirty-four to avoid removal from office if the House voted to impeach and proceedings moved to the Senate. In addition, House Judiciary Committee chairman, Peter Rodino (D-NJ), sent the White House a message that Nixon would not face criminal charges if he resigned. Morgan, *Nixon*, 187.

CHAPTER 9. EMERGENCY PRESIDENTIAL POWER AT ITS ZENITH

1. See chapter 12.

2. Barton Gellman, *Angler: The Cheney Vice Presidency* (New York: Penguin Press, 2008), 100.

3. Ibid.

4. Cheney was the ranking member on the House select committee investigating the Iran-Contra affair. He did not personally write the minority report, but later explained that the views expressed in the report "[were] very good in laying

out a robust view of the President's prerogatives with respect to the conduct of especially foreign policy and national security matters." Vice President Cheney's Remarks to the Traveling Press, December 20, 2005, Office of the Vice President, http://georgewbush-whitehouse.archives.gov/news/releases/2005/12/20051220-9.html.

5. Lee H. Hamilton, Chairman, House Select Committee, and Daniel K. Inouye, Chairman, Senate Select Committee, *Report of the Congressional Committees Investigating the Iran-Contra Affair* (Washington, DC: U.S. Government Printing Office, 1987), 3–22.

6. Ibid., 18–19.

7. Ibid., 457 (minority report).

8. Ibid., 469 (minority report).

9. Ibid., 457 (minority report).

10. Ibid., 459 (minority report).

11. Stephen M. Griffin, "The National Security Constitution and the Bush Administration," *Yale Law Journal Online* 120 (March 25, 2011): 367, 378–379.

12. James P. Pfiffner, *Power Play: The Bush Presidency and the Constitution* (Washington, DC: Brookings Institution Press: 2008), 220–221.

13. Christopher S. Kelley, "Rethinking Presidential Power: The Unitary Executive and the George W. Bush Presidency," paper prepared for the annual meeting of the Midwest Political Science Association, Chicago, April 2005, 4, http://www.users.muohio.edu/kelleycs/paper.pdf.

14. Robert J. Spitzer, *Saving the Constitution from Lawyers: How Legal Training and Law Reviews Distort Constitutional Meaning* (New York: Cambridge University Press, 2008), 94–96, quoted in Pfiffner, *Power Play*, 220.

15. Scholars also discuss the idea of a "unitary executive" in another context to argue that presidents have plenary control over the executive branch, including the power to control and to remove all executive branch officials. See Steven G. Calabresi and Christopher S. Yoo, *The Unitary Executive: Presidential Power from Washington to Bush* (New Haven, CT: Yale University Press, 2008). The unitary executive theory discussed here is a different idea that describes a much broader vision of presidential power, as explained in this chapter.

16. U.S. Const., art. II, § 1, cl. 1.

17. U.S. Const., art. I, § 1 (emphasis added).

18. Yoo, *Crisis and Command*, xv.

19. Pfiffner, *Power Play*, 220, citing Kelley, "Rethinking Presidential Power," 4. See also chapter 3.

20. Kelley, "Rethinking Presidential Power," 6–8.

21. Mark Tushnet, "A Political Perspective on the Theory of the Unitary Executive," *University of Pennsylvania Journal of Constitutional Law* 12 (2010): 313, 323–324. Tushnet calls this a "super-strong theory of the unitary executive" in contrast with Calabresi and Yoo's weak theory of the unitary executive, which is described in note 15. Ibid., 315. Tushnet distinguishes between (a) the idea that the Take Care Clause empowers the president to set aside legislation "that in his view

encroached on authority the Constitution gave to the President alone" and (b) the idea that the Take Care Clause requires the president "to take care that the nation be preserved, to which the duty to take care that the laws, including the Constitution, be faithfully executed, is subordinate." Tushnet concludes that each of these views "became embedded in the super-strong theory of the unitary presidency with which the Bush administration became identified." Ibid., 324.

22. Fisher, *Defending Congress and the Constitution*, 14–15. David Gray Adler argues, however, that inherent power is not, strictly speaking, extraconstitutional since "[t]he claim of inherent executive power, however specious it may be, represents an effort to locate within the executive constitutional authority that exceeds the textual grant of enumerated powers, as well as implied authority that flows from that grant, but that, nonetheless, is derived from article II of the Constitution." "The Framers and Executive Prerogative: A Constitutional and Historical Rebuke," 378. On either view, however, inherent powers are not limited in the way that express or implied powers are.

23. Pfiffner, *Power Play*, 79.

24. U.S. Const., art. II, § 2.

25. *Youngstown*, 343 U.S. at 579, 640–641 (Jackson, J., concurring). Jackson noted that Article II expressly assigns the president the authority to "require the Opinion, in writing, of the principal Officer in each of the executive Departments, upon any Subject relating to the Duties of their respective Offices." Jackson asked why it would be necessary to specifically assign this power to the president if the Vesting Clause had already assigned *all* executive power to the president. The fact that the Framers spelled out this and other specific presidential powers "is a strong indication that they had not, by the vesting clause, already given the president extensive executive powers not specified in the Constitution." Pfiffner, *Power Play*, 79.

26. Fisher, *Defending Congress and the Constitution*, 13.

27. "The Framers and Executive Prerogative: A Constitutional and Historical Rebuke," 379–381. Adler concludes that "To the extent that there was a debate on 'executive power,' it centered almost entirely on the question of whether there should be a single or a plural presidency [i.e., whether one or more than person should wield executive power]." Ibid., 381. Adler also rejects the Take Care Clause as a basis for broad emergency presidential power, noting that "[t]he proposition that the duty to execute the laws carries with it the power to defy, violate, or create them would have surprised the framers." Ibid., 383.

28. Pfiffner, *Power Play*, 66.

29. Yoo, *Crisis and Command*, 3–4.

30. Pfiffner, *Power Play*, 79.

31. Scott M. Matheson Jr., *Presidential Constitutionalism in Perilous Times* (Cambridge, MA: Harvard University Press, 2009), 86.

32. Barron and Lederman, "The Commander in Chief at the Lowest Ebb—A Constitutional History," 948 (arguing that for most of American history, presidents did not make "preclusive claims of authority," in other words, claims of inherent

or plenary power allowing them to disregard laws they believed intruded on presidential power).

33. *Meet the Press* Transcript for September 14, 2003, http://www.msnbc.msn .com/id/3080244 (Vice President Cheney declaring during interview with Tim Russert that "9/11 changed everything").

34. Griffin, "The National Security Constitution and the Bush Administration," 379–380.

35. The Franklin D. Roosevelt administration asserted a claim of inherent power (i.e., claimed power to disregard statutory limits on presidential authority) when, during oral argument before the Supreme Court in the *Quirin* case (see chapter 5), Attorney General Francis Biddle suggested that the president could set aside statutory limitations imposed by Congress on military tribunals. Barron and Lederman, "The Commander in Chief at the Lowest Ebb—A Constitutional History," 1051–1052. However, Biddle backed away from this argument when challenged by Chief Justice Stone and the Court, in deciding the case, did not endorse the notion of unilateral presidential power to set aside statutory limits. Ibid., 1052–1055. Barron and Lederman assert, however, that the *Quirin* Court left open the question of whether presidents may sometimes set aside congressional limitations on presidential power. Ibid., 1053. Barron and Lederman note that other presidents made claims of inherent or plenary power after Roosevelt, but, "[c]ertainly there was no sustained practice of actually disregarding statutes similar to [what] we have seen since September 11, 2001." Ibid., 1099.

36. Several key memoranda were released in 2009. "Secret Bush Memos Releases," April 2, 2009, http://www.huffingtonpost.com/2009/03/02/secret-bush-memos-release_n_171221.html, and Sam Stein, "Bush Torture Memos Released by the Obama Administration: See the Complete Documents," June 9, 2009, http://www.huffingtonpost.com/2009/04/16/bush-torture-memos-release _n_187867.html. A more complete list of Bush-era OLC memoranda, including some that are still secret, appears at "The Missing Memos," http://www.propub lica.org/special/missing-memos.

37. Gellman, *Angler*, 133–134.

38. David Cole, ed., *The Torture Memos: Rationalizing the Unthinkable* (New York: New Press, 2009), 11.

39. Griffin, "The National Security Constitution and the Bush Administration," 383–384; see also Matheson, *Presidential Constitutionalism in Perilous Times*, 87, discussing influence of Vice President Cheney and executive branch lawyers on national security issues.

40. Gellman, *Angler*, 177.

41. Public Law 107–40, 115 Stat. 224 (2001), passed by the House and Senate on September 14, 2001, and signed into law by the president on September 18, 2001. The AUMF provided, in part, that the president "is authorized to use all necessary and appropriate force against those nations, organizations, or persons he determines planned, authorized, committed, or aided the terrorist attacks that occurred on September 11, 2001, or harbored such organizations or persons, in

order to prevent any future acts of international terrorism against the United States by such nations, organizations or persons." On September 23, 2001, President Bush declared a national emergency "with respect to persons who commit, threaten to commit, or support terrorism." The declaration of national emergency was renewed by President Obama on September 11, 2012. Continuation of the National Emergency with Respect to Persons Who Commit, Threaten to Commit, or Support Terrorism, 77 Fed. Reg. 56519 (November 16, 2001), https://federal register.gov/a/2012-22710.

42. September 25, 2001, Yoo memo.

43. Polk also sought and obtained congressional authorization for the use of military force against Mexico in the form of a declaration of war.

44. September 25, 2001, Yoo memo.

45. Ibid.

46. Ibid.

47. Yoo's memorandum was not made public for more than two years. Once the memo was made public, one commentator suggested that it had been intended to justify the later invasion of Iraq. Michael Isikoff, "2001 Memo Reveals Push for Broader Presidential Power," *Newsweek*, December 18, 2004, http://www.global policy.org/component/content/article/154/25721.html.

48. September 25, 2001, Yoo memo.

49. Yoo's memorandum was addressed to Timothy Flanigan, Deputy Counsel to the President. Flanigan was part of the "core legal team," along with Alberto Gonzales, the White House counsel, and David Addington, counsel to the vice president, that worked with Vice President Cheney to develop legal justification for broad presidential power after the September 11 attacks. See Gellman, *Angler*, 132–136.

50. Note: Louis Fisher observes that Jefferson's order was in fact "based on congressional authority." Fisher, *Presidential War Power*, 33.

51. Eric A. Posner and Adrian Vermeule, "A 'Torture' Memo and Its Tortuous Critics," *Wall Street Journal*, July 6, 2004, http://www.ericposner.com/torture memo.html.

52. Jack Balkin, "Vermeule and Posner Defend the Torture Memo," *Balkinization*, July 15, 2004, http://balkin.blogspot.com/2004/07/vermeule-and-posner-defend-torture.html.

53. *Youngstown*, 343 U.S. at 641–642 (Jackson, J., concurring).

54. Ibid. at 645.

55. Fisher, *Defending Congress and the Constitution*, 251–255.

56. In addition to other war powers, such as the authority to raise and support armies, traditionally assigned to the British king. Pfiffner, *Power Play*, 71.

57. September 25, 2001, Yoo memo.

58. Farrand, ed., *The Records of the Federal Convention of 1787*, vol. 2, 318–319; see also Pfiffner, *Power Play*, 77.

59. Fisher, *Defending Congress and the Constitution*, 241.

60. Ibid.

61. M. Andrew Campanelli, Kai Draper, and Jack Stucker, "The Original Understanding of the Declare War Clause," 24 *Journal of Law and Politics* 24 (Winter 2008): 49.

62. Rakove, *Original Meanings*, 263.

63. Pfiffner, *Power Play*, 68, see also Fisher, *Defending Congress and the Constitution*, 241.

64. Matheson, *Presidential Constitutionalism in Perilous Times*, 40: "In the *Prize* Cases, the Court in a 5-4 decision upheld Lincoln's actions on the narrow ground of presidential power to repel sudden attacks arising from domestic rebellion before Congress can be assembled."

65. Pfiffner, *Power Play*, 75.

66. Ibid., quoting John Jay, Federalist No. 4.

67. Pfiffner, *Power Play*, 74-75, quoting Gaillard Hunt, ed., *The Writings of James Madison* (New York: G. P. Putnam's Sons, 1900-10), 6:174.

68. Pfiffner, *Power Play*, 74, quoting *Helvidius* in *The Writings of James Madison*, 6:146 (emphasis in original).

69. Pfiffner, *Power Play*, 70-71; see also Fisher, *Defending Congress and the Constitution*, 235-241.

70. Pfiffner, *Power Play*, 74, quoting *The Works of Alexander Hamilton*, ed. John C. Hamilton (New York: John F. Trow), 3:746 (emphasis in original).

71. *The Federalist Papers*, Federalist No. 69, 193-195 (emphasis in original). See also Pfiffner, *Power Play*, 74, quoting Federalist No. 69.

72. A point Yoo has emphasized in subsequent writing. In *Crisis and Command*, Yoo emphasizes the "importance of *practice* as a source of constitutional meaning." Yoo, *Crisis and Command*, xvii.

73. September 25, 2001, Yoo memo.

74. Ibid.

75. Fisher, *Presidential War Power*, 100.

76. Ibid., 81.

77. Ibid., 91.

78. Ibid., 101, quoting Edward S. Corwin, "The President's Power," *New Republic*, January 29, 1951, 16.

79. Pfiffner, *Power Play*, 70.

80. Yoo, *Crisis and Command*, xvii.

81. Posner and Vermeule, *The Executive Unbound: After the Madisonian Republic*, 74.

82. Matheson, *Presidential Constitutionalism in Perilous Times*, 8, quoting Justice Frankfurter's concurring opinion in *Youngstown*.

CHAPTER 10. DETAINING AND TRYING
SUSPECTED TERRORISTS

1. Geneva Convention Relative to the Treatment of Prisoners of War, adopted August 12, 1949, http://www2.ohchr.org/english/law/prisonerwar.htm.

2. Ibid.

3. Ibid. Under the GPW, "[e]very prisoner of war, when questioned on the subject, is bound to give only his surname, first names and rank, date of birth, and army, regimental, personal or serial number, or failing this, equivalent information."

4. GPW, Article 17.

5. As the Supreme Court explained in *Hamdan v. Rumsfeld*, "[t]he term 'conflict not of an international character' is used here in contradistinction to a conflict between nations." 548 U.S. 557 (2006). In other words, a conflict between a nation and a group that is not a nation is "conflict not of an international character," that is, conflict that is not between nations.

6. Court decisions discussed in this chapter refer to prisoners as "detainees." The two words are used interchangeably in this chapter. A prisoner is not necessarily a prisoner of war.

7. Prepared text of Attorney General Eric Holder's March 5, 2012, speech at Northwestern University School of Law, http://www.justice.gov/iso/opa/ag/speeches/2012/ag-speech-1203051.html.

8. Note: a central question is whether prisoners are, in fact, terrorists. Philbin's opinion assumes that they are. Prisoners whose status has not yet been determined would be better referred to as "suspected terrorists."

9. Note: Article 21 provides: "The provisions of this chapter conferring jurisdiction upon courts-martial do not deprive military commissions, provost courts, or other military tribunals of concurrent jurisdiction with respect to offenders or offenses that by statute or by the law of war may be tried by military commissions, provost courts, or other military tribunals." As we'll see, the Supreme Court later concluded that this provision did *not* give the president unlimited authority to set up military commissions at his or her discretion.

10. Note: this historical discussion is factually incorrect, as discussed later.

11. Note: "with even stronger reason."

12. Recall the critique of inherent powers offered by Louis Fisher, as mentioned in chapter 9.

13. Scott Horton, "Six Questions for Louis Fisher, Author of *The Constitution and 9/11*," *Harper's Magazine*, January 5, 2009, http://www.harpers.org/archive/2009/01/hbc-90004121.

14. Fisher, *Military Tribunals and Presidential Power*, 65–69.

15. The memo itself was kept secret at the time, and was not released for several years. Gellman, *Angler*, 136, n. 36.

16. Military Order of November 13, 2001: Detention, Treatment, and Trial of Certain Non-Citizens in the War against Terrorism, 66 Fed. Reg. 57,833, November 16, 2001, http://www.fas.org/irp/offdocs/eo/mo-111301.htm.

17. Ibid.

18. A standard that could include hearsay evidence or evidence obtained through coercion or torture.

19. Military Order of November 13, 2001.

20. Ibid.

21. Matheson, *Presidential Constitutionalism in Perilous Times*, 130.

22. The president's order did not directly apply to U.S. citizens but included the provision that "Nothing in this order shall be construed to . . . limit the lawful authority of the Secretary of Defense, any military commander, or any other officer or agent of the United States . . . to detain or try *any* person who is not an individual subject to this order." Military Order of November 13, 2001, emphasis added. The president ultimately claimed this authority to designate U.S. citizens as enemy combatants and to detain them indefinitely, as discussed in the *Hamdi* case, discussed later in this chapter.

23. Ibid.

24. Military Commission Order No. 1, March 21, 2002: Procedures for Trials by Military Commissions of Certain Non-United States Citizens in the War against Terrorism, http://www.defense.gov/news/Mar2002/d20020321ord.pdf.

25. The Order avoided referring to them as "defendants."

26. Military Commission Order No. 1, March 21, 2002.

27. Ibid.

28. Ibid.

29. Matheson, *Presidential Constitutionalism in Perilous Times*, 129.

30. Gellman, *Angler*, 171; see also Pfiffner, *Power Play*, 99.

31. *Johnson v. Eisentrager*, 399 U.S. 763 (1950).

32. Joseph Margulies, *Guantanamo and the Abuse of Presidential Power* (New York: Simon and Schuster, 2006), 49–50.

33. Most prisoners placed in the military system were simply detained rather than tried. During the Bush administration, just three prisoners were convicted by military tribunals. By contrast, nearly two hundred terrorists were convicted in federal civilian courts. Richard M. Pious, "Prerogative Power in the Obama Administration: Continuity and Change in the War on Terrorism," *Presidential Studies Quarterly* 41, no. 2 (June 2011): 272.

34. Ibid.

35. Tom Lasseter, "America's Prisons Often Held the Wrong Men," *McClatchy Newspapers*, June 15, 2008, http://www.mcclatchydc.com/guantanamo/story /38773.html?storylink=MI_emailed.

36. As of January 2012, 171 detainees remained in Guantanamo. About eighty of these have been cleared for release but are still being held. Forty-eight have been deemed too dangerous to release, though there are no plans to try them. Dina Temple-Raston, "Guantanamo at 10: U.S. Weighs Future of Detainees," *NPR*, January 11, 2012, http://www.npr.org/2012/01/11/145011208/guantanamo-at-10-u-s-weighs-future-of-detainees.

37. Shafiq Rasul himself was released from custody before the court issued its opinion in the case that bears his name.

38. *Rasul v. Bush*, 542 U.S. 466, 473 (2004), *superseded by statute*, Detainee Treatment Act of 2005, Pub. L. No. 109-148, div. A, 1001-06, 119 Stat. 2680, 2739, quoting 28 U.S.C. §§ 2241(a), (c)(3).

39. *Rasul*, 542 U.S. at 474.

40. Ibid. at 474–475.

41. Justice Kennedy wrote a separate opinion, concurring in the judgment.

42. *Rasul,* 542 U.S. at 480–481.

43. Ibid. at 506.

44. Ibid. at 485.

45. Most applicable constitutional protections—for instance, the Sixth Amendment right to a speedy jury trial and the Fifth Amendment Due Process Clause—are not expressly limited to citizens only. However, in some cases, courts have recognized greater protections for citizens during time of war—in part, because of the Alien Enemies Act, which authorizes detention and deportation of "enemy aliens" during wartime.

46. Margulies, *Guantanamo,* 156.

47. Note: the Non-Detention Act, passed by Congress in 1971 and intended to prevent the United States from establishing internment camps again, as was done with 110,000 Japanese Americans during World War II.

48. Note: in contrast with the standard in civilian criminal cases, which places the burden on the government to prove the defendant's guilt beyond a reasonable doubt.

49. Note: "During war, law is silent."

50. Note that this claim went even further than the president's Military Order of November 13, 2001, which only specifically asserted the president's authority to unilaterally designate noncitizens as enemy combatants. The November 13 order reserved the president's right to designate *any* individual as subject to detention, a power which was ultimately exercised with regard to U.S. citizens, such as Hamdi.

51. Posner and Vermeule, *The Executive Unbound,* 35.

52. Fisher, *The Constitution and 9/11,* 196.

53. Louis Fisher observes that the allegations against Hamdi, even if true, "describe[d] Hamdi as involved in a civil war between the Taliban and Northern Alliance, not a terrorist's action directed against the United States." Ibid., 191.

54. Margulies, *Guantanamo,* 156. The government never fully explained either why Hamdi had been detained or why he was released, saying only that "considerations of United States national security did not require his continued detention." Jerry Markon, "Hamdi Returned to Saudi Arabia," *Washington Post,* October 12, 2004, http://www.washingtonpost.com/wp-dyn/articles/A23958-2004Oct11.html. To gain his release, Hamdi had to agree to renounce his U.S. citizenship, to move to Saudi Arabia, and not to sue the U.S. government. Fisher, *The Constitution and 9/11,* 196–197.

55. Deputy Secretary of Defense Paul Wolfowitz, Memorandum for the Secretary of the Navy: Order Establishing Combatant Status Review Tribunal, July 7, 2004 (hereinafter July 7, 2004, Wolfowitz memo), http://www.defense.gov/news/Jul2004/d20040707review.pdf.

56. Ibid.; see also Margulies, *Guantanamo,* 159–170.

57. Margulies, *Guantanamo,* 169.

58. July 7, 2004, Wolfowitz memo.

59. Ibid.

60. Margulies, *Guantanamo*, 162.

61. Ibid., 163–164.

62. Ibid., 164–165.

63. Ibid., 167.

64. This is distinguished from the beyond a reasonable doubt standard used in criminal trials. The preponderance of the evidence standard is met by showing it is "more likely than not" that the position of the party bearing the burden of proof is correct. Generally, this means showing better than a 50–50 chance that the claim is correct. In other words, CSRT members would find the prisoner to be an enemy combatant if they concluded this was "more likely than not" the case. The beyond a reasonable doubt standard is far more demanding.

65. July 7, 2004, Wolfowitz memo. For further discussion of the CSRT process, see Mark Denbeaux and Joshua Denbeaux, "Report on Guantanamo Detainees: A Profile of 517 Detainees through Analysis of Department of Defense Data," February 8, 2006, http://law.shu.edu/publications/guantanamoReports /guantanamo_report_final_2_08_06.pdf; Mark P. Denbeaux and Joshua Denbeaux, "Second Report on the Guantanamo Detainees: Inter- and Intra-Departmental Disagreements about Who Is Our Enemy," March 20, 2006, http://law.shu.edu /publications/guantanamoReports/second_report_guantanamo_detainees_3_20 _final.pdf.

66. Pub. L. No. 109–148, 119 Stat. 2739 (2005); Pub. L. No. 109–163, 119 Stat. 3136 (2006). The Detainee Treatment Act was "enacted pursuant to both the Department of Defense, Emergency Supplemental Appropriations to Address Hurricanes in the Gulf of Mexico, and Pandemic Influenza Act, 2006 (P[ub].L. [No.] 109–148, Title X), and the National Defense Authorization Act for FY2006 (P[ub].L. [No.] 109–163, Title XIV)." Michael John Garcia, "Interrogation of Detainees: Requirements of the Detainee Treatment Act," Congressional Research Service, August 26, 2009, http://www.fas.org/sgp/crs/intel/RL33655.pdf.

67. Pub. L. No. 109–148, 119 Stat. 2739; Pub. L. No. 109–163, 119 Stat. 3136.

68. Ibid.

69. Ibid.

70. Ibid.

71. The DTA provided that the Department of Defense would need to provide for periodic review of new evidence, but said nothing about judicial review of new evidence. Ibid.

72. Ibid.

73. A successor to the 2002 Military Commission Order discussed earlier.

74. Pub. L. No. 109–148, 119 Stat. 2739; Pub. L. No. 109–163, 119 Stat. 3136.

75. Pfiffner, *Power Play*, 106.

76. Chief Justice Roberts recused himself because he had participated in the case as a judge on the D.C. Circuit Court of Appeals before joining the Supreme Court.

77. Note: from Chief Justice Chase's concurring opinion in *Milligan*.

78. Note: when the Articles of War were revised.

79. Fisher, *The Constitution and 9/11*, 239; see also Glenn Greenwald, "The Significance of Hamdan v. Rumsfeld," *Unclaimed Territory*, June 29, 2006, http://glenn greenwald.blogspot.com/2006/06/significance-of-hamdan-v-rumsfeld.html.

80. The bill that the Bush administration supported initially contained language stating that "[t]he President's authority to convene military commissions arises from the Constitution's vesting in the President of the executive power and the power of the Commander in Chief of the Armed Forces." Fisher, *The Constitution and 9/11*, 241, quoting S. 3861, 109th Cong., § 2(3) (2006). Fisher observes that the administration's approach to the legislative process ignored the limits the court had attempted to place on executive power in *Hamdan*. Fisher, *The Constitution and 9/11*, 239. The Bush administration continued to assert a view that broad, unilateral executive power provided the foundational authority for a military tribunal system. The proposed language quoted here was removed from the bill that was ultimately enacted as law.

81. Fisher, *The Constitution and 9/11*, 239–240.

82. Statement by Lieutenant Commander Charles D. Swift, JAGC, U.S. Navy, during hearings before the Senate Committee on the Judiciary, 109th Congress (2006), quoted in Fisher, *The Constitution and 9/11*, 240.

83. Pfiffner, *Power Play*, 108.

84. Pub. L. No. 109-366, 120 Stat. 2601 (2006), § 948c.

85. Ibid., § 948a(1)(A)(i) and (ii).

86. Ibid., § 949a(a).

87. Ibid., §§ 948i and j.

88. Ibid., §§ 948k, 949c(b)(3).

89. Ibid., § 949a(b)(2)(A).

90. Ibid., § 949a(b)(2)(D)(i).

91. Ibid., § 949a(b)(2)(E)(ii).

92. Unless they were used against a person accused of torture.

93. Ibid. (2006), §§ 948r(b) and (c).

94. Ibid., § 948r(c).

95. Ibid., § 948r(d).

96. Fisher, *The Constitution and 9/11*, 243.

97. Pub. L. No. 109-366, 120 Stat. 2601 (2006), § 949d(f).

98. Ibid., § 949d(f)(2)(A).

99. Ibid., § 949d(f)(2)(B).

100. Fisher, *The Constitution and 9/11*, 243.

101. Pub. L. No. 109-366, 120 Stat. 2601 (2006), § 6(a)(3)(A).

102. Ibid., § 6(b)(1)(B)(1).

103. The 2006 MCA provided for a newly created Court of Military Commission Review to review decisions by military commissions before they could be appealed to the court of appeals. The Court of Military Commission Review would be composed of military judges. Ibid., § 950f.

104. Though now, under the 2006 MCA, those provisions were created, at least in part, by Congress.

105. Ibid., § 950g(c). The 2006 MCA also provided that both the court of appeals and the Court of Military Commission Review could "act only with respect to matters of law." Ibid., §§ 950f(d), 950g(b).

106. Ibid., § 950g(d).

107. Ibid., § 7(a).

108. Ibid., § 7(b).

109. The 2006 MCA has since been supplanted by the Military Commissions Act of 2009.

110. *Boumediene v. Bush*, 553 U.S. 723, 743 (2008).

111. Ibid. at 745.

112. Ibid. at 765.

113. Ibid. at 765.

114. Ibid. at 767.

115. Ibid. at 768–769.

116. Ibid. at 771.

117. Ibid. at 783–784.

118. Ibid. at 777.

119. Ibid. at 785, quoting *Frank v. Mangum*, 237 U.S. 309, 346 (1915) (Holmes, J., dissenting).

120. Ibid. at 786.

121. The court observed that the possibility that a prisoner might be denied access to evidence that became available after the CSRT proceeding was "not a remote hypothetical. One of the petitioners, Mohamed Nechla, requested at his CSRT hearing that the Government contact his employer. The petitioner claimed the employer would corroborate Nechla's contention he had no affiliation with Al Qaeda. Although the CSRT determined this testimony would be relevant, it also found the witness was not reasonably available to testify at the time of the hearing. Petitioner's counsel, however, now represents the witness is available to be heard." *Boumediene*, 553 U.S. at 790.

122. Ibid. at 785.

123. Ibid. at 795.

124. Glenn Greenwald, "Supreme Court Restores Habeas Corpus, Strikes Down Key Part of Military Commissions Act," *Salon.com*, June 12, 2008, http://www.salon.com/2008/06/12/boumediene.

125. The Bush administration had itself released or transferred more than 500 detainees once held at Guantanamo Bay. Bill Adair, "More than 500 Guantanamo Detainees Were Released or Transferred Under Bush," Politifact.com, June 18,

2009, http://www.politifact.com/truth-o-meter/statements/2009/jun/18/steny-hoyer/hoyer-correct-500-guantanamo-detainees-were-releas/.

126. Gellman, *Angler*, 171.

CHAPTER 11. TORTURE IN THE WAR ON TERROR

1. Pfiffner, *Power Play*, 128.

2. Cole, *The Torture Memos*, 8, quoting Cofer Black, director of the CIA's Counterterrorism Center, testifying in 2002 before Congress.

3. Ibid., 5; see also Tom Lasseter, "U.S. Abuse of Detainees Was Routine at Afghanistan Bases," McClatchy Newspapers, June 16, 2008, http://www.mcclatchydc.com/detainees/story/38775.html.

4. Pfiffner, *Power Play*, 146–149.

5. Ibid., 147.

6. This opinion was rejected, in a different context, by the Supreme Court in the *Hamdan* decision, which concluded that the Common Article 3 of the Geneva Conventions *does* apply to captured members of Al Qaeda. See chapter 10. In addition to the provisions addressed in the *Hamdan* decision, Common Article 3 prohibits parties to the Geneva Conventions from causing violence to any prisoners who have laid down their arms, including through "cruel treatment and torture," and protects prisoners from "outrages upon personal dignity, in particular humiliating and degrading treatment."

7. Memorandum opinion from Alberto Gonzales to the President, *Decision Re: Application of the Geneva Conventions on Prisoners of War to the Conflict with Al Qaeda and the Taliban* (January 25, 2002), http://www.gwu.edu/~nsarchiv/NSAEBB/NSAEBB127/02.01.25.pdf.

8. Ibid. The federal War Crimes Act of 1996, 18 U.S.C. § 2441, defines a "war crime" as a "grave breach" of the Geneva Conventions, including a grave breach of Common Article 3. The War Crimes Act specifically defines torture, cruel or inhuman treatment, and the intentional causation of serious bodily injury as grave breaches of Common Article 3. 18 U.S.C. §§ 2441(d)(1)(A), (B), (F). Violations of the War Crimes Act are punishable by a prison sentence for life or some shorter period or by the death penalty. 18 U.S.C. § 2441(a).

9. FBI interrogators relied on more traditional interrogation methods based on gaining the prisoner's trust, as opposed to using the methods discussed here. There are also reports of disagreement within the CIA, suggesting that not all CIA interrogators supported the use of waterboarding. David Johnston, "FBI, CIA Tussled over Interrogation: Interviews Show Agents Disagreed on How to Question al-Qaida Henchman," *Houston Chronicle*, September 10, 2006, 4 Star edition, http://www.chron.com/CDA/archives/archive.mpl/2006_4187675/fbi-cia-tussled-over-interrogation-interviews-show.html; see also Spencer Ackerman, "Former FBI Agent Testifies to CIA Contractor Push for Harsh Interrogation," *The Washington Independent*, May 13, 2009, http://washingtonindependent

.com/42903/former-fbi-agent-testifies-to-cia-contractor-push-for-harsh-interrogation. A 2005 Justice Department memorandum states that "[t]he CIA used the waterboard extensively in the interrogations of [Khalid Sheikh Muhammed] and [Abu] Zubaydah, but did so only after it became clear that standard interrogation techniques were not working." Memorandum opinion from Principal Deputy Assistant Attorney General Stephen G. Bradbury to Senior Deputy General Counsel of the CIA John Rizzo, *Re: Application of United States Obligations under Section 16 of the Convention against Torture to Certain Techniques That May Be Used in the Interrogation of High-Value al Qaeda Detainees*, May 30, 2005, http://media.luxmedia.com/aclu/olc_05302005_bradbury.pdf.

10. 18 U.S.C. §§ 2340–2340B. The federal antitorture statute applies to torture committed outside the United States; already existing criminal law was deemed "sufficient to prohibit torture committed within the United States." Matheson, *Presidential Constitutionalism in Perilous Times*, 197 n. 36.

11. 18 U.S.C. § 2340(1).

12. 18 U.S.C. § 2340A(a).

13. Gellman, *Angler*, 174–179, 182–184.

14. Cole, *The Torture Memos*, 14.

15. The government later concluded that Abu Zubaydah was not a high-level Al Qaeda official and not even an "official" Al Qaeda member, though he did work with Al Qaeda after the September 11, 2001, attacks. Peter Finn and Joby Warrick, "Detainee's Harsh Treatment Foiled No Plots," *Washington Post*, March 29, 2009, http://www.washingtonpost.com/wp-dyn/content/article/2009/03/28/AR2009032802066.html?nav=hcmodule.

16. Marc Ambinder, "What the CIA Did," *The Atlantic*, April 16, 2009, http://politics.theatlantic.com/2009/04/the_torture_memos.php. The insect tactic, though approved, was apparently never used. It is strikingly similar to the book *1984*'s infamous fictional account of Winston Smith's torment by rats in Room 101. Orwell's Room 101 contained whatever a prisoner feared most (for Smith, it was rats). See Scott Horton, "Revealing the Secrets in Room 101," *Harper's Magazine*, April 18, 2009, http://www.harpers.org/archive/2009/04/hbc-90004803.

17. Eric Weiner, "Waterboarding: A Tortured History," *NPR*, November 3, 2007, http://www.npr.org/templates/story/story.php?storyId=15886834.

18. Evan Wallach, "Waterboarding Used to Be a Crime," *Washington Post*, November 4, 2007, http://www.washingtonpost.com/wp-dyn/content/article/2007/11/02/AR2007110201170.html.

19. *United States v. Lee*, 744 F.2d 1124 (5th Cir. 1984).

20. Memorandum from Assistant Attorney General Jay S. Bybee to Acting General Counsel of the CIA John Rizzo, *Interrogation of al Qaeda Operative* (August 1, 2002) (hereinafter August 1, 2002, Bybee memo), http://media.luxmedia.com/aclu/olc_08012002_bybee.pdf.

21. Waterboarding is used to train members of the U.S. military in order to prepare them for the possibility that they might be captured and waterboarded.

Frederick A. O. Schwartz Jr. and Aziz Z. Huq, *Unchecked and Unbalanced: Presidential Power in a Time of Terror* (New York: New Press, 2007), 84.

22. Spencer Ackerman, "Former Navy Instructor Offers Another Waterboarding Primer for Mukasey," *TPM Muckraker*, October 31, 2007, http://tpmmuckraker.talkingpointsmemo.com/archives/004617.php.

23. Megan Lane and Brian Wheeler, "The Real Victims of Sleep Deprivation," *BBC News Online Magazine*, January 8, 2004, http://news.bbc.co.uk/2/hi/3376951.stm.

24. Ibid.

25. Ibid.

26. *Ashcraft v. Tennessee*, 322 U.S. 143 (1944).

27. Ibid. at 154.

28. Ibid. at 150 n. 6.

29. Ibid. at 155.

30. August 1, 2002, Bybee memo.

31. Ibid.; see also Cole, *The Torture Memos*, 15.

32. Memorandum from Assistant Attorney General Jay S. Bybee to Alberto R. Gonzales, Counsel to the President, *Re: Standards of Conduct for Interrogation under 18 U.S.C. §§ 2340–2340A*, August 1, 2002, http://www.justice.gov/olc/docs/memo-gonzales-aug2002.pdf. Although Bybee signed the memo, John Yoo drafted it. David Cole, "The Torture Memos: The Case against the Lawyers," *New York Review of Books*, October 8, 2009, 14, http://www.nybooks.com/articles/archives/2009/oct/08/the-torture-memos-the-case-against-the-lawyers/?pagination=false. Accordingly, I will refer to it as the "Yoo-Bybee memo." The Yoo-Bybee memo is a companion to the previously discussed but separate memorandum also dated August 1, 2002, which I refer to as the August 1, 2002, Bybee memo.

33. Matheson, *Presidential Constitutionalism in Perilous Times*, 90.

34. Cole, *The Torture Memos*, 14–17.

35. Ibid., 21.

36. Yoo-Bybee memo.

37. Ibid.; see also Cole, *The Torture Memos*, 21–22.

38. Gellman, *Angler*, 183; see also Cole, *The Torture Memos*, 23–24.

39. "Abu Zubaydah," *New York Times*, Times Topics, updated April 20, 2009, http://topics.nytimes.com/topics/reference/timestopics/people/z/abu_zubaydah/index.html.

40. Scott Shane, "Waterboarding Used 266 Times on 2 Suspects," *New York Times*, April 19, 2009, http://www.nytimes.com/2009/04/20/world/20detain.html.

41. Ibid.

42. Cole, *The Torture Memos*, 21–22.

43. If convicted of torture, a defendant faces a fine or up to twenty years' imprisonment or both. If, however, the act resulted in the victim's death, a defendant may be sentenced to life imprisonment or to death. See 18 U.S.C.A. §§ 2340A(a). . . . [Note: this note appears in original text as footnote 1.]

44. Note: CAT and the antitorture law provide criminal penalties only for torture, not for cruel, inhuman, or degrading treatment or punishment.

45. Note: after this memo was written, there was a prosecution under the anti-torture law. Elise Keppler, Shirley Jean, and J. Paxton Marshall, "First Prosecution in the United States for Torture Committed Abroad: The Trial of Charles 'Chuckie' Taylor," *The Human Rights Brief* 15, 3 (2008), http://digitalcommons.wcl .american.edu/hrbrief/vol15/iss3.

46. Yoo-Bybee memo.

47. Department of Justice, Office of Professional Responsibility Report: Investigation Into the Office of Legal Counsel's Memorandum Concerning Issues Relating to the Central Intelligence Agency's Use of "Enhanced Interrogation Techniques" on Suspected Terrorists, July 29, 2009, 230, http://judiciary.house.gov /hearings/pdf/OPRFinalReport090729.pdf.

48. Christopher H. Schroeder, testimony to the Subcommittee on the Constitution, Civil Rights and Civil Liberties, Committee on the Judiciary, U.S. House of Representatives, June 26, 2008; see also Balkin, "Vermeule and Posner Defend the Torture Memo."

49. Matheson, *Presidential Constitutionalism in Perilous Times*, 105.

50. Ibid., 104.

51. Shane, "Waterboarding Used 266 Times on 2 Suspects."

52. Ambinder, "What the CIA Did."

53. Cole, *The Torture Memos*, 16.

54. Ibid.

55. Bob Woodward, "Guantanamo Detainee Was Tortured, Says Officials Overseeing Military Trials," *Washington Post*, January 14, 2009, http://www .washingtonpost.com/wp-dyn/content/article/2009/01/13/AR2009011303372 .html.

56. Ibid.; see also Cole, *The Torture Memos*, 16.

57. Mark Tran, "FBI Files Detail Guantanamo Torture Tactics," *The Guardian*, January 3, 2007, http://www.guardian.co.uk/world/2007/jan/03/guan tanamo.usa.

58. Susie Madrak, "Trickle-Down Torture: Rumsfeld Memo Used to Justify Torture in Gitmo, Afghanistan and Iraq," *Crooks and Liars*, April 22, 2009, http:// crooksandliars.com/susie-madrak/trickle-down-torture-rumsfeld-memo-us.

59. Lasseter, "U.S. Abuse of Detainees Was Routine at Afghanistan Bases."

60. Cole, *The Torture Memos*, 17.

61. Ibid.

62. "U.S. Operatives Killed Detainees during Interrogations in Afghanistan and Iraq," American Civil Liberties Union, October 24, 2005, http://www.aclu .org/human-rights-national-security/us-operatives-killed-detainees-during- interrogations-afghanistan-and-.

63. Scott Horton, "The Bush Era Torture-Homicides," *Harper's Magazine*, May 7, 2009, http://www.harpers.org/archive/2009/05/hbc-90004921.

64. Ambinder, "What the CIA Did."

65. Glenn Greenwald, "Eric Holder Announces Investigation Based on Abu Ghraib Model," *Salon.com*, August 24, 2009, http://www.salon.com/2009/08/24/holder_9/.

66. Scott Lemieux, "Torture without Accountability," *The American Prospect*, September 3, 2012, http://prospect.org/article/torture-without-accountability.

67. See Scott Horton, "Overseas, Expectations Build for Torture Prosecutions," *Harper's Magazine*, January 19, 2009, http://www.harpers.org/archive/2009/01/hbc-90004233.

68. "Extraordinary rendition" is the practice of transferring suspected terrorists to other countries for interrogation and detention—in the case addressed by the Italian court, CIA agents seized a Muslim cleric in Italy and sent him to Egypt, where he was tortured. The countries where detainees are sent are often seen as places that use interrogation methods not in compliance with the law—in other words, countries that torture. See, e.g., Schwartz and Huq, *Unchecked and Unbalanced*, 97–123.

69. "CIA Agents Guilty of Italy Kidnap," *BBC News*, November 4, 2009, http://news.bbc.co.uk/2/hi/europe/8343123.stm.

CHAPTER 12. WARRANTLESS WIRETAPPING

1. Formally known as the U.S. Senate Select Committee to Study Governmental Operations with Respect to Intelligence Activities. See Pfiffner, *Power Play*, 172; see also "The Church Committee and FISA," *Bill Moyers Journal*, October 26, 2007, http://www.pbs.org/moyers/journal/10262007/profile2.html.

2. Operation Shamrock ran from August 1945 through May 1975. Louis Fisher, *Constitutional Limitations on Domestic Surveillance*, Statement before the House Committee on the Judiciary (June 7, 2007), 2, http://loc.gov/law/help/us conlaw/pdf/tsp-house-judiciary.pdf; see also Katelyn Epsley-Jones and Christina Frenzel, "The Church Committee Hearings and the FISA Court," *PBS Frontline: Spying on the Home Front*, May 15, 2007, http://www.pbs.org/wgbh/pages/frontline/homefront/preemption/churchfisa.html.

3. Jon Ponder, "Operation Shamrock: NSA's First Domestic Spying Program Was Revealed by Congress in 1975," *Pensito Review*, May 13, 2006, http://www.pensitoreview.com/2006/05/13/operation-shamrock-nsas-first-domestic-spying-program-was-shut-down-by-congress-in-1975.

4. Gellman, *Angler*, 141.

5. FISA also addresses physical searches and other methods of gathering foreign intelligence not relevant for our purposes.

6. U.S.C. § 1809.

7. FISA defines a "foreign power" to include foreign governments, groups engaged in international terrorism or preparations for international terrorism, entities controlled by foreign governments, and foreign based political organizations. 50 U.S.C. § 1801(a).

8. 50 U.S.C. § 1802.

9. 50 U.S.C. § 1805(e)(1)(D). When FISA was first enacted, in 1978, the attorney general could authorize emergency surveillance for up to twenty-four hours without a warrant. That window was enlarged to seventy-two hours in December 2001 and has since been enlarged to seven days under the current FISA, as amended.

10. 50 U.S.C. § 1811.

11. There is also an appeals court, the Foreign Intelligence Surveillance Court of Review.

12. 50 U.S.C. § 1803(a).

13. 50 U.S.C. § 1805(a)(2). An "agent of a foreign power" can include, among other things, a U.S. citizen or legal resident who is engaged in "sabotage or international terrorism" on behalf of a foreign power. 50 U.S.C. § 1801(b)(2). However, no U.S. citizen or legal resident "may be considered a foreign power or an agent of a foreign power solely upon the basis of activities protected by the first amendment to the Constitution of the United States." 50 U.S.C. § 1805(a)(2)(A).

14. The FISC almost never denies an application for a warrant; in fact, between 1978 and 2005, the FISA court granted more than eighteen thousand warrant applications and denied just five. Pfiffner, *Power Play*, 175.

15. Gellman, *Angler*, 141.

16. Enacted in October 2001.

17. For one perspective on roving wiretaps, see Julian Sanchez, "PATRIOT Powers: Roving Wiretaps," Cato@Liberty, October 15, 2009, http://www.cato-at-liberty.org/2009/10/15/patriot-powers-roving-wiretaps.

18. Gellman, *Angler*, 142–143.

19. "Unclassified Report on the President's Surveillance Program," July 10, 2009, http://www.globalsecurity.org/intell/library/reports/2009/psp-oigs_090710.pdf.

20. The description of these activities later in this chapter, including quoted statements, is derived from the July 2009 Inspectors General report. Ibid.

21. Fisher, *Constitutional Limitations on Domestic Surveillance*, 9. The Gang of Eight consists of each party's leaders in the House and Senate as well as the chairs and vice chairs of the intelligence committees. During these briefings, congressional leaders were not permitted to bring staff members and were not permitted to take notes or to discuss the program with other members of Congress. Ibid. There is disagreement as to whether the Gang of Eight was fully briefed on the program: former Representative Jane Harman (D-CA) says the briefings covered "the operational details of the program" but not the "legal underpinning." Transcript, "Congress Granted Oversight for NSA Surveillance Program," *PBS NewsHour*, February 8, 2006, http://www.pbs.org/newshour/bb/politics/jan-june 06/nsa_02-08.html. Former Senator Bob Graham (D-FL) similarly claimed that "[t]here was no reference made to the fact that we were going to . . . begin unwarranted, illegal, and I think unconstitutional eavesdropping on American citizens." Sidney Blumenthal, *How Bush Rules: Chronicles of a Radical Regime*

(Princeton, NJ: Princeton University Press, 2006), 316. Another Gang of Eight member, Senator Jay Rockefeller (D-WV), raised concerns about the program in a handwritten note he gave to Vice President Cheney. Ibid.

22. Presiding Judge Royce Lamberth was eventually read in when James Baker, the Justice Department's chief liaison to the FISC, "stumbled across the program." Baker insisted that Judge Lamberth be told about the surveillance program. Around Christmas 2001, David Addington, counsel to Vice President Cheney, agreed that Judge Lamberth, but no other judge on the court, could be read in. OLC attorney Yoo subsequently briefed Judge Lamberth on the program. Yoo asserted that FISA did not and could not limit the president's authority to order intelligence gathering because FISA improperly sought to limit presidential power in the area of national security. In Yoo's view, Congress simply did not have the power to forbid the president to conduct warrantless surveillance in the area of national security. Judge Lamberth later said that his understanding was that the program "was a very short-term emergency thing, perhaps until we got a legislative fix, and certainly not something that would end up going on for years." The Bush administration agreed to keep Judge Lamberth and then his successor, Judge Kollar-Kotelly, fully informed about the surveillance program and further agreed not to use evidence gained by warrantless surveillance as the basis for an application for a warrant. Baker, the Justice Department liaison to the FISC, was not sure the administration fulfilled these promises. Gellman, *Angler*, 151–153, 307–308.

23. This included a threat assessment document that was known as the "scary memo" because it described terrorist threats that were "sobering and scary."

24. Fisher, *Constitutional Limitations on Domestic Surveillance*, 10.

25. Ibid.

26. Pfiffner, *Power Play*, 170.

27. Yoo concluded that, since warrantless surveillance under the PSP was "reasonable," it did not violate the Fourth Amendment, which prohibits "unreasonable searches and seizures." Yoo pointed to Supreme Court opinions permitting warrantless searches when it comes to drug testing for employees and student athletes, as well as sobriety checkpoints for drivers, circumstances in which the Court has concluded that "special needs, beyond the normal need for law enforcement, make the warrant and probable-cause requirement [of the Fourth Amendment] impracticable."

28. An unclassified Department of Justice white paper also cites inherent presidential power and the sole organ doctrine to justify the warrantless surveillance program: "The NSA activities are supported by the President's well-recognized inherent constitutional authority as Commander in Chief and sole organ for the Nation in foreign affairs to conduct warrantless surveillance of enemy forces for intelligence purposes to detect and disrupt armed attacks on the United States." *Legal Authorities Supporting the Activities of the National Security Agency Described by the President*, January 19, 2006, http://www.justice.gov/opa/whitepaperonnsa legalauthorities.pdf.

29. As noted at note 21, there is disagreement as to how complete these briefings were.

30. Daschle said that Gonzales's account "does not conform to my recollection. It is completely untrue." Representative Harman claimed that the Gang of Eight was "not briefed on the legal underpinnings. . . . I was never told, I figured this out after the briefings basically stopped, that they had substantially failed to follow FISA over the years." Gellman, *Angler*, 301.

31. Ibid.

32. Foreign Intelligence Surveillance Act of 1978 Amendments Act of 2008, Pub. L. No. 110–261, 122 Stat.2436 (2008).

33. Gellman, *Angler*, 302.

34. Foreign Intelligence Surveillance Act of 1978 Amendments Act of 2008, Pub. L. No. 110–261, 122 Stat.2436 (2008), codified at 50 U.S.C.§ 1881a. A "United States person" is defined by FISA as a U.S. citizen, a permanent resident who is a citizen of another country but has been lawfully admitted to the U.S., a corporation incorporated in the U.S., or an unincorporated association with "a substantial number of members [who] are citizens of the United States or [permanent residents lawfully admitted to the U.S.]." 50 U.S.C.§ 1801(i). Corporations or associations directed and controlled by a foreign government are not U.S. persons under the law. Ibid.

CHAPTER 13. DETENTION AND MILITARY COMMISSIONS UNDER THE OBAMA ADMINISTRATION

1. Barack Obama, "Review and Disposition of Individuals Detained at the Guantanamo Bay Naval Base and Closure of Detention Facilities," Executive Order 13492, 74 Fed. Reg. 4897, January 22, 2009, http://www.fas.org/irp/offdocs /eo/eo-13492.pdf.

2. Pious, "Prerogative Power in the Obama Administration: Continuity and Change in the War on Terrorism," 272.

3. Charlie Savage, "Accused 9/11 Mastermind to Face Civilian Trial in N.Y.," *New York Times*, November 13, 2009, http://www.nytimes.com/2009/11/14 /us/14terror.html?pagewanted=all.

4. Jonathan Tracy, "The Real Problem with Khalid Sheikh Mohammed's Military Commission," *ABA Human Rights Magazine* 38, no. 1 (winter 2011), http://www.americanbar.org/publications/human_rights_magazine_home /human_rights_vol38_2011/human_rights_winter2011/the_real_problem_with _khalid_sheikh_mohammed_military_commission.html.

5. National Defense Authorization Act for Fiscal Year 2011, Pub. L. No. 111–383, § 1032, 124 Stat. 4351 (2011); Department of Defense and Full-Year Continuing Appropriations Act, 2011, Pub. L. No. 112–10, 125 Stat. 38 (2011); see also Michael John Garcia, Jennifer K. Elsea, R. Chuck Mason, and Edward C. Liu, "Closing the Guantanamo Detention Center: Legal Issues," Congressional Research Service, July 6, 2011, 13, http://fpc.state.gov/documents/organization/169054.pdf.

6. President Obama signed the legislation itself, the National Defense Authorization Act for FY 2011 into law, although he included a signing statement explaining that he signed the act "because of the importance of authorizing appropriations for, among other things, our military activities in 2011." However, Obama further stated that he had "strong objection" to the provisions that barred the use of funds to transfer Guantanamo prisoners to the U.S., even for purpose of prosecution, and he stated that "my Administration will work with the Congress to seek repeal of these restrictions, will seek to mitigate their effects, and will oppose any attempt to extend or expand them in the future." January 7, 2011, statement by the President on H.R. 6523, the Ike Skelton National Defense Authorization Act for Fiscal Year 2011, http://www.whitehouse.gov/the-press-office/2011/01/07/statement-president-hr-6523.

7. Anne E. Kornblut and Peter Finn, "Obama Advisers Set to Recommend Military Tribunals for Alleged 9/11 Plotters," *Washington Post*, March 5, 2010, http://www.washingtonpost.com/wp-dyn/content/article/2010/03/04/AR2010030405209.html.ol.

8. Charlie Savage, "Detainees Will Still Be Held, but Not Tried," *New York Times*, January 22, 2010, http://www.nytimes.com/2010/01/22/us/22gitmo.html?hpw.

9. Barack Obama, "Periodic Review of Individuals Detained at Guantanamo Bay Naval Station Pursuant to Authorization to Use Military Force," Executive Order 13567, 76 Fed. Reg. 13275, March 10, 2011, http://www.whitehouse.gov/the-press-office/2011/03/07/executive-order-13567-periodic-review-individuals-detained-guant-namo-ba.

10. *Hamdi*, 542 U.S. at 507, 516.

11. Executive Order 13567.

12. Ibid.

13. Ibid.

14. Sam Stein, "Civil Libertarian Rips Obama Speech: All Bells and Whistles," *Huffington Post*, June 21, 2009, http://www.huffingtonpost.com/2009/05/21/civil-libertarian-rips-ob_n_206343.html.

15. Joseph Heller, *Catch-22* (New York: Simon and Schuster, 1994). In Heller's book, men serving in the U.S. Army Air Force during World War II can be sent home if they tell a military doctor that they are crazy, but anyone who would want to be removed from combat duty can't really be crazy.

16. Jennifer K. Elsea and Michael John Garcia, "The National Defense Authorization Act for FY2012: Detainee Matters," Congressional Research Service, April 10, 2012, 11, http://www.fas.org/sgp/crs/natsec/R42143.pdf.

17. Critics might respond that the habeas access recognized in *Boumediene* has turned out to be a mixed bag at best as implemented by the lower federal courts, therefore making it more important that prisoners receive some other meaningful review process. See Stephen I. Vladeck, "The D.C. Circuit after Boumediene," *Seton Hall Law Review* 41 (2011): 1451. The Supreme Court "has provided scant guidance on these questions, consciously leaving the contours of the substantive

and procedural law of detention open for lower courts to shape in a common law fashion." *Al-Bihani v. Obama*, 590 F. 3d 866, 870 (D.C. Cir. 2010). In other words, it has been up to the lower federal courts to determine what it means for a prisoner at Guantanamo to have access to the courts on a habeas petition. In practice, lower federal courts have permitted the government to meet its burden of proving that a prisoner is an enemy combatant by a preponderance-of-the-evidence standard instead of the more exacting beyond-a-reasonable-doubt standard typically used in criminal cases. Lower courts have also permitted the government to use hearsay evidence in justifying its claim that a prisoner may be detained as an enemy combatant. Ibid., 590 F. 3d at 875–881.

18. *Hamdi*, 542 U.S. at 519–521. ("[W]e understand Congress' grant of authority for the use of 'necessary and appropriate force' to include the authority to detain for the duration of the relevant conflict, and our understanding is based on longstanding law-of-war principles. If the practical circumstances of a given conflict are entirely unlike those of the conflicts that informed the development of the law of war, that understanding may unravel. But that is not the situation we face as of this date [in 2004].")

19. Pub. L. No. 112–81, 125 Stat. 1298 (2011). Section 1023 of the law requires the secretary of defense to submit procedures for implementing the PRB process and further requires that these procedures provide certain clarifications regarding the purpose of the PRB process (for example, that its purpose was to determine not whether a prisoner was properly held pursuant to the laws of war but only whether, as a discretionary matter, the PRB could determine that the prisoner did not pose a continuing threat to U.S. security).

20. The 2001 AUMF did not expressly address detention; however, as discussed in chapter 10, the Supreme Court concluded in *Hamdi* that the AUMF implicitly provided the president with authority to detain enemy combatants.

21. Pub. L. No. 107–40, 115 Stat. 224 (2001).

22. Pub. L. No. 112–81, 125 Stat. 1298 § 1021 (b)(2) (2011). In September 2012, a federal district court ruled that this section of the 2012 NDAA is unconstitutional and permanently enjoined its enforcement. *Hedges v. Obama*, 2012 U.S. Dist. LEXIS 130354 (S.D.N.Y. 2012). The 2nd Circuit Court of Appeals vacated the district court decision, concluding plaintiff lacked standing. 2013 U.S. App. LEXIS 14417.

23. Ibid., § 1021 (c)(1). They could alternatively be tried before military tribunal or transferred to the custody of another country, though this is not required. Ibid., § 1021(c). The 2012 NDAA does not permit funds to be used to transfer Guantanamo prisoners to the United States for trial. Ibid., § 1026.

24. See *al-Bihani*, 590 F. 3d at 872–873 (concluding that the president had authority to detain as an enemy combatant a man who served as a cook for a paramilitary group allied with the Taliban that included Al Qaeda members as the cook was "substantially supporting" enemy forces—even if the man could arguably be considered a civilian contractor). Subsequent decisions have cast some doubt on *al-Bihani*'s conclusion.

25. Glenn Greenwald, "Three Myths about the Detention Bill," *Salon .com*, December 16, 2011, http://www.salon.com/2011/12/16/three_myths_about_the _detention_bill/singleton.

26. Ibid.; see also Elsea and Garcia, "The National Defense Authorization Act for FY2012: Detainee Matters," 16.

27. However, it may be difficult to try prisoners held at Guantanamo in federal court in the United States. As discussed, Congress has prohibited the use of funds to transfer prisoners from Guantanamo to the United States for trial. In addition, section 1022 of the 2012 NDAA required, with limited exceptions, military detention for any prisoner taken into custody two months or more after the act took effect. Such prisoners either could be held indefinitely under the law of war or, if tried, could be tried only before military tribunals. The Obama administration objected to this requirement, arguing it would make it more difficult to combat the threat of terrorism by depriving the executive branch of the option of criminal prosecution in civilian courts. Ibid., 17–22.

28. Frank James, "Obama's Gitmo Tribunal Move: From Campaign Poetry to Governing Prose," *NPR: It's All Politics*, April 4, 2011, http://www.npr.org /blogs/itsallpolitics/2011/04/04/135123729/obamas-military-tribunal-move-shows-shift-from-poetry-to-prose; see also Jonathan Tracy, "The Real Problem with Khalid Sheikh Mohammed's Military Commission," *ABA Human Rights*, 38, no. 1 (winter 2011), http://www.americanbar.org/publications/human_rights _magazine_home/human_rights_vol38_2011/human_rights_winter2011/the _real_problem_with_khalid_sheikh_mohammed_military_commission.html.

29. They were first revised in the 2006 Military Commission Act, one section of which was struck down by the court in the *Boumediene* decision, as discussed in chapter 10. The 2006 MCA has since been replaced by the 2009 MCA.

30. Pub. L. No. 111–84, § 948b(a), 123 Stat. 2190, codified at 10 U.S.C. chapter 47A (2006).

31. 548 U.S. 557 (2006).

32. Ibid. at 613–615.

33. They are called "military commissions" under the 2009 Act, but the term "military tribunal" is used interchangeably.

34. 10 U.S.C. §§ 949a(a), (b)(1). See also Jennifer K. Elsea, "Comparison of Rights in Military Commission Trials and Trials in Federal Civilian Courts," Congressional Research Service, November 19, 2009, http://fpc.state.gov/documents /organization/133509.pdf.

35. 10 U.S.C. § 949d(c)(2)(a).

36. 10 U.S.C. § 949(a)(b)(2).

37. At least four other military officers must be assigned to a noncapital case, and, in most circumstances, at least eleven other officers must be assigned to decide capital cases. 10 U.S.C. §§ 948m(a), 949m(c).

38. 10 U.S.C. § 949a(b)(3)(d).

39. 10 U.S.C. § 948(b)(d).

40. 10 U.S.C. § 949l(c).

41. 10 U.S.C. § 948r. However, statements obtained through coercion falling short of torture or cruel, inhuman, or degrading treatment could be used as evidence.

42. 10 U.S.C. § 948c.

43. 10 U.S.C. § 950g.

44. Or, one might argue, why not simply hold enemy combatants without trial of any kind—assuming a system of indefinite detention is legally justified?

45. Prepared text of Attorney General Eric Holder's March 5, 2012, speech at Northwestern University School of Law, http://www.justice.gov/iso/opa/ag/speeches/2012/ag-speech-1203051.html.

46. Ibid.

47. Attorney General Holder suggested that using military tribunals could harm relations with other countries that refuse to "cooperate with the United States in certain counterterrorism efforts . . . if we intend to use that cooperation in pursuit of a military commission prosecution." Ibid.

48. This includes some prisoners who have been cleared for release: the Obama administration suspended transfer proceedings for twenty-nine Yemeni nationals after the attempted bombing of an airliner en route to Detroit focused attention on Al Qaeda in the Arabian Peninsula, which is active in Yemen. Although the government does not allege that these men are enemy combatants, they are still being held at Guantanamo. Peter Finn, "Guantanamo Detainees Cleared for Release but Left in Limbo," *Washington Post*, November 8, 2011, http://www.washingtonpost.com/national/national-security/guantanamo-detainees-cleared-for-release-but-left-in-limbo/2011/11/03/gIQAJivMM_story.html.

49. It may prove difficult for courts to identify when the conflict with the Taliban and/or Al Qaeda and/or supporting forces has ended—in a recent case decided by the D.C. Circuit Court of Appeals, the court concluded that "[t]he determination of when hostilities have ceased is a political question" to be decided by the president and Congress. *al-Bihani v. Obama*, 590 F. 3d at 874–875.

CHAPTER 14. THE STATE SECRETS PRIVILEGE

1. Including the secret legal memoranda discussed in chapters 9–12.

2. U.S. House of Representatives, Committee on Government Reform—Minority Staff, Special Investigations Division, "Secrecy in the Bush Administration," September 14, 2004, 31, quoting David C. Vladeck.

3. Cary Coglianese, "The Transparency President? The Obama Administration and Open Government," *Governance*, 22, no. 4 (September 2009): 529–544, doi: 10.1111/j.1468-0491.2009.01451.x.

4. Trevor Morrison argues that the Obama administration reined in power in certain areas, including in the areas of interrogation (the Obama administration banned waterboarding and other interrogation methods used at times during the Bush administration), the criminal prosecution of suspected terrorists captured in

the United States (the Obama administration has exclusively used civilian courts in these cases), and access to habeas corpus for prisoners at Guantanamo (the Bush administration fought against this in the courts, the Obama administration has not). However, Morrison also concedes that "there are of course many points of consistency between the Bush and Obama administrations." "Obama v. Bush on Counterterrorism Policy," *Lawfare*, November 11, 2012, http://www.lawfareblog .com/2012/11/obama-v-bush-on-counterterrorism-policy/.

5. *Arar v. Ashcroft*, 585 F.3d 559, 606 (2d Cir. 2009) (Sack, J., dissenting).

6. 345 U.S. 1 (1953).

7. Louis Fisher, *In the Name of National Security: Unchecked Presidential Power and the Reynolds Case* (Lawrence: University Press of Kansas, 2006), 98, 104.

8. In the judge's chambers, privately.

9. Fisher, *In the Name of National Security*, 1–3, 29–30, 50, 53, 55–56. Fisher notes that "[t]he accident report, submitted October 18, 1948, was originally classified as Restricted. Of the four [classification] levels—Top Secret, Secret, Confidential, and Restricted—Restricted was the lowest. Some of the documents were upgraded to Secret on January 3, 1949, but returned to Restricted on September 14 or 15, 1950. In later years, in response to Freedom of Information Act requests, the government began to release heavily redacted reports. In the 1990s, the government declassified the . . . documents and made them available to the public at a price." Ibid., 60.

10. Fisher observes that "[t]he analogy to Great Britain was misplaced because the U.S. Constitution recognizes values and principles that broke with British history and practice, including an independent judiciary capable of deciding against the executive branch, even in cases of national security. The American framers [of the Constitution] considered the British legal model, which placed all of external affairs, foreign policy, and the war power in the executive, and firmly rejected it." Ibid., 61.

11. Ibid., 56–62, 64–66, 72, 77, 91.

12. Ibid., 79–80, 82–84, quoting *Reynolds v. United States*, 192 F.2d 987, 996 (3rd Cir. 1951).

13. Fisher, *In the Name of National Security*, 84.

14. Ibid., 97–100 (emphasis in original), quoting "Petition for a Writ of Certiorari to the United States Court of Appeals for the Third Circuit," *United States v. Reynolds*, No. 21, Supreme Court October Term, 1952, at 42–43.

15. Fisher, *In the Name of National Security*, 84–85.

16. The three justices who dissented—Black, Frankfurter, and Jackson—did not write a separate dissent. The reported decision explains only that they "dissent, substantially for the reasons set forth in the opinion of Judge Maris [writing for the Third Circuit] below." *U.S. v. Reynolds*, 345 U.S. at 12.

17. Ibid. at 6–8, 10–11.

18. Ibid. at 11–12.

19. Fisher, *In the Name of National Security*, 111, quoting *Reynolds*, 345 U.S. at 8.

20. Ibid., 112.

21. Ibid.

22. After the Supreme Court's decision, "[t]he widows settled for less money than they had been previously awarded by [the district court]." Ibid., 117.

23. Ibid., 177–179.

24. Ibid., 177. The government denied that it had lied, arguing that the claim of privilege did not "[make] any specific representation concerning the contents of . . . [the accident report and the witness statements." Ibid., 190–191, quoting Brief in Support of Defendant's Motion to Dismiss in *Herring v. United States* (E.D.Pa. 2004).

25. Fisher, *In the Name of National Security*, 119, 165. For many years, the executive branch invoked "national security" or "foreign affairs" rather than "state secrets" in arguing that documents could not be made available in litigation. However, since the September 11, 2001, terrorist attacks, "the government now routinely cit[es] 'state secrets' as the ground for denying private litigants access to agency information." Ibid., 212.

26. Even after *Reynolds*, courts evaluating a claim of state secrets privilege "have a range of options, including *in camera* review. Depending on the type of case—criminal or civil—the government faces a number of hurdles and may find that invoking the state secrets privilege can cause it to lose the case." Ibid., 226. In *Reynolds* itself, of course, the court's deference to the state secrets privilege did not require dismissal of the case.

27. Christina E. Wells, "State Secrets and Executive Accountability," *Constitutional Commentary* 26 (2010): 625.

28. Dahlia Lithwick notes that the state secrets privilege was asserted fifty-five times before 2001 but was used at least thirty-nine times in eight years by the Bush administration alone. Dahlia Lithwick, "See No Evil," *Slate.com*, February 10, 2009, http://www.slate.com/articles/news_and_politics/jurisprudence/2009/02 /see_no_evil.single.html, citing David Kravets, "New Attorney General Orders Review of Bush-Era State Secrets," *Wired.com*, February 9, 2009, http://www .wired.com/threatlevel/2009/02/ag-holder-deman. Robert M. Chesney reaches a different conclusion, rejecting the assertion that the Bush administration's use of the state secrets privilege was unprecedented. Robert M. Chesney, "Enemy Combatants after *Hamdan v. Rumsfeld*: State Secrets and the Limits of National Security Litigation," *George Washington Law Review* 75 (2007): 1249, 1252. Chesney argues that "[t]he quantitative inquiry is a pointless one in light of the significant obstacles to drawing meaningful conclusions from the limited data available, including in particular the fact that the number of lawsuits potentially implicating the privilege varies from year-to-year." Chesney also concludes that the Bush administration did not make claims of state secrets privilege that were qualitatively different from those made in the past. However, he notes that whether or not the Bush administration was doing something new in this area does not answer the question of whether use of the state secrets privilege is justified. Ibid. at 1252–1253.

29. Extraordinary rendition involves sending a prisoner to another country for purposes of interrogation, often by means of torture. It is differentiated from ordinary rendition, which is the extradition of a criminal suspect, pursuant to legal process, to another country for purposes of trial before a court. Extraordinary rendition is not carried out through legal means (i.e., it is not done pursuant to an extradition treaty) and is done for the purpose of interrogation and torture rather than trial. See Louis Fisher, "Extraordinary Rendition: The Price of Secrecy," *American University Law Review* 57 (2008): 1405.

30. These claims have been substantiated by a Council of Europe report, which concluded that "El-Masri's account of his rendition and confinement was substantially accurate." *El-Masri v. United States*, 479 F.3d 296, 302 (3rd Cir. 2007), *cert. denied*, 552 U.S. 947 (2007).

31. *El-Masri*, 479 F.3d at 300; see also Fisher, "Extraordinary Rendition," 1442–1443.

32. *El-Masri*, 479 F.3d at 301–302, 308.

33. Ibid. at 302–305.

34. Ibid. at 309.

35. Ibid. at 310.

36. Ibid. at 311.

37. Ibid. at 305–6, 311, quoting *Reynolds*, 345 U.S. at 8 and at 10.

38. Ibid. at 309.

39. Ibid. at 312.

40. Ibid.

41. Ibid.

42. *Arar v. Ashcroft*, 585 F. 3d 559 (2d Cir. 2009) (*en banc*), *cert. denied*, 130 S.Ct. 3409 (2010).

43. His claims were reviewed by the Canadian government, which issued an 822-page judicial report concluding that "Canadian intelligence officials had passed false warnings and bad information about Arar to the United States." The report further concluded that Arar had no involvement in terrorism and that there was no evidence he was a security threat. In January 2007, Canada's prime minister issued a letter of apology and provided $9.75 million in compensation to Arar. Fisher, "Extraordinary Rendition," 1441–1442.

44. *Arar*, 585 F.3d at 565–566; Fisher, "Extraordinary Rendition," 1436–1439.

45. Fisher, "Extraordinary Rendition," 1440.

46. *Arar*, 585 F.3d at 563.

47. See Gordon Silverstein, "Bush, Cheney, and the Separation of Powers: A Lasting Legal Legacy?," *Presidential Studies Quarterly* 39, no. 4 (December 2009): 878–895, doi: 10.1111/j.1741-5705.2009.03712.x.

48. Lithwick, "See No Evil." The case is *Mohamed v. Jeppesen Dataplan, Inc.*, discussed in this chapter.

49. Government Defendants' Motion to Dismiss in *Jewel v. NSA* and supporting memorandum, https://www.eff.org/files/filenode/jewel/jewelmtdobama .pdf (at 12 of memorandum); see also Steven D. Schwinn, "Obama Administration

Claims State Secrets Privilege (Again)," *Constitutional Law Prof Blog*, April 9, 2009, http://lawprofessors.typepad.com/conlaw/2009/04/obama-administration-claims-broad-state-secrets-privilege-again.html.

50. Zachary Roth, "Expert Consensus: Obama Mimics Bush on State Secrets," *Talking Points Memo*, April 9, 2009, http://tpmmuckraker.talkingpointsmemo.com/2009/04/expert_consensus_obama_aping_bush_on_state_secrets.php?ref=fp1; see also Glenn Greenwald, "The 180-Degree Reversal of Obama's State Secrets Position," *Salon.com*, February 10, 2009, http://www.salon.com/2009/02/10/obama_88/.

51. Memorandum from Attorney General Eric Holder to Heads of Executive Departments and Agencies and Heads of Department Components (September 23, 2009) (hereinafter September 2009 Holder memorandum), http://www.justice.gov/opa/documents/state-secret-privileges.pdf; see also Wells, "State Secrets and Executive Accountability," 640–646.

52. September 2009 Holder memorandum, 1.

53. Ibid.

54. Ibid., 2.

55. Ibid.

56. 92 U.S. 105 (1876). See also Steven D. Schwinn, "ACLU's Ben Wizner Talks about Mohamed v. Jeppesen, Extraordinary Rendition, and State Secrets," *Constitutional Law Prof Blog*, April 30, 2009, http://lawprofessors.typepad.com/conlaw/2009/04/aclus-ben-wizner-talks-about-mohamed-v-jeppsen-extraordinary-rendition-and-state-secrets.html.

57. *Reynolds*, 345 U.S. at 11.

58. *Totten v. U.S.*, 92 U.S. 105 (1876).

59. *Tenet v. Doe*, 544 U.S. 1, 8 (2005).

60. This narrow category would seem to include cases where plaintiff's allegations could be proved only through the disclosure of secret information that plaintiff had initially agreed to keep secret—for instance, the disclosure of an espionage agreement in *Totten* itself.

61. *Mohamed v. Jeppesen Dataplan, Inc.*, 614 F.3d 1070 (9th Cir. 2010), *en banc, cert. denied*, 131 S.Ct. 2442 (2011).

62. *Mohamed*, 614 F.3d at 1074. "Publicly available evidence support[s] [much of] th[e] [plaintiffs'] allegations, including that Jeppesen knew what was going on when it arranged flights described by one of its own officials as 'torture flights.'" Ibid. at 1095 (Hawkins, J., dissenting).

63. Ibid. at 1076.

64. *Mohamed v. Jeppesen*, 579 F.3d 943 (9th Cir. 2009).

65. *Mohamed*, 579 F.3d at 953. The alleged secret agreement in *Mohamed* involved support Jeppesen provided to the government regarding transportation of the men who were subjected to torture after being sent to other countries through the extraordinary rendition program.

66. Ibid. at 954.

67. Ibid.

68. Ibid. at 955.

69. Ibid.

70. Ibid.

71. Ibid.

72. Ibid.

73. Ibid. at 957.

74. *En banc* review means that all members of the court consider the case. The initial panel decision was before a three-judge panel only.

75. *Mohamed*, 614 F.3d at 1084 (emphasis in original).

76. Ibid. at 1085.

77. Ibid. at 1086.

78. Ibid. at 1090.

79. Ibid.

80. Ibid. at 1087, citing *El-Masri*, 479 F.3d at 312 (emphasis in original).

81. Ibid. at 1090.

82. Ibid. at 1088–1089 (emphasis omitted).

83. Ibid. at 1089. One concurring judge would have dismissed the case under *Totten*. Ibid. at 1093.

84. Ibid. at 1089, quoting *Totten*, 92 U.S. at 107.

85. *Mohamed*, 614 F.3d at 1091–1092.

86. *Mohamed*, 614 F.3d at 1101 (Hawkins, J., dissenting).

87. Ibid. at 1095 n. 1.

88. Ibid. at 1097, 1099; see also Benjamin Bernstein, "Over before It Even Began: *Mohamed v. Jeppesen Dataplan* and the Use of the State Secrets Privilege in Extraordinary Rendition Cases," *Fordham International Law Journal* 34 (2011): 1400, 1426 ("[T]he court [in *Mohamed*] expanded the Reynolds state secrets privilege to become the functional equivalent of *Totten*. A case can now be dismissed if there is a risk that state secrets may be divulged.").

89. *Mohamed*, 614 F.3d at 1098 (Hawkins, J., dissenting).

90. Ibid. at 1098.

91. Ibid. at 1095–1096.

92. Ibid. at 1097.

93. Ibid. at 1093.

94. Ibid. at 1094.

95. Ibid. at 1094.

96. The Supreme Court declined to review the Ninth Circuit's *en banc* decision. 131 S.Ct. 2442 (2011).

97. Memorandum in Support of Defendant's Motion to Dismiss, *Al-Aulaqi v. Obama*, Civ. A. No. 10-cv-1469, United States District Court for the District of Columbia, filed September 25, 2010, http://www.aclu.org/files/assets/Al-Aulaqi _USG_PI_Opp__MTD_Brief_FILED.pdf.

98. Tara McKelvey, "Inside the Killing Machine," *Newsweek*, February 13, 2011, http://www.thedailybeast.com/newsweek/2011/02/13/inside-the-killing-machine.htm.

99. *Al-Aulaqi v. Obama*, 727 F.Supp.2d 1, 2–11 (2010).

100. Gregory Johnsen, "A False Target in Yemen," *New York Times*, November 19, 2010, http://www.nytimes.com/2010/11/20/opinion/20johnsen.html.

101. Ibid.

102. Memorandum in Support of Defendant's Motion to Dismiss, *Al-Aulaqi v. Obama*, Civ. A. No. 10-cv-1469, 46.

103. Ibid. at 43–59.

104. Ibid. at 51.

105. Ibid.

106. Ibid. at 52.

107. Ibid. at 53.

108. Ibid.

109. However, as we will see, administration officials discussed the kill list with a reporter.

110. In this case, as in *Reynolds* and *Jeppesen*, the government provided the court with classified declarations explaining *why* the state secrets privilege applied but did not provide the information itself that the government claimed was shielded by the state secrets privilege. See *Al-Aulaqi v. Obama*, 727 F.Supp.2d at 1, 53. The classified declarations were not made available to plaintiff or his attorneys. Ibid. at 54. The government assured the court that "the privilege has been invoked only after that careful review and adherence to the mandated procedures under the Attorney General's [September 2009] policy." Ibid.

111. Ibid. at 1. The district court's decision was not appealed. See Benjamin Wittes, "No Appeal in Al-Aulaqi," *Lawfare*, February 22, 2011, http://www.lawfareblog.com/2011/02/no-appeal-in-al-aulaqi. However, a wrongful death lawsuit was filed by the government after Al-Aulaqi was killed, as discussed later.

112. Ibid., 727 F.Supp.2d at 53.

113. Ibid., quoting *Jeppesen*, 614 F.3d at 1083.

114. *Al-Aulaqi*, 727 F.Supp.2d at 53, quoting *Jeppesen*, 614 F.3d at 1079.

115. Charlie Savage, "Secret U.S. Memo Made Legal Case to Kill a Citizen," *New York Times*, October 8, 2011, http://www.nytimes.com/2011/10/09/world/middleeast/secret-us-memo-made-legal-case-to-kill-a-citizen.html?pagewanted=all.

116. Amy Davidson, "An American Teen-Ager in Yemen," *New Yorker*, October 18, 2011, http://www.newyorker.com/online/blogs/closeread/2011/10/an-american-teen-ager-in-yemen.html.

117. Complaint in *Al-Aulaqi v. Panetta*, U.S. District Court for the District of Columbia, July 18, 2012, http://www.ccrjustice.org/files/July-18-2012-Nasser-Al-Aulaqi-Complaint.pdf.

118. Tom Junod, "For Obama's Lethal Presidency, New Suit Aims at Justice," *Esquire.com*, July 18, 2012, http://www.esquire.com/blogs/politics/aclu-drone-lawsuit-10785942.

119. Holder, March 5, 2012, speech at Northwestern University School of Law.

120. Ibid.

121. Ibid.

122. Ibid.

123. Pious, "Prerogative Power in the Obama Administration: Continuity and Change in the War on Terrorism," 263, quoting President Obama speech of May 21, 2009. As a U.S. senator, Barack Obama criticized the Bush administration for making unilateral decisions about, for example, the power to detain U.S. citizens as enemy combatants, without allowing meaningful judicial review. Senator Barack Obama floor statement of September 27, 2006, http://obamaspeeches.com/091-Floor-Statement-on-the-Habeas-Corpus-Amendment-Obama-Speech.htm.

124. Holder, March 5, 2012, speech at Northwestern University School of Law.

125. Glenn Greenwald, "Attorney General Holder Defends Execution without Charges," *Salon.com*, March 6, 2012, http://www.salon.com/2012/03/06/attorney_general_holder_defends_execution_without_charges/singleton.

126. Glenn Greenwald, "Leon Panetta's Explicitly Authoritarian Decree," *Salon.com*, January 30, 2012, http://www.salon.com/2012/01/30/leon_panettas_explicitly_authoritarian_decree/singleton.

127. Ibid., citing Charlie Savage, "Secret U.S. Memo Made Legal Case to Kill a Citizen," *New York Times*, October 8, 2011, http://www.nytimes.com/2011/10/09/world/middleeast/secret-us-memo-made-legal-case-to-kill-a-citizen.html?_r=1&hp.

128. Michael Isikoff, "Justice Department Memo Reveals Legal Case for Drone Strikes on Americans," *NBC News*, February 4, 2013.

129. Department of Justice White Paper, "Lawfulness of a Lethal Operation Directed Against a U.S. Citizen Who Is a Senior Operational Leader of Al-Qa'ida or an Associated Force" (undated but released in 2013), http://msnbcmedia.msn.com/i/msnbc/sections/news/020413_DOJ_White_Paper.pdf.

130. Ibid., 1–2. In fact, the 2001 AUMF did not provide authority to use force against forces *associated* with Al Qaeda: such authority was only provided by the 2012 NDAA, which was enacted after al-Aulaqi was killed. Public Law 107-40, 115 Stat. 224 (2001) (AUMF); (Public Law 112–81, section 1021(b)(2) (2011) (2012 NDAA). Note also the suggestion that the president possesses inherent power to defend the nation; John Yoo made a similar claim during the Bush years.

131. Holder, March 5, 2012, speech at Northwestern University School of Law.

132. Greenwald, "Attorney General Holder Defends Execution without Charges."

133. Pious, "Prerogative Power in the Obama Administration: Continuity and Change in the War on Terrorism," 275. Pious notes that, while the Bush administration also had some form of a kill-or-capture list, "it seems that until 2009 no American was ever placed on the list." Ibid., 274–275.

134. Ibid., 274.

135. Mark Hosenball, "Secret Panel Can Put Americans on 'Kill List,'" *Reuters*, October 5, 2011, http://www.reuters.com/article/2011/10/05/us-cia-killlist-idUSTRE79475C20111005.

136. Pious, "Prerogative Power in the Obama Administration: Continuity and Change in the War on Terrorism," 274.

137. Hosenball, "Secret Panel Can Put Americans on 'Kill List.'" Obama's decision to create this panel without statutory authority suggests that the administration relied on some form of implied or inherent emergency presidential power, but the administration did not fully explain its rationale.

138. Holder, March 5, 2012, speech at Northwestern University School of Law. However, the details are somewhat unclear. Some officials said that President Obama did not personally approve the panel's decision to place a U.S. citizen on the kill or capture list, while others said President Obama was notified of the panel's decision and had the opportunity to overrule it. Hosenball, "Secret Panel Can Put Americans on 'Kill List.'"

139. The Department of Justice white paper that was publicly disclosed in February 2013 also presented this argument, though it relied on an incorrect description of the authority granted to the president under the 2001 AUMF—that authority did not, in fact, extend to forces "associated with" Al Qaeda (like AQAP). Compare Department of Justice White Paper, 2 with Public Law 107–40, 115 Stat. 224 (2001) (AUMF). The white paper also suggested that inherent presidential power provided authority for the decision to kill al-Aulaqi, though there is some ambiguity on this point—ambiguity that could be resolved by the undisclosed OLC memo(s). Department of Justice White Paper, 1.

140. Presumably *Quirin* and *Hamdi*, although the cases were not specifically identified in Savage's article.

141. See chapter 11, discussing the legal doctrine of necessity in the context of torture.

142. Savage, "Secret U.S. Memo Made Legal Case to Kill a Citizen."

143. Glenn Greenwald, "The Awlaki Memo and Marty Lederman," *Salon. com*, October 9, 2011, http://www.salon.com/2011/10/09/the_awlaki_memo_and_marty_lederman/singleton. See also Louis Fisher, "Why Classify Legal Memos?," *National Law Journal*, July 14, 2008, http://www.loufisher.org/docs/ssp/447.pdf (criticizing arguments made to keep other legal memos secret).

144. Greenwald, "The Awlaki Memo and Marty Lederman."

145. However, Attorney General Holder's March 5, 2012, speech did not rely solely on the AUMF in claiming that the president can determine when it is necessary to order the targeted killing of a U.S. citizen. Holder suggested that his asserted justification could be based simply on his reading of Article II powers assigned to the president when he claimed that "[t]he conduct and management of national security operations are core functions of the Executive Branch." That sounds closer to the unitary executive theory that John Yoo put forth, as Holder's argument did not seem to rely only on congressional authorization for presidential action. The Department of Justice white paper similarly seems to rely in part

on something that resembles a claim of inherent presidential power. Department of Justice White Paper, 1.

146. Ibid., 2.

147. Greenwald, "The Awlaki Memo and Marty Lederman."

CHAPTER 15. THE OBAMA ADMINISTRATION AND MILITARY ACTION IN LIBYA

1. Memorandum opinion for the Attorney General from Caroline D. Krass, Principal Deputy Assistant Attorney General, *Authority to Use Military Force in Libya*, April 1, 2011, 1 http://www.justice.gov/olc/2011/authority-military-use-in-libya.pdf (hereinafter April 1, 2011, Krass memo).

2. Ibid.

3. Ibid.

4. Ibid., 2, quoting Dan Bilefsky and Mark Landler, "Military Action against Qaddafi Is Backed by U.N.," *New York Times*, March 18, 2011, http://www.nytimes.com/2011/03/18/world/africa/18nations.html?pagewanted=all&_r=0.

5. Louis Fisher, "Military Operations in Libya: No War? No Hostilities?," *Presidential Studies Quarterly* 42, no. 1 (March 2012): 176.

6. Ibid.

7. Ibid., 178.

8. April 1, 2011, Krass memo, 6.

9. Ibid.

10. Fisher, "Military Operations in Libya: No War? No Hostilities?," 177, quoting Charlie Savage, "Barack Obama's Q & A," *Boston Globe*, December 20, 2007, http://www.boston.com/news/politics/2008/specials/CandidateQA/ObamaQA.

11. April 1, 2011, Krass memo, 14.

12. Ibid., 1, 6.

13. Ibid., 10–12.

14. Ibid., 6 (emphasis added).

15. 50 U.S.C. § 1541(c).

16. Although the WPR also contains language suggesting that the president may order the use of military force for any reason for up to sixty days (or, in some circumstances, for ninety days). 50 U.S.C. §§ 1543(a), 1544(b). This may simply be the result of imprecise drafting.

17. Louis Fisher, "Teaching the Presidency: Idealizing a Constitutional Office," *PS: Political Science and Politics* 45, no. 1 (January 2012): 29; see also Pfiffner, *Power Play*, 68.

18. April 1, 2011, Krass memo.

19. As mentioned in chapter 9, however, some of Hamilton's writings emphasize *limits* on presidential power.

20. April 1, 2011, Krass memo, 7.

21. Ibid., 6.

22. Ibid., 7.

23. And, in fact, President Obama did provide such a report to Congress. President Obama noted that he was "providing this report as part of my efforts to keep the Congress fully informed, consistent with the War Powers Resolution." March 21, 2011, letter from President Obama to the Speaker of the House of Representatives and President Pro Tempore of the Senate, http://www.whitehouse .gov/the-press-office/2011/03/21/letter-president-regarding-commencement-operations-libya.

24. April 1, 2011, Krass memo.

25. Ibid., 8.

26. Ibid., 13.

27. Ibid.

28. Ibid., 8. Louis Fisher points out that "[u]nder OLC's analysis . . . [i]f U.S. casualties can be kept low—no matter the extent of physical destruction to another nation and loss of life—war to OLC would not exist within the meaning of the Constitution." "Military Operations in Libya: No War? No Hostilities?," 180.

29. Under the WPR, when the president unilaterally authorizes military action, operations must normally terminate within sixty days (or ninety days in the case of military necessity involving the safety of armed forces) unless Congress takes action. 50 U.S.C. § 1544(b).

30. Charlie Savage, "2 Top Lawyers Lost to Obama in Libya War Policy Debate," *New York Times*, June 18, 2011, http://www.nytimes.com/2011/06/18/world /africa/18powers.html?_r=2&partner=rss&emc=rss.

31. Ibid.

32. It was unusual, even "extraordinarily rare," for President Obama to disregard OLC's legal conclusions. Typically, OLC's legal opinions are seen as legally binding on the executive branch, though the president may sometimes set them aside, as he did here. Ibid.

33. Fisher, "Military Operations in Libya: No War? No Hostilities?," 181, quoting *United States Activities in Libya*, June 15, 2011, report submitted by the Obama administration to the House of Representatives, 25, http://www.nytimes .com/interactive/2011/06/16/us/politics/20110616_POWERS_DOC.html ?ref=politics.

34. Fisher observes that it is strange to use the word "further" given that the Obama administration had not received any *prior* congressional authorization. "Military Operations in Libya: No War? No Hostilities?," 181.

35. Ibid., quoting *United States Activities in Libya*, June 15, 2011, report.

36. Testimony by Legal Adviser Harold Hongju Koh, U.S. Department of State, on Libya and War Powers before the Senate Foreign Relations Committee, June 28, 2011, 4–5, http://www.foreign.senate.gov/imo/media/doc/Koh _Testimony.pdf.

37. Ibid., 5.

38. Ibid., 7–11.

39. Ibid., 10–11.

40. Ibid., 12.

41. Ibid., 7, 13–14.

42. Ibid., 13.

43. Ibid.

44. Fisher, "Military Operations in Libya: No War? No Hostilities?," 181.

45. Ibid., citing Thomas F. Eagleton, *War and Presidential Power: A Chronicle of Congressional Surrender* (New York: Liveright, 1974).

46. Fisher, "Military Operations in Libya: No War? No Hostilities?," 182.

47. Ibid., 183. Fisher acknowledges that the Obama administration might argue that circumstances changed when the United States transferred responsibility for operations to NATO. However, Fisher asserts, "[n]o one could deny that NATO was engaged in 'hostilities' against Libya[,]" so the U.S. "was at least *supporting* hostilities" (emphasis in original). In addition, Fisher observes that NATO is not an independent organization and depends on the United States for much of its funding.

48. Koh testimony before Senate Foreign Relations Committee, June 28, 2011, 13.

49. Ibid., 12.

50. Jennifer Steinhauer, "House Deals Obama Symbolic Blow with Libya Votes," *The Caucus: The Politics and Government Blog of the New York Times,* June 24, 2011, http://thecaucus.blogs.nytimes.com/2011/06/24/house-takes-up-a-rebuke-to-obamas-libya-policy.

51. Ibid.; see also Juan Cole, "House Libya Vote: Anti-War or Just Anti-Obama?," *Informed Comment,* June 25, 2001, http://www.juancole.com/2011/06/house-libya-vote-anti-war-or-just-anti-obama.html.

52. April 1, 2011, Krass memo.

53. Ibid., 8 n. 1.

54. Ibid., 10.

55. Ibid. In the case of Libya, the OLC concluded, the last two important national interests "were at stake."

56. Ibid., 8.

57. It is possible that one could conclude that Obama's *initial* decision to use military force in Libya was justified but that continuing operations without congressional approval were not justified after the sixty-day WPR window expired. In fact, reporting suggests that this is what Principal Deputy Assistant Attorney General Caroline Krass concluded. See Savage, "2 Top Lawyers Lost to Obama in Libya War Policy Debate."

58. Koh testimony before Senate Foreign Relations Committee, 7–11.

59. Fisher, "Military Operations in Libya: No War? No Hostilities?," 181–182.

60. Koh testimony before Senate Foreign Relations Committee, 5.

61. Ibid., 9–11.

62. Ibid., 5.

63. Fisher, "Military Operations in Libya: No War? No Hostilities?," 181–182.

64. Koh testimony before Senate Foreign Relations Committee, 12.

65. Fisher, "Military Operations in Libya: No War? No Hostilities?," 181.

66. "An Interview with John Yoo," 2005, http://www.press.uchicago.edu /Misc/Chicago/960315in.html (Yoo stated that "The three branches almost seem to agree that the WPR is either unconstitutional or irrelevant").

67. President Nixon, Veto of the War Powers Resolution, October 24, 1973, http://www.presidency.ucsb.edu/ws/index.php?pid=4021#axzzm16LmoK.

68. "An Interview with John Yoo."

69. Koh testimony before Senate Foreign Relations Committee, 5.

70. Fisher, "Military Operations in Libya: No War? No Hostilities?," 177.

INDEX

Article I in Constitution (*cont.*) 203, 275n4, 287n32, 290n9; Vesting Clause in, 126–128, 281n10

Article II in Constitution: summary of, 3, 17, 280n60; emergency presidential power and, 3, 18–19, 30–32, 60, 285n20; executive power and, 275n1; Framers and, 5, 12–17, 22, 128, 279n41, 279n47, 280n56, 286n23, 286n28, 307n25, 307n27; Framers' principles and, 17–18; implied presidential power and, 4, 8, 277n4; inherent executive power and, 4, 9, 127–128, 276n8, 277n13, 307n22; interrogation methods and, 222; limited emergency presidential power, 8–9, 277n7; Lockean prerogative and, 30; Oath Clause in, 31, 127; Take Care Clause of, 102–103, 127, 306n21, 307n27; unilateral emergency presidential power and, 9–10, 17–18, 30–32, 60, 271–273, 278nn21–22, 280n60; Vesting Clause in, 104, 127–128, 281n10, 302n12, 307n25. *See also* Commander in Chief Clause in Article II

Article III in Constitution, 46

Article 4 in Geneva Convention Relative to the Treatments of Prisoners of War or GPW, 145, 146, 311n3

Articles of Confederation, 5, 12, 15–16

Ashcraft v. Tennessee (1944), 209–210

Ashcroft, John, 210, 230–233

associated forces, 180, 238–239, 259, 261, 263

attorney general, 226, 228, 230–233. *See also* Justice Department; *and specific attorney general*

Authorization for the Use of Military Force (AUMF) of 2001: detention/trials of suspected terrorists and, 180, 236, 238, 308n41, 326n20; PSP and, 230, 232; targeted killing of citizens and, 261–263, 335n130, 336n139; unilateral emergency presidential power as claimed and, 130–131, 180; warrantless surveillance and, 230, 232

Baker, James, 323n22

Balkin, Jack, 138, 222

Barnhart, Edward N., 298nn21–22

Barron, David, 263, 284n8, 287n32, 292n7, 307n32, 308n35

Bauer, Robert, 268–269

Begin, Menachem, 208

Bellia, Patricia L., 116, 302n4, 303n11, 303n18

Bernstein, Benjamin, 333n88

Biddle, Francis, 67–68, 84, 308n35

Bill of Rights: due process and, 87, 88, 255, 258–264, 260, 283n35, 299n45, 313n45, 335n123; emergency presidential power and, 7, 10, 62, 291nn24–25; free speech and, 25–26, 322n13; national security threats and, 25, 26, 283n36; noncitizens and, 25, 283nn35–36; searches and seizures and, 225–229, 232–234, 258, 323n27, 324n34; trials and, 283n35, 313n45. *See also* Constitution

Blackstone, William, 11, 12

blockade of Confederacy (*Prize Cases* [1863]), 46–49, 140–142, 290nn86–87, 299n91, 310n64

Boumediene v. Bush (2008), 200–204, 327n29

Brookings Institution, 119, 304n16

Buchanan, James, 29, 276n5

Burleson, Albert, 62, 291nn24–25

Bush, George W.: AUMF and, 130–131; death of detainees under, 205, 206, 208, 210, 223; emergency presidential power and, 129–130; extraordinary rendition under, 223, 247–249, 321n68, 331nn29–30, 331nn42–43; Iraq invasion and, 309n47; limited emergency presidential power and, 62; Military Order of 2001 and, 156–159, 311n16, 311n18, 312n22, 313n50; OLC memoranda and, 130, 308n36; targeted killing of citizens and, 262, 335n133; unilateral emergency presidential power and, 147; unitary executive theory and, 126–131, 203, 306n21, 308n35. *See also* detention and trials under Bush; extraordinary rendition under Bush; interrogation methods under Bush; Office of Legal Counsel (OLC), and Bush; state secrets privilege under Bush; warrantless

288n55–56, 289n64; Supreme Court and, 7, 203

Hamdan, Salim Ahmed, 183

Hamdan v. Rumsfeld (2006): DTA of 2005 and, 197, 200; enemy combatant framework and, 183, 197, 198, 200, 239–241, 317n6; evidence and, 183, 199, 239; excerpts from, 183–196, 315nn77–78; justices' lack of unity on, 197, 241, 315n176; MCA of 2009 and, 239–240; tripartite framework and, 197–198; UCMJ and, 183, 197, 239; unitary executive theory and, 197–198

Hamdi, Yaser, 161, 180, 313n54

Hamdi v. Rumsfeld (2004): AUMF and, 180, 263, 326n20, 336n140; citizen detainees and, 160–161, 179–180, 239, 313n45, 313n50, 313n53; enemy combatant framework and, 161, 180–182, 236, 239, 259; excerpts from, 161–179, 313nn47–49; Fifth Amendment or due process and, 161, 202, 238, 259, 261; justices' unity on, 161, 179–180, 183, 313n50; perpetual detention and, 238–239, 326n18; unitary executive theory and, 161, 179–180, 313n50, 326n20; *Youngstown* case and, 180

Hamilton, Alexander, and topics discussed: Article II in Constitution, 21, 281n9; Articles of Confederation, 16; congressional war powers, 141; executive power, 5, 13–14, 16, 21, 141, 267, 279n41, 279n47, 281n9; federal government, 16; implied presidential power, 21; judicial review, 16, 118; limited emergency presidential power, 141, 337n19; limited emergency presidential power of Jefferson, 284n7; neutrality proclamation by Washington, 21–22, 281n14

Hawaii, and martial law, 298n18

Hayden, Michael, 211

Heller, Joseph, *Catch-22*, 238, 325n15

Hirabayashi, Gordon, 85, 88

Hirabayashi v. United States (1943), 85–90, 299n36, 299n45, 299n49, 300n59

historical context: for Framers, 10–13, 278n25, 279n31, 279n35, 279n41, 279n47; for separation of powers,

11–12, 15–16, 22–23, 141–142, 201, 280n53, 282n17–18, 282n21, 310n82

historical practice (precedent): for detention/trial of terrorists, 5, 80–81, 140, 144–147, 154–155, 157, 308n35, 336n140; for emergency presidential power, 5, 8–9, 26, 33, 60, 79, 141–142, 267–270, 272–273, 291n16, 295n56, 310n72

Holder, Eric, 223, 240–241, 249–250, 259–263, 328n47, 336n145

Hosenball, Mark, 336n138

Hughes, John, 84, 304n16

Huston Plan, 118, 304n8

Immigration Restriction Act of 1924, 83, 296n12

impeachment, and Nixon, 124, 305n32

implied presidential power: summary of, 10; Constitution and, 4, 8, 277n4; flaws in, 119–120, 210–211; flaws in theory of, 28, 119–120; Framers and, 17; Hamilton on, 21; Lincoln and, 8–9, 28, 30–32, 45–46, 289n64; Polk and, 28; Supreme Court and, 59; Washington and, 21. *See also* emergency presidential power

inherent executive power: Constitution and, 4, 9, 127–128, 276n8, 277n13, 307n22; Iran-Contra affair and, 125–126, 305n4; targeted killing of citizens and, 261, 262, 335n130, 336nn137–138; warrantless surveillance and, 323n28

intelligence gathering, and warrantless surveillance under Obama, 249. *See also* Foreign Intelligence Surveillance Act (FISA) of 1978; warrantless surveillance under Bush

interbranch practice, 269, 272, 273. *See also* separation of powers

internment of Japanese Americans: apology and restitution to internees and, 301n67; citizens and, 86, 100, 298n28; Constitution and, 90–100, 300n63, 300n66, 301nn67–68, 303n31; curfew and reporting violations, 85–90, 295n55, 299n36, 299n45, 299n49; detention camps and, 84–85, 298n18; Executive Order 9066 and, 84–85; historical

internment of Japanese Americans (*cont.*)
context for, 82–84, 86–89, 296n5, 296nn9–12, 297nn14–15, 298n22; loyalty of Japanese Americans and, 82, 87–91, 295n4, 299n49, 300nn59–60; martial law in Hawaii and, 298n18; national security threats claims and, 82, 84–86, 89, 293n22, 295nn2–3; noncitizens and, 86, 100, 298n28; Non-Detention Act of 1971 and, 301n71, 313n47; statistics, 85, 89, 313n47; tolerance/intolerance of Japanese Americans and, 84, 90–91, 100, 298nn21–22. *See also* Japanese Americans; *Korematsu v. United States* (1944)
interrogation methods under Bush: Abu Ghraib and, 210, 222–223; Afghanistan detention camps and, 205, 223, 247; Al Qaeda and, 205–207, 210–211, 222, 317n6, 317n9, 318n15; antitorture law of 1994 and, 206, 210, 318n10, 319n43, 320nn44–45; Article II authority and, 222; CAT and, 206, 320n44; CIA and, 206, 210–211, 222–223, 317n9, 321n68; description of, 206–210, 318n21; extraordinary rendition and, 223, 321n68; FBI and, 317n9; Geneva Conventions and, 205–206, 317n6, 317n8; Guantanamo and, 204, 205, 210, 222; necessity defense and, 210; OLC memoranda on, 205–207, 210, 317nn6–8, 319n32; tripartite framework and, 222; unilateral emergency presidential power and, 205–206, 223–224; War Crimes Act and, 206, 317n8; waterboarding and, 204, 207–208, 210–211, 222, 317n9, 318n21; Yoo-Bybee memo and, 210–222, 319n43. *See also* Bush, George W.
Iran-Contra affair, 125–126, 305n4
Iraq, 210, 222–223, 309n47
Irons, Peter, 84, 296nn10–11, 298nn21–22, 299n49, 300n59
Italian Americans, 86, 100, 298n28
Italian courts, 223, 321n68

Jackson, Robert H., and topics discussed: Commander in Chief Clause, 138–139;

Curtiss-Wright case in context of limited foreign aid, 64–66, 139–140; executive power, 10–11, 17, 115–116, 278n25, 303n31, 303n33; foreign affairs and executive power, 64–66, 116, 139–140, 292n7; Framers intent, 10–11, 17, 128, 278n25, 307n25; guidance to presidential advisers, 116; private company seizures, 116; tripartite framework, 115–116, 139, 222, 229, 278n22, 303n31, 303n33; unilateral emergency presidential power, 64–66, 116, 139–140, 292n7; *Youngstown* case, 115–116, 138–139, 303n20, 303n27, 303n31, 303n33
Japanese American Citizens League (JACL), 83, 297n14
Japanese Americans: loyalty of, 82, 87–91, 295n4, 299n49, 300nn59–60, 300n63; martial law in Hawaii and, 298n18; military service by, 82, 295n4; tolerance/intolerance of, 84, 90–91, 100, 298nn21–22. *See also* internment of Japanese Americans
Jay, John, 15, 141
Jefferson, Thomas: Alien (Friends) Act and, 25; limited emergency presidential power, 28–29, 284nn7–8, 309n50; on neutrality proclamation by Washington, 20, 22, 281n4, 281n14; Sedition Act of 1798 and, 25–26; unilateral emergency presidential power and, 29, 284n8; vice presidential elections and, 24, 282n29
Jeppesen Dataplan, Inc. *See Mohamed v. Jeppesen Dataplan Inc.* (2010)
Johnsen, Gregory, 256
Johnson, Andrew, 154–156
Johnson, Lyndon B., 117, 304n1, 304n11
Johnson v. Eisentrager (1950), 158, 160, 201, 312n31
judicial power. *See* courts; Justice Department; *and specific courts*
Judiciary Act of 1789, 34, 159, 288n48
Justice Department: attorney general and, 226, 228, 230–233; Commander in Chief Clause and, 323n28; extraordinary rendition and, 249–250; inherent executive power and, 323n28; interrogation

methods and, 222–223, 247, 317n9; Japanese American school segregation and, 296n9; military commission created by Washington and, 155; Offices of Inspectors General for, 227, 228; OLC and, 130; Palmer raids by, 62; separation of powers and, 15, 23, 50, 80, 114–115, 302n15, 303n24; sole organ doctrine and, 323n28; targeted killing of citizens and, 261, 263, 336n139, 336n145; on Vesting Clause in Article II, 302n12; warrantless surveillance and, 227, 228, 232, 233, 249, 323n22, 323n28; WPR and, 340n66. *See also* courts; separation of powers; *and specific attorney general*

Kashima, Tetsuden, 295n3, 298n18
Khan, Samir, 258
killing of citizens under Obama. *See* targeted killing of citizens under Obama
Knox, Frank, 84
Koh, Harold H., 268–270, 272–273
Korematsu, Fred, 301n67
Korematsu v. United States (1944), 90–100, 300n63, 300n66, 301nn67–68, 303n31
Krass, Caroline, 266–268, 339n57
Kruman, Marc W., 279n37

labor disputes, 102–103, 302n5, 302n11
Lamberth, Royce, 233, 323n22
Lederman, Martin, 263, 284n8, 287n32, 292n7, 307n32, 308n35
"Legality of the Use of Military Commissions . . ." or memo of November 2001 (Philbin): citizens as suspected terrorists and, 160–161; courts and, 147, 160–161; detention system and, 147, 158; excerpts from, 147–154, 311nn8–11; location of military commissions and, 156, 158; military commissions and, 147, 154–156, 158, 197, 311n9; rules for military commissions and, 147, 197; suspected terrorists' status and, 147, 311n8; UCMJ and, 147, 154, 311n9; unilateral emergency presidential power and, 147, 154–156, 158, 197, 311n9; unitary executive theory and, 154

Lend-Lease Act of 1941, 66, 292n10
limited emergency presidential power with retroactive congressional approval: Adams and, 26–27, 283n48; Bill of Rights and, 62, 291nn24–25; Bush and, 62; Commander in Chief Clause and, 266, 268, 338n23, 338n29; emergencies as contrived and, 61, 276n9, 291n19; Framers and, 17, 131, 277n7, 286n28, 287n33; Jefferson and, 28–29, 284nn7–8, 309n50; Lincoln and, 28–33, 40–41, 48–49, 131, 276n5, 284n10, 285n12, 285n14, 287n30, 287nn32–33, 287n38, 290n91; Obama and, 62, 266, 268, 272–273, 338n23, 338n29, 339n57; Truman and, 115–116, 303n31, 303n33; Washington and, 23, 155. *See also* Congress and congressional power
Lincoln, Abraham: Commander in Chief Clause and, 31, 64; constitutional emergency presidential power and, 30–32, 60; emergency presidential power and, 5, 8–9, 30–35, 41–46, 58–61, 277n2, 287n32, 290n10, 291n16; evaluation of war-time actions of, 44–46; habeas corpus suspension by, 32, 34–35, 41–44, 277n2, 287n32; historical practice and, 5, 8–9, 33, 60, 291n16; implied presidential power and, 8–9, 28, 30–32, 45–46, 289n64; limited emergency presidential power and, 28–33, 40–41, 48–49, 131, 276n5, 284n10, 285n12, 285n14, 287n30, 287nn32–33, 287n38, 290n91; *Merryman* decision as disregarded by, 40–41; Message to Congress by, 41–44; military trial of assassination conspirators and, 154, 155–156; national security threats and, 46–49, 140–142, 290nn86–87, 299n91, 310n64; naval blockade and, 5, 29–30, 33, 46–49, 131, 290nn86–88, 299n91; Polk's use of unilateral emergency presidential power compared with, 28, 29; prisoners held indefinitely without trial and, 44; *Prize Cases* and, 46–49, 140–142, 290nn86–87, 299n91, 310n64; Supreme Court's limits on emergency presidential power

Milligan, Lambdin, 50–51. *See also Ex parte Milligan* (1866)

Milwaukee Social Democratic Pub. Co. v. Burleson (1921), 62, 291nn24–25

Mohamed v. Jeppesen Dataplan Inc. (2010): *en banc* review and, 252, 254, 255, 258, 333n74; extraordinary rendition and, 249, 251–255, 331n48, 332n62, 332n65, 333n74, 333n88, 333n96, 334n110; targeted killing of citizens and, 256–257, 334n110

Montesquieu (Charles de Secondat, Baron de Montesquieu), 11–13, 279n35

Montgomery Ward & Co., 103

Morgan, Iwan, 304n2, 304n4, 304n17, 305n32

Morrison, Trevor, 328n4

Mueller, Robert, 231–232

Muhammed, Khalid Sheikh, 204, 222, 235–236, 239, 317n9

Muskie, Edmund, 119, 120, 304n17, 305n20

Nance, Malcolm, 207, 318n21

National Defense Authorization Act for FY 2011, 236, 325n6

National Defense Authorization Act (NDAA) for FY 2012 or 2012 NDAA, 238, 326nn22–23, 327n27, 335n130

National Security Agency (NSA), 225, 227, 228

national security threats: summary of, 3–6; Adams and, 25, 27; Bill of Rights and, 25, 26, 283nn35–36; Buchanan and, 29, 276n5; FDR and, 63–66, 82, 84–86, 89, 292nn3–4, 292n7, 292n10, 293nn20–22, 295nn2–3; Framers and, 287n30; Iran-Contra affair report and, 125–126, 305n4; Lincoln and, 46–49, 140–142, 290nn86–87, 299n91, 310n64; McKinley and, 61, 291n19; Nixon and, 118–119; Obama and, 249–250, 260–261; Polk and, 28–29, 31, 61, 131, 284n10, 309n43; pre–Civil War era and, 284n2; Schlesinger on, 284n2, 287n30; Washington and, 20–23, 21, 23, 26–27, 281n2, 281n4. *See also* warrantless surveillance under Bush

NATO (North Atlantic Treaty Organization), 266, 269, 272, 339n47

naval blockade of Confederacy, 5, 29–30, 33, 46–49, 131, 290nn86–88, 299n91

Nazi saboteurs. *See Ex parte Quirin* (1942)

NDAA (National Defense Authorization Act) for FY 2012 or 2012 NDAA, 238, 326nn22–23, 327n27, 335n130

necessity defense, 210

Neutrality Act of 1937, 292n3

neutrality proclamation, by Washington, 20–23, 26–27, 281n2, 281n4, 281n14

9/11 terrorist attacks, 129–130, 204, 222, 235–236, 239. *See also* detention and trials under Bush; detention and trials under Obama; interrogation methods under Bush; state secrets privilege; targeted killing of citizens under Obama; unitary executive theory; war on terror; warrantless surveillance under Bush

Nixon, Richard: citizen detainees and, 301n71, 313n47; elections as rigged and, 119, 120, 124, 304n17, 305n20; emergencies as contrived during escalation of Vietnam War and, 118–119, 304n11, 304n16; FBI's opposition to, 118, 124; impeachment likelihood and, 124, 305n32; implied presidential power flaws and, 119–120, 211; national security threats and, 118–119; noncitizen detainees and, 301n71; popular will and, 117–118, 119, 304n4; resignation of, 124, 305n32; secret tapes subpoena by Congress and, 120, 124, 305n26, 305n28; unilateral emergency presidential power and, 118–120; unitary executive theory and, 126; *United States v. Nixon* and, 120–124, 126, 305nn29–30; warrantless surveillance and, 118–119, 304n17; Watergate burglary and, 119, 120, 124; WPR and, 273

noncitizen detainees: Congress and, 100, 301n71; detention and trials for, 158–160, 180–181, 200–204, 316n121, 327n29; executive power and, 84–86, 100, 298n28; Fisher on, 300n66, 301n71; internment of Japanese Americans as, 86, 100, 298n28; Nixon and, 301n71; Supreme Court and, 100, 158, 160, 202–203. *See also* citizen detainees noncitizens, and Bill of Rights, 25, 283nn35–36. *See also* noncitizen detainees

Non-Detention Act of 1971, 301n71, 313n47

North American Aviation plant, 102–103, 116

North Atlantic Treaty Organization (NATO), 266, 269, 272, 339n47

NSA (National Security Agency), 225, 227, 228

Oath Clause in Article II, 31

Obama, Barack: Afghanistan projected withdrawal by, 238; Commander in Chief Clause and, 263, 336n145; due process and, 255, 258–264, 260, 335n123; emergency presidential power and, 129–130, 260–261; enemy combatant framework and, 262; extraordinary rendition as defended by, 249–255, 331n29, 331n48, 332n60, 332n62, 332n65, 333n74, 333n88, 333n96, 334n110; on Fifth Amendment or due process and, 260, 335n123; Justice Department white paper and, 261, 263, 336n139, 336n145; limited emergency presidential power and, 62; national emergency renewal by, 130, 308n41; national security threats and, 260–261; searches and seizures, 258; unilateral emergency presidential power and, 9; unitary executive theory and, 260, 335n123; warrantless surveillance under, 249; waterboarding ban by, 328n4. *See also* military action in Libya; Office of Legal Counsel (OLC), and Obama; targeted killing of citizens under Obama; *and specific cases, OLC members and memoranda*

Office of Legal Counsel (OLC), and Bush: Cheney and, 130; Constitution and, 138; interrogation methods under Bush and, 205–207, 210, 317nn6–8, 319n32; Justice Department and, 130; secrecy and disclosures of memoranda and, 130, 308n36, 309n47, 311n15; unilateral emergency presidential power and, 130–131; warrantless surveillance and, 130, 228–232, 322n21, 323nn22–23. *See also* Office of Legal Counsel (OLC),

and Obama; *and specific members and memoranda*

Office of Legal Counsel (OLC), and Obama: CIA interrogation and, 223; Commander in Chief Clause and, 266–268, 338n32, 339n57; military action in Libya and, 266–270, 338n28, 338n32, 339n55, 339n57; targeted killing of citizens by Obama and, 261–264, 336nn139–140, 336n145. *See also* Office of Legal Counsel (OLC), and Bush; *and specific members and memoranda*

Office of the Director of National Intelligence, 227, 237

Olson, Keith W., 305n20

Operation Shamrock, 225, 321n2

Ozawa v. United States (1922), 296n10, 296n12

Palmer, Mitchell A., 62

Patriot Act of 2001, 227

Pelosi, Nancy, 230–231

Pentagon Papers, 118–119, 304n11

Periodic Review Board (PRB), 237–238, 325n15

perpetual detention: Bush and, 157, 328n48; Obama and, 236–239, 242, 325n15, 326n18–20, 326nn22–24, 327n27, 328n44

personal representatives, for detainees, 237

Pfiffner, James, 128, 141–142, 229, 307n25, 309n56, 322n14

Philbin, Patrick, 229–231. *See also* "Legality of the Use of Military Commissions . . ." or memo of November 2001

Pine, David A., 104

Pious, Richard M., 262, 292n10, 312n33, 335n133

Polk, James, 28–29, 31, 61, 131, 284n10, 309n43

popular will, 5, 117–118, 119, 304n4

Posner, Eric A., 138, 142

post-9/11 war on terror. *See* detention and trials under Bush; detention and trials under Obama; interrogation methods under Bush; state secrets privilege; targeted killing of citizens under Obama; unitary executive theory; war on terror; warrantless surveillance under Bush

334nn109–110; *Al-Aulaqi v. Panetta* and, 258, 334n117; AUMF and, 261–263, 335n130, 336n139; Commander in Chief Clause and, 263, 336n145; due process and, 255, 258–264, 260, 335n123; emergency presidential power and, 260–261; enemy combatant framework and, 262; inherent executive power and, 261, 262, 335n130, 336nn137–138; Justice Department white paper and, 261, 263, 336n139, 336n145; *Mohamed* case and, 256–257, 334n110; national security threats and, 260–261; OLC and, 261–264, 336nn139–140, 336n145; *Reynolds* and, 257, 334n110; searches and seizures, 258. *See also* Obama, Barack; state secrets privilege under Obama

Tateishi, John, 296n9, 297n15

Temple-Raston, Dina, 312n36

TenBrock, Jacobus, 298nn21–22

Terrorist Surveillance Program (TSP), 227–229

Texas-Mexico border disputes, 28–29, 31, 61, 131, 284n10, 309n43

tolerance/intolerance, of Japanese Americans, 84, 298nn21–22

torture. *See* interrogation methods under Bush

Totten v. United States (1876), 250–255, 332n60, 333n88

transfer or release of detainees: detention/trials under Bush and, 159, 180, 312n36, 313n54, 316n125; detention/trials under Obama and, 236, 326n23, 328n48

trials (Sixth Amendment), 283n35, 313n45. *See also* courts; Justice Department

tripartite framework: detention/trials under Bush and, 197–198; interrogation methods under Bush and, 222; warrantless surveillance and, 229; *Youngstown* case and, 115, 139, 197–198, 222, 229, 303n27

Truman, Harry: Commander in Chief Clause and, 102, 138–139; inherent executive power, 102, 277n13; limits of executive power and, 101–102, 277n13; unilateral emergency presidential power claims and, 101–102, 142, 301n3;

unitary executive theory and, 126, 142. *See also Youngstown Sheet & Tube Co. v. Sawyer* (1952)

TSP (Terrorist Surveillance Program), 227–229. *See also* Terrorist Surveillance Program (TSP)

Tushnet, Mark, 306n21

unclassified reports, on warrantless surveillance, 227, 323n28

Uniform Code of Military Justice formerly Articles of War (UCMJ), 67–71, 147, 154, 157, 183, 197, 239, 294n33, 311n9

unilateral emergency presidential power: Article II and, 21; Bush and, 9, 147, 248, 330n28; Constitution and, 9–10, 17–18, 30–32, 60, 271–273, 278n21, 278n22, 280n60; detention/trials under Bush and, 159; diplomacy and, 24; extradition treaties passed in Congress and, 9, 18, 27, 65, 140; foreign affairs powers and, 9, 18, 24, 65, 140; Framers and, 8, 17, 131; interrogation methods under Bush and, 205–206, 223–224; Jefferson and, 29, 284n8; *Merryman* case and, 35, 40–41, 46, 278n21; military action in Libya and, 267–270, 271; Nixon and, 118–120; Obama and, 9; OLC and, 130–131; sole organ doctrine and, 9, 18, 64–66, 138–140, 323n28; state secrets privilege and, 9, 248, 330n28; warrantless surveillance and, 118–119, 227–229, 304n17; Washington and, 20–22, 155; *Youngstown* case and, 104–105, 115, 116. *See also* executive power

unitary executive theory: Bush and, 126–131, 203, 306n21, 308n35; Cheney and, 129; Commander in Chief Clause and, 131, 138; description of, 126–129, 131, 306n15, 306n21, 307n32; detention/trials under Bush and, 161, 179–180, 197–198, 313n50; Nixon and, 126; Supreme Court and, 126. *See also* executive power; "President's Constitutional Authority to Conduct Military Operations . . . , The" memorandum of 2001 (Yoo)

United Nations Security Council, 142, 265–266

UN Convention against Torture and Other Cruel, Inhuman or Degrading Treatment or Punishment (CAT), 206, 320n44

U.S. citizens. *See* citizen detainees; targeted killing of citizens under Obama

U.S. Congress. *See* Congress and congressional power

U.S. Constitution. *See* Constitution; Framers of Constitution

U.S. Department of Defense. *See* Defense Department

U.S. Department of Justice. *See* Justice Department

U.S. District Court for the District of Columbia, 201

U.S. embassies attacks in 1998, 142

U.S. Supreme Court. *See* Supreme Court

United States v. Curtiss-Wright (1936), 9, 18, 64–66, 139–140

United States v. Nixon (1974), 120–124, 126, 305nn29–30

United States v. Reynolds (1953): summary of, 242–247, 328nn8–10, 329n16, 330n22, 330nn24–25; extraordinary rendition as insulated by, 242–243, 247–248, 250–251, 253–255, 333n88; state secrets privilege and, 247, 330nn25–26; targeted killing of citizens as insulated by, 257, 334n110

United Steelworkers union, 102. *See also Youngstown Sheet & Tube Co. v. Sawyer* (1952)

USS *Maine*, 61, 291n19

Vallandigham, Clement, 60, 290n5, 291n14, 294n45

Vermeule, Adrian, 138, 142

Vesting Clause, 104, 126–128, 281n10, 302n12, 307n25

vice presidential elections, 24, 282n29

Vietnam War, 117–119, 270, 273, 304n1, 304n11

Vladeck, Stephen I., 290n91, 325n17

War Crimes Act of 1966, 206, 317n8

War Labor Disputes Act of 1943, 103, 302n9

war on terror, 5, 6, 115, 129–130, 204, 206, 247, 330n28. *See also* detention and trials under Bush; detention and trials under Obama; interrogation methods under Bush; state secrets privilege; targeted killing of citizens under Obama; unitary executive theory; warrantless surveillance under Bush

War Powers Resolution (WPR) of 1973, 125, 266–273, 278n22, 290n87, 337n16, 338n23, 338n29, 340n66

warrantless surveillance: under Nixon, 118–119, 304n17; under Obama, 249

warrantless surveillance under Bush: summary of, 232–234; Al Qaeda and, 228; attorney general's role in, 228, 230–233; AUMF and, 230, 232; Church Committee and, 225, 321n1; CIA unclassified reports and, 227; Commander in Chief Clause and, 229–230, 231–232, 323n28; FBI and, 231–232; FISA and, 226, 321n7, 322n9; Gang of Eight and, 228, 230–231, 322n21, 324nn29–30; inherent executive power and, 323n28; Justice Department and, 228, 323n22; NSA and, 225, 227, 228; OLC and, 130, 228–232, 322n21, 323nn22–23; Operation Shamrock as precursor to, 225, 321n2; private companies and, 225, 232; PSP and, 227, 229–232, 323n27; roving wiretaps and, 227; searches and seizures, 225–229, 232–234, 323n27, 324n34; sole organ doctrine and, 323n28; tripartite framework and, 229; TSP and, 227–229; unclassified reports on, 227, 323n28; unilateral emergency presidential power and, 227–229. *See also* Bush, George W.; Foreign Intelligence Surveillance Act (FISA) of 1978; national security threats; warrantless surveillance

warrants for surveillance, 226–227, 322nn13–14. *See also* Foreign Intelligence Surveillance Act (FISA) of 1978; warrantless surveillance; warrantless surveillance under Bush

Washington, George: André's military commission and, 154–155; congressional war powers and, 22–23; implied presidential power and, 21; limited emergency presidential power and, 23, 155; national security threats and, 21; neutrality proclamation by, 20–23, 26–27, 281n2, 281n4, 281n14; unilateral emergency presidential power and, 20–22, 155

waterboarding, 204, 207–208, 210–211, 222, 317n9, 318n21, 328n4

Watergate burglary, 119, 120, 124

Wilson, Woodrow, 61–62, 102

World War I, 61–62

World War II. *See* internment of Japanese Americans; Roosevelt, Franklin D. (FDR)

WPR (War Powers Resolution) of 1973, 125, 266–273, 278n22, 290n87, 337n16, 338n23, 338n29, 340n66

Yoo, Christopher S., 281n4, 292n7, 310n72

Yoo, John C., and topics discussed: Commander in Chief Clause, 138–139; congressional war powers, 138; foreign affairs and executive power, 26, 138; Geneva Conventions and Al Qaeda, 205; historical practice of emergency presidential power, 141–142, 268, 310n72; inherent executive power, 9; neutrality proclamation by Washington, 26–27; sole organ doctrine, 138–140; unilateral emergency presidential power, 9, 17, 26, 130–131, 138–142, 229, 267–268, 309n56, 310n64; unitary executive theory, 138–143, 306n15, 306n21;

warrantless surveillance, 228–230, 323n22, 323n27; WPR, 273, 340n66. *See also* "President's Constitutional Authority to Conduct Military Operations . . . , The" memorandum of 2001 (Yoo); Yoo-Bybee memo of 2002

Yoo-Bybee memo of 2002, 210–222, 319n43

Youngstown Sheet & Tube Co. v. Sawyer (1952): Commander in Chief Clause and, 138–139; emergency presidential power and, 102, 103–104, 114–115, 302n4, 302nn10–12, 303n24; excerpts from, 105–114, 303n23; foreign affairs and executive power and, 115, 116; Framers intent and, 10–11, 17, 115, 128, 278n25, 307n25; judicial power in context of emergency presidential power and, 104, 115, 278n25, 303nn17–18; justices' lack of unity on, 104–105, 303n20; labor disputes and, 102–103, 302n5, 302n11; limited emergency presidential power and, 104, 115–116, 180, 302n15, 303n31, 303n33, 304n17; Lockean prerogative and, 104, 303n18; separation of powers and, 142, 310n82; tripartite framework and, 115–116, 139, 197–198, 222, 229, 303n27; unilateral emergency presidential power and, 104–105, 115, 116; unitary executive theory and, 126, 143. *See also* Truman, Harry

Zubaydah, Abu, 206–207, 210–211, 222, 317n9, 318n15